SEVEN SUMMITS

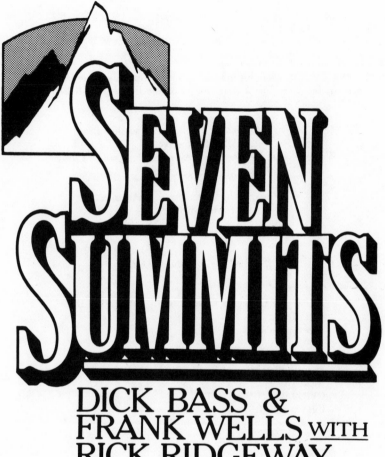

SEVEN SUMMITS

DICK BASS & FRANK WELLS WITH RICK RIDGEWAY

WARNER BOOKS

A Warner Communications Company

The excerpts on pages 3 and 208 from "A Rolling Stone" and the excerpt on page 90 from "The Men Who Don't Fit In" are reprinted by permission of Dodd, Mead & Company, Inc. from *The Collected Poems of Robert Service* by Robert Service

Warner Books, Inc., 666 Fifth Avenue, New York, NY 10103

W A Warner Communications Company

Printed in the United States of America
First Printing: April 1986
10 9 8 7 6 5 4 3 2 1

Designed by Giorgetta Bell McRee

Library of Congress Cataloging in Publication Data
Bass, Dick.
  Seven summits.

  1. Mountaineering. 2. Mountaineers—United
States—Biography. I. Wells, Frank. II. Ridgeway,
Rick. III. Title.
GV200.B37 1986   796.5'22   85-43162
ISBN 0-446-51312-1

Our love and appreciation
to our families,
to David Breashears,
and, especially, to Marty Hoey

CONTENTS

A PERSONAL NOTE

Rick Ridgeway, to whom alone credit is due for the massive undertaking encompassed in these covers, has done so thorough a job of capturing our motives and feelings about the Seven Summits that even to try to elaborate would be without purpose. Instead, we simply say—he got it right—just the way it was—just the way we felt—and why we did it. We thank him deeply.

The dedicatory page speaks for itself. To that page we add just these few further expressions of deepest gratitude.

To Nansey Neiman of Warner Books, who with unfailing energy saw through to completion the editing and publishing of this book. To Steve Marts who was always there—ahead of us with all of his camera equipment on every climb in '83—all the way to the top; tireless; climber as well as photographer (and without whom FGW would never have made it to the top of Elbrus). He is so totally unique that it would take half another book to convey his qualities and contributions to this odyssey.

And, of course, to Giles. This book *does* do him justice and he deserves it all—together with our undying appreciation. We thank him and all the climbers, especially the indomitable Phil Ershler, as well as the many others whom you will meet in these pages.

FGW
RDB

Snowbird, Utah
January, 1986

ix

INTRODUCTION

Their goal was to climb the highest mountain on each of the seven continents. It was an imposing list: Aconcagua in South America, Everest in Asia, McKinley in North America, Kilimanjaro in Africa, Elbrus in Europe, Vinson in Antarctica, Kosciusko in Australia.

Everest would be the most difficult because of the extreme altitude, over 29,000 feet. Vinson would be the greatest logistical challenge because of its location deep in the interior of frozen Antarctica. But the other peaks were not to be discounted—McKinley, for example, at over 20,000 feet and close to the Arctic Circle, has some of the most severe weather on earth.

No one had ever scaled all seven summits. To do so would be an accomplishment coveted by the world's best mountaineers.

Thus it was even more improbable that Frank Wells and Dick Bass proposed to try it, both of them having so little climbing experience they could hardly be ranked amateur much less world-class. And if that wasn't enough, Frank was a few months from his fiftieth birthday, and Dick had already reached fifty-one.

What made them think they had a chance? Part of it was naivete—they knew so little about high altitude mountaineering they didn't realize just how preposterous their proposal was. But part also

1

was their strong conviction that with enough hard work and perseverance they could accomplish anything they set their minds to. It was a conviction that for both of them had led to successful business careers; Frank was the president of Warner Brothers Studios, Dick an entrepreneur with an oil business in Texas, a ski resort in Utah, and coal interests in Alaska. They figured that if it worked in business, why not in mountain climbing.

So with the attitude that anything is possible, the two set out to accomplish the impossible.

But why? Why risk their lives on the frozen, barren slopes of the world's most remote mountains? Especially when both could justifiably take pride and pleasure in their success in the business world?

When they first started their adventure, Frank and Dick weren't that sure themselves. By the time they had finished their Seven Summit odyssey, however, they had no doubt. They were so charged from their experiences they were eager to share them with anyone willing to listen.

Dick told his friends how in his business it often took years before he could enjoy the successful completion of a project. "Look at my Snowbird Ski Resort. I've been in it fourteen years, and I've got at least that many more before I see it reach its manifest destiny. And when you're involved in long-term projects, sometimes you feel you're on a treadmill in a dark tunnel and you don't know when you're ever going to break out into the sunlight.

"With mountain climbing, I've discovered a tangible, short-term goal. It's me and the mountain, and that's it. There are no bankers or regulatory officials telling me what I can and can't do. It's just me and my own two feet, my own physical strength and my own mental resolve.

"At the same time it's only rewarding if the mountain is a real one. Podunk hills don't count. I'm trying to make up for the frustration I face in the lowlands, and to do that I've got to have a challenge, something to gut up for, something that forces me to strain. There has to be a spirit of adventure to it, too, and an element of uncertainty and risk. Then when I persevere and prevail, when I overcome and make it, I come back down to the lowlands, back to the bankers and the regulatory officials, and by golly I'm recharged and ready to take them all on."

Frank, too, told friends and acquaintances about the unexpected lessons, the surprises.

"It all started as a challenge," he said. "And probably a good bit of macho as well. But it became much, much more. It became travel, adventure, true camaraderie. It was all about going high, as high as you can get. When I spent three nights on the South Col of Everest, at 26,200 feet, I was probably the highest human on the face of the earth those particular days. But it was also the sheer fun, and it was especially the magic moments, the surprises that came over the next rise.

"It was the first time I saw Everest after dreaming about it for thirty years, when in a truck out of Lhasa we came over a pass and there it was, higher than anything around, with that great and ever-present cloud plume streaking off the summit.

"It was beating our way in a storm up to 16,000 feet on McKinley and getting to the top of the ridge to suddenly break into the clear and see what looked like all of Alaska spreading below us.

"It was being ushered into the presence of the High Lama of Tengboche Monastery in Nepal, and having our expedition blessed, and receiving a blessing for ourselves.

"And of course it was the summits. It was standing on top of Aconcagua, the first time I had finally made the summit of any of our peaks, hugging Bass. It was marching in lockstep with Bass to the summit of Elbrus—having not made it the year before—reciting in unison one of Dick's favorite poems, Kipling's 'Gunga Din.'

"And perhaps most of all, it was on Kilimanjaro, where my dream to someday climb the Seven Summits had started nearly thirty years before. It was a night at our last high camp huddled around the fire with twenty near-naked African porters when Bass decided to recite another one of his favorite poems.

" 'Have you heard "The Rolling Stone" by Robert Service?'

" 'No,' we told him, 'somehow that one's gotten by.'

"So he recited it:

> " 'To scorn all strife, and to view all life
>   With the curious eyes of a child;
> From the plangent sea to the prairie,
>   From the slum to the heart of the Wild.
> From the red-rimmed star to the speck of sand,
>   From the vast to the greatly small;
> For I know that the whole for the good is planned,
>   And I want to see it all.'

"And I guess that's the answer. We wanted to see it all, and we knew no better way than from the tops of the tallest mountains on each of the seven continents."

THE DREAM

It was a sunny July morning in 1981, and Dick Bass had no inkling whatever that before the day was over he would receive a phone call that would send him on the beginning of an incredible series of adventures to the most remote corners of every continent on earth.

He arrived in his downtown Dallas office expecting the same frustrations he had suffered all month. Herbert Hunt, one of his two partners in an Alaska coal lease, had been so busy with other far-flung business involvements he hadn't had time to close the sale of the lease to a mining company; Dick needed no one to remind him that if the contract wasn't signed by September 1 he would have no way of coming up with the $4 million needed to meet the loan payment on his Snowbird Ski Resort in Utah. The thought of losing his life's overriding purpose and passion left him with a numbing sense of desperation. He loved Snowbird. There was nothing that made him happier than seeing people swooshing down the finest powder skiing in the world. And nothing equalled the satisfaction of knowing he had created the place from scratch.

It would be a few more years, though, until Snowbird was through its initial growth so it could carry itself. Meanwhile it was sapping

4

every penny Dick could scrape up from his oil and ranching interests in his home state of Texas. If he didn't come up with the $4 million it wouldn't be just Snowbird down the tubes, but all of his other assets as well.

Oh well, Dick thought to himself, as Molière said, "Men spend most of their lives worrying about things that never happen."

Amazing, though, is that all the stress had little effect on Dick's health. Perhaps it was because of his congenital optimism, which gave him an ability to smile in the face of adversity and always believe that with hard work and a lot of faith things would work out. Then, too, he had a physique made for his high-stakes entrepreneurial life. At five foot ten, with a medium build, he had very low blood pressure and a resting pulse of only forty-one, "except that it goes up to forty-eight when I start talking, which is most of the time. That's why they call me 'Large-Mouth Bass.' " And at age fifty-one, even without disciplined exercise—nothing more than an occasional ten minutes of stretching in the morning—he seemed always to be in good shape. He had shown that a little over a month before when he climbed to the summit of Mount McKinley—at 20,320 feet the highest point on the North American continent—without any prior conditioning.

Dick had not always been an avid mountain climber. In fact, McKinley was only the third peak he had ever scaled, the other two being a hike to the top of Fuji when he was an ensign in the navy, and two overnight guided ascents of the Matterhorn, the last one with his two sons and twin daughters. But those earlier ascents had whetted an interest, and Dick was quick to take advantage of an opportunity to climb McKinley when it presented itself.

The opportunity came about one evening when he was regaling some of the Snowbird employees with stories about his second climb of the Matterhorn with his kids. The climb was actually part of a larger five-month around-the-world adventure that had included things like swimming two and half miles across the Hellespont and jogging for thirty-one miles over the original route of Phidippides when he carried the Marathon victory message to the Athenians. As always, Dick was loquacious, gesturing with his hands and arms as he carried on about his adventures and his climb. About twenty minutes into the story one of the employees said, "Dick, did you know Marty here is the only female guide on Rainier and McKinley?"

Dick glanced over to Marty Hoey, sitting by herself with what looked like a scowl painted on her face. Dick didn't know much about

Marty other than that she was head of the safety patrol during the ski season.

"Gosh, Marty, I didn't know you were a climber, much less a guide on McKinley," Dick said.

Marty replied only with a curt nod, and Dick added, "I'd love to climb McKinley some time. Would you be my guide?"

Dick really knew little about McKinley other than that it was in Alaska and the highest peak in North America. He wasn't fully aware that because it is 20,320 feet high, and only a little more than a hundred miles from the Arctic Circle, it has some of the most savage weather in the world, making it a very serious mountaineering undertaking by any route. So Dick was a little surprised by Marty's reply.

"Bass," she said icily, "your hot air won't get you up that mountain."

Thrown off-balance, Dick couldn't fathom why someone who worked for him, whom he had never really known before, would be so impertinent. Turning back to the others, he wound up his story in five minutes instead of the usual hour, then excused himself as politely as he could. Later, he talked to Bob Bonar, Marty's boss on the ski patrol, to find out why she had made such a remark.

Bonar laughed and said, "Marty just categorized you as a braggadocio city slicker, even if you are her employer. She's a mountaineering, outdoor type who mistrusts city people who talk a lot—especially ones with money."

"Well, she's thrown down the gauntlet. Makes me really want to climb McKinley, just to have her eat crow."

Dick paused, then added, "Didn't you climb McKinley a couple of years ago?"

"Yeah, I did."

"Well why don't you take me up?"

"The only reason I climbed it was because I was going with Marty at the time. She took me up. I'm really no guide. But find someone who is, and I'd be glad to go back with you."

"How are things with you and Marty now?"

"That's all over, but we're good friends."

"Then what do you say if you and I go, and also I'd like to bring my four kids, and you see if you can get that arrogant female to be our guide. Then I can watch her eat crow in person."

It took several attempts before Marty finally agreed to talk to Dick.

When she did, she said she would only consider taking him if he were to enter into a serious training regimen.

"And your kids should come only if they want," she added. "Not because you force them to."

The more hardboiled this five foot six, dark-haired twenty-nine-year-old with striking features and very strong legs became, the more Dick resolved to prove her wrong in her judgments about him.

"Okay," she finally said, "we'll go. But you had better start getting in shape. That place is really high and cold. We each have to carry a full share of the load. And I don't think you can make it. When you get as far as I feel you should go, that'll be it. You'll just have to camp and wait while the rest of us go on to the top. And there will be no appeal."

If this young lady was anticipating giving her boss his comeuppance, Dick was totally determined to never give her any justification to "camp" him on the mountain. Dick knew he always did his best when he had a challenge right in front of him to focus on, and Marty's contempt would be just the carrot. He felt he could do anything she could; what he didn't realize, though, was that he was taking on superwoman.

He found out quickly at the beginning of the very first day of the climb that all his low altitude confidence was based on extreme naivete. They had flown in a ski-equipped Cessna 185 to the 7,000-foot elevation on McKinley's Kahiltna Glacier. Besides Marty, Bob Bonar, and three other Snowbirders, Dick's two sons, Dan and Jim, and twin daughters, Bonnie and Barbara—all in their early to mid-twenties—joined the team, each thinking it would be a great chance to follow up their around-the-world odyssey of two years before with another great adventure.

They unloaded their equipment, stuffed their backpacks and sleds, then fastened the bindings on their alpine touring skis to begin the long, slow trek up the gradually inclined glacier. The first ten feet and Dick couldn't believe it. His pack had to weigh about seventy pounds and his sled a good thirty-five. He felt his leg muscles strain and his stomach muscles tighten. How was he ever going to make it several miles to the glacier head, then the 8,000 vertical feet further up the steep ridges and slopes to the summit? He made another fifty feet and felt his heart pounding and his breathing quicken.

Good Lord, he thought, what have I gotten myself into?

Another fifty feet and he felt his pulse pounding in his temples.

The Arctic sun reflected off the snow, and the heat took him by surprise. The salt from his sweat, mixed with sunscreen, burned his eyes. He wondered if he could even make it through the first day.

Then an unexpected thing happened. Fifty more feet and he found a way to think of something besides the agony. Dick was very fond of poetry—part of the enormous weight in his pack was three hardback volumes—and now he found distraction, even inspiration, with one of his favorites, Kipling's "If." He recited from memory each stanza as he continued to place one foot in front of the other: If . . . *step* . . . you . . . *step* . . . can . . . *step* . . .

> *If you can dream—and not make dreams your master*
> *If you can think—and not make thoughts your aim;*
> *If you can meet with Triumph and Disaster*
> *And treat those two imposters just the same . . .*

Dick was in a near trance reciting the poem over and over, and he was startled from his reverie when Marty announced arrival at the day's campsite. He felt an immense relief sweep over him, a deep physical fatigue, but now it was a good feeling. The first day was behind him, he had purged his mind of all defeatist thought, and he now felt he might have a chance of making the rest of the distance.

As he found out, though, that distance was a long one. For two more days he carried the heavy pack and pulled the awkward sled like a workhorse towing a canal barge. Then the climb up the ridge started and, though they left behind their sleds, they now began the arduous task of humping heavy pack loads—carrying supplies to a higher campsite one day, going back down to the last camp and sleeping, then next day moving the camp up to the new site. Marty was relentless, pushing for one hour, two hours, three hours without rest. But each day Dick found he could recite his poems and find a rhythm. Each day he found himself feeling a little stronger, despite the increasing altitude. Thirteen days later he still had the rhythm as he made the last step to the 20,320-foot summit. It was 4:00 P.M., the temperature was 37 below zero, and Dick stood gazing across hundreds of square miles of glaciers and ice-encrusted peaks, every single one below him. In addition to Marty and the other Snowbirders, his two sons also reached the top, and his daughters came very close. Waving his ice axe, Dick let out with his trademark Bass Tarzan call: Aah-eah-eaahhh, aah-eah-eahhh!

On the way down he realized he had gotten more from the climb than he had ever anticipated. Beyond the satisfaction of proving to himself—and to Marty—he could handle the physical and mental strain, and beyond the joy of standing on top and seeing the world fall away from his feet in all directions, he found the climb had been a perfect antidote to his frenzied, high-pressured business life. It occurred to him he ought to start planning other climbs every once in a while in order to keep his head screwed on right.

He was in sight of the tents at the 17,200-foot camp when the idea hit him. He had just finished reaching the summit of the highest peak on the North American continent. What if he made it a goal to try to climb the highest peak on every continent? He had no idea whether anyone had ever done it, but that didn't matter. It would keep him busy for a number of years. Every time he felt the pressure of business closing in, the grind of the daily round wearing him down, he could get away by checking another climb off the list.

Dick reached the tents around 10:00 P.M. on the first rope team. It was still light at that latitude, and he put on his down jacket and pants—it was now 45 below zero—and started melting snow for anyone wanting a hot drink or instant soup, but his mates had already collapsed in their sleeping bags. He was so pumped up from his triumphant success—despite all the cynics and naysayers—that he couldn't think of getting horizontal yet, especially not until Marty had arrived and he could have the moment he had been waiting months for.

About forty-five minutes later Marty came trudging in at the lead of her rope team. Everyone immediately dove for their bags except Marty, who put on her down clothing and started coiling the rope. Dick waited for what seemed an aeon or two for her to say something. Finally he couldn't stand it any longer.

"Hoey, you told me I couldn't make it."

Marty glanced up from coiling the rope, waddled in all her bulky clothing like a penguin over to Dick and gave him a hug and a peck on the cheek.

"Bass, I don't believe you. You're an animal," she said, giving him the ultimate mountaineering compliment.

Dick swelled up as if someone had just stuck a helium nozzle in his down jacket.

"Marty, I not only made it, I felt like gangbusters all the way up and down."

"Yeah, I saw it. But I don't understand it."

"Well, I'll tell you why. It's because it was only me and the mountain and the weather. You don't have any idea, Marty, what I've got to go through down there in the lowlands. I've got knots on my head and bruises on my shins from dealing with bankers and radical environmentalists. Don't get me wrong, I truly love my fellow man in general, but some of them can be like hairshirts that scratch like crazy. Up here I was free for once from all the human barriers. Also, this climb gave me a definite goal in a short timeframe. We don't get report cards out of school, Marty, and after being in the long black tunnel of Snowbird without a glimmer of light at the end of it, I finally found something really big to give me a tangible sense of accomplishment—*now*! I'm telling you, this climb has given me a newfound sense of self-respect and self-confidence. And by golly, I feel ready to go back and face the world."

Marty answered with a wan look and a feeble grunt.

"And one more thing which you'll probably scoff at just like you did my McKinley idea. I had a great idea coming off the summit, just a little while ago."

"What's that?"

"It hit me that since I've just climbed McKinley, the highest point in North America, I'm going to try to climb the highest mountain on each of the other six continents."

Marty paused. She was obviously exhausted, but mustering all the strength she could, said, "That's a fantastic idea. In fact, I'd like to go too."

"Well, I'll tell you what, you clean up your act and start treating me decently, and I'll take you with me."

Once back in Dallas, though, the demands of business pressed so tightly Dick had no time to think about future climbs. Each day the clock on the Snowbird loan ticked louder, and Dick knew his only hope was making a deal on his coal lease in Alaska. As June passed, then most of July, and the deal still didn't close, and the September 1 deadline on the loan got closer each day, Dick put any thoughts of mountain climbing onto the back burner.

Until that sunny day in late July when he went to his office expecting the same hassles, and instead, out of the blue, got an unbelievable phone call.

"Someone named Jack Wheeler on line two," Dick's secretary said.

"Jack who?"

"Jack Wheeler. Says he's the professional adventurer you met a few months ago at a party here in Dallas."

"Oh, yeah. Okay, but I can only give him a few minutes."

Dick picked up the phone. "Hello?"

"Hi Bass, Wheeler here."

Dick was a little put off by the slick tone, but then he dismissed it, remembering this Wheeler fellow had said he was from Southern California, and Dick just figured they were all the same out that way.

"How ya doin'," Dick said.

"Fine. Listen, when we met you said you were about to go to McKinley. I was wondering if you did."

"Yes, I went." There was a pause, and Dick sensed this Wheeler fellow was hesitant to ask the obvious next question. Maybe he doesn't want to embarrass me, thinking maybe I didn't make it, Dick thought.

"Well, uh, er, did you climb it?" Wheeler finally asked.

"That's what I went there for, isn't it?"

"You mean you made it?"

"Of course I made it."

"You did? You don't mean it! I mean . . . Well, was it hard?"

Dick saw his chance to return a little of Wheeler's bravado. "Heck no, it wasn't any hill for a climber," Dick said, wanting this Southern Californian to know that Texans were not to be underestimated.

Wheeler exclaimed, "That's just fantastic! Listen Bass, how old are you?"

"Fifty-one."

"Perfect. I recently met someone here in California who said he would be interested in meeting you. He's almost fifty, and a successful businessman; he's president of Warner Brothers Studios. His name's Frank Wells, and I met him through our mutual friend Clint Eastwood. Frank has this dream, and part of it is climbing McKinley. Would you mind talking to him, maybe giving him some pointers?"

"Sure, I'd be glad to. But what's his dream?"

"He wants to climb the highest mountain on each continent."

Dick nearly fell out of his chair. He had known, as soon as he had returned from McKinley, that his fantasy of climbing the highest peak on each continent would probably remain just a fantasy. It was simply a question of too many irons in the fire. But now, from out of nowhere, this: a partner, somebody to help him with the planning, the financing, the logistics. Someone to share the whole adventure from beginning to end. It was like some kind of divine intervention.

"Tell Frank Wells I'll talk to him. In fact, tell him I'd like to come out to California and meet him. Right away."

• • •

Although the center of Frank Wells' universe was very much the presidency and co-chief-executive-officership of Warner Brothers Studios, he had an interest in mountain climbing that dated back thirty years to his undergraduate days at Pomona College when he used to daydream about becoming the first to climb Everest, even though at the time his only experience had been a hike to the top of Mount Whitney, in California's Sierra Nevada. One day while studying for graduation finals Frank's fraternity brother, who also shared the Everest fantasy, called and said, "Well, we blew it. Some guy named Hillary just climbed it."

That put Frank in a deep funk, but not for long. After graduating *summa cum laude* and Phi Beta Kappa from Pomona he won a Rhodes Scholarship to Oxford University, where he found an American friend who shared his passion for adventure. After spending Christmas skiing in the Alps they started wondering what to do for spring break.

"I've got it," Frank's buddy said. "Africa! Listen, I've got my pilot's license, so we'll pool our money, buy a cheap plane, and fly from here to Cape Town and back."

They found a tiny two-seat airplane for $600. It had no navigation equipment and no radio. It also happened to be all they could afford. With eight weeks remaining before Easter break, Frank was in charge of visas and landing permits, which turned into a full-time job. With a maximum range of 500 miles, they were going to have to land in twenty to thirty countries, principalities, caliphates, and assorted chiefdomships.

The day before departure Frank's buddy said, "Oh, there's one more thing you'll have to be in charge of because I haven't had time to learn how."

He handed Frank a book on air navigation. Frank was up all night reading furiously and finished the book only after they were airborne. He honed his navigational skills with the dividers and parallel rule as they hopscotched across France, over Corsica and Sardinia and on across the Mediterranean into North Africa, gunkholing to Libya, Egypt, and then down to the Sudan and Uganda. Approaching Nairobi they could see due south the glistening snow on the summit of Kilimanjaro.

"Let's climb it," Frank said impulsively.

A week later they ascended via the established Kibo trail, although in 1954 the mountain wasn't climbed enough for the trail to be labeled the tourist route. Near the top Frank was nauseous, throwing up every ten minutes, but too close to turn back. They both made it.

They continued toward Cape Town and shortly after had to make an emergency landing in a farmer's field. The plane flipped upside down and was totally destroyed, but they walked away unscathed and hitched a ride on a British military air transport back to England.

It was a glorious adventure, and Frank was hot to follow it up with an even better sequel, an idea that had come to him while descending Kilimanjaro. Hillary had climbed Everest, so he couldn't be the first to do that. But Frank was sure nobody had ever climbed the highest peak on each continent. He had just done the highest in Africa, so why not try for the other six?

The demands of Oxford, though, precluded any other extensive adventures, and then one thing led to another—the army, law school, legal practice, and eventually Warner Brothers Studios, where he started in the business affairs department. At six foot four, with a cordial but sincere smile, and the habit of cutting extraneous fat from phone calls, meetings, or any conversation in order quickly to get to the heart of the matter, Frank's career at Warner Brothers had been a steady rise to the presidency.

But he had never forgotten that mountain climbing fantasy. Years went by, but in 1980 he had managed to get a couple of weeks off to travel to Europe and attempt Mont Blanc, the highest peak in Western Europe. He made the top, and it rekindled what was now a twenty-five-year fantasy about doing the highest peak on each continent.

One day he mentioned this interest to his friend Clint Eastwood. Clint told him about a fellow named Jack Wheeler, who helped him scout locations in the high Arctic for his next film, *Firefox*. Eastwood explained that Wheeler had some experience mountain climbing, and he thought the two of them might like to meet.

"Send him over," Frank said.

When he met Wheeler, Frank told him about his highest-peak-on-each-continent fantasy.

"Now I'm the first to admit I don't have much experience," Frank said. "Other than Kilimanjaro and a guided climb up the Matterhorn, the only other mountain I've climbed was Mont Blanc, last year. And that was with a guide and I was throwing up near the summit just from exhaustion. But I made it—the highest peak in Europe—so I've got two crossed off the list."

"There's only one problem," Wheeler said. "That's not the highest mountain in Europe."

"What do you mean?"

"Europe is measured as everything west of the Ural Mountains. The highest peak in Europe is Elbrus, in Russia's Caucasus Mountains between the Caspian Sea and Black Sea."

"Well, fine."

"What do you mean, fine?" Wheeler had clearly expected a different reaction.

"That means there's still another mountain to climb to reach my goal, and Russia itself sounds like an adventure."

Why not try Elbrus right away, Frank figured. If it could be done in ten days or so, he could check that peak off his seven summits list without compromising his company responsibilities. He had no time to organize such a thing himself, but here was someone who claimed to be a professional at doing just that.

A deal was struck and Wheeler started to investigate what it would take to organize climbs to the other peaks.

It was while researching that idea that Wheeler remembered this Dick Bass fellow he had met at the Dallas party a couple of months earlier, the one who had said he was going to climb McKinley. Thinking he might be a good source of information on that peak, Wheeler called Dick and was astonished to learn that Dick had the same fantasy about climbing the highest mountain on each continent.

Wheeler immediately called Frank, who quickly latched onto the possibilities: he would have a climbing companion, and there was a good chance they could share costs.

"Should I set up a meeting?" Wheeler asked.

"As soon as possible."

When he hung up Frank mused, Of all the luck, to find someone with the same outrageous fantasy, about the same age, and in a financial position to afford making the fantasy come true.

You could have put all the names in the world into a computer and still not come up with such a pairing.

That had been a week before, and now, as Frank pulled his Mercedes in front of Warner headquarters he thought about his lunch that day with Dick Bass. He was anxious to meet him, but didn't dwell too long on it: he had a full day's business agenda, and Dick Bass was just an item scheduled between noon and one.

In his office Frank's secretary came in with the list of yesterday's calls and the morning's schedule, starting with an informal meeting with the four other Warner execs to discuss a picture having a slow start. Should they put more money into advertising or concede the picture didn't have "legs" and drop it? They decided to drop it. Next item was a completed film they could pick up at a good price, but one that had a questionable potential—20th Century-Fox had just passed on their option.

"What's it about?" Frank asked.

"Basically it's a story set around the 1924 Olympics about a couple of runners with different backgrounds who compete against each other; one's a Jew and the other's a Scot Presbyterian."

"Sounds like some blockbuster," Frank hooted.

"I've seen it, though, and it does have good music."

"Maybe we should get it over for a screening just in case it might be worth our while."

"What's it called?"

"*Chariots of Fire.*"

The meeting over, Frank returned his calls; then it was time for lunch. In a few minutes Frank's secretary escorted in Dick Bass.

Dick was impressed, not by the office, but by Frank. Raw-boned and rangy looking, Dick thought. But Dick didn't know whether that was from climbing or from weathering the rigors of the movie-making business.

After some brief small talk, Frank looked at his watch and stated peremptorily they had better get over to the corporate dining room right away: "We've got a lot to talk about."

In the private lunchroom Dick took a seat while Frank remained standing. Frank had just finished Jack Wheeler's report on how they could climb the highest peak on each continent—the Seven Summits, as he started calling them—and now Frank was ready to explain the proposal to Dick.

"First, after checking into it a little, we've found that no one has ever climbed all seven summits. So for whatever it's worth, we would be going after a first-time record."

"Second, other than Everest and the Vinson Massif, the highest peak in Antarctica, all these climbs should be relatively easy to organize. Aconcagua, the highest in South America, is climbed each year by dozens of parties. You know about McKinley, of course, and I can tell you Kilimanjaro is a long, long day when you go for the summit but really nothing more than a grueling hike. Kosciusko in Australia actually has a road almost to the top of it, and as for Elbrus, it shouldn't be too hard either. But I'll get back to that in a minute. First, though, the problems with Everest and Antarctica . . ."

Dick sat in his chair staring up at Frank. An old neck injury started acting up, and despite the growing discomfort Dick made an effort to stay politely attentive.

"Now with Jack Wheeler's help I've been checking into Everest. If you can believe it, there are so many climbers who want to try Everest they're waiting in line. The mountain sits on the border of Nepal and Tibetan China, so you can attempt it from either side, but as the two governments only allow a couple of teams on different routes each season the permits are presently backed up all the way to 1990. The only way to get one is wait or tie-in with a group that already has one, and I'm checking into that . . ."

Dick couldn't believe it. He was the one who almost always did the talking when he first met people, but now he felt out-gunned. What Frank was saying was interesting, though, and he was obviously serious about the seven climbs. But he kept talking . . . for ten minutes, fifteen minutes . . . and the pain in Dick's neck was getting worse.

". . . as for Antarctica, as you may know, our government's National Science Foundation has a chartered mandate to direct and oversee the U.S. bases there, and the most direct way to get to Vinson would be on board one of the C-130s operated by the navy out of McMurdo Station. I'm checking into it; I've got a few friends in Washington, and . . ."

My God, Dick thought to himself. This guy is more like me than I am. Meanwhile, lunch had been served, so Dick could look down and give his neck a rest. Frank ignored his food and continued to talk.

". . . so if the N.S.F. doesn't work out we've got this backup plan with a converted DC-3, retrofitted with brand new turboprop engines—three of them, including one in the nose—and ski-equipped because it was built to fly support for U.S. bases in the high Arctic out of Alaska's north slope. It's privately owned and although there are lots of problems, I'm investigating what it would take to charter it and have it flown from its home base near here in Santa Barbara down to the tip of South America, across the Magellan Strait, to Antarctica, and on to Vinson. The biggest hurdle there looks like refueling in Antarctica, and to solve that we have a handful of possibilities . . ."

Twenty minutes nonstop. This guy must think he's chairing a board meeting.

". . . and so we could do the seven climbs in that order. But I still think we should climb Elbrus right away, for practice. Then go back to it later, if we want to do them all in a row in one year. If something happens to U.S.-Soviet relations and we can't get back into Russia we'll have it under our belts. I think we can get the Elbrus permit arranged in three weeks. What do you think?"

Without waiting for a reply Frank sat and started wolfing down his lunch. Dick said he had a trip coming up in two weeks to Europe, to examine mountaintop restaurants in the Alps for a possible similar installation at Snowbird, and it would be easy for them to rendezvous over there and travel together to Russia.

"Fantastic," Frank said as he finished his lunch. "I've got a good friend, Jack Valenti, who's president of the Motion Picture Association and knows Dobrynin, the Soviet ambassador to the U.S., quite well, so the permit shouldn't be a problem. Make sure you take your climbing gear with you to Europe."

Then Frank looked at his watch and said, "This has been a fantastic meeting, and I wish I had all day, but I really must get to another appointment." Walking back, Dick considered all that Frank had said. While Frank had certainly taken over their first meeting, that really didn't bother Dick, as it would probably be an advantage to have someone like Frank to help organize the seven expeditions. And just as important, it seemed Frank was in a position to share expenses.

"Frank, what do you think this whole thing might cost?"

"I'm guessing it will come in at about half a million."

"Well, if you want, you've got yourself a partner," Dick said, extending his hand. Frank smiled—if there was anything he liked it was a man willing to make up his mind quickly—and taking Dick's hand he said, "You're on."

With that, Frank returned to his office, and Dick caught a plane back to Dallas. They both had full schedules, and there would be time later to pause and think about what they had just done.

ELBRUS '81

Frank Wells had several weeks before he was to rendezvous with Dick Bass in Europe and then travel to Moscow for the Elbrus climb. That should be sufficient time to get the permit, especially since he would have his friend Jack Valenti ask Dobrynin to speed things up. But there wasn't much time to get into shape or, more important, to try to learn more about mountain climbing. Still, Frank decided he should do as much as his busy schedule allowed.

He had just finished reading a book I had written about an American ascent of Everest, and learning I lived in Southern California he asked Wheeler to get in touch with me. At the time Wheeler called I was working on a mountain climbing documentary in post production at the Burbank Studios, the same lot that houses Warner Bros. In addition to writing about outdoor adventures, I had started making films on the same subjects, and had managed to support myself from my interest in climbing and adventuring. In addition to the Everest expedition I had also climbed K2, the world's second highest peak, and had been on climbs in many remote places around the world, including Antarctica.

After Wheeler told me of Frank's interest, I flip-flopped in my sandals and Aloha shirt over to the inner sanctum of the Warner headquarters and was ushered into his office. A group of men were huddled over a black onyx table looking at storyboards for what seemed to be a *Superman* sequel. The office was first cabin: posh carpeting, original art, skylights, indoor palm trees, wet bar.

"Frank, Mr. Ridgeway is here."

Frank looked up with a smile and walked over to shake my hand. "Wow, what a pleasure," he said.

"Likewise," I said, still staring around the room.

Frank then turned to the others, "Okay boys, meeting's over. I've got some important business."

After Frank outlined his plan to me, I said, "Maybe you ought to go on a one-day climb first. You know, to see if you like it." He agreed.

We got together the next weekend at Sespe Gorge, a rock cliff near my hometown of Ventura. I brought my neighbor Yvon Chouinard and another visiting climber, Al Steck. Both are among the best-known climbers in the United States. (Frank later said it was like getting invited to your first golf game with Arnold Palmer and Jack Nicklaus.)

Chouinard and Steck went off on another route and I took Frank up a crack in the 400-foot-high wall that had a 5.7 rating, meaning it was easy-to-moderate by mountaineering standards—to Frank it looked impossibly vertical. About halfway up, he was having trouble. The technique on such a climb is to jam your hands and feet in the cracks, but Frank was pawing the rock searching for footholds, his hands bleeding from incorrectly jamming them. Panting hard, he looked up and said, "What do you say we practice that thing where you slide down the rope. What do you call it—rappel?"

"Sorry, but we have to finish. Otherwise you'd be disappointed in yourself."

Frank paused to absorb this.

"I took Tom Brokaw up this climb a few weeks ago. He zoomed right up. It was his first rock climb too."

"So you mean if I don't make this, word gets out that Brokaw does the climb and Wells wimps out."

"You said it, not me."

Frank made another move and suddenly his foot shot out and in an instant he was hanging from the rope.

"Go ahead and hang there for a minute and rest your arms and legs. Then try it again, but this time don't hug the rock. That way you'll stay in balance and won't pop off that foothold."

"What foothold?"

"That edge just above your right knee."

"You mean this? It's a quarter-inch wide!"

"Yeah, it's a big one all right. So just put the edge of your shoe on it and press up."

Frank tried again, and fell again. The third time he made it, but he looked very awkward. When we finally reached the top he had several nasty scrapes on the backs of his hands, his knees were bleeding and he had what climbers call sewing machine leg, meaning his legs were vibrating as fast as a needle on a Singer. But he also had a wall-to-wall smile.

"I'm glad as hell you made me stick to it. Still, do I really need to learn how to climb rock cliffs in order to get up these seven peaks?"

"Not really, I suppose. They're all mostly walk-up snow slopes with ice axes and crampons. Altitude, avalanches, and crevasses will be your biggest dangers."

"Then thanks again for taking me on my first—and last rock climb."

As we drove back to Ventura, Frank explained how everything was set for the Russia climb. He had the permit, and his partner Dick Bass was already in Europe. He was checking on a couple of possible ways to get to Antarctica, and he had just contacted a Spanish team going to Everest next year and was hopeful he and Dick might be able to join them.

I listened, agreeing it was a great idea and a wonderful project, but at the same time wondering if someone who had just shown by all indications that he had absolutely no natural ability as a climber could really get very far on something as grand as what he proposed. Especially a peak like Everest. I had been up above 8,000 meters —26,200 feet—an altitude in mountaineering that is a kind of red line above which any climbing becomes not only extremely difficult but also extremely dangerous, where the severely thin air confuses your perception and judgment, where often even the world's best climbers make fatal mistakes. And listening to Frank, I was certain he had no real idea what it was like up there in what climbers call the death zone.

Still, it was such a wonderful idea, I didn't want to denigrate it. Moreover, I knew that if Frank and Dick were going to have a real chance of climbing even a few of these peaks, they were going to have to hook up with people who knew what they were doing. Although we didn't discuss it at the time, I had a notion I might just get a chance to become part of this crazy adventurous scheme.

• • •

Dick Bass stood on the sundeck of the Kleine Matterhorn Restaurant Complex in Zermatt. Spreading his arms to encompass the view he exclaimed, "Just look at this, Hoopie. I'm telling you, we'll have the same thing at Snowbird and people will flock to it."

Until then Hoopie, Snowbird's mountain manager, who was accompanying Dick on this tour of mountaintop restaurants, had doubted the possibility of a similar installation at Snowbird. But now, caught between Dick's contagious enthusiasm and the inspiring view of the Matterhorn, he was beginning to sway.

"I'll admit, it's impressive."

"I knew you'd come around," Dick said. "You're just like the rest—always doubting me at first."

It seemed to Dick he was always facing an uphill battle convincing people not only about the mountaintop restaurant but about most of the visions he had for Snowbird (just as he had had a hard time convincing people he could climb McKinley).

With so many nay-sayers it had been tough finding financing, and Dick had sunk every penny of his own money into the project. That had put a tight squeeze on his personal life, and even contributed to his first wife's leaving him, he thought. He was now married again, but the money pressures were still there.

He was absolutely convinced, though, that someday the ski area would not only stand on its own legs but be the greatest year-round mountain resort on earth. He was almost evangelistic about it. He would tell you that when he had gazed on the aspen- and evergreen-covered slopes in Little Cottonwood Canyon, outside of Salt Lake City, his mind's eye saw a system of chairlifts, gondolas, and aerial trams beyond what anyone thought possible. He knew it would probably take another twenty years to see Snowbird the way he dreamed it, but that was okay: he was only fifty-one years old.

Dick felt his tour of mountaintop restaurants in Europe had been such a success that he could put Snowbird out of his mind for a couple of weeks and turn to this mountain climbing project. He had just received word from Frank in California and learned that everything was "go"; Frank had given him instructions to meet at the Copenhagen airport en route to Russia and the Caucasus.

Dick had his twenty-five-year-old son Dan with him to go on the climb as well, and together they arrived in Copenhagen and spotted Frank and Jack Wheeler waiting at the neighboring baggage carousel. The clockwork-precision rendezvous was an auspicious beginning.

Once they had Frank's and Jack's gear they could board Aeroflot to Moscow. When the baggage started down the conveyor, however, Dick got a little skeptical, thinking the luggage looked pretty fancy for a true climber.

Mostly that top-drawer Abercrombie and Fitch stuff, Dick thought.

Then a large metal case trundled down.

"What in the world is that?"

"The camera."

"The camera? Look, Frank, we're here to climb a mountain, not lug something that big."

"Let me explain. This isn't for the mountain."

"Then what's it for?"

"My friend Clint Eastwood is making this movie about a navy pilot who dresses himself up as a Russian officer and sneaks into the country to steal one of their top-secret fighter jets. He's asked me to take a few establishing shots for him in Red Square."

"Do you know how to use this thing?"

"Jack's had some lessons."

"You've got a permit to do this, don't you?"

"No, we're going to sneak it."

"Sneak it! We'll be run out of Russia and never climb Elbrus!"

"Don't worry," Frank said. "Nothing's going to happen."

Dick didn't say more, but he hated this kind of unnecessary anxiety. He had enough of that back home, and he came on these climbs to get away from such things. Now he felt that familiar knot in his stomach.

The flight to Moscow was uneventful, as was their passage through customs. The camera box wasn't even opened. They were greeted by the chief of Russia's Mountaineering Committee, Mikail Monastersky, who introduced the two climber-guides on Elbrus. It couldn't have been a more friendly reception, and on the way to the hotel, Monastersky said to Frank, "Next time you come to Russia, you can contact us directly. There's no need to go through such high channels." Apparently Dobrynin's request had gotten through.

As they had only two days in Moscow, Monastersky made sure they packed in the circus, the Bolshoi, St. Basil's. They were so busy Frank decided to store the camera in Moscow and get Eastwood's shots on the way home. That was a relief to Dick's nervous system. At least he could put the camera thing out of his mind until after the climb. After all, this was supposed to be the time when he enjoyed the simplicity of a pure physical challenge, and he didn't need any new worries, especially since he had worked so successfully before leaving to clear his calendar of the problems that had been pressing him, primarily the payment on the Snowbird loan. Now, if they did get into trouble filming, they would have Elbrus checked off their list.

The first payment on the Alaska coal deal had arrived on a Friday only twenty minutes before the bank closed and his loan payment would have become delinquent, but Dick had still taken a few extra minutes to have a picture taken of himself holding the check under the office portrait of his father before he sprinted the five blocks to the bank. Dick had no doubt that if his father were still alive he would have been mortified to see how far his son was in hock to his creditors. On the other hand he had no doubt his father would have been pleased to see he had built a personal code around the other values the old man had so rigorously inculcated. Dick's father was among the pioneer drillers in the Oklahoma oilfields, and he used to tell his son that a man's capital is not measured by financial wealth but by "integrity, hustle, and friends." Dick grew up a kid who worked hard in school, loved athletics, and was born with a gregarious bent and ease at making friends.

In high school, despite his slight stature, he went out for every sport on the roster. No matter how hard he tried, though, he just wasn't big enough or good enough, until finally in his senior year he made the football team—only to get his face smashed in a scrimmage at the beginning of the season.

Dick was keenly disappointed, but not discouraged. At this time he saw a poem in the Dallas *Morning News.* He was fond of poetry, and some lines from this one, simple though they were, had a lasting influence: "Ability and brain and brawn/all play a certain part/but there is nothing better than/to have a fighting heart." Dick decided he would have one more try. The only sport he hadn't gone out for was swimming. This time it worked. He finally found something where his low pulse rate, quick recovery, and determination paid off, and he got his letter.

He also ran for the president of the student council, but lost. His uncle sent words of commiseration and encouragement, again giving Dick an aphorism he would carry the rest of his life: "Just remember, 'men are made strong not by winning easy battles, but by losing hard-fought ones.' "

There was one other thing he learned, although it was less a lesson than a self-realization. All through high school he had been a top student, and now he was heading for Yale at 16, two years younger than normal. But he hadn't gotten those grades just because he was smart and liked schoolwork. The main reason had been a girl. She had motivated him, but not with words of love. In fact, she loved someone else, she told Dick, because this other fellow was "so smart and got such good grades." That had done it: Dick set out to show her, and from then on he never came home with anything less than an A. He realized there was nothing that energized him more than the desire to show someone he could do something, especially when that someone doubted him.

That was one of the main things that kept him in Snowbird— showing all those who had doubted him. That was what had got him up McKinley—because Marty had told him his hot air wouldn't get him up the mountain.

And that was what would help get him up the seven peaks: a lot of friends and business associates already were telling him he was crazy, that at best this mountain climbing was nothing more than a midlife crisis, a quixotic fantasy, and at worst possibly the ruin of his businesses from which he could ill afford so much time away.

The Elbrus team—Frank, Dick, Dick's son Dan, and Jack Wheeler—checked into the Sports Hotel, built for the Moscow Olympics of 1980. (The charge for hotels, transportation, including domestic airfare, interpreters, and climbing guides was only $850 per person for the entire eleven-day trip.) Their Russian hosts couldn't have been more gracious and they repeatedly asked that they tell other American climbers to come and visit Russia.

They caught a flight south past Stalingrad to the town of Mineral Vody (Mineral Water), from where they made a two-hour drive to the quick-flowing Baxan River, draining the north and east slopes of Elbrus into a valley wooded with evergreens and here and there deciduous trees beginning to yellow with fall color. Their microbus followed the river to the head of the valley, where they checked into a drab five-story resort owned and operated by a labor union and available to tourists. The Russian guides told them that next morning they would begin with an acclimatization hike.

At dawn the guides awakened them, and after a quick breakfast they left for their hike. The natural beauty of the upper Baxan Valley was a surprise. Perhaps the leaden sky and dull architecture of Moscow, succeeded by the arid landscape outside Mineral Vody, had dampened their expectations, but here they found a trail through an enchanting forest with streams and rivulets cascading down the steep walls of the canyon. The temperature was in the low 80's, and as the hike progressed through the morning Frank worked up a sweat and found he was falling behind.

"Maybe you ought to take off that heavyweight underwear you're wearing," Dick suggested at the next rest stop.

"I'll be all right," Frank said.

"Whatever you say." Dick was trying to share some of the things he had learned from Marty Hoey on McKinley, such as how important it is to dress so as never to get overheated and dehydrate by sweating, or lose too much heat and use up energy needlessly trying to stay warm. Dick had learned that in the mountains things like that count.

What Dick hadn't yet learned, though, was that Frank didn't pay much attention to such things. Frank's wife had actually bought most of the outdoor clothing for this trip, just as she always bought all his clothes, and always packed for him. He hated doing things like that, just as he hated to be concerned with what he considered petty details in the home, like cooking, furnishings, and the like. He just focused on grander schemes.

As they continued Frank once again fell behind, and now he stopped long enough to shed the top of his underwear. But that wasn't the only thing holding him back. No matter how hard he tried, he couldn't keep up. He knew he wasn't in great shape, but he had diligently worked out for two weeks before coming on the climb, so he thought he should be in shape to handle this level of climbing. In fact, soon after he had agreed with Dick to do the Seven Summits, he decided to test himself: he got up each morning at 6:00 sharp and ran hard for one hour. Frank hated running and he hated getting up that early, but he felt if he could do both for two weeks he could also find the stamina to climb the seven peaks.

He fulfilled this pact with himself, and felt confident for the climb. More important than the physical benefits from this exercise, though, was Frank's experience on his earlier climbs of the Matterhorn, Kilimanjaro, and Mont Blanc. On the summit day of each of those climbs he had been nauseous and exhausted but had pushed on anyway and made the tops. From that he had concluded that on this new project the worst he could expect would be a total of seven bad summit days.

But now that he was having trouble keeping up on just the practice hike he was becoming less sanguine about the summit climb. At the next rest stop he found the others waiting for him, and he was concerned he was holding them up. He sat down, breathing hard, and now took off his long underwear bottoms.

"Well, Frank," Dick said with a smile as he gestured toward Frank's slightly overweight waist, "you'll lose that before the year's out."

Frank knew Dick intended no malice, but sensitive as he was to falling behind, the comment had a barb to it. Frank's ego was not bolstered by the Russian guides, either, whose contemptuous silence needed no translation.

Dick was of course aware the Russians weren't too impressed, and indeed he himself was beginning to wonder about Frank. But he put it out of his mind, thinking that the next two days would be the real test; he would withhold judgment until then.

The following day they had a comfortable morning, eating from a breakfast selection of porridge, yogurt, bacon, salami, and canned fish and fruit. Frank only picked at his food, though, not finding much to his liking. The six of them, including Danny Bass, Wheeler, and the two Russian guides, left at 8:00 A.M. and took a nearby aerial tram from 8,000 feet to nearly 11,000 feet, followed by a short chairlift, before actually walking at a comfortable pace another 2,000 vertical feet to the shelter where they would spend the night. It was a peculiarly rounded three-story building sheathed in raw sheet metal that looked like a giant Airstream trailer.

"We sleep now," the Russian guides said as soon as it was dark. "We leave early."

True to their word, the two guides woke them at 3:00 A.M., and although they were out of the hut and on their way by 4:30 the guides grumbled because they were already an hour behind. The weather was good though, and the clear predawn boded a fine summit day. There was just enough starlight to follow the snowy path. There was no wind, and the only sound was their boots crunching on hard snow. An hour from the hut twilight revealed neighboring peaks across the adjacent valley. The tallest, now only slightly higher than the level they were on, had twin summits that looked like ears on the famous Cheshire cat; the tips of those ears caught the dawn's first rays, and a soft pink moved slowly down the cat's face.

Dick and the senior guide soon began to work ahead of the others.

Danny, having trouble with a frame pin in his pack, was behind, as was Wheeler; Frank, along with the younger Russian, further yet. In three hours Dick and the older guide reached what the Russian indicated was a regular rest stop.

"You good. You strong," the Russian said. Dick puffed at the compliment even though he knew he was gaining his rating only in comparison to his weaker companions. But still he couldn't deny he was feeling great.

Wheeler arrived and soon Danny caught up and they juryrigged a missing pin to hold his pack to its frame. Frank and the younger guide were now too far back for the others to wait, so they carried on. It was a separation that continued to grow as the day progressed.

Elbrus is an old extinct volcano that for the most part is really nothing more than a long walk up extensive, gradual snow slopes. The technique was to find a comfortable pace, placing one foot after the other, breathing rhythmically between steps. Even though they were now at 16,500 feet, and they had climbed to that altitude with little acclimatization, Dick and his guide continued to make good progress and by noon crested the long slope that led to a saddle just below the final summit rise. Wheeler and Dan soon caught up, and they continued. Afternoon cumulus obscured the valleys below but the snow summit was brilliant against blue sky, and in little more than an hour Dick was making the final steps. Though he had been climbing with only an occasional rest for nearly nine hours, and with little more than a short snack since breakfast, he felt no exhaustion. There were no thoughts of Snowbird, of bankers, of loan payments, of payroll deadlines; this was the catharsis that drew Dick to climbing mountains. Here it had been only himself against these snow slopes, a simple one-on-one he had met and overcome. He stepped on top.

18,481 feet, the highest point in Europe. He looked east, across the transverse Caucasus range, toward the landlocked Caspian Sea, then west toward the Black Sea. He thought how this was another of the Seven Summits—now he had done two of them. Then Dan made the top. That made all of them except Frank and his guide. It was now 2:00 in the afternoon, and Dick knew there was little chance Frank would make it. They stayed on the summit for a half hour, then their guide pointed to his watch and they turned to the descent.

At that moment Frank was 1,500 vertical feet below them, still moving upward but at a tortoise pace. Frank didn't realize it, but the high altitude was clouding his perceptions. He and his single guide stopped to rest at an abandoned hut just before the final and steepest slope.

I can stay here tonight, Frank thought, then in the morning after a rest keep going to the top.

He was too fatigued to realize that the hut's roof was destroyed, that the inside was filled with snow, that he had no pack, no sleeping bag, no food, no stove, and consequently no water. Staying at the hut—or what was left of it—made no sense whatsoever.

After a few minutes, the guide motioned to Frank it was time to strap crampons on their boots, but Frank was so exhausted he remained lying on his back until the guide came over and strapped the crampons on for him. Then they stood, and although Frank walked like a member of a death march, they continued climbing.

I'll play a game, Frank thought. I'll take thirty steps. Count each one . . . two, three, four.

Frank got to thirty and tried to talk himself into another thirty. He made five, but couldn't do any more. He collapsed on his back, breathing hard. Frank watched as the guide, now fifty feet above him, uncoiled a rope.

What's he doing that for? Frank wondered.

The guide then tossed the rope, and the end landed next to Frank. He stared at it, wondering why the guide threw it down.

Maybe he's trying to dry it out, Frank thought.

The guide waited five minutes, then ten. Frank didn't move, but continued to breathe hard and stare at the rope. Finally the guide motioned it was time to turn around.

Frank felt no sense of disappointment; instead, there was relief it was ending, that soon he would be back in the refuge, in bed. Shortly the others, on their way down, caught up, and as they descended together Frank started feeling better and the dreamlike fatigue that had swept him like a drug began to fade. They reached the refuge at dusk.

Even though he was improving, that evening Frank was running a temperature and told everyone he was too exhausted to think about another attempt.

"Maybe I can come back here next year when I'm in better shape," he said.

The next day they descended the tram and began the trip back to Moscow. Oddly, Frank still experienced no disappointment—he felt he had given the attempt his best effort—but he realized he would have to retract his former belief that with an all-out, determined effort he could force himself to push to the summits of the seven peaks. This time it hadn't worked. Instead of feeling demoralized, though, he decided the thing to do was try to get in better shape and then give the future climbs his best shot and be content with that. He felt good about his self-realization, and back in Moscow he called his wife, Luanne.

"Darling, even though I didn't make it, I have really good news about the climb."

"What could possibly be good about this mountain-climbing business?"

"That it was the easiest thing in the world for me to turn back, that I didn't feel defeated, or even disappointed, that the rest of the climbs won't be do-or-die efforts like I said, but that I'll just give each one my best shot."

Frank didn't know Dick well enough yet to confide these thoughts to him, but Dick nonetheless sensed that Frank's failure on Elbrus hadn't dampened his enthusiasm to follow through with their plan. Dick knew that even if Frank couldn't make some of the summits, or even most (after all, Elbrus was among the easiest), there would probably always be on each expedition other mountaineers who could accompany Dick. If he had to leave Frank behind, well, that was life. He would certainly prefer a partner he could go arm-in-arm with to the top of each peak but he also realized how extraordinarily lucky he was to have anyone with whom to share the dream of trying the Seven Summits.

Before leaving Moscow, Frank made another call to his office and learned he was needed immediately in California.

"There's just one thing we haven't done yet," he said to the others. "Would you guys please get that movie camera and get Clint's footage of Red Square?"

Now Dick was doubly pleased he had climbed Elbrus because once again he was afraid that without a film permit they would be caught and blacklisted from ever returning to Russia. It was a gray, misty morning as Wheeler stealthily unboxed the camera in a removed corner of Red Square while Dick kept lookout for the trenchcoated KGB officials he was certain were going to nab them any moment. Then Wheeler used Dick's shoulder for the camera rest as he filmed. No Russians interfered after all, and some months later, when *Firefox* was released, there were a few brief seconds on the wide screen of their Red Square footage.

ACONCAGUA: THE FIRST EXPEDITION

Frank realized his best hope of getting up the Seven Summits was to get into better shape, and he knew the best way to do that was to climb. A few weeks after Elbrus he was on his annual family vacation on the island of Hawaii, and he decided to take a day hike up Mauna Loa.

He started in the morning but by late afternoon realized he had misjudged the distance and wouldn't make the top by nightfall, so he turned back. He knew he couldn't reach his rental car before it got dark, and having forgotten to take a flashlight he groped down the lava trail, tripped, and went nose first into the jagged lava rock. He held his hand over his face, feeling the warm blood gush. It took an hour back to the car, and by the time he pulled into a nearby army camp he was in shock. It took fifteen stitches and another two hours before he finally got back to the hotel.

"Oh, my God," Luanne said when she opened the hotel room door.

"Not exactly a good start on my climbing career, darling."

But Frank was undaunted. As soon as he got back to his office he called Dick.

"It's a question of getting in shape," he said.

"You just need a few more practice climbs," Dick agreed.

"And I've been thinking," Frank continued, "that once I do get in shape we definitely should plan on doing all the climbs one after another in one year. Otherwise if we spread them out over a few years it'd be hard to maintain that conditioning."

It wasn't the first time Frank and Dick had kicked around the idea of doing all seven climbs in one calendar year. It was an attractive idea for several reasons. First, as Frank just said, it would be a lot easier to maintain conditioning by climbing them back to back. Second, they would have all their gear and equipment organized, and third, neither of them was getting any younger.

"Kind of makes a nice packaged chapter in our lives," Dick said.

Frank asked Jack Wheeler to research the logistics of the idea, to make sure the climbing seasons on the various mountains fit together; Wheeler reported it was feasible.

"Nineteen eighty-three should be the year to shoot for," Frank now said to Dick. "That would give us this year to make all the plans, plus give me a chance to go on more practice climbs. And speaking of that, got any ideas where we might go next? How about that friend of yours, Marty Hoey? Maybe she could take us up Rainier."

Finding Marty wasn't easy. Her movements were unpredictable, as though she purposefully threw red herrings across her path. A friend told Dick she was climbing somewhere in the Pacific Northwest, another said he had seen her recently in Alaska, high on McKinley. Dick left messages, but before any of them found her Marty happened on her own to call Dick.

"I've got something you might be interested in," she said, "a way you can get to Everest."

"Are you serious?"

"With the Rainier Mountaineering Guides. Lou Whittaker (who co-owned the guide service) has a permit from the Chinese to try Everest from the Tibet side, next spring. We're looking at the Great Couloir on the North Wall—nobody's ever climbed it. Now Lou's having trouble raising funds, and I just had this thought. What if you were to partially underwrite the expedition in exchange for coming on the climb?"

"Marty, that sounds fantastic."

Dick then told Marty about his chance acquaintance with Frank Wells, and how they had agreed to do the Seven Summits together and that they had just gone to Elbrus.

"Maybe he could join the team, too," Dick said.

"Possibly," Marty replied. "I'll ask about both of you."

"That would be great, Marty. But listen, when you're talking to

Whittaker and those guys, don't mention the Seven Summits. It might sound presumptuous, and I don't want them thinking we're a couple of blowhards. Also, we want you to take us up Rainier sometime soon."

After hanging up, Dick broke into his uncontained smile. He couldn't believe his good fortune. First he meets Frank, and now this.

Must be God's will, Dick thought.

But things like this were typical in Dick's life. He could make a full-page checklist just to wad it an hour later because an unexpected phone call—a new opportunity—was suddenly sending him in a different direction. Over the years he had learned to keep his nose to the wind for such things because many of the major breaks in his life, such as Snowbird and the Seven Summits, had been the result of unexpected encounters. But Dick knew things didn't happen just because you had chance encounters: the trick was to recognize their potential and then do something about them.

Dick knew immediately this had enormous potential. One of the biggest hurdles planning the Seven Summits was getting to Everest, since the mountain was booked until 1990. An attempt to get on board with the Spanish team who had a spring 1982 permit for the Nepal side had come to naught, as the Spaniards weren't interested in having two Americans on their climb, no matter what they chipped in toward expenses.

And now this manna from heaven.

Dick called Frank, who was immediately enthusiastic. The only drawback was the route. It would be a major challenge for Dick and Frank to attempt the so-called normal South Col route on the Nepalese side—the one Hillary had pioneered on the first successful ascent in 1953—but the Whittaker group was proposing an unclimbed line right up the enormous North Wall.

"But even if we don't make it, it'll be a fantastic learning experience for when we do all our seven summits in eighty-three," Frank said.

"Well partner," Dick said, "You wanted me to find you a practice climb!"

A few days later Frank and Dick were at a restaurant near the base of Rainier to meet Whittaker and a few members of the Everest team. Lou Whittaker was fifty-two, stood six foot five, and with a lumber-jack's build looked as fit as the younger guides who worked for him. Lou had climbed Rainier over 200 times. Most of the other team members were professionals with the Rainier Mountaineering Guide Service who climbed nearly every day of the season. They were deeply tanned by the strong sun off Rainier's glaciers and obviously very fit. One member, though, who was notably not a guide, was Jim Wickwire, a Seattle attorney. Wickwire was best known as one of the summit climbers on the first American ascent of K2, the world's second highest peak, and also noted as the one who made an emergency bivouac near the summit, without sleeping bag or tent. It was a severe ordeal that cost him part of a big toe to frostbite, and also part of his left lung, later removed in surgery.

"One thing to clear at the outset," Whittaker said, "is even though you two guys will be paying part of the expenses, you'll be coming on this climb like any other member of the team. We know you won't be doing any of the lead climbing, but once the ropes are fixed you will be expected to do your share of load carrying. We want this to feel like one team, not one team plus two guys who are paying for part of it."

Frank and Dick were pleased; the last thing they wanted was to be pampered. Both were sensitive to buying a slot on the expedition when everyone else had gained it from years of hard work. "Just treat us like the others and we'll be happy," Frank said. There was one other item: would it be possible to bring Jack Wheeler? Here the Everest team demurred; the addition of each new person upped the logistic requirements, and everyone felt they were already at their limits.

The rest of the meeting was spent discussing those logistics: buying and packing for seventeen people for three months, ordering oxygen bottles, clothing, tents, ropes, and special oxygen regulators, and shipping everything to Peking in advance of their departure. Most of the team had experience with these types of things and there would be little for Frank or Dick to do other than get in shape and hopefully work in some practice climbs.

"Understand you've made a deal with Marty to take you up Rainier in the morning," Whittaker said. "This is a good place to start your practice."

It was a two-day climb, but as they left the hut on the summit day, Frank again fell behind.

"Try to get into a rhythm," Marty suggested. "Make a step, then take a deep breath and force it out through pursed lips. Move your ice axe, then make the next step."

Frank practiced this "pressure breathing," inhaling and exhaling loudly, but he was still too slow to keep up. Finally Marty ordered him to turn around and go back down with one of the other guides while she took Dick to the summit.

Rainier was strike three for Frank, but again he felt far from being called out. He was convinced all he needed was yet more practice climbs. It was Wickwire who came up with the idea of going to Aconcagua. It was perfect. The mountain was in the southern hemisphere, so they could go there in December or January, two months before Everest. It was also the highest peak in South America, and even though Frank and Dick didn't make a point of it, they were attracted to the idea of getting practice on another of their Seven Summits. In addition to Wickwire, a couple of the others on the Everest team, including Marty, said they would like to go.

At 22,835 feet Aconcagua is not only the highest peak in South America but the highest in the western hemisphere. Lying in Argentina but close to the border with Chile and only a little north of the latitude of Santiago, Aconcagua is a massive volcanic peak with a complex of faces, ridges, and glaciers. They knew the "ruta normal" was easy, maybe too easy since they were looking for pre-Everest training. On the other side of the mountain the Polish Glacier route would have climbing challenges similar to Everest but on a smaller scale. It sounded like the best objective. They decided to make the climb in January 1982, two months before leaving for Everest.

There was little for Frank and Dick to do but arrange their business lives in order to take the time off. For Dick that meant trying to get as much advance work done as possible on the next development stage of Snowbird: a time-share condominium then only in blueprints. For Frank, though, it was a different problem. There was no way to get his work done in advance, since it was a continuing process that each day needed full attention. Just to get time off for the Elbrus climb had been difficult. Now he was looking at three weeks for Aconcagua followed by three months for Everest followed by much of the following year for all seven summits in 1983. It would be unfair to ask either his colleagues at the studio or the chairman of parent Warner Communications, Steven Ross, for that kind of sabbatical. He realized he was looking at a choice: Seven Summits, or the presidency of Warner Bros. But not both.

Frank's working career spanned twenty-five years from Stanford Law School to a job in a firm specializing in entertainment law, to the other side of the negotiating table working for Warner Bros. He worked very hard, a habit begun as a student when he was at the top of his class at Pomona College as a Phi Beta Kappa *summa cum laude* political science major, at Oxford as a Rhodes Scholar where he received a coveted "first," and at Stanford Law School where he was a note editor of the law review and in the Order of the Coif. In the entertainment law firm and later at Warner Bros., Frank most days worked twelve to fifteen hours, six or seven days a week with two weeks vacation a year—unless work cancelled the ski jaunt to Vail or the beach break on Hawaii.

And Frank loved it. He thrived on the thrill of an industry that was at heart a gambler's Eden, where you risked $15 million on a picture that belly-flopped with a whack that left your ears ringing until the next quarter showed your $6 million dollar picture had grossed $45 million in its first six weeks. He enjoyed, too, the residuals that were part of the chiefdomship in an industry synonymous with glamour. It was not so much the tangible perks (he was too aligned with social welfare concerns and liberal politics to feel comfortable with too much ostentatious show of success), but the intangible enjoyments of corporate life: the authority, the pleasure of having bright associates to execute plans, the ability to make important decisions quickly and then move on to the next problem.

So in the fall of 1981 Frank Wells had a great job, a wonderful wife, two bright, athletic, and polite kids, a Beverly Hills home, a weekend beach house, condos in Vail and Sun Valley, interesting and often famous friends, a loving mother still alive, and financial security. Looking back there was nothing he would have done differently. He had no regrets. He was successful, and proud of it. In short, there was nothing in his profile that suggested midlife crisis. Yet he sensed he was about to make a decision that would be a radical life passage, a buoy around which the course bearing of his life could very well sail in a different direction. And if anyone would have asked why he was considering such a change at the height of his corporate career, all he would have been able to answer was that it just plain felt right. Furthermore, at age forty-nine, he knew it was now or never.

If Frank Wells and Dick Bass had anything important in common it was their belief in following their hunches when a choice presented itself. When it came to decisions both men shunned a brooding analysis and preferred a quick, instinctual action. They took risks on visceral hunches. It was a modus operandi that had made their careers not only successful but also fun.

When the chance came to join the Everest expedition, forcing him either to go with or give up the Seven Summits dream, he thought about it for two days. Not full-time for two days—his schedule was much too busy for that. There were no long walks on the beach. He considered the tradeoffs, when he had a free moment to think about them, and found the balance weighed in favor of climbing. He would never have a similar chance. Besides, he told himself, how tragic it would be if someday he looked back and regretted not going with the opportunity. That thought did it: He met with Steven Ross.

"The other mountains, aside maybe from Antarctica with its logistics, I can get on my own," Frank told Ross. "But Everest, with all the problems getting permits, is a chance I can't pass. It's an American group too, and through China and Tibet, which will be very interesting and is another reason I'm doing this. And I would never think of doing it if I didn't know we had great management in place who can replace me and do it even better."

"I don't know anything about mountain climbing," Ross said, "but I can understand your feelings. When do you want to do it?"

"I don't want it to leak out. So we should announce it very soon, effective January one."

The next day Ross and Frank called a meeting of the top thirty executives in the company, and Frank announced his decision. The following morning Frank came downstairs to his breakfast table to find the industry paper *Variety* with the headline, "*Wells Quits Warners to Scale Mountain.*" With that, he crossed his Rubicon.

The Aconcagua team was set. In addition to Frank and Dick, there would be Marty Hoey, George "Geo" Dunn (another Rainier guide), Jim Wickwire (the Seattle attorney), and Chuck Goldmark (a partner in Wickwire's law firm).

For Frank, the climb would be his first exposure to really high-altitude, expedition-style mountaineering. Elbrus had been more like the European Alps where climbs are one-to-three-day affairs, often with guides and usually taking advantage of huts. But Aconcagua via the Polish Glacier had all the elements of an expedition climb: an approach march of several days through wilderness to the foot of the glacier where base camp would be established, another week or more establishing camps each a day's climb apart, ferrying loads between these camps to stock them. They planned to set two or three camps above their base camp. The first camp would be stocked with enough provisions so the climbers could move into it and from there work up to the site of the next camp. Then they would ferry up more supplies. When this next camp was ready, they would occupy it and again scout the way to the next higher camp, from which they hoped to be in position to attempt the summit. In this way the establishment and provisioning of camps on a big mountain reflects in a sense the pyramidal shape of the mountain itself, where the lower camps are stocked with a far broader and larger quantity of supplies, and the upper camps contain just the narrow minimum necessary to support a summit team. In part because of the need to make several ferries of food and supplies from one camp to the other, and in part because of the need to move slowly to give time to adjust physically to the increasing altitude, the climb would take between two to three weeks if the weather was favorable.

One of the joys of expedition mountaineering is traveling to exotic places through offtrack regions, often accompanied by local porters or animal drivers. On Aconcagua the approach began at a trailhead off the trans-Andean highway connecting Merida and Santiago, where they hired mule drivers to pack their food and equipment to base camp. These mule drivers were dressed like the gauchos who ride the open ranges of Argentine Patagonia: legs sheathed in heavy leather chaps, boots armed with sharp spurs, heads protected with wide-rimmed hats, shoulders draped with ponchos woven of alpaca. Each carried on his saddle a three-ball bola, the South American lasso that can bring down with a quick flick any errant mules. The approach would take three days, and as they started out the two mule drivers herding the pack animals brought up the rear. It was January, the height of the austral summer, and the country was bare-rocked and dry save for the muddy Vacas River flowing in full flood.

Although Dick had been on one expedition climb (his ascent the previous spring of McKinley), this approach on foot through exotic countryside was also for him a new experience. They set a comfortable pace, sharing stories as they went, Dick doing most of the talking, including reciting poems and singing a wide range of songs. Here and there the trail steepened or passed around boulders that demanded coordinated, concentrated footwork, and Dick had no trouble balancing across any difficulties without missing a sentence. But if Dick showed a natural sense of balance, Frank was awkward and depended on the two ski poles he carried as walking sticks. That Frank seemed a bit klutzy wasn't lost on the other climbers either, and in whispered speculation there was concern about the climb ahead, for if he did something wrong it wouldn't be just Frank's neck, since at least one of the others would be tied on the same rope.

They reached base camp without incident. Even with the few days' experience on the approach setting up camp each night, it still took Frank and Dick over two hours to level a platform and pitch their tent, mainly because Frank was tired and assumed a supervisory role. The team took the next day off to give themselves time to acclimatize to the 13,500-foot elevation, and also time to organize equipment and divide it into loads. The next day they each took one of the loads, between twenty and forty pounds, and followed the morainal scree toward the location of camp 1. It was a six-hour trip, and Frank was again by far the slowest.

"Let me take some of your weight," Marty told Frank.

He didn't protest, but even with a lighter pack he couldn't keep up. They cached their loads and returned to base camp, and that evening Wickwire observed that Frank hardly touched his dinner. That was a bad sign, and in his journal that night Wickwire wrote, "Frank is going to have to improve if he is to have a chance at the summit. He seems almost incapable of taking care of himself, and Bass has to look after him when we don't. Nonetheless, his gumption is there, and that's to be admired."

During the next three days they moved up to camp 1, then carried loads to the site of camp 2. They told Frank he could take a day off if he liked, but Frank insisted on trying to keep up.

Dick was doing very well, though, maintaining the pace, carrying as much weight as anyone. He was excited to be climbing with such hotshots as Wickwire, and as always he had great admiration for Marty. He marveled each time he saw this sprightly 125-pound gal strap onto her back a pack loaded as heavy as any of those the guys carried, and then not just keep the pace but often as not get out in the lead and set it. Since his climb with her up McKinley Dick held for Marty a tremendous admiration, and more than ever she was to him a source of great inspiration.

If that gal can do it, he kept telling himself, I sure think I can!

One afternoon it fell to Dick and Marty to melt snow for the evening's brew. At altitude, where the dry air dehydrates you and the lack of oxygen creates chemical imbalances in your blood that have to be flushed out by a high liquid intake, it is necessary to drink four or more quarts of water a day, and the job of melting that much snow is time consuming. Dick and Marty had their work cut out for them, and they passed the time chatting.

"I haven't told anyone about your Seven Summits dream," Marty said. "You're still hot on it, aren't you?"

"You bet we are. Between you and me, Frank and I recognize there isn't a great chance we'll get up Everest this try, especially on a new route, so now we're talking about setting aside eighty-three and doing all seven peaks in one calendar year."

"I'd still love to be a part," Marty said. "You want me along?"

"Absolutely! How'd I ever expect to climb them without you?"

"Well, I'd love to do it. First, though, I guess we'd better concentrate on this initial Everest trip."

"Yeah, and I'm just not sure about it," Dick admitted candidly. "I know a person's abilities are only limited by their self-doubts, but when it comes to Everest I can't help having a few."

"To be truthful, I don't know how I'll do, either," Marty said.

"As long as we're confessing," Dick said, "there's something else I haven't told anyone. I don't want you to think I'm involved in some kind of mumbo-jumbo, but for some years my wife has been seeing this psychic, a well-known one around Dallas. Now again, I don't want you to think I'm dealing in the occult, but in the past I've had a few experiences with psychics telling me about what my business life is going to be like, and the accuracy of those predictions just makes my hair stand on end.

"Well, my wife insisted I go see this psychic before leaving on these climbs," Dick continued, "and this one predicted that on Everest we are going to have a tragedy, and somebody is going to get killed. So now my wife is up in arms, telling me not to go. The logic side of my brain tells me not to pay attention, but nevertheless I can't get away from it, and I guess it makes me feel better to share it with someone."

"I don't believe you can just dismiss those things, either," Marty said. "You never know. And this climbing business is even more dangerous than you presently realize. I think something like two out of three expeditions that tries Everest loses at least one person."

There was a silence, then Marty said, "You know, Bass, I might not come back from Everest."

"Don't be silly, Marty. I didn't mean to put ideas in your head."

"You never know. But if I should make the big mistake, make sure they leave me on the mountain. And another thing, I wouldn't want any mourning. In fact, I would want all my friends to have a wake, but to have it as a big party and not to be sad. Because if I should happen to make the big mistake, I would be going out doing what I love the most, and that's really not that sad."

If it were in the cards for someone to make a fatal mistake even on this Aconcagua climb, lack of experience and climbing ability would seem to have placed Frank Wells in favored position. If he had been awkward on the approach march to the Polish Glacier route, then he was clumsy and unbalanced on the hard snow, where they had to strap crampons on their boots. The only other time Frank had worn crampons was on Mont Blanc (on Elbrus he had turned back before needing them). It takes some experience to learn to step comfortably with ten steel spikes protruding from the bottom of your boot, and Frank was finding himself not only mistakenly edging his crampons (causing them to slip out from underneath him) but also sometimes hooking the points on the inside of his opposite calf. On the lower glacier, where the slope was low-angled, tripping yourself like that was only an inconvenience; up near the summit, however, it could be fatal.

This climbing business was not child's play, as was all too clearly brought home to them by a frozen, weathered body they passed near the bottom of the glacier above camp 2. Ten days after beginning the climb they had established camp 3, their high camp, at 20,500 feet, and were ready in the morning for a summit attempt. That was, weather permitting. Until then every day had been brilliantly clear, but now clouds brought afternoon hail and there was concern a major storm would develop. Still, Wickwire made plans in case the dawn brought clear skies.

"We'll go in two ropes of three," he told everyone. "Marty with Dick and Chuck, me with Frank and Geo."

In this way Wickwire would keep each rope team at maximum strength. He knew he had the big challenge, getting Frank to the top of the mountain, but Marty, who had been tied to Frank all day, said he was doing better. Everyone felt good, too, and that evening they ate a hearty meal, had an extra cup of cocoa, and were to sleep early.

At 4:00 A.M. Wickwire poked his head out of the tent and saw a clear night sky. The morning star was so bright it cast a thin line of light on the glacial ice. It was absolutely still and quiet.

"Okay, everybody, we got our break. Let's get ready."

After a breakfast of instant oatmeal followed by several cups of tea and cocoa (knowing even with that they would be dehydrated before day's end) the climbers dressed and left camp. First light exposed the clear sky. There was no talk; each person kept his or her own thoughts; the only sound was of the cold steel spikes of their crampons squeaking as they bit into the icy dawn glacier. For a hundred feet their movements were mechanical, until they could walk out the night's stiffness and dispel that slight nauseous feeling that comes from predawn departures at high altitude. The brilliant light of the morning star held long after other stars had disappeared, but finally it too was absorbed into day and soon direct sun was on them. They made their first stop to shed parkas.

Above they could see the angle steepened to 30 degrees, and sometimes even 40 degrees. There were several large sections that showed the telltale gleam of hard ice. Normally this would have been no cause for concern, but as climbing ice (as opposed to snow) requires more expert technique, there was the question of how Frank could get past these sections. George Dunn led across the first; the others followed. As expected, Frank had problems.

Dick could see Frank was incorrectly keeping his ankles rigid instead of bending them so all ten points of his crampons bit evenly. When it got steeper Frank tended to weight the uphill edge of his boot even more. This was probably habit from downhill skiing, but in climbing such technique is disastrous. Dick mentioned this, but his advice didn't seem to make any difference. It was similar to the incident on Elbrus with the heavyweight underwear, and as he had then Dick began to wonder about his Seven Summits partner.

The others were also wondering. Frank was tied on a rope with Wickwire and Geo, and if Frank were to slip on the slick ice it was questionable whether they could hold him. Wickwire looked down the slope and imagined the long ride, certain to end in injury at best. But if they stopped to anchor the rope and give Frank a safety belay up each section, the time required would eliminate any chance of reaching the top in time to descend before nightfall.

Wickwire realized it had been a mistake to choose the Polish Glacier route. He wondered if perhaps they could traverse west and connect with the easier ruta normal. They decided to try, and with Wickwire leading they crossed a fan of scree that was like trying to traverse a sand dune. It was hard going, but at least safe. Spotting a gully that looked like it might connect to the summit ridge on the regular route, Wickwire went to scout it while the others waited.

"Bad news," he said when he got back. "It's a cul-de-sac."

"I'd like to keep traversing anyway," Marty said. "See if we could connect at a lower altitude."

"It'd be a long way," Wickwire pointed out. "And it's eleven-thirty already."

"It would be a good reconnaissance if nothing else," Marty countered.

"I'll go with you," Geo offered.

"Why don't we all go?" Frank said.

"Are you serious?" Wickwire stated incredulously. "It'll be extremely close if Marty and Geo don't get stuck bivouacking."

But Frank was serious. It was as though in his limited experience he could not realize just how slow and awkward he really was. Frank knew he was the weak link but what he didn't know was how easy it would be for him to push himself into a position he couldn't get out of.

"I'll take the others here back to camp," Wickwire told Marty.

"You're giving up on a summit try, then?" she asked.

"No. I might solo the Polish Glacier route in the morning."

Now it was the others' turn to be incredulous, but they knew Wickwire was experienced enough to judge such matters. Without further discussion the team split, Marty and Geo continuing on the traverse, the others descending to high camp.

They were quiet as they worked their way down a broad slope. Back at camp the mood was glum. Even Dick was too disappointed to strike up conversation. Frank collapsed outside his tent in the sun and was soon asleep. Wickwire got the binoculars and starting scanning the upper slopes to see if he could locate an alternate route on the Polish Glacier free of crevasses so he could make a solo attempt the next day. One way looked possible but still would involve crossing the bergshrund, the wide crevasse where the head of the glacier separated from the mountain.

To keep his mind off his disappointment, Dick concentrated on reading an account of a previous climb up the Polish Glacier, figuring such background might prove helpful. But he knew his chances were slim. If Marty and Geo came back too tired, and if Wickwire was going to solo in the morning, there was no hope that he could climb the mountain by himself. Obviously, Frank and Goldmark, both having trouble with the altitude, were out of it.

Maybe I ought to tell Wickwire how much I'd love to go with him, Dick thought.

But he hesitated.

No, he thought, I'm the neophyte and I'd better stay in my place.

Dick read the article for the third time, then noticed Frank was getting sunburned.

"Frank, wake up," Dick yelled.

"Huh?"

"You've got to learn to watch after yourself. You're getting sunburned."

Frank wouldn't move, so Dick got Wickwire to help drag him inside their tent, where he lay motionless the rest of the afternoon. Dick went back to the article. About 5:30 Marty and Geo returned, looking exhausted, and sat down on their packs without saying anything. Dick wasn't sure how far up they had made it, but he figured they looked so wiped out there was no chance they'd want to try it again tomorrow. Wickwire started the stove to make the pair a hot drink.

Marty looked over to Dick and said, "Whoever said this mountain is an easy walk up is full of it."

"What do you mean?"

"I mean it's a long way up there."

"You mean you made it?"

"Yeah, we made it." Marty was too exhausted even to grin.

"Well why in the heck didn't you say so?" Dick hooted.

Dick's excitement was dampened a moment later when he realized that now there really was no way they would go back up. He looked over to Wickwire, who again seemed deep in thought.

The bergshrund was bothering Wickwire. There was no safe way around it, and he had promised his wife he would never again take an unnecessary risk, not after he had nearly died on that high bivouac on K2. That time he had spent the night out alone at 28,000 feet with no sleeping bag or tent. At dawn he had been so exhausted from the ordeal all he had wanted to do was lie back and go to sleep, but an image in his mind of his wife and kids going to the airport and seeing all the team except him returning home gave him the strength to get up and continue the descent.

Wickwire looked toward Marty and said, "Do you think Bass could make it?"

Marty was still bent over with exhaustion, staring at her tea cup. Without looking up she said, "Bass can go, he can make it."

Dick wanted to hug and kiss her.

"Hey Bass," Wickwire called over. "You want to climb this thing with me in the morning?"

• • •

Dick moved to Wickwire's tent that evening, and at midnight he peered out the tent door. The night was cloudless, and he crossed his fingers, hoping the clear skies would hold. Now he was like a little kid waiting for dawn to bring Christmas morning. At 4:15 he shook Wickwire.

"Time to get ready, Wickwire."

It took two hours to melt the snow necessary for several rounds of hot tea and cocoa. Although they got away later than he would have liked, Wickwire was optimistic. Dick had shown the previous several days he was strong and could climb quickly, and besides they would be moving even faster because they were carrying next to nothing, only three liters of water and four candy bars. Soon they reached yesterday's high point, where they had traversed off the Polish Glacier, but now they continued upward. The ice was smooth and getting steeper.

When climbing steep ice it is sometimes necessary to front-point, to kick in the two crampon points that protrude from the toe of the boot like prongs on a pitchfork. When the ice is hard these points go in only a quarter inch or so and it takes experience to judge how much or little they will hold. When first tried it can be unnerving, and front-pointing was altogether new to Dick.

Wickwire showed Dick how to belay the rope, and then started up the first steep section, kicking in his front points and at the same time giving Dick a little on-the-job instruction.

"Keep your heels down, otherwise you put the wrong angle on the front points and they might pop."

Dick watched, trying to remember at the same time what Wickwire had told him about belaying the rope in case Wickwire should fall.

Was I supposed to hold firm with this hand, Dick thought, or this other hand?

"Swing your ice axe like this. You'll know by the feel when the bite is good."

"If you say so."

Please don't fall, Wickwire, Dick thought.

Minutes later Wickwire reached the end of the rope length, set up a belay and yelled to Dick, "Belay's on. Your turn."

Dick reached with his ice axe, swung it and felt the pick bite the ice. Then he kicked his boot but the points glanced off. He tried again and this time felt the points stick. He stepped up, and kicked in the other boot.

"That's the way," Wickwire called down encouragingly.

Dick was connected to the mountain only by the prongs of his front points and the tip of his ice axe—none of which was in the ice more than a half inch—and he welcomed any words of encouragement. He pried the ice axe loose, moved it up an arm's length, and swung again. It glanced off, and he tried again. Another glancing blow.

"Hold the shaft firmly, and swing with an even arc."

This time it held. Dick next moved his crampon points higher, first kicking one boot, then the other. In this vertical crab-crawl he climbed toward Wickwire, stopping once to look down to see the glacier falling away under his boots with only the four thin prongs connecting him to the mountain. He quickly looked back up and decided to pay attention only to the work directly in front of him.

Dick reached Wickwire and they repeated the same cycle, climbing four more rope lengths until the angle lay back and they could continue simultaneously. Wickwire set a fast pace, and occasionally Dick would yell for a rest, but his stops were always brief. Wickwire was impressed.

"Bass, if only I can be as strong when I'm fifty-two."

At this point the trick was to place your mind almost in a trance, to move one foot in front of the other at a pace slow enough to minimize rest stops and fast enough to reach the summit with enough daylight remaining to get down. Here Dick had experience; on McKinley he learned to push his body beyond what he thought possible. Dick found it amazing that with only a little water and two candy bars a person could accomplish so much work.

Eventually they came to the bergshrund Wickwire had spotted earlier through binoculars. The crevasse was wide and deep, and the only crossing appeared to be over a narrow snow bridge only a few feet thick. Wickwire took Dick's ice axe and drove it into the snow, showing Dick how to belay the rope around it and over the top of his boot, to hold him in case the bridge broke. Then Wickwire started across, probing as he went with his ice axe to test the snow. With careful steps, he crossed. On the other, higher side he set up the same ice axe–boot belay, and Dick started over.

"Follow my exact steps," Wickwire said.

Suddenly Dick's foot punched through and in a heartbeat the bridge started to crumple. Reflexively Dick leaped while at the same instant he swung his ice axe and dug in his front crampon points; they hit home in the opposite wall just as the rest of the bridge gave way into the deep crevasse. Dick pulled himself up on the axe shaft, wormed over the crevasse edge and joined Wickwire at the safe belay.

"Great going, Bass! Done like a real mountaineer," Wickwire said as he gave Dick a pat on the shoulder. Dick didn't know whether to just feel relieved he had made it, or be buoyant because he had performed so well.

Wickwire looked across the now bridgeless chasm but judged that on the way down with the uphill advantage they could probably jump it.

They guessed they were close to the top. A few hundred feet higher they could see a crest of snow with nothing behind or around it. They set a slow, even pace, making one step, breathing a few times, making another. Dick was elated, thinking how only yesterday afternoon he had nearly given up hope of reaching this point. He looked up. There was the crest, now only thirty more feet. He made a few more steps, then looked up again.

"Oh, my gosh," Dick said.

He was hoping his eyes were deceiving him, but he knew better. The crest wasn't the summit at all. Beyond it was another ridge, several hundred feet long, with another crest maybe a hundred feet higher. They continued their slow step, breath, step.

Dick was starting to feel exhausted. Haven't I been through enough not to have to suffer through this ordeal, Dick said to himself in a kind of half thought, half prayer.

Dick felt he was too close not to make it, however, and mustered the will to keep making more steps, resolving to make the summit no matter what. Now he only had forty more feet, thirty more . . .

"Oh, no! Another false summit."

The ridge continued higher, to another crest at least a hundred feet higher and again several hundred further. Dick felt himself sink, the elation he had felt seconds ago changed to dismay, even doubt.

I'm not going to make it, he thought. This close, and I'm not going to make it.

But he did make another step, then another. He tried to ignore his fatigue, his aching legs and lungs. Step, breath, breath, step.

I was tired just below the summit of McKinley, he told himself, and I made that. So I know I've got it in me to make this one, too.

Step, breath, step, breath.

Each step now seemed like it took minutes. He knew it wasn't that much time, but the fatigue made it seem that way. He thought about looking up from his feet again, but decided not to. He couldn't bear another disappointment. He made a few more steps. He changed his mind, and glanced up quickly.

What's that on top of the crest just in front, he wondered. A cross? Yeah, it's a cross. That means it's got to be the summit.

Wickwire had now stopped, and Dick caught up to him. With twenty steps left they interlocked arms around each other's shoulders and side-by-side walked to the summit of Aconcagua.

The highest point in the western hemisphere: 22,835 feet.

"Bass, this has been one of the best summit days I've had. It's been a real pleasure climbing with you."

Dick beamed with pride and felt a tear in his eye. Coming from a veteran like Wickwire, it made him feel like he had really won his spurs. Below them through building clouds they could see the sweep of snow mountains extending north and south, a view to match Dick's joy.

"Aah-eah-eaahhh," Dick bellowed.

Storm clouds, then snow hampered their descent. Belays down a steep, icy section next to the Piedra Bandera, a prominent rock mass on the east side of the glacier, took two hours and they found themselves at nightfall groping their way across heavily crevassed portions of the glacier back toward their camp on the west side—which they had left over thirteen hours earlier.

Both of them were lightly clothed and Dick had real concern not only about the crevasses, but about not finding their camp as well. It would be just my fate, he thought, after climbing this mountain, to freeze to death in this storm. This wasn't just an idle or "nervous Nellie" concern, either; not too far below them lay the body they had seen coming up. Possibly the man had perished just this way the year before. Dick could see the corpse clearly in his mind, spread-eagled on its back.

All of a sudden, George Dunn came out of the darkness right in front of them. Marty and the others had descended that morning, but he had waited at high camp for them because of the storm and finally couldn't stand the anxiety any longer, deciding to go look for them with a tent and some food in his pack. He knew it would be difficult to survive the night without some help, but he really didn't think he could find them on such a large glacier, at night and in the middle of a snowstorm.

They all hugged, roped one to the other, and Geo led them out of their trial—at least this trial of finding camp. For Dick, though, another trial was about to begin.

Just as he was making his last step from the hard, pocked glacier ice onto the rock of their campsite, his left foot dropped abruptly into a hole he hadn't seen in the dark. He yelled and toppled over, sliding downhill while clutching his left calf. Geo and Wickwire immediately leaped back onto the glacier and fell on top of him, arresting his movement with their crampons and ice axes.

He had really torn it, literally and figuratively. His gastrocnemius muscle was shredded and so was any reasonable chance of getting off the mountain, particularly with the tortuous route that lay below.

That night his lower leg swelled up like a balloon and the slightest jar would give him pain. Early next morning they were pondering what to do, when Dick asked if they had any pain pills, so he could move enough to go to the bathroom. Fortunately, Wickwire had some triple Empirin with codeine, which Dick started taking. Within fifteen minutes he was able to move slowly, so long as he didn't put any weight on his left leg; it was aching, but only had sharp pain if he jerked or vibrated, or accidentally put weight on it. Encouraged, Dick told them he would try to descend the mountain on his good right leg, using his two ski poles for support. Actually, there was no alternative; they certainly couldn't carry him.

For the next two days he tediously made his way down from 20,500 feet through sections that were challenging enough on the ascent, when he had two good legs. At times he would stumble or fall, and the pain would knife through him so badly he couldn't get his breath, but he finally reached the Vacas River at 10,000 feet. There they met with an Argentine mountaineering detachment that was on training maneuvers, and the soldiers considerately put him on one of their mules. The next day he rode the remaining twenty miles to the highway and civilization.

For Dick, his summit success as well as his gutsy descent, bolstered his confidence, and reduced his anxiety about Everest, although it didn't eliminate it, assuming his leg would heal in time. He was concerned about Frank, though, because for him this would be another to add to his growing list of failures. He hoped Frank wasn't becoming discouraged. He had enjoyed Frank's company in Russia, and on this climb too, and if Frank should lose enthusiasm Dick knew he could never find a replacement.

Dick was pleased, then, when Frank said he still had a full head of steam.

"I'm disappointed, sure, but not discouraged," Frank said.

He told Dick he still felt it was a question of conditioning, that all he needed was to go home and work out harder and then spend two or three months on Everest. After that, he would be ready for the Seven Summits year.

Dick certainly hoped Frank was right. But he couldn't help but note that Frank really did seem unaware of just how bad he had been on this climb. Frank didn't even seem to suspect that he was the reason everyone had turned back that day of their first summit attempt, not only because of his slowness, but also his inability to learn to use his crampons and ice axe, to manage a rope, and most of all, to judge the limits of his strength.

Dick decided not to say anything. He was just glad Frank still wanted to go through with the Seven Summits plan, and, being the optimist he was, hoped that things would work out, that maybe on Everest Frank would somehow change and get a lot better.

Two weeks after Frank and Dick left Aconcagua a Canadian climber named Patrick Morrow arrived to climb the mountain. By coincidence, Morrow also had come to Aconcagua as conditioning for an Everest expedition. He was a member of a large Canadian team that had a permit from the Nepalese government to attempt the mountain in the coming fall of 1982.

Morrow was twenty-eight years old, and made his living as a photojournalist specializing in outdoor adventure subjects, especially mountaineering. It was a tough way to make a living, and he had developed a habit of always thinking about things he could do that would interest his editors. He reached the summit of Aconcagua without any difficulty, and while making his descent a particularly appealing idea hit him. He had just climbed the highest mountain in South America. The year before he had climbed McKinley, the highest mountain in North America. He was on his way to try to climb the highest mountain in Asia. If by chance he did manage to get up Everest, why not try to climb the highest peak on each of the remaining continents?

He was sure no one had ever done it. What he didn't know, of course, was that an Oxford Rhodes scholar nearly thirty years before had had the same idea while coming off Kilimanjaro, and that a Dallas businessman in his fifties had had the same idea only the previous spring while coming off McKinley. And he had no idea he was now following their footsteps on Aconcagua.

He wouldn't find that out until he was far along toward realizing his own dream of being the first up the Seven Summits.

EVEREST: THE NORTH WALL

Dick Bass relaxed in his dinette seat, lulled by the metronomic kla-klack, kla-klack, kla-klack of the train's wheels and the wistful whistle of the steam locomotive. Out the window the rows of tall poplars bordering cotton fields cast blinking shadows on the curtains of their first-class sleeper. With sunset light on the water they crossed a steel trestle over the great Huang, China's celebrated Yellow River.

"Two days on a train is just what I needed," Dick said to Frank. "I don't think I got more than two hours sleep out of the last 72 before we left."

As always the demands of Snowbird had kept Dick juggling on a tightrope. He thought of his frenzied pace and how he hadn't been able to spend any time training for this once in a lifetime experience. So many people assumed he was related to the affluent Bass family of Fort Worth and would probably think this was just another diversion to tide him over the midlife crisis, much like they thought Snowbird was just another hobby. This hurt him. Enduring his perpetual roller-coaster ride wouldn't be nearly as wearing if people only knew the sacrifices Snowbird had required these past thirteen years. And the climbing was actually just a means of trying to keep his head screwed on straight, so he could hang in there on the Bird. Anyway, he wouldn't have to keep the pins in the air now, at least not for the next two months. He had left his business manager, Thurman Taylor, to deal with it, and he now felt free to concentrate on Everest.

Dick still felt a vague unease when he thought of the thin atmosphere above 22,835 feet—the summit of Aconcagua, which was now his personal best altitude record. These last few weeks had been so hectic, though, he really hadn't dwelled on it; now, with more time, he again felt that uncertainty, but in typical Bass fashion pushed it aside, telling himself Everest would be like any other project. Albert Schweitzer had said, "Every start upon an untrodden path is a venture which only in unusual circumstances looks sensible and likely to succeed."

If, for Dick, Everest was an untrodden path, for Frank it was a potential landmine. Following his return from Aconcagua, Frank did begin to realize somewhat how far it was he had to go if he were to have any success at all on the Seven Summits. Although it wouldn't be until much later when he would look back with more experienced eyes that he would see he really had no hope of ever climbing Aconcagua on that first attempt, he was sensing there was only the remotest chance he could get up Everest. But he was committed to performing much better than he had on Aconcagua, to carry as many loads to the highest camps as possible. In the few weeks between Aconcagua and departure to China he had upped his exercise regimen to two hours a day.

The train sped into the night, and the darkness outside shrank their world to the eight-by-twelve confines of their sleeper. The train passage from Peking to Chengdu was more indulgence than necessity, as the team could have as easily flown, but everyone had felt it would be fun to see the countryside. Frank was surprised to find himself enjoying the ride; normally he would have lacked patience for a gratuitous two-day extension to a schedule.

Frank was also enjoying the camaraderie of this relaxed interlude and the talks with Dick and the others. Here was Marty Hoey, stopping by their stateroom for a chat. Frank was impressed by Marty's ability to always be one of the guys yet at the same time always be the lady on the team. She had a smile that matched the pretty features of her oval face, yet she could just as quickly raise her left eyebrow with an authoritative skepticism. She could move with grace and femininity, yet her shoulders were strong and her legs powerful. On a

climb she would move her feet with firm placement and plant her ice
axe with precision. Yet also on a climb she would be careful to have
her hair always under a freshly laundered scarf, and a pendant from
a fine chain around her neck.

Frank considered how this young lady was in position to become
the first American woman to climb Everest, and later with him and
Dick, she might also become the first woman to climb the Seven
Summits. Frank's mind went back to a visit Marty had made to L.A.
just before they had left for Aconcagua, and to a morning when she
accompanied him on his run up Mulholland. Frank was determined
to show he was getting in shape, and set the fastest pace he dared
up the hill. She stayed with him, but he had the impression she did
so only out of courtesy. On each curve Marty took the outside, chiding
Frank to do the same: a fast car on a blind curve might not have time
to swing wide. That was like Marty, always cautious, always planning
the safe strategy, always being the guide. Near the top she could no
longer restrain herself, and breaking to a near-sprint had dashed the
last quarter mile, then waited politely for Frank to catch up.

It was late afternoon on the second day when the train descended
from the steep hills to the rich riceland basin of Central Szechwan,
and nightfall when they pulled into Chengdu station. They were
escorted to the Jin Jiang Hotel, seven high-ceilinged stories reminiscent of the austere architecture they had seen in Russia. Probably
the place had been built in the fifties, when Soviet influence yet
prevailed. Two days later they were again reminded of the old geo-
politics when they boarded a vintage Russian Ilyushin turboprop for
the four-hour flight to Lhasa.

The eastern margin of the high Tibetan Plateau rises abruptly a
short distance out of Chengdu and on occasional clear days rice
farmers in their paddies can see in the distance the shimmering snows
of a peak called Minya Konka, rising to over 24,000 feet elevation.
Through the plane's window the team spotted this precipitous peak
—first climbed in 1932 by an intrepid team of young Harvard
students—looking like a shark's fin cutting the rarefied atmosphere.
Beyond Minya Konka lay a sea of summits quite beyond anything
they had seen before. In the compressed folds of the peaks lay the
valley headwaters of four of the world's great rivers: the Irrawaddy,
the Salween, the Mekong, the Yangtze. Below their wings were unknown regions, peaks even the Chinese knew little or nothing about.

They landed outside Lhasa and drove into town in a microbus

provided by the Chinese Mountaineering Association. Their hosts put them in a recently finished tourist guest house, and in a way it again reminded Frank of Russia where so many things were half-finished: here were fixtures for hot water but no hot water, flush toilets that didn't flush. Unlike Russia, however, these accommodations came with a high price.

When the Chinese first opened their mountains to foreign climbers, in 1979, there was much speculation why they had so suddenly reversed their long xenophobia. Perhaps it was a political move, an extension of the thaw that started with the invitation of the U.S. Ping-Pong team. When the first American expeditions returned from their climbs in 1980, however, it was apparent the Chinese had their sights on something else: foreign currency.

Unable to resist a mischievous jab, Frank cornered the liaison officer appointed to accompany the team to base camp. "When we were in Russia last year," he said, "we had two weeks with all hotels, buses, airfare, food, and two guides, for eight hundred dollars apiece. You guys charge eight thousand, maybe more."

Actually Frank didn't care if the Chinese were overcharging. He found it more interesting than annoying, and what he was really trying to do was get the liaison officer into a conversation on his favorite subject, politics.

Frank also thought the accommodations were adequate. It wasn't the Ritz, but then two months in tents strung up and down Everest wasn't going to be, either. He and Dick unpacked, then visited the others before turning in. Tomorrow they would have time to tour Lhasa, then the following day load into a minibus and start the four-day drive toward Everest base camp.

One of Marty's roommates had his cassette machine playing a forties tune.

"My kind of dancing music," Dick said.

"Wish I knew how to dance to this," Marty replied.

"Well, I can teach you."

Dick, who felt confident in his ability to lead even the shyest woman on the dance floor, was glad for the opportunity to reverse the teacher/student roles with Marty. Soon he and Marty were fox-trotting on the worn carpet floor of this Lhasa cottage. But, like a little girl, Marty kept saying she couldn't do it, and he was tempted to repeat back to her what she had put on him whenever he said he didn't have time to train: "No excuses, Bass. Your friends don't need any, and your enemies won't believe them." It was interesting, this trait she had of alternating between helpless maiden and pile-driving martinette. He recalled seeing her in a dress for the first time at a party at Snowbird and how feminine she looked. "Gosh, Marty, I've never seen you in a dress before," he told her. Marty replied, "I love dresses, Bass, but I can't afford them because you pay such paltry wages." Then Dick thought how next day she went back to her jeans, back to the mountain, back to being a real take-charge leader, demanding of the personnel who worked under her their best performance, and also feeling for them a responsibility, making sure when the season slowed they were the last to get laid off.

That was Marty: one minute acting like a helpless little girl, the next "wearing the pants" like a superconfident leader. Now she literally had pants on again, but he noticed she also wore the earrings he had bought for her in Chile, after Aconcagua. He had been in a jewelry store getting a gift for his wife, and Marty had happened in and was admiring the earrings but said she couldn't afford them. So when Marty left Dick had bought them and later surprised her. Now, as he taught her the basic fox-trot in that spartan room high on the Tibetan Plateau, he noticed she had them on, those simple but elegant lapis lazuli earrings.

They were seventeen climbers and six tons of food and equipment, and it took a minibus followed by a caravan of bulbous fendered Chinese flatbeds to move them across the Tibetan Plateau. In places the road crossed rocky streambeds and they had to get out and help push the trucks through. On the fourth day, they crossed a pass and had their first close look at the mountain they had traveled half the world to climb.

Even at thirty miles the great summit dominated the skyline; on this north side the sweep of its pyramid was unobstructed, rising white and black, snow and rock. From the top the emblematic plume boiled to leeward a mile or more, like a banner off the lance of a royal knight: it marked the great altitude where the summit punctured the jet stream.

The climbers yelled to the truck driver to stop. They stared at the mountain in silence. It was a couple of minutes before anyone spoke.

"The Great Couloir looks straightforward but it might be a tricky exit."

"I bet we can get it with five camps. Top one about twenty-six five, then go for it."

"Long summit day, though."

"It's going to be tough, oxygen or no oxygen."

Tough, but exciting. The adrenaline charge from that first view lasted until about nine in the evening two days later when they finally lumbered into base camp, the trucks wheezing in the thin air. If the trucks were feeling the altitude, the climbers were faring better, having benefitted from the days in Lhasa and then the overland drive, all at more than 12,000 feet. They quickly pitched tents, and settled in for a good night's sleep.

There was another team sharing the base camp site, a small but powerful four-man British group lead by the indomitable Chris Bonington. They proposed to climb the unscaled northeast ridge of Everest, and would be hiking upglacier with the North Wall team to a point where they would then diverge on a subsidiary glacier leading to their route. Bonington was England's best-known mountaineer and the veteran of at least eight Himalayan expeditions. He had been the leader of two previous Everest climbs, the last of which, in 1975, made the first ascent of the mountain's formidable southwest face. He had never personally reached the top, however, and he was hopeful this time he would make it.

The two teams spent the next day swapping stories while they worked around camp. The Americans had to sort gear and divide loads for yaks to carry to advanced base camp, to be located about eight miles up glacier, at a site just under 19,000 feet elevation.

Yaks, the shaggy-haired oxen of Tibet and Central Asia—once described by a climber as the Mack Truck of the Himalaya—are temperamental but strong, able to carry 120 pounds on rocky, icy trails between 12,000 and 22,000 feet. In fact, they seem to perform better the higher they go; if a yak is taken to lower elevations it becomes sickly. Word went out that the climbers would need dozens of these beasts to carry loads up the margin of the Rongbuk Glacier, and soon the animals and their nomadic owners arrived.

For much of the distance the team hiked alongside a long chain of ice towers up to a hundred feet high, a fairybook icescape caused by diurnal freezing and melting. Even though the route gained little elevation, 8 miles at over 17,000 feet was still a bone-wearying long way, and for Frank and Dick the campsite came none too soon. Despite the available yak transport, both Frank and Dick had chosen, as had everyone else on the team, to carry heavy packs, to help them get in shape. This set the pattern for the next three weeks. While the lead climbers shared the job of scouting the best route from advanced base another 5 miles upglacier to camp 1, and then from there to the site of camp 2, at the foot of the great North Wall at 20,300 feet, everyone else including Frank and Dick shared the tiresome task of ferrying from one camp to the next the several tons of food and equipment.

Frank noticed this load-carrying was done with a tacit but barely concealed competition, and that an individual's performance—or lack of it—did not escape unnoticed. Thus, when Jim Wickwire, struggling with a heavy pack, was slowly approaching advanced base camp and Lou got up to walk down the route and help him with part of his load, another team member stopped him: "Everyone has to carry their own weight around here." Thus Lou Whittaker, transporting equipment from camp 1 to 2, pulled two sleds instead of the normal one and was careful upon arriving in camp to leave them fully loaded and on display in the circle of tents. Without experience to compare, Frank assumed this was part of the stamina-building strategy necessary to climb high-altitude peaks (he would later learn that it had more to do with the inherent competitiveness of a team of professional guides who had among them a hierarchy of rank and skill). Without fully realizing it, Frank little by little became determined to prove his mettle. He told himself that while he might not have the stuff that would get him to the top, he would show everyone he could carry heavy loads between the lower camps, day after day.

For two weeks he did just that, carrying thirty to forty pounds a day, usually from camp 1 to 2. Meanwhile the lead climbers fixed ropes toward the Great Couloir.

Dick also was working hard carrying loads but edged ahead of Frank delivering food, equipment, and oxygen tanks first to camp 2 and then to 3. Dick found each day he was a notch stronger, and as he acclimatized he increased his payload to equal what the lead climbers were hauling, sometimes more than fifty pounds. At this rate he judged he might have a shot at the top, especially if the lead climbers fixed ropes most of the way. Maybe it would even work out that he could team with Marty as they had planned at Snowbird, but he didn't want to build any unrealistic expectations.

While Dick gained strength, Frank found each day he was weakening. After three weeks he had lost nearly twenty pounds and had a cough he couldn't kick. But determined as ever, he took only one rest day a week. Those were days to be cherished, days when you slept in, then with great laziness washed your clothes, perhaps yourself, and, unless you took a nap, read a book or wrote a letter home.

The mail service on Everest, if you could call it that, had disappointed everyone; up to then, Frank was the only one who had received a letter, and at least it had contained good news from his former colleagues at Warner Bros. They had won the best picture Oscar for *Chariots of Fire*.

Even though he didn't receive much mail (they found out later it had by mistake been held up) that didn't discourage Frank from writing home. Twenty-eight days after reaching base camp, Frank wrote to his family a progress report:

20 April

Dear Family,

There are eight of us here at base camp on "R&R." No one is at camp 1 at the moment, but five are in camp 2, carrying each day to camp 3 where three are staying and trying, despite our first bad weather, to finish locating camp 4 at 23,700 feet. The ropes to camp 4 have already been fixed up a 45-degree slope, and now platforms for the tents have to be built in the snow. Each day decisions are made over the radio as to who should be in what camp and what supplies should be carried to the next higher camps, and things are in a constant change depending on the physical condition of each of the sixteen climbers, and the weather.

The next step is to locate camp 5 at the edge of the Great Couloir, then camp 6 at the top of the Couloir, about 26,500 or 27,000 feet. That will be the last stopping (sleeping point) before the summit. We plan to begin using bottled oxygen above camp 6. This is a good deal higher than most expeditions start using it, but there have been three people who have summitted without using oxygen at all, and some of our young bucks may have a go at trying it this way as well.

It is also significant that our expedition, unlike all but one previous Everest attempt, is using no Sherpas or porters (they're only available on the Nepal side). Since the yaks left our gear here at base camp, we have been on our own, and so far we're pleased with our progress.

Now here are a few other things you may find interesting.

First, despite my fairly intense training for eight months, I am not even close to the physical condition of the others, particularly the ten "hotshots" (my term) who as professional climbing guides have taken clients up Mount Rainier anywhere between 100 and 200 times each. You can't imagine what it's like "humping" thirty-five pounds from camp 1 to 2, moving as well as you can (but still slow, still breathing very hard) and to have someone like Marty Hoey come blazing past you whistling, yes whistling, some tune!

Second, I simply lack the technical climbing knowledge these people have. I'm not the one who rigs the fixed ropes to ice screws; I'm not the one who picks the routes and campsites. This was understood at the outset, and I decided from the start it would be best to give my all to humping loads of equipment between the lower camps. So during the first seventeen days of the climb, I carried fifteen loads between base camp, camp 1, and camp 2. I was urged to take a few days off, but I felt strongly I had to do more carries than anyone to make up for my deficiencies.

Well, all this came to a crashing halt a few days ago when our team doctor, Ed Hixson, sleeping in the next tent, heard my coughing all night and next day gave me a physical. I'd lost thirty pounds. That was no mystery, really, as it's common to lose weight at high altitude. You really need to eat 6,000 calories a day just to hold even, but it's hard when the food isn't great, when you don't feel like eating—because of the altitude—and when it's easy to skip lunch when you're in the middle of a carry. So I am weak from the weight loss, but my cough may also be beginning pneumonia. As a result, Hixson said, "No more carrying for now, down to base camp, lots of food, pills for the coughing, and I'll tell you when you can start carrying again."

I guess I have to be honest and say it's a relief. Lou himself is here in advanced base for a rest, and he has told me I have already done so much more than anyone expected from a fifty-year-old novice. You have no idea how important these words were to me—said before half the team. I know, though, I have simply no chance of being one of those who reach the top. But if I leave feeling I have done my share of the work, and the team is successful, I will be completely fulfilled.

So for the next month I will first repair myself, then begin again with fairly light carries. Then maybe in a couple of weeks or so, just maybe, on a nice clear day, I can go to camp 3, and from there—this is all speculation, as I doubt I'll make it—maybe camp 4. But I do assure you, one and all, that the route, with fixed ropes laid, is totally safe.

So sometime around late May or early June, I'll be home. My God, you do get homesick, too, for so many, many things you haven't even thought about for so long. So I'll be home, maybe not much wiser, certainly a bit lighter, and probably a touch more content.

> Much love to you all,
> Frank

Dick Bass rested his forearms on his knees to relieve the weight of his pack; he didn't have to bend far since the snow slope was steep. The jumar clamp he used to ascend fixed rope was cammed firmly onto the line, and attached by a nylon webbing sling to his waist harness so he was secure in case he should slip. Looking up he could see, a few hundred feet beyond, the tents at camp 4. There was a climber leaving camp, beginning to rappel down the line; that would have to be somebody off the lead team who had been working to establish camp 5, probably coming down for a rest at a lower camp. Dick could see they would cross on the rope in a few minutes.

With his ice axe Dick cut a small platform in the snow and then unshouldered his forty-pound pack and balanced it on the level, connecting with a carabiner to his jumar so it wouldn't take off if he happened to bump it. With the pack's shoulder straps off he breathed freely and leaned on his knee against the steep slope to enjoy a well-earned rest.

As it had for Frank (until his illness, anyway), this expedition for Dick distilled down to a daily exercise of carrying loads at ever-increasing altitudes. He didn't begrudge the duty, for he knew that all the while he was learning—learning to handle the steep route, learning to pace himself, learning how his body reacted to high altitude. On that last point he was especially pleased; it seemed he was physically gifted for this sort of thing, and he was feeling stronger each day despite the altitude of almost 24,000 feet.

Still, he knew there was little chance he would reach the top. First, the expedition was struggling to get to camp 5, and above that, camp 6. The climbing was tough, and without any porters or Sherpas to help carry loads much of the expedition's strength was expended on that job. Dick was realizing that each pound of food or equipment that was ultimately delivered to the high camp represented considerable toil: it was a pound that had gone from one camp to the next, carried by climbers who were also burning the stove fuel and eating the food to get the energy to carry more food and fuel. Then when he considered the effort that would be required once they started breathing oxygen, above camp 6, out of cylinders that weighed seventeen pounds each, that had also been carried up one camp to the next, each camp a day's climb apart, the full scope of the task really sank in. It was easy to see how they had been working for thirty-five days and still had a long way to go.

So Dick was quite certain that when the time came there would be available provisions only for a few of the strongest climbers to attempt the top, and it was obvious that such a formula would exclude him, as it should. Even without a climb to the summit it was all marvelously worthwhile, not only because of the knowledge and experience that would be invaluable when he and Frank returned again to Everest as part of their Seven Summits dream (although they still had no idea exactly how they would do that), but also because of the unusual adventure, because of moments like this. Moments when you had a short rest from hard work, work that freed you instead of shackling you, good physical work that was half the world away from the bankers telling you what you could or couldn't do. Work that seemed to clear your brain of the fog that down below often muddled how you saw things. Up here the view was sharp-edged and crystal. Up here you sat on a perch like an eagle in an aerie, gazing over a domain of ice and rock. Over the Rongbuk Glacier, that frozen river moving inexorably toward the Tibetan Plateau, ice overlaying desert. Over the immense North Wall, that 10,000 vertical feet of rock and ice.

Dick looked up. That figure he had seen earlier coming out of camp 5 had now grown to a recognizable human with shining black hair emerging from a freshly laundered babushka.

"Marty, it's great to see you."

"Hi, Bass."

Dick hadn't seen Marty for over a week. She had been working to put in the high camp while he was hauling loads at mid-elevations. It was curious how on the climb you often went two weeks or more without seeing some of your companions; Dick hadn't seen Frank, for example, since he had contracted pneumonia two weeks ago. But he knew Frank was better and starting to carry again, and would probably be up to this level soon.

"Bass, I've been getting reports about how you've been carrying all these heavy loads. I'm proud of you."

Dick swelled up like a male grouse on display. "Marty, you don't know how much your compliment means to me."

"I'd have to be blind to miss that. You haven't forgotten about our deal have you? We're still going to the top, you know, me and you."

"Marty, I don't know. I think when the moment of truth comes there may only be room for a few selects on the summit teams and you'd have a lot better chance with someone more experienced."

"No way. Deal's a deal."

"We'll see when the time comes, but whatever God wills I want you to know I appreciate your still wanting to take me."

"How's everyone else? Seen Lou?"

"We came up to three together yesterday. Paid me a heck of a compliment, said I handled the rope better than anyone he'd been tied to this trip. But then that's because I had a good teacher."

Marty smiled. Dick continued. "Then we tented together, and his appreciation waned when I started to recite poetry. He kind of rolled over and cold-backed me. Guess he didn't want a large-mouthed Bass laying a poem on him at 23,000 feet."

"His problem. What poem?"

"Well, I've put Lasca to memory."

"Lasca! Bass, you know that's my favorite, well, one of my favorites. I've got the Xerox of "Evolution" you gave me in my pack. Boy, Lasca is a lot to memorize. I don't see how you did it."

"Unless you can sleep fourteen hours a day there's a lot of time lying awake in your sleeping bag."

"Think you could recite it now?"

"Thought you'd never ask."

Although there was no audience on the climb he would have preferred to Marty, he also knew how much she loved the poem so he made a silent prayer he didn't screw up. He recited it, though, without missing a word of the poignant story told by a cowboy of his half-breed woman who gave her life to save him in a cattle stampede.

Marty was thrilled.

"Dick, do those last lines again."

Dick recited the last lines over:

> *"And I wonder why I do not care*
> *For the things that are like the things that were.*
> *Does half my heart lie buried there*
> *In Texas, down by the Rio Grande."*

Marty pursed her lips and fought back a tear. "Thanks Dick. That was great."

She turned and continued down the rope, and Dick noticed she was wearing those lapis earrings, and they matched her blue babushka.

Camp 5 was established at the base of the Great Couloir. After several days rest, Marty was back up the mountain, and with some of the others started the effort to establish camp 6 at about 26,500 feet. Once that camp was in and sufficiently stocked they would be in position for the first summit attempt. The team for that first effort was now chosen: Larry Nielson (the team member with perhaps the strongest physical endurance), Jim Wickwire, Marty Hoey. Dick and Frank were both excited for Marty; she was now in position to accomplish her dream of becoming the first American woman on top of Everest.

Meanwhile Dick had stayed in camp 3, each day humping loads up to 4, and now Frank moved up to join him. There was a third person in camp 3, Steve Marts, a Seattle-based climber and documentary filmmaker who was a one-man cinematography team shooting and recording a 16mm film of the expedition. Both Frank and Dick had been impressed watching Marts, using a camera with a sound recorder strapped on and a microphone attached to the top, single-handedly get synced-sound coverage of the expedition, including the climbing up to about 25,000 feet.

This was the first time since his illness that Frank had seen Dick, and as Marts was crowded by himself in the cook tent, Frank moved in with Dick. They were both pleased at the chance to share time together. They were the neophytes, the outsiders in a sense. Conversation relating to sex and mountains was interesting enough, but nevertheless they both had other common interests which they enjoyed talking about.

But while they shared much, they were also very different from each other in some significant ways. Dick was open and gregarious, while Frank had a certain brusqueness that kept people at bay. Then, too, the pair were opposites when it came to the way they organized their lives. Frank was a delegating generalist, Dick the finicky, nit-picking do-it-himself type. Finally, they were at opposite ends of the political spectrum. Frank was a flaming liberal, Dick the arch conservative. And that led to some lively badinage during the many weeks they spent sleeping in the same two-man tent.

"Frank, what I don't understand is why you can't be more intellectually honest about human nature and get past your bleeding heart advocacy of socialism."

"I don't advocate socialism. I advocate social welfare."

"Welfare! The only way you'll help man is to get man to help himself."

Steve Marts, listening in his nearby tent, thought, Boy, these two really are The Odd Couple.

"Look," Dick continued, "it's not the duty of the government to support the people, but rather the duty of the people to support the government."

"You got to admit, though, Kennedy was more eloquent."

"But he didn't practice what he preached. Frank, I'm telling you, you're wearing blinders. Now I figure you and I have a lot of tent time coming up together if we're going to do these Seven Summits, and by golly if there's one thing I want to accomplish it's to turn you around politically."

Now Marts yelled over, "What's Seven Summits?"

Other than Marty, Frank and Dick really hadn't discussed their Seven Summits dream with anyone. It wasn't that they wanted to keep it a secret as much as they felt sheepish talking about such a bold plan in front of some of the world's best climbers, especially when they themselves were such amateurs. But now that the cat was out of the bag they saw no harm in describing the project to Marts.

"Come on over here and we'll explain it," Dick said.

Dick told Marts about the plan, and when he finished he suddenly had an idea. He was annoyed it hadn't occurred to him earlier, but here he was about to commit a great deal of time, risk, and money and he ought to have a film of it, if for no other reason than to show it to his children and grandchildren, and to remember his adventures once he was an old man. He visualized how it would be when he was ninety-five. He'd be in a rocker, and all he'd have to do was push a button and a screen would come down and the movie would start, and he'd rock back and forth pointing at the screen yelling, "Look at that boy go."

"Marts, by golly, we've got to film the Seven Summits!"

Marts didn't say anything for a moment. Dick could tell he was mulling the idea over. Then he answered, "Dick, that's a fantastic story line. I mean it's commercial: two businessmen at age fifty either give up or jeopardize their successful careers to try to climb the highest peak on each continent. Do you realize with a film you could pay for your climbs?"

"You've got to be kidding!"

"Not only that, but you'd be a folk hero."

Dick nearly gagged at that.

"Marts, you're full of B.S."

"No, I mean it."

"You really think so?" Dick then looked over to Frank, who was reading a book. "What do you think, Frank?"

"It'll never sell."

"Wells, sometimes you're such a wet blanket. What do you mean?"

"First, it's hard as hell to even make your money back on an expensive documentary. Second, we're probably going to have to climb Everest in the wrong sequence. Our most likely chance is to hook up with one of the groups going next spring, and that means the drama will be backwards. You want the hardest to come last, so it climaxes. The way we're doing it, we go up Kosciusko last, and that's a hike up a trail to only 7,300 feet. In fact, there's a gravel highway going up it. The whole thing's scripted wrong."

"Frank, I've been telling you what my life is like back home, with people always telling me I can't do this or that, dampening my enthusiasm, and here I am at 24,000 feet on the side of Mount Everest and the same thing's following me up here. Now you might be some great Hollywood movie mogul but that doesn't mean you know everything about this stuff, and Marts here, who has years of experience in this documentary business, says it will go over like gangbusters. He even says we'll be folk heroes."

Frank smiled condescendingly and went back to his book, but Dick wasn't about to give up.

"You've got to think positive. There's a solution to this getting the sequence in order."

While Frank read, Dick lay thinking of possible solutions and forgot the time. He looked at his watch and said, "Darn, forgot to turn on the radio for the afternoon call. I wanted to get news on how they're doing above."

"We'll get the morning call," Frank said, and went back to his book. Dick slept hardly at all that night, pondering the film problem; at first light he shook Frank.

"I got it," Dick said.

"Got what?"

"Got how to end this film. How we're going to climb Kosciusko last and still have a great ending. You and I'll put on running shorts with packs on our backs and we'll jog up there—that'll give it some interest—and while we're doing that we'll have had our wives and best friends flown over there and get the longest black limos we can find and they'll be in tuxes and evening dresses, see, and while you and I are jogging up the road they'll come by in this limo and lean out the window and the sun will glisten on their studs and jewelry and we'll be sweating—that'll get a good laugh—and when we get to the top I have this Swiss chef named Hans who is the consummate sculptor and can take a huge hunk of ice and carve it into a horse's head or an eagle—any darn thing you want—like no one you ever saw, so we'll get him down there and have an ice carving on the summit and a banquet table waiting for us. It'll be a feast that would make Nebuchadnezzar envious, and the others will be waiting . . ."

"I'll get my mother, too," Frank said, "and a few other friends . . ."

". . . and then we'll go behind a rock," Dick continued, "and out will fly our T-shirts and jock straps and then you and I will emerge looking resplendent in our tuxes, then we'll hug our wives and friends and we'll go to the food spread where there'll be a pig with an apple in its mouth, pheasant under glass, oysters and shrimp and caviar piled high—remember the eating scene from *Tom Jones*, Frank? Heck, that'll be nothing, this will be sensual like that—gorging ourselves on gourmet delights while overlaying this—now close your eyes and imagine it—overlaying this are scenes of us with ice in our beards, and the wind blowing snow, and all this misery we got up here right now eating gruel out of tin cups, it'll be the juxtaposition of the incongruous that'll make it hilarious, Frank, and then we'll pop the bubbly and fade out, walking down the road into the sunset with our backpacks on over the tuxes and champagne in our hands."

Frank was smiling. "Not bad, Bass, not bad. That might work."

Buoyed with enthusiasm for his plan, Dick started dressing for that day's carry up to camp 4. Marts was in the other tent making breakfast for the trio. It looked like it would be another fine day and Dick wondered how things had gone yesterday.

"Get your mush," Marts yelled.

Dick crawled out and brought back two bowls of oatmeal and finished dressing while he ate. He thought again about the climbers above. If they managed to get camp 6 in yesterday they could be in position for the first summit bid tomorrow or the day after. Which reminded him, time for the radio call. Frank picked it up and turned it on. Almost immediately Whittaker's voice from camp 1 came on the air.

"Hello camp 3. Camp 3. Frank or Dick. Do you read?"

"Morning, Lou. Frank here."

"We've been trying to get you guys since yesterday evening. I'm afraid I have some very, very bad news. We had a tragedy late yesterday afternoon, just below camp 6. We're not sure yet exactly what happened, but apparently her waist harness came unsecured and Marty fell to her death."

Dick dropped his oatmeal and stared at the tent wall.

Dick felt as if somehow his nerves now extended through his skin so each pore burned as though he might incinerate on the spot, vaporize and disappear. He prayed he could purge his memory of what he had just heard, that he could edit out that overwhelming despair, that he could come back and things would have returned to the way they were before. But the burning stayed and he started to scold her, saying to himself, Marty, damn you, why did you foul up? You are the one always preaching safety, always yelling at me on McKinley about the proper use of my ice axe and crampons and rope. How can you expect me to listen if you don't follow your own preaching? How can we ever go and climb the Seven Summits now that you've done this? Without you . . .

Then he was swept with guilt. He hadn't told Frank, or anyone except Marty, about the psychic in Dallas and what he'd said, that there would be a tragedy on Everest and someone would die. But he had told Marty back on Aconcagua, and she had said that that someone just might be her and now it had all come true, and was it somehow because he had told her in the first place about the prediction? Was he somehow an unwitting agent who created in her a self-fulfilling prophecy?

Then he started to cry. Frank too.

Wickwire showed up a short time later, visibly shaken, and told them the details.

"The others were about a hundred feet above, looking for a site for camp 6, and Marty and I were at a rock in the middle of the Great Couloir. The weather was deteriorating and we could see the others only intermittently through the mist. I heard a call down from above for more rope, and I was just moving to put my pack on when Marty said, 'Let me get out of your way.' Then I heard this rattling of carabiners and I looked over to see her falling backwards. She grabbed for the fixed rope but couldn't quite reach it. She really gathered speed and then was gone. I looked back and saw her jumar still attached to the rope and to it her open harness, just hanging there. I guess she didn't loop the belt back through the buckle, and it pulled through when she leaned back. I'm sure she went the whole way, 6,000 feet of vertical."

Over the radio Whittaker told everyone to take the day off, and Dick and Frank descended with Wickwire to camp 1. Some of the others climbed over to the base of the North Wall to see if they could spot anything. There was no sign, and it was felt that Marty had probably disappeared into the heavily crevassed area that separated the wall from the glacier. In camp there was quiet mourning. Nearly everyone on the team had worked with Marty for years, and to some she was a best friend.

There was some talk of what to do regarding the expedition, and everybody was agreed that the next day they would resume the climb. They were now in position to make the first summit bid, and they knew Marty would have been upset had they passed on such a chance, especially after working so hard. But of more immediate concern was how best to get word to Marty's parents. Marty's mother—the Mayor, they called her—had already lost two of her kids, and now her third and last. They knew she would, of course, want whatever possessions Marty had left, so Dick and some others circulated around camp and collected them. There wasn't much, as Marty didn't cotton to material possessions, owning only what she needed. There was something, though, that Dick looked for in particular. Something he couldn't find. And that was good, because it meant she had them with her when she fell, and that's the way Dick wanted it. She had to be wearing those lapis earrings.

EARTHBOUND

The day after Marty's death Larry Nielson, who after the accident had stayed at camp 5, was joined by two others of the lead climbers and together they made the first attempt to reach the summit. They climbed from camp 5 back up to their previous high point at camp 6, 26,500 feet. The next day they awoke early to make preparations to leave for the summit, but it was so cold they feared a predawn start would end in certain frostbite. Worse, their oxygen cylinders showed 25 percent less pressure than they should have, and without a full charge they decided it made more sense to leave the heavy bottles behind.

So at the late hour of 7:00 A.M. the three set out. Even without oxygen Nielson kept a good pace. One of the other climbers, Eric Simonson, however, had an injured knee and couldn't keep up, so the second man, Geo Dunn, stayed with him while Nielson continued solo.

Climbing without a rope, he made steady progress. As he got higher, though, he found the climbing increasingly steep and difficult. At one place he was forced to remove his mittens so he could grip the rock, and it only took a few seconds before he felt his fingers start to freeze. He realized his only chance of success was if the climbing difficulties higher above would ease. But soon he encountered a section in the rock band that was near-vertical.

This would require careful consideration. He glanced down the steep North Wall below his feet.

He thought, It's a one-bouncer if I slip.

That was an estimate of how many times he might bounce before hitting bottom. A slight exaggeration, perhaps, but a good reminder that without a rope any fall was fatal.

He sat on a small ledge to think it out. Was it worth the risk? He looked at his fingers: they were already frozen. Continuing would result in almost certain amputation. And if he did manage to get to the summit, would he be able to get back down?

Still, he was now at about 27,500 feet, and he might never again get the chance. This was the summit of his dreams, the peak he wanted more than any.

He sat for thirty minutes weighing both sides.

Finally he decided this was not to be the day he climbed Everest. He stood up, and started down.

During the summit bid Frank and Dick continued to carry loads to the intermediate camps. Frank was now fully recovered from his sickness, and knowing he had no chance of reaching even high camp, he set himself a new goal. He would be content if he could get as high as camp 4.

Lou Whittaker had promised Frank he would take him up, but now Frank sensed Whittaker wasn't interested in going back up the mountain, so Frank enlisted world-class mountaineer, and chief guide on Rainier, Phil Ershler.

"I would suggest one thing, though," Ershler told Frank, "and that's not to worry about carrying a load to camp 4, but go light."

To Frank, accustomed as he was by now to heavy packs, the near-empty pack felt weightless and he made good time up the fixed ropes.

This was not only the steepest slope Frank had ever been on but the biggest. The wall fell away below him 4,000 feet to the glacier; by now Frank had been on enough lesser slopes that the exposure didn't bother him, and, in fact, he found the bird's-eye view exhilarating. He managed to keep up with Ershler too, who was pleasantly surprised and told Frank he was climbing strongly, adding to Frank's growing confidence.

From camp 3 they reached the edge of camp 4 by noon, two tents perched on small platforms cut into the steep snow face. Wickwire was in camp and greeted them. Ershler unclipped from the fixed rope, and with a sigh of relief pulled off his pack and sat down. Frank made the last few moves up the rope and onto the platform, then following Ershler's lead unclipped his jumar.

Frank was lackadaisical taking his pack off. Wickwire had noticed that Frank sometimes had a tendency to get a little sloppy once he thought he was out of danger, or past the point that demanded vigilance. Wickwire was just about to say something when suddenly Frank started slipping toward the edge.

"Frank . . .!"

Wickwire judged in a flash he was too far to make a lunge to catch Frank. His breath held in his throat as he watched, and his mind quickly played the scenario, so much like what had happened to Marty: the uncontrolled slide, the lightning-fast acceleration, then over the edge, into the abyss, still gaining speed, tumbling, tumbling . . .

Just as suddenly as it had started Frank crabbed his hands into the snow and his crampons bit the surface. He stopped.

For a moment no one said anything. Then Wickwire, trying to find his voice, said, "Don't ever, ever unclip from that rope until you know without any doubt you have both feet planted firmly on the surface."

Frank said he understood but Wickwire wasn't sure he fully realized how close he had come. After they had rested, Ershler scrutinized Frank as he connected his descending ring to the fixed rope and began the rappel back to camp 3.

As he slid down the rope Frank was no longer thinking of his near mishap. Now his feet were moving effortlessly one before the other as he hopped down the slope. He gazed across the valley, past the glacier to distant peaks, feeling as though he were flying. It was another mark of his inexperience that he wasn't in any way shaken, that even in the wake of Marty's death he hadn't registered the fine line you balance on while climbing, the ease with which the guard that keeps that balance can let down, and the speed in which you can be one moment at complete ease enjoying the view and the next saying to yourself, just as you gather speed, "No, no, this isn't really happening to me, is it?"

If Frank hadn't realized how close he had come to crossing over that fine line himself, soon he was reminded how real the danger was when more bad news arrived, this time from a different direction.

Chris Bonington, the English climber whose small expedition had been working valiantly to establish a new route on the neighboring northeast ridge of Everest, unexpectedly showed up in camp with one of his team members. It took only a glance at his face to know something was wrong.

"Pete and Joe," Bonington said, referring to Peter Boardman and Joe Tasker, two members of his team who were Himalayan veterans and considered among the best high altitude mountaineers anywhere. They were also two of his closest friends.

"We last saw them through our scope at about 27,000 feet," Bonington explained, "climbing behind a pinnacle. It was close to nightfall, and next morning there was no sign of them. We've been looking for several days now. I was hoping they somehow might have come down this way. But then that wasn't a very real hope, was it?"

Tears then came to Bonington's eyes. Combined with Marty's death, it was for Frank and Dick a very sobering introduction to Himalayan climbing. But if they had now seen in a tragically intimate way just how dangerous this game of high altitude climbing really was, they also witnessed how tenacious its players were. Nielson's failure notwithstanding, Wickwire and two more lead climbers headed back up for another summit attempt. But this time they only got to 24,500 feet when a heavy storm turned them back. It appeared the monsoon had arrived, and everyone agreed that in the face of it there was no real hope of reaching the summit. Whittaker announced the expedition was over.

Before leaving base camp at the foot of the Rongbuk Glacier the team erected a stone cairn in memory of Marty, and gathering around it they paid their last respects.

Dick wanted to say a eulogy that was distilled and concise, like a poem.

And that gave him an idea. He recalled that last stanza of Lasca, the one Marty had asked him to repeat. If he could just substitute a few words, he prayed he could find a way to convey his own emotions. When it came his turn, he spoke briefly of Marty's meaning to Snowbird, and then finished with

> "And I wonder why I do not care
> For the summits that are like the summits that were.
> Does half my climbing heart lie forever afar
> By Everest North Face, below the Great Couloir."

As Dick finished, residual clouds from the latest storm cleared from the summit of Everest, while here and there shafts of sunlight through the scattering clouds spotlighted the glacier and the huge fluted snow faces.

It was a place of incomparable beauty, but at the moment Frank and Dick had to question whether it was a place they ever wanted to return to.

Dick had just said that the summits that are (ahead) would never quite be like the summits that were (behind). Should he and Frank, then, continue to pursue their Seven Summits dream? Or was it hopelessly, foolishly, quixotic?

Following Marty's accident, they both had agreed not to make a decision until they had returned home. But already, despite the melancholy cast by Marty's death, both of them were toting up a positive and negative balance for the expedition's ledger.

For Frank, he would always remember the previous day when he walked by himself from advanced base camp down to base camp, along the eastern margin of the glacier. His only company was the ice towers standing on the glacier like a legion of silent sentinels; the only sound the occasional rattle of a falling rock loosened by the otherwise imperceptible downward creep of the glacial ice. His senses were honed by the weeks of living on the razor's edge. He felt his muscles work without complaining, and he was proud of his lean body, hardened and conditioned more than at any time in his adult life.

It was a day that was reason enough for wanting to come back.

But what about the danger? If it could happen to Marty, it could certainly happen to either of them. They told themselves that Marty's accident had been a human error and that proper vigilance on their part would prevent such a thing happening again. Even acknowledging that mistakes do happen, even acknowledging there was always the risk it could happen to them—as it almost had to Frank only a few days before—it was a risk they still felt was sufficiently remote that it weighed lightly against both the adventure of the life they had led these last three months, and the thought that perhaps, if they tried again, they might just have a chance at reaching the top. Especially if they could get on an expedition going up the easier South Col route.

They had told each other they would wait until they got home, but before reaching Peking they began to talk it over.

"I know that Marty would have wanted us to have a go at it," Dick pointed out. "After all, that's part of the mountaineer's credo, to carry on even in the wake of a tragedy. Look at how her fellow guides kept going on this trip, even after the accident. And I know that part of the reason was they knew Marty would've wanted it that way."

"I'm all for following through," Frank said. "My only concern is Luanne. In view of the accident, she's going to have a hard time accepting the idea."

"I guess that's one of the advantages of remarrying when you're fifty," Dick said. "My wife Marian knew what she was getting into —at least I think she did."

Actually Marian was no more excited or accepting about mountain climbing than Luanne was. Both women were terrified by the danger and risk, and Marian had decided the best way to cope with it was to distance herself from it. She preferred, then, to stay home and receive news as it came; the less she knew about the expeditions, the less she had to worry about.

Luanne, however, had decided to meet the group in Peking, and Frank knew she would be there when they arrived. So he decided the best strategy was probably to be up-front about his intentions and tell her right off the bat he wanted to go back.

"Darling," he said when he met her, "it was the saddest thing to lose Marty, more than I can tell you. But it was also the greatest adventure you could imagine, and I know you're not going to like this, and it's hard for you to understand, but we've got to go back, Dick and I, next year."

Luanne was cool to the idea. But she sensed the depth of Frank's commitment to his dream, and knew that she couldn't say no.

As Frank and Dick returned home, then, they still hadn't made a final pact between them to carry on with their plan, but they both knew in their hearts they were going to do it.

It took only a week after returning from Everest before they had decided to follow through with the Seven Summits. They would divide duties. Frank would organize Kilimanjaro, Antarctica, and Russia; Dick would tackle McKinley, Everest, and Aconcagua. Kosciusko would only require buying airline tickets to Australia.

A few weeks later, though, in July 1982, Dick, in one of his almost daily phone calls to Frank, told him he was having problems.

"Frank, my business manager's telling me if I take off in 'eighty-three to do all these climbs, Snowbird will fold. Can't we put it off until 'eighty-four?"

"I quit my job to do this," Frank said. "I can't wait around another year."

"Well, I'll try. But no promises, and I doubt I'll have a lot of time to help organize things."

"Dick, don't worry about it. I've expected for some time this would come up."

Even while they were dividing the duties, Frank knew in the back of his mind this would happen, and he had prepared himself to take on the whole job, or at least the lion's share of it. He had long since realized that to know Dick Bass was either to love him or to be frustrated as hell with him. Dick was perpetually overcommitted, "Just heading down life's highway pell-mell," as he cheerfully admitted, "juggling like crazy and winging things right and left."

It wasn't going to be easy for Frank to take on that much work, as he still had some responsibilities with Warner Bros. as a part-time consultant on special assignments. But he felt he could do it, and he felt as long as he was going to do it, it wasn't unfair asking Dick to bend a little and do all the climbs in '83. Besides, he knew Dick still liked the idea of doing them all within a calendar year. As Dick had said, "It'll make a neat, packaged chapter in our lives." And as Frank had added, "Plus prevent it from dragging on, so I can get on to other things, like trying to find a job."

With that question settled, then, Frank laid out the itinerary: "We'll start January 1, 1983, with Vinson Massif in Antarctica. Then as part of the same trip we'll knock off Aconcagua on the way home. Then six weeks later, on to Everest from the Nepal side, with the German group. Then home for two or three weeks, and off to McKinley, followed by a quick flight to Africa a month later to get up Kilimanjaro, and from there a shuttle to Russia to knock off Elbrus. Back home again for a few weeks, then we'll wrap the year with the banquet on top of Kosciusko."

"Aah-eah-eaahhh," Dick yelled over the phone. Whatever hesitation he had felt a moment before about doing the climbs in '83 was lost to the excitement following Frank's itinerary.

Frank knew the hard nut to crack would be Antarctica. Everest would be a lot of work, certainly, but their chances looked good of hooking up with the German group that held the permit for the spring '83 climbing season. And with the permit, the rest would be a perfunctory organization of the team, food, equipment, oxygen, transport, and porters. Certainly the difficulty of climbing on Everest above 26,000 feet would still be the same, but so many groups had now gone up the South Col route season after season that the organization of the expedition would be almost a kind of climb-by-the-numbers procedure.

Antarctica, however, was another matter. The climb itself shouldn't be difficult—the mountain had been scaled twice, and both teams had reported no unusual technical difficulties—but getting there would be a real challenge. There had never been a privately organized and financed expedition to the interior of Antarctica. Since he had a contact at the National Science Foundation, the agency that oversees U.S. operations in the Antarctic, Frank had his fingers crossed that they would provide transport. And although Frank wasn't certain they would need it, Chris Bonington was at the moment approaching the British Antarctic Survey for possible support, namely refueling at their Rothera Base on Adelaide Island.

Bonington had traveled out from Everest the same time as the North Wall team, and Frank and Dick asked him if he would be interested in joining their Antarctica expedition. Bonington had not given an immediate answer, so Frank and Dick had been pleased, even surprised, to receive a short time after they got home a letter from Bonington saying he would be thrilled to be counted in. Frank and Dick had thought that after Bonington's own grim experiences on his Everest attempt his enthusiasm to pursue another climbing expedition might have waned, at least for a while. But they learned that was not Bonington's style. He stayed at it even though, probably more than any climber, he had suffered tragedy after tragedy as his closest climbing companions died. It was a long list: in 1972, on his climb of Annapurna, a close friend killed under a collapsing ice block; in 1975, on his first ascent of Everest's enormous southwest face, a close companion lost on a summit bid; in 1978, on an attempt on K2, another dear friend killed in an avalanche; and now again on Everest, two more close friends.

But Bonington seemed eager for Antarctica, and his inclusion on the team was an important step toward Frank and Dick's strategy to get on each climb the most capable mountaineers they could find. It was a plan they felt would increase not only their chances of getting to the summits but also their chances of getting back down alive. So in addition to Bonington they started calling other climbers to fill spots on all the expeditions.

Gerhard Lenser, leader of the German Everest expedition, indicated he would be willing to allow Frank and Dick to bring two or three other Americans, so they asked Wickwire and Ershler if they would like to go. Like Bonington, Wickwire had also experienced firsthand a number of deaths in the mountains—Marty had been the fourth—but like most who are drawn to high altitude mountaineering, he had long before made his personal pact with the odds. Frank and Dick knew he was hungry for Everest's summit, and they were pleased he accepted, although he voiced some apprehension about going with a group of Germans who none of them knew. Ershler too yearned for the summit, and he accepted as well.

About this time I got a call from Frank inviting me to join any of the Seven Summits expeditions, and I accepted both Aconcagua and Antarctica. My friend Yvon Chouinard also expressed interest in Aconcagua, and Frank was thrilled to have him along.

Finding people to join the expeditions, then, was easy (at least at first); harder, much harder, was figuring how to get to Vinson Massif. Frank contacted his connection at the National Science Foundation only to learn the agency had a blanket policy of refusing to assist or support in any way private expeditions to the Antarctic; Frank's contact said their reason was that if anything went wrong with a private group, the NSF would have to disrupt their scientific programs, at great cost of time and money, as well as risk to life, to rescue them. The contact further told Frank it would be useless to plead for an exception; the policy was unbending.

Frank found this curious since he knew that the climbers, all private individuals, who had made the first ascent of Vinson and several other peaks in the area in 1966 had been fully supported by the NSF and the U.S. navy. They had been flown to the mountain in Navy C-130s, provided with skidoos, fuel, radios, and other gear, then picked up and flown back to McMurdo when they were finished climbing. Wanting to know more about it, Frank called Nick Clinch, the San Francisco Bay Area lawyer who had led that expedition.

"First," Nick explained, "it was the NSF who contacted us. Apparently they had been hounded by so many climbers wanting to get to Vinson that they decided it would be easiest just to sponsor someone to do the first ascent so everyone would get off their back. They contacted the American Alpine Club, who contacted me, and I contacted several of my friends, and we had the time of our lives."

Frank then queried other people who, since Nick's expedition, had sought NSF assistance for private ventures; he learned that not only in each case had they been refused support, but the NSF had actively tried to sabotage the plans of at least one expedition. Frank therefore decided to avoid the NSF at all costs. But how, then, to get to Vinson?

Frank still had another card: that privately owned DC-3 retrofitted with new turboprop engines, including a third one in the nose, and ski-equipped, that flew support each summer for U.S. bases in the high Arctic. Frank knew the plane was, theoretically, capable of making it to Vinson if it could be refueled somewhere along the route. The other consideration, however, was that the plane had been built in 1942. Still, if there was no alternative . . .

But an alternative did develop, beginning with a tip to Frank that another party led by Japanese adventure-skier Yuichiro Miura, known best from his movie *The Man Who Skied Down Everest*, was trying to get to Vinson. Apparently Miura had a long-term project to ski down the flanks of the highest peak on each continent, and he had worked a deal with the Chileans to charter one of their C-130s to Vinson. Frank called Dick to ask if he knew anything about Miura.

"Heck, yes. He's a longtime skier at the Bird. Let's call him right now."

Over the phone Miura told them the only hitch in his plan was that the Chileans' C-130 didn't have skis, and he didn't have any way to obtain them. But Miura had an idea. If Frank and Dick could find the skis, perhaps they could join expeditions and together travel to Vinson.

"I'm telling you, Frank," Dick said, "That's how things work. Right when you can't figure how to solve a problem, a solution will come out of the blue." Frank was relieved. The Everest trip looked on track, too, for the German leader seemed receptive to the idea of a joint expedition.

Fifty-five-year old German mountaineer Gerhard Lenser had received from the Nepal government the permit to attempt Everest in the premonsoon spring season of 1983. Making the application was easy: he had paid the $1,500 "peak fee," and had the German Alpine Club verify he was of sound mind and body. More difficult had been finding the money to fund the climb, as a normal Everest expedition costs between $150,000 and $250,000.

So Lenser was warm to Frank and Dick's proposal to pick up a share of the costs in exchange for making it a joint expedition. He seemed pleased when Frank and Dick added Wickwire and Ershler, and when Wickwire added two of his friends. This then had been the core of the 1983 German-American Everest expedition when, in August, Lenser arrived at Snowbird to meet the team, and also to travel with Dick to Wyoming for an ascent of the Grand Teton.

Lenser was about five foot seven and lean, almost skinny in his torso, but with superstout legs. His light, gray-streaked hair was carefully trimmed. He wore metal-rimmed glasses that, with his habit of buttoning his shirt collar and wearing over that a plain but neat V-neck sweater, gave him a studious appearance. He spoke slow but carefully enunciated English and his manner was generally serious and cautious, but when he smiled or laughed, he showed great warmth and sense of humor.

Frank and Dick had assumed—correctly, as it turned out—that Lenser was uneasy having added to his expedition several foreigners about whom he knew little or nothing, and so they were careful to show him, as Dick called it, "some good old American hospitality." They preceded the climb of the Grand with a western barbecue at an outdoor chuckwagon on the edge of the National Park, and made the two-day climb up the regular Exum route with the company of a guide. Although hard to read through his sober countenance, Dick thought Lenser was enjoying himself, and when they reached the summit Dick was pleased when Lenser gave him a hug. Things looked good for Everest, too.

"Murphy's Law," Frank said to Dick over the phone. "Can you believe it? Those C-130 skis are classified strategic weapons by our government. God knows why, but it would take a presidential decree to get a pair for the Chileans. And it took me fifty calls just to find that out."

"What now?" Dick asked.

"I'm checking into the DC-3."

"You mean that jalopy built in 1942?"

"At least it's proven. The owner says he'd be willing to lease it, but only if we get insurance and this pilot named Clay Lacy, an entrepreneurial soldier-of-fortune-of-the-air with a Lear Jet charter service here in Burbank. He showed up a few years back at one of those air shows where they race planes barely off the ground, only he came in his DC-7 and just about beat everyone. Anyway, he likes the idea of going to Antarctica."

"How much does the plane owner want for a charter?"

"It ain't gonna be cheap. Up to a hundred grand."

"Holy Jehoshaphat."

"But I got a couple of ideas. First, there's always the chance, although it's an outside one, we can make a profit if we follow through on your idea to make a film. A better shot is to try to line up some kind of corporate sponsorship, and on that front I may have a deal going with Budweiser."

Frank had contacted Budweiser to see if they might be interested in sponsoring the Seven Summits; Frank offered to take a six pack to the top of each peak, with the idea Bud could work an ad campaign around it. The Bud people were interested.

"But here's an even better idea," Frank continued, "that at least would reduce costs. I think Miura has some money from Japanese TV, so let's invite him to join our expedition—especially since he was kind enough to ask us to join his—and split the charter fifty-fifty."

"And let's also sell seats to some of those climbers who've been contacting us to take them to Antarctica." Word was just getting out in climbing circles that Frank and Dick were trying to get to Vinson, and a few climbers, including Reinhold Messner—considered the best in the world—had asked if they could join.

"I thought of that," Frank said, "but there's only limited space on the plane because of all the fuel it has to carry, which is the main problem. Somehow we've got to arrange a refueling along the Antarctic Peninsula. But I just had a brainstorm. If the Chileans were willing to charter us their C-130, maybe we could still charter it to parachute a few dozen fuel drums at some prearranged point on the Peninsula.

"Don't worry," Frank concluded, "I'm all-out on this one. As we say in the movie business, it's time to start working the phones."

It was now September, four months before departure to Antarctica, and although it was a great relief to breathe new life into the plans for that expedition, at almost the same time plans for Everest began to gasp. Call it Murphy's Law, bad karma, or plain bad luck, that universal tendency that turns order to chaos now let loose its furies on the Everest plans. Given Lenser's apparent amiability during his visit, Frank and Dick were now surprised to find him vehemently refusing their every suggestion about organizing the climb, and worse, threatening to pull out of his agreement. It sounded as though Lenser was convinced Frank and Dick were trying to take over the expedition (which in part was true, as they would have most of the members and be supplying most of the equipment, gear, and food).

In an attempt to pacify Lenser, Frank sent him a cable that opened: "Gerhard Lenser is leader of the 1983 German Everest Expedition in name and in fact." When that failed, Frank, during an overseas phone conversation with him, lost his patience and yelled, "What do want me to do, Gerhard, click my heels and salute?"

"I almost said, 'What do you want me to do, seig heil you?'" Frank confessed to Dick. It didn't matter; the message had gotten through, and things went from bad to worse. Dick suggested it might be more politic if he were to deal with Lenser. He felt he had a more conciliatory way of dealing with people because he had learned over the years as an independent entrepreneur that the best way to get people to do what you wanted was to use friendly persuasion. So Dick called Lenser in Germany and after an hour conversation thought he had him pacified.

But they no more than had Lenser back on board when they received the next blow. Wickwire, sensing a debacle if this combustible combination of people mixed for three months on a high altitude climb, pulled out, and with him went the other climbers he had brought to the project. It was now late November, only three and a half months before the Everest expedition was to depart, and they had purchased no food, no equipment, no oxygen, and only Ershler remained on their team. Both Frank and Dick knew that normally an Everest expedition takes about three years for such preparations, not three months. But they also knew they were used to putting together business deals under the pressure of a ticking clock, and they felt the Everest climb, as well as the Antarctica project, could be handled much the same way.

So, despite Dick's heavy workload trying to get Snowbird in shape so he could leave for most of the coming year, he spent time keeping Lenser pacified, while Frank worked on locating a new Everest team. Frank also continued single-handedly figuring out how to get the DC-3 to Antarctica, and Dick realized that even if he had more time to spend on the Seven Summits he wouldn't have been able to match Frank's performance with a challenge like Antarctica where Frank's background as a corporate executive was essential. He was indomitable; whenever he encountered a new hurdle, he just found a solution, refusing to accept from anyone an opinion that something was impossible. Like the great turn-of-the-century Antarctic explorer Ernest Shackleton, Frank too felt that "Obstacles are merely things you overcome."

But the list of those obstacles seemed only to grow. The last of November Frank called Dick to update him on Antarctica. "The single biggest problem is Clay Lacy. He's nearly impossible to get on the phone. His Lear Jet business has him hopping, he's a United pilot too, and he's got all these movie jobs going. I'm scared to death that at the last minute he'll say he can't go. We did get a fantastic co-pilot, a Brit named Giles Kershaw. He has more flight time in Antarctica than anyone, nearly 5,000 hours. Flew last year for that British Trans-Globe expedition, the one that went around the world over the poles. Kershaw wasn't easy to get ahold of either. After a dozen phone calls I finally located him in Oman, where he'd been flying supplies for some oil exploration. I'm also working on an inertial navigation system—the plane doesn't have one, and compasses won't work that far south. Then we need maps, and I'm scared Washington will put their foot down if I make a request. The logistics of our refueling are getting detailed—we have to calculate the correct landing zone for our intermediate stop. What's really got me worried is Chile. General Lopatequi, who is handling this, tells me not to worry, but I just don't know how far to trust that. Then there's insurance. The plane's owner won't let it off the ground without one hundred percent coverage. Lloyds is interested, but it's taking time to determine the risk factor, as you can imagine, and they're not confident they can sell it to their underwriters."

Organizing Antarctica was becoming a paramilitary operation more like a wartime invasion than a mountaineering expedition, and Frank was now working longer hours on Seven Summits than he had as president of Warner Bros. He didn't mind it, though; it was a challenge and he thrived on hard work. What he found enervating was his emotional stake. He had quit his job, and he had told all his friends and colleagues he was going, and if somehow he failed to put this thing together, it would seem like he had made such a terrible mistake.

But he knew those were feelings it was best to keep to himself. It was important to show, outwardly, no sign of doubt: Frank knew that when you have a deal to put together that involves simultaneous cooperation from a number of people, the only way to get everyone at once on your bandwagon is to inspire confidence that there is no doubt whatever your deal is going to happen.

Still, Frank couldn't help on occasion pausing to wonder if at some point a hurdle would appear that he couldn't get over, that would prevent him from even getting to Vinson. Each time he found himself brooding like that, however, he tried to put it out of his mind. He would tell himself that so far he had been able to solve each problem that came up, so chances were he could continue to do so.

And at the moment, not only Antarctica but also Everest was back on track. Lenser seemed, at least for the moment, mollified. He now agreed to let Frank and Dick choose all the team members, and he added that while he still insisted on being the expedition's leader, he would probably remain in base camp the duration of the climb.

This was all good news to Frank and Dick. Equally encouraging, they had found a new team, all good men by the sound of it. Each was busy with an assigned task—gathering or setting up food, equipment, oxygen, medical supplies, transportation—and it was all going well. They were to meet in a few weeks in Snowbird, to get acquainted and to compare checklists before Frank and Dick left for Antarctica and then Aconcagua.

Clay Lacy finally returned Frank's call, apologizing for not getting back sooner, but adding that he had been so busy with his other businesses he hadn't had time to do much work on Antarctica, which he was eager to try. Worse, the Chileans were still noncommittal about organizing the fuel drop because of scheduling uncertainties in their own Antarctic program. Frank now realized that time was so short it seemed he had no choice but to postpone the expedition.

Frank had always held this possibility as his last card, but he hated to play it, since he'd be left with no backup option. Worse, Miura had just held a big press conference in Japan announcing his departure, and Frank would be embarrassed to have to tell him he now had to wait nearly a year, especially since Miura had been so dependable coming through with his half of the financing. Still, there might be no choice.

So the first climb of the year would be Aconcagua, and Antarctica would be scheduled for the beginning of the next austral summer, in November and early December 1983. At least the plan had the benefit of giving them more time to prepare Everest.

Fortunately *those* preparations were on schedule. Frank and Dick rendezvoused in Snowbird with their new Everest team on New Year's Eve, a few days before both of them were to leave for South America. They gathered in Dick's living room, where each man introduced himself and gave a brief summary of his climbing background. Phil Ershler, whom Frank and Dick had asked to be climbing leader of the expedition, mentioned his many years as chief guide on Rainier. Ershler had also arranged to get Larry Nielson on board, and although Nielson was still recovering from the frostbite he had suffered on his solo attempt (he had lost the end of a thumb and part of one toe to amputation), he said he was confident he would be back up to speed when the time came. In addition there was Gary Neptune, owner of a mountaineering shop in Boulder, Colorado; Gerry Roach, veteran of a 1976 Everest attempt; Jim States, who had recently got very high on Makalu, the world's fifth-highest peak; and Peter Jamieson, another Colorado climber. Ed Hixson (from the North Wall team) would again be expedition doctor. And they had decided to make their documentary film, so Steve Marts would be cinematographer (and not just on Everest, but on all seven expeditions). Each man was an experienced Himalayan veteran, and each man was eager. They reported that most of their assigned organizational chores were nearing completion. Soon the only thing remaining would be to climb the mountain.

Later that night Dick stood in his living room with the lights out so he could see the glow of the full moon illuminating the ski runs across the valley, thinking how those used to be Marty's runs when she was head of the safety patrol. It wasn't going to be the same without her, but Dick knew in his heart she was going to be with him in spirit on the way up every one of those seven peaks.

Frank walked up and stood next to Dick. "Well, partner," he said, "the clock just struck twelve."

"The first day of what's going to be the best year of our lives." Dick grinned.

It was also going to be an exciting year for the Canadian Pat Morrow. Three months before that New Year's—on October 6, 1982—he had reached the summit of Everest. He had scaled the mountain by the so-called normal route on the southeast ridge, the same way Frank and Dick were planning. In a single day he had gone from the 26,200-foot level to the summit and back down to 22,000 feet, and the following day had descended to base camp. There he had collapsed in exhaustion, but after sleep and a good meal he felt much better, and as he started his homeward trek he began to make his plans.

He had now climbed three of the seven summits, including the highest and hardest. Of the remaining four, three would be easy. He could pick off Kilimanjaro, Elbrus, and Kosciusko anytime in 1983. The only remaining hurdle was to figure how to get to Antarctica. Morrow had not yet heard about Frank and Dick, so his plan at that time was, once he got back home, to contact one of the air services that fly in the high Canadian Arctic and see if they had any idea how to get to the Antarctic. Realizing it was too late to get there in late '82 or early '83, he hoped to make his attempt the following season.

It was more or less the same timetable Frank and Dick had in mind.

ACONCAGUA '83:
ONE DOWN

The morning we were to leave for Aconcagua my wife and I arrived according to plan at Frank's Spanish-style home located on a lovely Beverly Hills street lined with tall jacaranda trees.

"Perfect timing," Frank said as the housekeeper escorted us into the breakfast room. Frank was seated at a table spread with papers.

"I need someone to witness the signing of my will," he explained.

"I thought updated documents might be a good idea," Frank's wife Luanne said as she arrived downstairs. Even at such an early hour Luanne looked impeccable. She sat down at the table with a grace that bespoke the days she had worked as a model, before she met Frank. They had been married twenty-seven years.

Frank, with a Cheshire cat grin, was clearly enjoying the melodramatic timing of his will-signing, but Luanne was sedate and I suspected took the matter seriously. She gave an effort at nonchalance, though, and as Frank and I loaded our gear in the rental van for the drive to the airport she said, "Just like sending the boys off to summer camp."

"See you in three weeks," Frank said, and gave her a kiss.

Then she started to cry. My wife put an arm around her.

"Don't worry," my wife consoled, "Rick says it's just a walk-up."

"Maybe," Luanne answered, still crying, "but it's a *23,000-foot-high* walk-up."

This was my first climbing departure since I had been recently married, and not wanting to worry my wife I had told her that Aconcagua was "a piece of cake, just a long hike, really," leaving out the altitude part. Now, as Frank and I drove out of the driveway, both women had tears running down their cheeks.

In the Miami airport we hooked up with Dick, cinematographer Steve Marts, Gary Neptune, and new team member, Dan Emmett. He was a forty-four-year-old real estate developer from Los Angeles who every year or so punctuated his work with an expedition either climbing, river running, or ski mountaineering. He was married with three children and a wife seven months pregnant. Both Emmett and I had been members of the 1976 Bicentennial Everest Expedition, and Frank had contacted him while planning the Seven Summits to ask if he had any tips. Emmett had told Frank that on the '76 expedition there were two groups on the team who climbed strongly, the guys in their twenties and early thirties, and the Sherpa porters, who were strong at any age. "No fifty-year-old Occidental," Emmett had added, laughing, "is ever going to climb Everest."

Frank took an instant liking both to Emmett's fearless opinionating and his convivial smile, and invited him to join any of the Seven Summits climbs (other than Antarctica, because of limited space on the plane). With his wife so close to delivery, going to Aconcagua had been a tough decision for Emmett, but he decided to come hoping the climb would go quickly, and if it didn't he would simply come home early. Emmett had also accepted Frank's offer to go on Kilimanjaro, Elbrus, and Kosciusko.

The last member of the Aconcagua team, Yvon Chouinard, was tied up in business meetings and had made arrangements to come late, hoping to catch us before we reached base camp. Chouinard was forty-five years old and had two businesses, one manufacturing climbing equipment and the other a line of outdoor clothing called Patagonia. He had annual sales of $30 million. Besides his entrepreneurial successes Chouinard was also a brilliant climber, regarded as a pioneer developer of modern ice climbing techniques, and was arguably the most internationally recognized climber in America. Despite business demands he managed to spend at least six months out of twelve pursuing his favorite sports, which in addition to climb-

ing included kayaking, surfing, telemark skiing, and fly fishing. When
Frank extended his invitation to join Aconcagua, Yvon had accepted
because it sounded like a fun group of people.

Both Chouinard and I knew that Aconcagua wouldn't offer any real
challenges in the way of technical climbing problems, but we still
hoped Frank would choose to try again the Polish Glacier route so
that at least we would have a bit of ice climbing and glacier travel
to look forward to.

"You've got that Everest experience behind you now," I said, "so
I bet you could handle it."

Frank hedged on deciding, and he queried the others to see how
they felt. Emmett was easy and said he was happy with any route.
Dick was the same. Neptune said he would go with either route but
had a preference for the Polish Glacier. Frank was afraid that without
the Polish route Chouinard might not come, and as he was looking
forward to having a climber of such stature on the trip, he agreed to
try the Polish.

As our plane approached Santiago, and we glimpsed the snow crest
of the Andes, Frank still wasn't certain he shouldn't have pushed
harder for the regular route.

Granted, I've been to twenty-four grand on Everest, he told himself,
and that's higher than Aconcagua. But still, what's important is that
I get this summit.

As Frank had left his office the day before, where he was still
doing some consulting for Warner Bros., his secretary said, "I hope
you get to the top of this one. Everyone is saying how you never make
it to the top on any of these climbs." And it wasn't just his reputation
with his friends, either, that was on the line, but his commitment to
the Seven Summits as well. With the hardships of three more months
on Everest coming up, and the work and money still needed to tie
up Antarctica, not to mention McKinley and Kilimanjaro and Elbrus,
he *had* to suceed on this first one. If he didn't, he didn't know if he
could muster the toughness and determination to go through with the
rest of it.

I should have stuck with the regular route, he thought again.

We spent an extra day in Santiago meeting with the Chilean military
to work out details of the fuel drop for the Antarctica trip later in the
year, then we were off in a minibus on the trans-Andean highway
which passes by Portillo close to Aconcagua. We entered the foothills,
climbing dozens of linked switchbacks up a narrow rocky defile. Near
the top of the pass the valley opened and the hills were colored with

spring grass and patches of yellow flowers. Things looked different from the way Frank and Dick remembered the year before. It had been a heavy winter, with record snowfall, and now with an unusually warm spring the rivers were in high flood. The railway running parallel to the road was washed out in several places, and soon our van was stopped in front of a 200-foot-wide tongue of mud oozing across the highway. The only way across was to wait for morning, after the night's temperatures had slowed the mud enough so that a bulldozer could plow a temporary swath.

The next day at the crest of the highway we rendezvoused with our two mule drivers and their pack animals to begin the three-day walk-in. These mule drivers told us no one had yet attempted to get up the Polish Glacier route this season, and they warned us the trail might be washed out. We took off ahead of the animals knowing they would soon catch us. An hour later we came to the first gray tongue of dried mud that covered the hillside, the hardened remnant of a huge flow that had come down during the spring thaws; it cut our trail for a quarter mile.

"Looks easier along the water edge," I yelled, raising my voice above the nearby Vacas River, roaring in full flood.

The churning water forced us against the mud cliff. I was in the lead, and turning a corner I could see ahead what looked like an impassable section where the raging water had cut vertically into the mudslide.

"Up here," Frank yelled, indicating a breach in the mud wall leading up to the surface of the slide. We had all been hesitant to make the traverse on the slope of hardened mud because it was covered with ball-bearing-like rocks, and a slip could send you off the edge into the turbulent rapids.

But there was no choice. We followed Frank up, then everyone fanned out across the mud slide, each man concentrating on his own footing. None of us were saying anything. It was like trying to walk across a floor tipped at an angle and covered with marbles. I glanced below to the eight-foot standing waves in the muddy torrent, and went through the mental drill of what to do should I plummet in: get my pack off, feet downriver, backpaddle for an eddy. But I knew if I got into one of those sucking ten-foot holes it would probably be all over.

I delicately placed one foot, then the other. Suddenly somebody was yelling, "Frank's going in!"

I spun and saw Frank on his belly sliding quickly toward the edge. Marts was below and off to the side, going for him. He reached and grabbed—and missed. Under the weight of his full pack Frank gathered speed, pawing the hard mud, trying to dig in with his fingers. He had twenty-five feet to the edge, and there was nothing any of us could do. Fifteen feet . . . ten . . . then his feet hit a small rock glued in the mud. He tried to brake on it, but his feet popped over. Five feet and he hit another rock . . . and stopped. He was on the very edge of the cliff.

"Don't move!"

Now I was closest. I took my pack off, braced it on a rock and worked across to Frank. With one hand on a rock I prayed was solidly glued and another grabbing Frank's pack frame I had him until Emmett could throw a rope.

Frank was motionless on his belly, breathing hard. His legs were shaking, and he had a nasty scrape on his thigh.

"Don't move until I get this rope around you."

No doubt feeling that flush of irrationality that sometimes hits you after a close call, Frank calmly said after we pulled him to safety, "You know, Rick, the last time my leg was shaking this bad I was with you too, on that rock climb in Sespe Gorge."

Then he looked up to Steve Marts and asked, "Did you get it?"

"Get what?"

"Get the scene on film?"

"Frank, you almost died and you're worried about the movie."

"I don't want to have almost died for nothing!"

Up-slope Gary Neptune found a better crossing, but further up, the trail became an obstacle course of avalanche debris. In several places we spotted carcasses of guanaco lying petrographically in the mud. They had apparently been caught in the slides and swept to their deaths. One baby guanaco had come to rest on a small flat and now, watered by the spring thaw, had a ring of yellow flowers around it. Late afternoon we came to a huge fan of avalanche mud that was clearly impassable; the only possible route might be across the river, but the rising torrent looked too treacherous.

"Let's try it anyway," Dick ventured.

"It's almost dark," Frank countered. "The river is swollen, we don't know how deep it is, and you want to cross."

"Heck, yes. Let's get this show on the road."

"That's my partner," Frank said, shaking his head.

"I'm not sure our mules are even going to make it this far," Emmett said.

He had a good point, and we decided to drop our packs and wait for the animals. By nightfall there was no sign of them so we spread our bags and bivouacked. In the morning we spotted the two mule drivers on horseback riding our way, but with no mules. When they got to us they said one of the mules had slipped and rolled over several times, fortunately without injury. Marts raised his eyebrows. I was acting as translator, and he asked me to ask if it had been the mule with the silver metal case, the one marked "camera equipment."

"Sí, señor."

Marts was crestfallen, but Frank perked up. Without the mules it was obviously impossible to continue toward the Polish route, and he knew the only alternative remaining would be to go back and try to get in by the easier regular route.

"Looks like the ruta normal," I said, voicing Frank's thoughts.

"I wouldn't mind seeing the other side of this mountain anyway," Dick added.

"And I wouldn't mind seeing the summit," Frank piped in, a wide grin on his face.

Fortunately Marts had done a good job packing his cameras and there was no damage from the mule tumble. Our reversal definitely had one advantage: Chouinard was able to catch up with us. As a complete team we were off again the next day, this time following a wide valley little affected by the avalanches that had turned us around on the other route. Despite the heavy snows and record runoff the surrounding cliffs were dry and barren. This was a high desert. On the second day of our hike the air above the flat floor shimmered under noon heat and it was easy to imagine from this a mirage of camels carrying turbaned riders with curved swords through their cummerbunds. The only reminder we were on our way to the base of the highest mountain in the western hemisphere was the tops of a few snow peaks visible above the valley rim.

We stopped for lunch in the shadow of a rock resting solitarily on the sandy expanse like a remnant of a Zen rock garden.

"You all look like you're in a natural theater in the open," Dick said. "How about I lay a poem on ya?"

"Let's hear it."

I smiled. It was great to be with someone with such unabashed romanticism.

"How about 'The Men Who Don't Fit In'?" Dick asked.

"Hear! Hear!"

Dick then recited from memory just as the mule drivers arrived, smiling as though they understood the words:

> *"There's a race of men that don't fit in,*
> *A race that can't stay still;*
> *So they break the hearts of kith and kin*
> *And they roam the world at will.*
> *They range the field and they rove the flood*
> *And they climb the mountain's crest.*
> *Theirs is the curse of the gypsy blood*
> *And they don't know how to rest."*

The next day we reached the end of the line for the mules, base camp at 13,700 feet, and we decided to spend at least two days there to acclimatize and also to sort loads. It would be important, in order to prevent mountain sickness, to climb at a slow rate; this was potentially even more a hazard here than on Everest because an easy route like this often lures people into climbing too high too fast. But then it looked like we might be in base camp for a few days whether we planned it or not. Telltale lenticular clouds forming over the summit presaged storm, and the next morning we awoke to several inches of new snow blanketing the rocks around camp.

"As long as we're going to get pinned down, it's fortunate we're already in base camp."

It was less fortunate, though, for the dozens of climbers caught higher on the mountain by the sudden and unseasonable weather. As the storm continued for the next two days they straggled in, four Venezuelans, three Basques, a Japanese team, three Swiss, two Brazilians, and an American couple from Arkansas. Many of them were novice, and they were suffering. The Brazilians had frostbitten hands with fingers starting to go black; another climber was suffering pulmonary edema, a potentially fatal accumulation of liquid in the lungs caused by high altitude; and even worse, there was a solo Korean missing, who had last been seen near the summit, just as the storm set in. "He was not climber," the Japanese reported. "Maybe just traveler who decides to climb mountain. No sleeping bag, no parka, no boots, only shoes like you wear in city. Maybe he have big trouble."

"I was afraid of this," Chouinard moaned. "Travel the length of the hemisphere just to get stuck in rescues."

I knew what Chouinard was talking about. As the most tenured climbers present, if anyone above were to get in trouble—and that seemed likely—the unwritten code of the mountain would have Chouinard, Neptune, and me up there trying to get them down alive. And we weren't in the mood. It wasn't that we had a dispassion for our fellow climbers as much as impatience for incompetents and fools who had no business on the mountain without guides. It was the same on McKinley. Each season so many people get in trouble that the better-equipped and more competent climbers often spend all their time in rescues and sometimes miss reaching the summit.

There was nothing we could do while the storm lasted, so we gathered in one of the larger tents and passed the days swapping stories. I told about my first adventure, when I had sailed a sloop to Tahiti with some other teenage friends, and how only one of us knew how to navigate, or claimed to know how, because after twenty days we sighted an island, but it wasn't Tahiti. When we asked our navigator, all he could do was shrug his shoulders, so we fashioned a directional antenna from a coathanger, tuned Radio Tahiti on our transistor, determined the direction of the strongest signal, and sailed that way. In the morning we sighted Tahiti and even before entering the pass through the fringing reef we heard the drums. Near the quay women were dressed in flowerprint wraps with hibiscus in their hair. Men chased women and women pushed men in the water. Everyone had a rum bottle. "This is it." "I knew it would be this way." "I'm never leaving." We all assumed it was just another typical day in paradise; none of us had ever heard of Bastille Day.

Chouinard had a story from his youth, too, when he was an itinerant climbing bum vagabonding from one mountain range to the next. He was in upstate New York, at the Shuwangunks cliffs, when he and his climbing pal took on an automobile delivery to New Mexico. They needed to get to Yosemite, and had just enough money to see them through the season there. The car kept breaking down, though, and all their money went to repairs. In New Mexico the car owner refused to pay them back, so penniless they set out hitchhiking toward Yosemite. In Winslow, Arizona, they were arrested for vagrancy and spent eighteen days in jail at hard labor, with only oatmeal to eat. By the time they got to Yosemite, Chouinard had lost twenty pounds and was too weak to climb.

"Those were the formative years," Chouinard concluded, "and to this day I can't get close to oatmeal."

"Dick, how about a story from your repertoire."

"Compared to you all," Dick said, "I've led a sheltered life. But I could tell you about the time I went around the world with my kids repeating the adventures of Richard Halliburton."

"Let's hear it."

"You younger guys might not know about Halliburton, but when I was ten years old his books really whetted my yearning for adventure. He had done all kinds of things like swim the Hellespont and the Panama Canal, ride an elephant over the Alps like Hannibal, and climb the Matterhorn. I knew he had done the Matterhorn in 1921 right after his college graduation, so when I was nineteen and going to Europe for the summer—that was 1949—I conned these three guys with me into giving it a try. Two of us made it—the other two got acrophobia—and on top I told our guide, Emil Perren, that someday I would come back and climb it again, with my kids.

"Now let's move up to 1973. I've got four teenage kids and all of a sudden my wife drops on me that she wants a divorce. It was a big blow, the two boys staying with me, the girls going with their mother. After that, the only time I ever saw all four kids together was Christmas dinner, so one year I said, 'You know, we need to go on a trip together. How about Switzerland to climb the Matterhorn!'

"They were all for it, so I cabled Emil Perren. He was almost seventy, no longer climbing, but he agreed to arrange guides. So that summer of seventy-eight we went over and gave it a try. We caught a midsummer snowstorm, though, and only got a third of the way up to the Schwarsee. But at the end of that year we were again at Christmas dinner and all the kids started saying what a great time they'd had so I said, 'Gosh, if you really enjoyed it that much let's go back and give it another try.'

"They leaped at the idea, and as we made plans I had the thought that as long as we were in Europe we might as well swim the Hellespont like Halliburton did, run the original route of Phidippides from Marathon to Athens, climb the pyramids in Egypt. And if we're going to do all that, why not go to Nepal and trek to the base of Everest, then to Japan to make the climb up Fuji.

"They thought it was a great plan. The only problem was the bank was talking about liquidating me to pay off my loans, and if I took off for several months, my business manager told me I would be finished. I told the kids we might not be able to do it. It was toss and turn in bed for me every night. The date came for our departure and I had to delay. The loan—with a new bank—that I needed to save everything still hadn't gone through. Finally on a night when I couldn't sleep at all I just said, This is it. Those bankers might be able to foreclose on my assets, but they're not going to foreclose on my memories. We left several days later.

"It was a Bass odyssey à la Halliburton. Around the world, we did it all. And I couldn't believe how we all became best friends. You see, the separation had left a kind of gaping hole in my psyche concerning the kids. It was like a mental cancer eating away at me, the thought of them growing up not knowing each other. But we made up for it. And when I reached the base of Everest and looked up at it, I got tears in my eyes and thanked the Lord for helping me set my priorities straight, as otherwise I would not have made the decision to go on the trip.

"While I was away my lawyer and my business manager finished the new bank loan, so I got home and everything was okay. The only thing that was a disappointment was we failed again to climb the Matterhorn—this time we got two thirds of the way up when another summer snowstorm forced us down. That was in 1979. Now in the spring of 1980 I asked Marian, whom I had been dating for five years, to marry me, and I had the idea to do it in the little Anglican chapel in Zermatt at the base of the Matterhorn. And that gave me another idea. Why not get married on the summit! I told her I'd have her helicoptered to the top, and our kids and I would climb up and we'd have the ceremony right there. Well, she put the nyet on that real fast, and when you're asking someone to marry you, you can't be too overbearing, so I yielded and agreed to get married in Dallas. But she agreed at least to have a follow-up ceremony in the little chapel in Zermatt.

"So the day after we were married we flew over. Emil Perren was down in the village cheering us on. And this time the weather was right and we climbed the thing—me and my two boys and twin girls—and we got to the summit before noon and were down by six-fifteen with just enough time for me to jump in the tub and soak my aching muscles and make the ceremony by seven. I was hobbling down the street on blistered feet as the church bells tolled, and inside I stood next to my new wife as sunset light filtered through the stained glass window behind the preacher. And when the preacher finished, he said, 'I feel compelled by circumstances to say a few words more. I don't know Dick here—as you can see he just arrived—but I realize this must be one of the great days of his life. Marian here, his new wife, has told me about his climbing the Matterhorn in 1949, his vow to return with his kids, and his two prior attempts. So if there's any final words to leave you with, I guess it's just to remember this: 'The third time works the charm.' "

With Dick's story finished, Frank and I left the group tent for the smaller two-man tent we were sharing. Outside we could see in the moonlight the huge west face of Aconcagua laced with fresh snow. The cloudless sky had opened the air to drafts of cold that slid from the upper slopes and we felt our cheeks glow and we could see our breath in puffs. The clear cold sky put an optimistic capper on a delightful evening: the barometer was climbing and all indications boded fair weather and a morning departure to locate camp 1. When we were warmly cocooned in our mummy bags I wished Frank a good night.

"You know, tonight has underscored for me the importance of choosing the right guys for these climbs," Frank said. "And I don't mean guys just because you know they can help you get to the top."

I thought, You're learning, Frank. There's a lot more to this mountain climbing than just that exhilarating moment you reach the summit. No, the parts that matter most are those intangible ones like tonight, those moments of camaraderie that are like sips of good brandy that give your body and spirit a nice, warm glow.

"Drink up boys," Chouinard said. "We'll need all the liquid we can hold today. It's going to be a hot one."

Chouinard had a four-quart pot full of steaming water for the morning brews. The dawn sky was cloudless, there was no wind, and although some of the upper slopes might yet be unstable with new-fallen snow the slopes leading toward camp 1 looked safe, and all of us were anxious to stretch our legs, since the storm had kept us tent-bound for three days. We planned to carry a load that day to the campsite, then the following day move up and occupy it. Then another load would be carried to camp 2, and the pattern repeated for another camp or two above that before we would be in position to attempt the summit.

"That way we should be acclimatized for the summit bid," Chouinard had said. "We'll take the mountain slow and easy, and drink like crazy the whole way."

Frank was encouraged. He was sure this route would be nothing more than a steep trail, and if he could get properly acclimatized, and if there were no long-term storms, and with the support from the rest of us, he should be able to make it. On that last point Frank was pleased none of us seemed overly disappointed changing from the Polish Glacier. In truth, it didn't really make that much difference any more because we were having such a good time enjoying each other's stories, and the challenge of a harder climb now seemed unimportant. Frank noticed that with this group there was none of the competitive jockeying that had colored the Everest climb, and he concluded there was more than one way to climb a mountain.

For Frank and Dick those weeks of carrying loads on Everest had paid off. Frank had about thirty-five pounds in his pack, Dick about forty-five, and finding that almost trancelike mind-set, they followed hour after hour the steps of us lead climbers as we switchbacked up the virgin snow. The white slopes reflected the noon sun and sweat dripped from our brows. We were down to our last layer of long johns and would have stripped to bare skin except we knew the sunburn would have been worse than the heat. For both Frank and Dick it had come as a surprise, when they first started mountaineering, to discover that often on high altitude climbs you suffer from heat as much as from cold.

We made a short stop to take a drink. Each man carried a plastic one-liter water bottle.

"Dick, could I borrow a packet of that energy stuff you put in your water?" Frank asked.

"How do you know I have any?"

"You always have at least two of everything. That's what I like about you."

"Frank, you've got to learn to bring your own things. I swear, you'll go to your grave still not knowing how to care for yourself. You know, just before we left on this trip Luanne pulled me aside and said, 'Dick, please look after Frank. He doesn't know how to take care of himself.' "

"And what did you tell her?" Frank asked with a sly grin.

"I said, 'Don't worry, we'll look after him.' "

"Well then, how about a packet of that stuff?"

After Frank had made his drink mix we rested a few more minutes, then saddled our packs and continued. The sun was past meridian when we found a good spot for camp 1. There was another tent at the campsite, but no one was home and we guessed they were up carrying a load to the next higher camp. We cached our loads of food and cooking fuel and returned toward base camp. Just above the tents Frank yelled ahead to Dick, "Bass, I've got fifty more yards, and if I make it this will be the first day of the trip I haven't stumbled and fallen."

"Well get your buns down here, then," Dick said. They joined arm-in-arm and came into camp whistling "Marching Along Together."

The next morning was again clear, and we packed up tents, stoves, personal equipment, sleeping bags, and clothing to move up to camp 1. We decided to leave a tent at base to store some of our backup food and equipment, and since the other climbers in camp who were recently returned from the upper mountain told us there were no technical sections above, we decided to save more weight and leave our ropes.

"But we can't leave our two sixpacks of Budweiser," Dick said. "That's how we're going to pay for this extravaganza."

Budweiser was still interested in sponsoring the Seven Summits. Frank had now talked to the executive vice-president of marketing and told him that for only two hundred grand he and Dick would take a sixpack on each climb and bring back footage of them toasting their success on the highest summit of every continent on earth. The vice-president loved the idea, and all he had to do was clear it with his other marketing people.

We knew we had all day to reach camp 1 so we took our time packing. When we were finally ready to go it was 11:00.

"Might as well cook a hot meal before we leave," Chouinard said. "Otherwise we'll just get started and have to stop for lunch."

"Away by the crack of noon," I quipped.

After finishing a full lunch it was even harder to get going, and once on the trail we complained of a malady common to climbers called high altitude foot disease: the inability to place one foot in front of the other. It was late afternoon when we finally reached the cache, and after we set up camp and made dinner it was 8:00 but still an hour before sunset. Some of us read or wrote in our journals, and Dick hauled out his blueprints for a future Snowbird addition, a high-rise hotel/condominium and restaurant complex he had now decided to call the Seven Summits Tower.

"I'm gonna have these penthouses called Summit Suites," he told us. "They'll be the McKinley suite, the Everest suite, the Aconcagua suite . . . I'll do up each one eclectically in the decor of its continent."

"I think it's great," Frank said impishly. "To be working on blue-prints of Snowbird while you're at 16,200 feet on Aconcagua."

"Wells, it's better than lying over there reading some paperback."

"You guys better come out here," Chouinard interrupted. "There's a fantastic sunset."

Anyone inside now crawled out to have a look. The sun was casting low slanting rays through Venetian-blind clouds that tinged the snow a pale yellow. The soft light glowed orange on the faces of Frank and Dick, placing a sparkle in their eyes and a warm gleam on their smiles.

"There's no place I'd rather be this moment," Frank said, "than right here doing what I'm doing."

That night a cold south wind buffeted our little tents. Morning brought clear skies and though the wind continued we carried loads to camp 2, halfway up the northwest side of the mountain. Returning to camp 1 we noted multiple lens-shaped clouds hovering to leeward of the summit, foreboding bad weather, and vapor streamers whisking over the bare rocks at 22,000 feet, indicating extreme winds at higher altitudes. It would not have been a good summit day.

Back at camp 1 it started to snow, and a 15-knot breeze made it uncomfortable. Chouinard and Emmett were on dinner detail and despite the grim weather chose to cook outside. Two Basque climbers on their way down stopped for a moment and told us a number of climbers were in the upper camps waiting for the wind to abate to try for the top. There was still no sign of the missing Korean, and the Basques thought he was surely dead.

"There's no way someone could survive up there in these conditions without a bag," Chouinard agreed.

It snowed through the night, then cleared next morning. It was windy and cold. Our plan was to dismantle camp 1 and carry the remaining gear to camp 2, at about 17,500 feet. The route was again up a low-angled snow slope, and the hours passed placing one cram-poned boot in front of the other. The slow pace seemed to agree with Frank, and both he and Dick carried substantial loads. All indications suggested Frank had a good shot at reaching the top of the first of his seven summits.

We set our three tents up on a flat bench free of snow. The altitude was now high enough to see beyond the bordering ridges to more distant mountains. Even at this elevation we were higher than most summits, and the multitude of lesser peaks spread to the horizon, interrupted here and there only by a few innocent cumulus. Aconcagua was clear, and the threat of storm had disappeared. That evening there was a strategy session, and as everyone was feeling well—other than Emmett, who had a sore throat—we talked about risking a direct move to the next camp, at 19,700 feet.

"So instead of ferrying loads we would pack everything tomorrow and move up in one carry," I explained.

"That would mean heavier packs," Chouinard added, "but since we would do it only once, and that way save at least a day, overall the weight would be less because we wouldn't need as much food."

"So if the weather holds, and it looks like it will," I continued, "we would make our summit shot day after tomorrow."

"So what happened to your idea of climbing the mountain slow and easy?" Frank asked. "That still seems best to me."

"Unnecessary work," Chouinard countered. "Because of the storm, we spent more days than planned at base, and that was a good altitude for acclimatizing. We should be in good enough shape now to shoot for the top and get out of here before any of us has a chance to get sick."

"This is turning into a bad weather year, and it makes sense to take quick advantage of a good spell," I added.

"What do you other guys think?" Frank asked.

Neptune and Marts didn't care one way or the other; they said they both felt strong. Dick was the same. Emmett, despite his sore throat, was anxious to get home to his expecting wife and favored the quick plan.

"Guess I'm out-voted," Frank said.

We broke camp the next day, caching all but the food, fuel, and clothing absolutely essential to our get-up-and-get-out strategy. Even so our packs still weighed in at fifty pounds and more, but we were all in good cheer as we moved at a plodding pace toward the next camp, known on the map as Camp Berlin. The slope steepened but the grade was still comfortable and the trail firm, so there was little danger of a slip or fall and no regret at having left our ropes at base camp.

Camp Berlin centered around a ruined hut whose roof was gone, and an interior filled with snow. We pitched our tents, started stoves, and collected snow to melt to water. Both Emmett and I weren't feeling well. I had a headache from the altitude, and Emmett now had congested lungs to add to his lulu of a sore throat. But neither of us felt our ailments were severe enough to keep us off the summit.

Other tents at the camp housed an international assortment of mountaineers: three Argentinians, two Basques, one Japanese, and two Alaskans. Dick introduced himself to the Alaskans and learned they had been the pair always one day ahead of us in the camps.

"I just want to thank you all," Dick said, "for such a marvelous job kicking that trail in."

They told Dick that Aconcagua was part of a climbing habit they had kept for several years of spending the northern summer on McKinley and the southern summer on Aconcagua. This was their fifth year in a row on Aconcagua.

The first Alaskan explained, "We come with lots of food and take our time. We meet a lot of intriguing folks. You wouldn't believe the goofballs on this mountain, and McKinley too."

The second Alaskan added, "Look at this Korean who's missing. I guess he made it to the top, but was slow coming down. There were a few other people to the top that day, but they came down at a faster pace. When they got back to this camp, the Korean never showed up, and then that storm came in. Everyone's been keeping an eye out for him, but so far no sign. Most people think he got stuck in the storm, crawled in some rock hole and froze."

The first Alaskan concluded, "Like we said, goofballs."

Dick took an instant liking to the pair and invited them to Snowbird.

While Dick was inviting the Alaskans, a solo Spaniard arrived, a slight, elfin man who had walked in to base camp the same time as we had but then worked ahead. He was now returning from the summit, and though clearly bone-weary he smiled and said the route to the top was straightforward and that none of us should have any difficulty. Encouraged, we finished dinner and turned in early, planning to wake about three, start melting snow for hot drinks, and get away by five.

That night was windy and cold, and Chouinard, wakened by Emmett's wrist alarm, started the stove and warmed his fingers over the blue flame. It took a half hour until the first drinks were ready, and another hour to eat breakfast and dress. We left in predawn and as we walked in a row up the pumice trail our bobbing headlamps, each suspended in blackness, looked like torches of a cabalistic procession. At one stop we turned off our lights and could see the southern sky: here, floating above the summit like two celestial cotton balls, the Magellanic Clouds, there, askew on its austral axis, the Southern Cross. Dawn revealed we were walking among black basalt towers, and as the sun rose behind the mountain we could see the giant shadow of Aconcagua cast for twenty miles across the blanket of lesser peaks that spread below us.

Though the sun was now clear of the horizon, the wind stole any warmth from the slanting rays, but moving at a steady pace we stayed comfortable. Ahead the trail switchbacked up a snow slope and disappeared behind a complex of jagged rock. Frank was slower than the rest of us, and on occasion we had to wait for him to catch up. We still made adequate progress, and soon arrived at Camp Independencia, a small wooden A-frame long destroyed by wind and weather. We were now at just over 21,000 feet. It was 9:00 A.M. and we decided to stop for a half hour and rest. With the increasing altitude our pace had slowed, but we still felt confident we had the summit.

Above the ruined A-frame the route followed a snow crest bifurcated by dark shadow and bright sun. Neptune led, walking the twilight edge into the shadow of the great summit pyramid. We knew the route worked around this formidable rock castle to a weakness in the rampart called the Canaleta, a lower-angled gully that led to the summit. After a half hour's climbing Neptune was at the end of the crest and the beginning of a long, steep snow slope at the base of the summit pyramid. Across this slope the snow trail sliced upward to the opening of the Canaleta. It was more exposed than we had reckoned, which wasn't a problem for those of us more experienced with using an ice axe, but for Frank and Dick a slip could mean a 2,000-foot slide to the base of the huge snowfield. And that wouldn't be something you would be likely to walk away from.

"Frank, you should go between Gary and me," Chouinard pointed out. "We don't want you lagging."

"We're all going to the top of this together," Emmett added.

Frank wasn't the only one moving slowly; I was suffering from the altitude, and had to push to keep up. Emmett still had a bad cough and was trying his best to ignore it. With Chouinard leading in the frozen steps of the established trail, the rest of us followed, inching our way across the traverse, pacing ourselves to Frank's rate. Dick was keeping his balance and feeling strong but Frank was awkward, adding a tension to the traverse that Emmett later described in his journal:

> *Frank scared us to death. His balance isn't that good, and he tottered for two hours across the abyss, just in front of me. He was at his physical limit as well as beyond his limited*

skill, but he kept going until we crossed the traverse, and then followed the others up some loose rocks to the base of the Canaleta.

Other than Neptune and Dick, both of whom seemed to gain strength with altitude, the rest of us felt the enervation of thin air. Frank, using the "pressure breathing" technique learned from the Rainier guides, sounded like a Lamaze trainee in labor. I was ashen and in beginning stages of mountain sickness. While the rest of us rested, Chouinard, also beginning to weaken, scouted around the corner into the base of the Canaleta. It was a mix of hard snow and loose rocks and while he nosed around for the best footing, a half dozen baseball-sized rocks whizzed by.

"I don't like the looks of it," Chouinard said. "Rockfall danger, hard snow, steep route, and no ropes or crampons. So much for our walk-up route."

Now we really regretted not bringing our ropes from base camp, and we also felt foolish leaving our crampons at the last camp. We had depended too much on what other climbers had told us, and not enough on our own experience.

But even if we had been equipped properly it wouldn't have helped my physical condition. My altitude sickness must have showed on my face.

"How you feeling?" Emmett asked me.

"Not too hot. Dizzy and nauseous."

Neptune, Marts, and Dick said they were okay, but Emmett and Chouinard admitted to feeling the altitude. And Frank was still not in good shape.

"Looks like we better bag it," Chouinard said.

"You mean give up and go back?" Dick asked.

"Yeah, back to Berlin and rest. Then maybe come up with crampons and ropes, and try again."

"In that case, I'm going to cache my load right here," Dick said.

"What do you have in that pack, anyway?"

"Why heck, I got the Bud for our summit movie and celebration."

Back at Camp Berlin Emmett announced he'd had his shot at the summit and was returning home.

"I'm feeling guilty with my wife only a few weeks from popping. And guilt is not something I usually subscribe to."

Neptune volunteered to go down with Emmett as far as base camp and come back with our ropes. He estimated he could easily get to base before nightfall, rest there, and since he would have a light pack, make it back to Berlin the following day. That would give the rest of us an extra day to acclimatize before again attempting the summit.

With Neptune and Emmett gone some of the conviviality left with them and we weren't quite the same merry band of storytellers.

"Feel better today?" Frank asked me.

"Much. It's amazing what one extra day of acclimatization can do."

"I just had an idea then. What if you and I were to climb up to Camp Independencia this afternoon. Then tomorrow when the others head for the summit, they could pick us up on the way. It would decrease the distance I have to climb on the summit day, and maybe increase my chances."

It sounded like a good idea so after lunch we set out, arriving at the A-frame with plenty of light to pitch our tent behind the ruined hut and begin the long job of melting snow. Frank was very tired, but I insisted he drink some hot soup, which perked him up a little. Back at Camp Berlin Neptune arrived just before sunset, having made it from base camp to Berlin in one day, a vertical gain of over one mile.

That night the sky was again jeweled with high-altitude stars and in the early predawn I started the stove to begin the brews. As planned, the lower team arrived at 7:30, and while they rested I served up a round of finger-thawing, as well as belly-warming, cocoa. Chouinard said he was still suffering a headache, but the rest were strong and we again completed the upward traverse to the opening of the Canaleta. This time we were prepared. Strapping crampons and tying with ropes into two teams we entered the gully.

In an unspoken arrangement I tied Frank on the end of my rope, and Neptune tied Dick on his. Chouinard and Marts, both comfortable without a rope, climbed on their own; this also allowed Marts the freedom to get the best camera angles.

Climbing a little faster, the others moved ahead while Frank and I set our own pace. I climbed up hard snow the length of the rope, found a place to anchor next to the rock that bordered the gully, and belayed the rope as Frank climbed. Frank was slow but steady, and when he reached the belay I again led the rope length while he rested.

An hour passed. Frank looked up to see Neptune and Dick several hundred feet higher, on the ridge that lead to the summit. Neptune's bright yellow parka was vivid against the cobalt sky. Frank knew he still had a long way, and lowering his head, returned to the task. He wasn't certain he could make it, but he kept telling himself to go at an even pace, to put one foot forward, balance, breathe five, six, seven times, then move the next foot. He could see I had stopped at the base of a large sweep of boulders, and was coiling the rope.

"We're off the snow from here," I said. "We'll leave the rope."

"How much further?"

"The others have disappeared over the ridge. I think they're on top. We should get there in an hour, I'd guess."

I led up the slope, balancing one rock to the next, waiting when Frank lagged. Soon we could see a figure in a maroon parka coming down. It was Chouinard. Had he turned back?

"You two better get up there," Chouinard shouted when he was a little closer. "They're waiting for you."

"You made it?"

"Yeah, but I've still got a terrible headache so I'm going down instead of waiting."

The altitude was now nearly 23,000 feet, and Frank could feel with each step the weight of his boots. I was just ahead, zigzagging between rocks. Frank picked out a rock thirty feet ahead, and started working toward it, as though it were the only goal that existed. When he reached it he breathed several times, then looked for another higher rock and drummed up the resolve to make it to this next goal. He wasn't sure he could keep going. He recalled what Dick had said about his climb the year before, how he had climbed several times toward what he thought was the summit only to discover it was a false crest. Frank now wondered if he had it in him to go from one false summit to the next.

Clouded in the amnesia of high altitude, Frank was forgetting that Dick had been on the other side of the mountain, that this side might be different. He glanced up and saw me going over the edge of the ridge, with only sky behind. He lowered his head again, hunched his shoulders and took another step, trying to set his mind to the long task ahead. He made three more steps, breathed several times, and glanced up.

Who was that? Was it Dick, looking over the edge? And what was that next to him? An aluminum cross?

"Get your bod up here, Pancho," Dick yelled. "We're freezing our buns off waiting!"

Frank leaned on his axe, breathing hard. When he thought he could speak he said, "You mean this is it?"

"Five more steps, Frank."

One, two, three . . . rest, a few more breaths . . . four, five. Dick grabbed him in a tight bear hug, and Frank slumped down onto the ground.

"Got to sit here. Just for a minute."

Frank sat next to the cross, breathing hard. After a few seconds he looked at Dick and holding his hands over his ears as though he were afraid his head might explode exclaimed, "You mean I made it? I mean, I made it!"

"I'm telling you, Pancho, this is the beginning of a streak. We're going to knock 'em all off. Where's Marts, anyway? Steve, get over here with that camera and turn it on. This is history."

With the camera going Dick reached in his pack and pulled out the sixpack of Budweiser. When Frank had sufficiently regained his breath Dick looked at him with a wide Texas grin and said, "Frank, this Bud's for you!" and popped the top. Nothing. "Keep the camera rolling," Dick said as he reached for another can. He popped it, and—nothing. All six cans were frozen solid.

"So much for the Bud idea," Dick laughed. "You got any other sponsors you're working on?"

Arm-in-arm they gazed around the points of the compass to the sea of snow summits extending north and south along the crest of the Andes. Every peak was below them, and not just those they could see, but those beyond as well. For at that moment, Frank Wells and Dick Bass were the two highest men standing on any point of land in the western hemisphere of the world.

"I told you all I needed was a little practice," Frank said.

"One down and six to go," Dick rejoined, and then he let out his Tarzan call.

"Aah-eah-eaahhh."

EVEREST '83:
THE ICEFALL

During the one year it would take to complete the Seven Summits odyssey Frank felt there would be two times when he would be, without doubt, sticking his neck out. Most of the climbs were not that dangerous. He shouldn't have any trouble on McKinley, for example. Kilimanjaro would be just a walk-up, as would Elbrus (Frank's earlier problems notwithstanding). Kosciusko was a walk in the park. The climbing on Vinson, too, should be relatively straightforward, based on reports of the first ascent party. But while the mountain itself might not pose any extraordinary hazard, getting there was another matter, and of the two things Frank feared, one was flying over 1,500 desolate miles of Antarctic ocean and ice in a 1942 DC-3.

The other was climbing through the notorious Khumbu Icefall on the south side of Everest. All the slopes of Everest would require vigilance, of course, since any climbing above 26,000 feet—8,000 meters, the so-called death zone—was hazardous simply because it's so easy to make mistakes when your brain is muddled from lack of oxygen. But that didn't bother Frank nearly as much as this other hazard he would face lower on the mountain, at the very beginning of the climb.

The Khumbu Icefall is a jumble of huge ice blocks, called seracs, which are formed when a glacier passes, during its inexorable downward march, over steep underlying bedrock. This causes the ice to split and fracture into these seracs that then sometimes shift or collapse, usually without warning. On the Khumbu Icefall, pressure occasionally builds over a large area, and sections an acre or more in size will slip, sending the seracs pell-mell. Anyone luckless enough to be in the Icefall when that happens will almost certainly be crushed, and Frank knew that of the people who have been killed attempting Everest from the south, most died in the Icefall.

Sometimes Frank wished he shared Dick's seemingly cavalier attitude about things like the Icefall. Dick in general seemed to approach uncertainties with a congenital optimism, a belief that when it came to big-ticket items like whether you live or die through the Icefall you were in the hands of your maker anyway, so it made no sense to worry. But that wasn't to say Dick was predisposed to cast his fate heedlessly to the elements. They both realized the risk in the Icefall was proportionate to the number of times a climber passed through it, and before leaving for Everest both of them promised their wives they would make the roundtrip only once.

The job of fixing a route through the maze of ice blocks was left to the other climbers, who didn't mind the arrangement, since neither Frank nor Dick would be of much use in the Icefall, as they lacked the necessary skills to rig ladders over the myriad crevasses and ropes around the labyrinth of seracs.

The Khumbu Icefall is unique in mountaineering as the only place that requires extensive use of aluminum ladder sections to span the dozens of crevasses. It wouldn't be necessary to rig the ladders if a team only had to go through once (although it would take longer, it would be possible to climb down, over or around the crevasses without ladders), but since the Sherpas had to make so many carries of food, fuel, oxygen, and equipment up and back, the ladders were essential. So along with the basic logistics—ten tons in all—there were added 40 eight-foot ladder sections.

As climbing leader, Phil Ershler had done a yeoman's job overseeing preparations, and after Frank and Dick returned from Aconcagua, the only tasks remaining were to arrange shipping to Nepal and to see if any sponsors could be found interested in backing the Seven Summits. The Budweiser deal had fizzled when the marketing people pooh-poohed the idea, so Frank sent a query letter to ABC

Sports, which he knew was interested in the possibility of covering an Everest climb.

For the previous year, ABC's *American Sportsman* series, headed by producer John Wilcox, had been working with a high-octane group of American mountaineers who proposed to climb Everest's West Ridge from the Tibet side, and the network had in mind a videotape coverage of the climb that would climax with a live transmission to North America, via microwave and satellite uplink, direct from the summit. Frank knew the expedition planned to be on Everest the same time his party would be (but on the opposite side), and he also knew ABC was having trouble obtaining from the Chinese permission to install an earth station in Tibet for the satellite uplink. Frank didn't want to do anything to jeopardize the other expedition's chances of securing sponsorship from ABC, but when he learned the deal was being dropped by the Chinese, Frank sent a proposal to the ABC producer that they cover the Seven Summits expedition rather than abandon the whole idea.

ABC already had a considerable investment in research and planning and rather than dump the money they accepted Frank's proposal. In exchange for rights to videotape the climb, ABC would partially underwrite the expedition. ABC explained that because time was now short they would not be able to install the several microwave relays necessary to get one hundred percent live coverage from the top of Everest to the satellite earth station they would install in Katmandu, so instead they proposed to have one of the team carry to the summit a small video camera and a two-pound microwave transmitter, and beam a signal to a receiving dish twenty miles away where it would be recorded, helicoptered to Katmandu, then beamed to New York. Not quite live, but as a live signal would arrive in New York at about 2:00 in the morning anyway, a few hours delay would probably increase the ratings.

Frank and Dick were delighted, and the other climbers approved although some voiced concern it might be a burdensome intrusion to have the extra television people. ABC assured them that they would send only experienced climbers. For the last six years I had worked on several mountain climbing shows for ABC, and I had been discussing for some time the possibility of working on the Everest show. When the coverage moved to Frank and Dick's expedition, I was offered the position of field producer and also on-air commentator, filing reports and on-location interviews. With the addition of two cameramen, David Breashears and Peter Pilafian, the crew was complete, and as there were only three of us and we were all experienced climbers whom many of the climbing team already knew, there was agreement among the expedition members to accept the TV sponsorship.

ABC next designed a production strategy. Steve Marts would still film the climb for Frank and Dick's Seven Summits documentary, but would also help when he could with the ABC coverage. Breashears, as high altitude cameraman, would go in with the team to tape the trek to base camp, rigging of the Icefall, and perhaps push to camp 2. Pilafian and I would go in later, when the bulk of the coverage would commence. In addition to us, there would be many more personnel both at the receiving station twenty miles from Everest and at the satellite uplink in Katmandu, including a team of Panasonic engineers, who were supplying camera and video recording equipment. Executive producer John Wilcox would shuttle between the receiving dish field location and the Katmandu nerve center. ABC's sport commentator Bob Beattie would be in Katmandu filing overview commentary, and in my final meeting with ABC I was instructed to end my reports with the line: "And now back to Bob Beattie in Katmandu . . ."

The day before departure Frank packed his gear himself, a new level of competence that greatly impressed Luanne. But Luanne wasn't the only one who noticed a change in Frank. At the Seattle airport, where Frank met with the rest of the team, Jim Wickwire had come to send them off, and noting that Frank was wearing cord pants and Nikes instead of Ralph Lauren slacks and Gucci shoes said, "Wells, you're even starting to *look* like a climber."

Dick was the only one missing (he would fly over a few days late because of last-minute business with Snowbird), so Frank handled the necessary chores in Katmandu, the bulk of which involved working with Gerhard Lenser, who was already there, to secure the final permits from the Nepalese for the ABC shoot.

As the team approached Katmandu they could see out the starboard side of the plane the great rampart of the Himalaya rising suddenly like a stupendous dam holding the Tibetan Plateau from spilling across the Gangetic Plain. To the east was what looked at first glance to be a great billowing cumulonimbus but closer scrutiny revealed to be the ridges and ice walls of the singular Kanchenjunga Massif, the third highest peak in the world. Moving their eyes back along the crest of the range they could see nestled among other high peaks a dark pyramidal summit that was the only one with a long snowplume banner tailing from its peak: only Everest punctured the jetstream.

Frank was about to land in a Marco Polo city plucked from the thirteenth century and set into the twentieth, a place with a thin skin of modernity over a body of timeless Hindu and Buddhist ritual. Katmandu had cars, but if your car happened to hit any of the hundreds of sacred cows that wandered the streets you were certain to go to jail (and the only way out was to prove to the court that the cow had intended to commit suicide). It was a city with an airport serviced by the latest jet aircraft, but they were planes that each year in a solemn ceremony were smeared with the blood of a goat or chicken sacrificed for the well-being of the plane and those who rode in it. It was a city where on Friday you could pick up a phone at your room in the Sheraton and get a satellite connection to New York, then on Saturday catch a taxi to the river to watch the weekly animal sacrifices at the Hindu temple. It was also a city, as Frank was about to learn, with a bureaucracy as byzantine as its medieval character.

Lenser had been in Katmandu for about a week and as far as Frank could determine, if he had accomplished anything it was to reverse whatever progress Frank felt he and Dick had made from the States toward expediting the expedition's passage through officialdom and onto the mountain. Frank once again felt his patience wear thin, but he knew the best policy was to restrain himself and wait for Dick.

When Dick arrived, Frank brought him up to date. "Gerhard says things are complicated because we need permits from all these different ministries for the satellite broadcast. We had things going pretty well until a couple of days ago when one of our guys was down at the airport trying to spring some gear out of customs and to speed things along signed some form with Gerhard's name, knowing Gerhard would approve it anyway. But when Gerhard found out he flipped, and then went around and told all the Nepalese what happened. So now the Nepalese are going crazy."

"That's because they think we're not taking them seriously," Dick said. "It's a matter of pride."

"They're already confused," Frank continued, "about us being the German Everest Expedition, aka the Seven Summits, with one German leader and twelve Americans who now want to import a twenty-thousand pound earth station to stick on top of the Sheraton. Worse, someone told ABC the way to do it is through diplomatic channels so they had the State Department contact the Nepalese foreign ministry and now the mountaineering ministry is up in arms because they think we're trying to go around them, and so Gerhard is saying ten times a day, 'See, you need me to take care of all this, to get your permit.' "

"Well that explains it then."

"Explains what?" Frank asked.

"It's just a question of money. Gerhard wants money for this last-minute involvement of ABC."

"Oh, I don't think so. It's a question of Germanic pride and his perception that we're treading on his authority."

"You watch. It'll come down to money, and I'd guess the amount will be about ten grand. And believe me it'll be worth it just to get his cooperation and keep this show moving."

The next day Lenser told Dick and Frank he needed to talk with them. He began an involved explanation about the steps yet necessary to gain the permit, and after about five minutes Dick interrupted and said, "Gerhard, how much money do you need to do all this?"

Frank leaned back in his chair. If money is what Lenser wanted, Frank was afraid it might be more than Dick's estimate. But Lenser wouldn't come out and say it directly; he went into a long rationale about how Dick and Frank could charge ABC about $10,000 for use of their Sherpas to help film the climb, Sherpas they had already hired anyway.

"So what are you saying?" Dick asked.

Lenser said that if they paid him $10,000, money they could recoup from ABC, that would cover his services. Dick glanced at Frank, then turned back to Lenser and told him that seemed a lot of money just to get the filming permit. Frank tried to hide his smile as Lenser was forced into another convoluted justification for the charge. Finally Dick figured they'd never get Lenser on their side without the payment and agreed to the figure. Lenser said it would take a few more days to get the permit, and that one of them would have to stay behind the extra time. Dick and Frank flipped a coin, and Frank won. He would get to leave in the morning, with Ershler, Nielson, and Neptune (the others had already flown out and started the ten-day walk to base camp).

Frank was pleasantly surprised that all it took was money to resolve the imbroglio with the Nepalese and Lenser. Frank and Dick had no intention of charging ABC to recoup the money, as Lenser had suggested, but it was worth every penny. At least now they had Lenser working with instead of against them, and there was still the understanding that even though Lenser was coming to base camp he would probably go no higher than that, and also be no more than a titular leader of the expedition.

Frank had hated to leave his partner in Katmandu, but the flip was fair and square. He first flew in a Twin Otter shuttle to a 9,000-foot dirt airstrip at Lukla, 120 miles east of Katmandu. From there he began the two-day walk to Namche Bazar, the principal Sherpa village on the way to base camp. It was a pleasant interlude. The trail was lined with Himalayan blue pine and deodar cedar, and with no automobile roads in the Khumbu, the stones on the trail were polished smooth by the passage of generations.

On the second day they finally crested a hilltop and could see the 100-odd two-story stone houses, arranged like concentric horseshoes on stair-stepped levels of a natural amphitheater, that formed Namche Bazar. Located above the confluence of the two major rivers in the region, at a junction of the trails that follow these drainages, Namche Bazar for over a hundred years had been the trading hub of the mountain Sherpas.

The trail to base camp is traveled by some 5,000 trekkers a year, and with so much traffic the route is divided into standard stages so that it usually takes just over a week to walk from Namche at 11,000 feet to base camp at 17,700 feet including a couple of layover days here and there to acclimatize. The next stage was a five-hour walk to the storybook Tengboche Monastery situated on a steep-sided ridge of land with a commanding view of many magnificent peaks, including the sword-summitted Ama Dablam, and further upvalley, Everest. Here Frank and some of the team members received a blessing for the expedition from the monastery's reincarnate lama.

Traditionally the monastery was supported by donations of labor and food from the Sherpas, but since the advent of trekking and mountaineering most local people were too busy to work at the monastery. It seemed only fair, then, that a principal source of funds was donations from various expeditions that received blessings, a consecration very important to the Sherpas working on the climb. Frank watched bemused as the lama carefully scribed a receipt for the donation, then stamped it.

Here we are nearly to the base of Everest, Frank thought, and even the lamas know about the IRS.

The following morning Frank and the others were on the trail, making good time. After three days they reached the lower Khumbu Glacier, which led to base camp. At the head of the glacial valley

Frank could see a 20,000-foot pass called the Lho La, and through the pass the tip of a peak that somehow looked familiar. He couldn't figure it out until he realized the peak was in Tibet, and that it was Changtse, the north satellite of Everest, a mountain he had camped under for two months the previous year. Until then, that other side of Everest—perhaps because the approach through Lhasa contrasted so with this southern route—had seemed a world removed.

While the glimpse of Changtse gave evidence of their proximity to last year's efforts, the first glimpse of base camp underscored the difference of climbing on this side of the mountain. In place of last year's spartan huddle of small mountaineering tents, the Sherpas had erected a tent city with a kitchen, an equipment warehouse, and separate dining areas for the Sherpas and the sahibs. As he entered camp a Sherpa boy greeted him with a metal platter holding a cup of steaming liquid. "Welcome to base camp, sahib. Would you like tea?"

Frank knew immediately that not only would he like tea, but he was going to like climbing Everest from this side in the company of these Sherpas.

"Tea, coffee, or cocoa, sahib?" Again, it was the same Sherpa cookboy, now poking his head in the tent. Frank glanced at his watch: 7:00 A.M. He had a slight headache from the altitude, but otherwise had passed a pleasant enough first night in base camp, and having cocoa served in bed (or more accurately, in sleeping bag) was a good way to start the first full day. Frank wrapped his fingers around the warm cup and considered the day ahead. There wouldn't be a lot for him to do, not today, or for the next week or two, since it was the Sherpas' task to complete the erecting of the remaining base camp tents, and the unloading of the yaks still arriving with food and equipment. Meanwhile, they had received notice it would be another two days before the lead Sherpa, the sirdar, arrived, along with the government liaison officer (or L.O., as he was called) who would stay at base camp the length of the expedition. As they legally couldn't start to climb above base camp until the L.O. was in camp, for the next two days even the lead climbers had little to do but help the Sherpas. No one was especially antsy though, since each day in camp their bodies gained valuable acclimatization to the high altitude.

It was now April 2, early enough that they should have sufficient time to keep to the climbing schedule dictated by pre-monsoon weather patterns. They guessed it would take them a week or so to get through the Icefall, then another few weeks to get up to camps 2 and 3, and finally to the South Col, from where they would be positioned for the first summit attempts. Unless there was unusually bad weather they should be able to make those first attempts in early May, well before the clockwork monsoon that arrives sometime during early June.

The L.O., Mr. Ale, arrived and introduced himself. He was a small, thin man in his late twenties who worked as personal secretary to the Minister of State. Being L.O. was a temporary appointment, a kind of vacation away from the desk. The lead Sherpa, Sonam Girme, also arrived, and he said that while the Sherpas would be happy to assist carrying ladders and rope for the lead climbers they would not sleep anywhere above base camp until after the puja, a Buddhist ceremony to propitiate the goddess of Everest, and to make the snows of Chomolungma—Mother Goddess of the World, as the Sherpas call Everest—safe for climbers. Sonam said they would wait to have this ceremony until everyone was in camp, including Dick. This would be no disruption to the schedule, as the Sherpas would not be required to sleep above base camp anyway until after camp 1 was well established, and that was at least a week away.

Before entering the Icefall the climbers studied through binoculars the maze of seracs to see if they could spot what might be the best route. Everyone was confident the route through the Icefall would "go" without any unusual difficulties—everyone except Jim States. For two weeks States had suffered forebodings of an accident, a tragedy someplace on the climb, most likely in the Icefall. The first premonition had been on the hike to base camp, when he had a powerful feeling someone was going to get hurt. From past experiences, States had learned to heed his premonitions. Once on Rainier he had been climbing a ridge running between ice and rock walls when he had a notion some disaster was pending. He talked his companions into a quick retreat, and they had only reached the abutting glacier when an avalanche broke above and in seconds buried the area where only minutes before they had been climbing.

"You get clues in the mountains," he told everyone. "I'm not sure how, but you do. It's kind of like how animals sense earthquakes. And I know it might sound strange, but I've really learned to pay attention to these feelings, and the premonitions I've been having the last week are so strong I'm thinking of leaving the expedition and going home."

"Maybe you should just take a couple of days off," Gerry Roach suggested. The others seconded Roach's advice, adding that they needed States' contribution to the climb but understood his feelings. Although at base camp he continued to wake each morning with the same vague foreboding, States decided for the time being to stay.

The next day climbing leader Phil Ershler gathered the team. "I've made a plan for the initial exploration of the Icefall," he said. "We'll divide into two teams and alternate so one group rests while the other climbs. Tomorrow Gerry Roach, Peter Jamieson, and Larry Nielson will make the first foray."

This would be the second time that Roach had explored a route through the Icefall; he had been a lead climber on that 1976 Everest Expedition, the same one Dan Emmett and I had been on. On that trip Roach had made it clear that more than anything in his life he wanted to climb Everest, but he awoke the day before his final departure from camp 2 complaining of stomach cramps, and switched places with one of the second summit team climbers to give himself an extra two days to improve. I had been a member of that second team, and when it was our turn for the attempt, Roach said his health was perfect. He was confident we could reach the top. As we gained the South Col, we met the first summit team on their way down. Two of them had summited, including the climber with whom Roach had traded places, but they told us there had been a mixup and no full bottles of oxygen remained in the upper camps. Furthermore, a wind storm was building, and I was having trouble breathing. We decided to retreat to camp 2, wait for the weather to clear, then go back up with another team of Sherpas carrying more oxygen. Back at camp, though, we learned the Sherpas were unwilling to go back up. So even though he was feeling strong there was nothing he could do to organize another attempt, and the expedition was concluded.

Now, seven years later, Roach was back, once again questing after that elusive square yard of real estate that forms the high throne of the planet, once again scouting the route through the Icefall. With the others, he left base camp in the black hours of predawn planning to finish work early and get back to camp before the sun warmed the ice, increasing the risk of avalanche. As first light illuminated the icy corridors they made rapid progress through the lower section of the Icefall, and by mid-morning they were perhaps a fourth of the way toward camp 1. Roach knew from past experience that this first section was easy and the real difficulties would start higher. But he was concerned they might be heading for trouble, since earlier that morning Larry Nielson had split with a few of the Sherpas and was now exploring an area Roach felt was dangerously close to the left margin of the Icefall, where avalanches frequently thunder off a bordering hanging glacier.

Later that day, when they had all returned to base camp, he spoke his mind: "It's a suicide route. Look what happened last year to Pat Morrow and the Canadians. They had their route over there and lost one climber and two Sherpas when an avalanche hit them."

"We're a hundred yards out of any avalanche zone," Nielson countered, "and in a place where there's a lot less risk from having a serac fall over and squash you."

As climbing leader, the ball was now in Phil Ershler's court, and consulting the Sherpas—many of whom had been on four or five Everest climbs—he learned the route normally did stay closer to center. Ershler decided that was the wiser strategy, and next morning, with Gary Neptune and Jim States, he got a predawn start, following the wand markers and fixed ropes to Roach's previous high point. There his group encountered a chaos of ice blocks, and one glance was sufficient to realize it would take at least two days to get through the maze; once past it, though, it appeared the route was less jumbled. They christened the section the Interconnect.

The following day Roach and Nielson were back, joined by Ershler and Peter Jamieson. Once again they split, Nielson and Ershler working straight up the Interconnect while Roach and Jamieson consolidated the route lower down, exploring an alternate one more toward the middle. Thinking he had found the best way Nielson came down to find Roach working on his alternate.

"It's much faster straight up," Nielson yelled from the top of a nearby ice block.

"And much more dangerous," Roach countered.

Nielson was fuming, as was Roach. Back at camp Ershler called a meeting. "Clearly we have some differences here so let's discuss the options."

Nielson stood and said, "There're four options, as I see it. One, we start listening to the climbing leader. Two, Gerry leaves this expedition. Three, I leave this expedition. Four, we go outside right now, Gerry, and I beat the shit out of you."

"Wrong," Roach fired back, jumping to his feet. "You forgot Five: we go outside and I beat the shit out of *you*."

"Hold on," Ershler said, now on his feet too. "As long as I'm climbing leader of this expedition nobody's going to beat the shit out of anybody."

When he had the pair calmed Ershler said they would return in the morning and have a look at both ways, then judge the best choice. Meanwhile there was enough work to do consolidating the distance they had already explored so that instead of alternating teams anyone who felt up to it should work each day, taking a rest day only when he felt he really needed one.

The next morning most of the lead climbers were in the Icefall rigging ladders and fixing ropes. Much of this work in the Icefall was mechanical, bolting ladder sections together, lowering them over crevasses, hammering in aluminum picket anchors, turning ice screws into the serac walls, and attaching long handlines of polypropylene rope. States was working to span a badly broken section in the Interconnect when Jamieson arrived to help.

"I'm going up that block to see how many more ladder sections we need," States said.

"Why don't you tie in first."

Jamieson belayed the rope while States balanced across the blocks. Getting to a block the size of a station wagon, States spanned his leg to reach it, and the second he transferred his weight the whole mass shifted. In a split second the block dropped quickly in a grinding roar, sending States falling into a maelstrom of car-sized ice blocks breaking about him. There was no sky, only the blue white shine of crunching ice blocks, and the noise. He held his breath, and waited for the crunch, for the awful sound of bones breaking. A big block pressed his right side, and he gritted his teeth, waiting for that final crunching shift.

Then it stopped. His right side was buried, pinning his arm and leg. The ice was pressing under his chin, forcing his head back. Was he hurt? He couldn't tell. Then in a grip of panic, he feared the blocks would shift again and complete the job of crushing him. With his free arm he started grabbing any loose hunks of snow and wedging them under the large block that pinned his right side, to keep it from shifting further. He was working furiously when he saw Steve Marts, who had been nearby filming, down in the hole muscling snow blocks.

"Hold on, Jim. We'll get you out."

Even with the smaller blocks moved the big one still pinned States, so Marts—disregarding his own safety—started hacking at it with his ice axe. In a few minutes States was out, and miraculously, other than a few bruises, he seemed uninjured. He was shaken, though, and told the others he was heading back to camp. As he left he passed one of the Sherpas, a young kid who looked under twenty, standing over the hole created by the shifting block, chanting a mantra and tossing sacred rice blessed by a lama.

The Sherpa kid's composure helped settle States's nerves, and on the way down States, knowing the physical work would bring his pulse closer to normal, forced himself to stop and adjust ropes and arrange ladders. Back at camp he decided to take up his teammates' earlier suggestion to take a couple of days off. While he recuperated he found, to his own surprise, that despite his earlier premonitions he now felt better about the expedition, and concluded that whatever had prompted his dark forebodings was now behind him, and that the rest of the climb would go safely.

While States rested, the others pushed the route higher, estimating they would reach the top of the Icefall in two or three days. Meanwhile Roach and Nielson waved a white flag and agreed to a truce, at least while the expedition lasted.

The days now became routine. The climbers would get to bed early so they could rise at three in the morning to breakfast and get away by four. The weather clouded in the afternoons and occasionally snowed lightly, but it cleared at night so that when the climbers left in the predawn the stars were brilliant through the vacuum-black sky, and the train of headlamps as they climbed above base camp made an eerie procession between the dim ice towers. The Sherpas, each freighting an eight-foot ladder section, would bring up the rear, chanting their Buddhist mantras and adding a kind of background hymn to the silent tension that came from knowing at any moment the ice blocks could explode in convulsing upheaval.

This ever-present threat of death in the Icefall made it like a frozen outdoor cathedral of some brimstone religion, a place that when witnessed at first dawn to the choral chanting of Sherpas had an unmatched siren call of beauty mixed with danger. It was a place that set a cutting edge to your senses so that at day's end, after you were returned to the safe harbor of base camp, you were left with a vague yearning, a kind of strange addiction cousin to whatever it is that lures men and women to take physical risk of their lives.

While the lead climbers worked on the Icefall, Frank had kept busy. One day he had hiked across the glacier to Kala Patar, a hilltop vantage with a commanding view of Everest. Then another day States had coached him up the side of a serac near base camp, to improve his ice axe and crampon technique. He kept busy reading, and was entertained by the assortment of trekkers who each day wandered into base camp. There was Bill Grant, the Scotsman who was on his fifth expedition looking for the yeti, the abominable snowman, and then the two Americans who rode in claiming the first bicycle ascent to the base of Everest. Another day an American visited camp who said he was a writer, working on a biography of Ingrid Bergman.

The writer triggered memories in Frank of the movie business he had given up to go climbing. For the first time since starting the Seven Summits he felt melancholic. Would he come to regret his decision, he wondered.

Later that afternoon he was rescued from his melancholy when he heard at the edge of camp that familiar Tarzan call, and stepping out of the dining tent he saw Dick approaching, wearing jogging shorts over long john underwear, a Snowbird visor hat, and a wide Texas grin.

"We secured all the loose ends in Katmandu," Dick said as he bear-hugged Frank. "We got the ABC permit, Gerhard is in a good mood, and I'm ready to climb this mother."

The full team was now in base camp and Sonam, the lead Sherpa, said next morning they would have the puja ceremony at the foot of the base camp altar, a stone pedestal the Sherpas had built on the highest point in camp and from which they had strung long lines of colored prayer flags. Here they kept a few boughs of juniper smoldering and whenever they left camp to go into the Icefall they paused to breathe the smoke. Like the chanting of mantras, this was thought to cleanse the soul of wrongdoing, or as one Sherpa put it, "to make sure you have good luck in the Icefall."

After breakfast the Sherpas gathered around the altar while one of them, chanting from a prayer book, reached in a sack and tossed handfuls of sacred rice in the air. After performing other ceremonious acts, they made an offering to the goddess of Everest of several glasses of chang, the local rice beer, a bottle of Remy Martin, and another of Johnnie Walker Red. When the ceremony was finished the Sherpas passed around the bottles, and when the liquor was polished off they proclaimed that the expedition could get fully underway.

Two days later the lead climbers established camp 1, at the top of the Icefall. It had taken nine days and while some sections were undeniably dangerous, especially the Interconnect, there was general agreement the route was a good one and the Sherpas could now begin carrying through it the hundreds of loads of food and equipment needed to provision the upper mountain. Gerry Roach and Peter Jamieson left to occupy camp 1 and begin the push into the Western Cwm (pronounced "Coom"), an enormous ice valley formed in part by the huge southwest face of Everest.

It was now April 19, and team leader Phil Ershler estimated they could be in position to make the first summit bid by the end of the month. It was time to think about selecting summit teams.

Ershler had been scrutinizing everyone's performance, earmarking those who had been working the hardest and therefore most deserved a position on the first summit team. He had also been wrestling with what to do about the Sherpas. He had listened carefully to Gerry Roach tell about the 1976 expedition when the Sherpas had refused to carry more oxygen to the high camps after the first summit attempt; Roach felt the problem stemmed from the Sherpas' feeling of being nothing more than hired hands. Sonam had also warned Ershler that if the Sherpas felt they were only beasts of burden, with no real hand in the climbing, they might quit early. It seemed critical to Ershler to devise a plan which included the Sherpas. And besides, all self-interest aside, he was fond of these warm-hearted, good-natured mountain people and felt they deserved a chance for success on this peak as much as the sahibs who had hired them.

He also had to consider Frank and Dick. Ershler recalled that when they had that New Year's team meeting in Snowbird, Frank had said at the time he and Dick wanted to be equals with other team members, and "all we expect is an equal chance at the summit." The team agreed without a single dissent. Now Ershler had to weigh how those terms might translate to a summit strategy. (Frank later told Dick that as soon as that meeting was over he regretted not being more specific in defining what an equal chance should be.) Ershler's view—shared by the other lead climbers—was that while Frank and Dick had paid for the expedition (other than personal airfare, which each member had covered for himself), they, the lead climbers, had contributed their share organizing the food and equipment, and more importantly had risked their lives to build the route through the Icefall. Given that no one had actually been hired to be Frank and Dick's guides, and as Frank had said, everyone was equal with an equal chance, Ershler felt he was on solid ground choosing from among the lead climbers the first summit teams. He called a meeting to announce his choices.

"I think the first team should be made up of those who have worked hardest getting through the Icefall," he said. "And I think those three guys are Gerry Roach, Peter Jamieson, and Larry Nielson. In addition, I think there should be one Sherpa on the first team, and I will get together with Sonam later to determine who that will be. Then the second team will be Gary Neptune, Jim States, myself, and another Sherpa. The third team will then be Dick Bass, Frank Wells, and Ed Hixson (the team doctor).

For a moment everyone was quiet, then Frank raised his hand.

"I respect the tough position you're in, Phil, and of course I respect your decision. But I have two comments. First, I think you should include yourself in the first team. You've earned it if anyone has. My second point: I don't think it's fair to exclude yourself from the first team, and either Dick or me from the second team, so a Sherpa can get a first shot. I realize your concern for the Sherpas, and for demonstrating to them how much we all appreciate their wonderful and valuable contribution here, but I can't help but weigh against that the work and expense Dick and I have put into making this thing possible, and I think one of us at least has earned a place on that second team."

"I'd like to comment on that too," Dick said. "I agree with my partner here that we've earned a spot on that second team, but I'd like to add further I'm perfectly happy on a third team because I feel confident I'm going to make it no matter where I fall in line. So I'd be happy to give that second-team spot to Frank here, although I sure wish we could climb the mother together so we could get that movie footage of us up there on the roof of the world arm-in-arm, in pure jubilation."

"Goddamnit Dick, if you weren't so unselfish sometimes you'd be easier to deal with," Frank said. "You should really be on that second team because you've got a much better shot at it than me. But my whole reason for wanting to be on that second team is that if I don't make it the first time I can come down and try again, and if that doesn't work, try a third time."

"Frank, there's no way you'll have it in you after one attempt to go back up and make another," Ershler argued.

"While you guys have been up in the Icefall," Frank countered, "I've been down here reading this mountaineering history of Everest, and in it there are plenty of examples of guys who have had a second shot and made it."

"But Frank, those are world-class climbers," Ershler said. "I was with you last year for three months on the other side of this mountain, and I hate to be blunt, but you ain't world-class."

"I know I'm not world-class, but I nevertheless feel I've earned a right to a second-team position."

Ershler then turned to Gary Neptune and said, "Gary, you're most likely to be the leader of the second team. What do you think?"

Neptune had been quiet, as was his style. He was a person who preferred to listen and not make waves. Two years before he had been on Ama Dablam, the sword-shaped summit near Everest, and after the first team made the summit, he didn't argue for another bid after the others wanted to go home. He simply climbed the peak solo.

Now he was uncomfortably on the spot. He was hesitant to state his true feelings—he didn't want to hurt or embarrass Frank—but he saw no way out. He hadn't forgotten his experience with Frank two months before on Aconcagua, when he had watched terrified as Frank awkwardly made the traverse of that steep snow slope leading to the Canaleta. Dick had been okay—Neptune hadn't minded going to the top of Aconcagua with him, and he wouldn't hesitate to do the same on Everest—but Frank was another matter.

"I don't know, Frank," Neptune said. "You weren't too strong on Aconcagua. You might be more acclimatized if you waited until the third attempt."

"That doesn't make sense. There's plenty of time to acclimatize."

"Well, I'm just not sure how you'll do."

"Gary, are you saying you wouldn't want to have me on your team?"

"Well, if you put it that way," Neptune said in a self-effacing tone, "I guess the answer is yes. I wouldn't be comfortable climbing with you."

Frank knew there was nothing more to say, and the meeting adjourned.

Frank held no grudge against Neptune, and decided if he couldn't get on the second team he would just live with his third-team position and do all he could to increase his chances of success there. He felt there were two ways to do that. One, to get as much oxygen as possible higher on the mountain. If any single thing would make it easier for him to climb Everest he felt it was that. Second, he began to lobby with Ershler for the establishment of an additional camp above the South Col—a camp 5 at around 27,500 feet—so he would have less distance to climb on his summit day. It was similar to his request on

Aconcagua, when he had asked me the day before our summit climb to go with him and overnight at that higher camp that was closer to the top.

Ershler had his hands full figuring which loads needed to go through the Icefall first, what climbers should be positioned where in order to always have a fresh pair in the lead, and how the Sherpas would best fit into the climbing strategy. He listened politely to Frank's requests, but his patience was wearing thin. Although he didn't tell Frank, he felt it was a waste of time making decisions about how much oxygen should go to the South Col, or when to put in a camp 5, because he doubted Frank would ever get high enough on the mountain to make use of those supplies, anyway. In fact, he wasn't even sure Frank would be able to get through the Icefall in one day, and if he couldn't do that, he couldn't get to camp 1.

That gave Ershler an idea. Next day he would insist Frank and Dick go with him through the Icefall; that way, when Frank saw for himself he couldn't make it, maybe he would stay off Ershler's back.

"You two have been sitting idle in base camp here too long," Ershler said to Frank and Dick. "What do you say in the morning you go with me through the Icefall. Get some exercise."

Despite their promise to their families to go through the Icefall only once, Frank and Dick felt it would be important for them to go along with Ershler. The next morning leaving camp Frank and Dick paused at the Sherpa altar to breathe juniper smoke. It wasn't that Frank and Dick had developed a belief in Buddhism, but rather they and everyone else on the team observed these rituals out of a combination of courtesy for the Sherpas and a sense that, as Frank put it, "It can't hurt."

There were two Sherpas with them who chanted mantras as they entered the shadowy frozen towers at the base of the Icefall. As Ershler had anticipated, he and Dick soon pulled ahead, leaving Frank with the Sherpas.

"Dick, the real reason I got you two up here this morning was to give Frank a test," Ershler confessed. "I know you can handle this okay but I want to see how well Frank does."

"Well, whatever," Dick said. "I'm just happy to be getting the experience."

Ershler didn't want to be unfair, but he still decided to set a good pace. He and Dick hooked into the fixed ropes with their carabiners and stepped out quickly up the trail, which was now well packed around the maze of blocks. It was a brilliantly clear dawn, and Dick paused to gaze across the glacial valley to the cone-shaped summit of Pumori bathed in a pink glow. They crossed the first aluminum ladder, and as Dick stepped on the first rung his crampon spike skated off and he caught his balance on the handline; next step he was careful to place his foot so the spikes straddled the rungs. There was a kind of eerie silence to the Icefall, the only sound the crunch of their boots in the dawn snow and the whistle of their quickened breathing. It was not particularly cold; in fact, dressed in long john underwear, a pile fabric coat, and a windsuit, Dick was almost too warm as he steadily plodded along behind Ershler. They paused to look back and see how Frank and the Sherpas were doing.

"I can't believe it," Ershler said.

Frank was only a few dozen yards behind. Ershler turned to keep climbing. Thirty minutes later he paused again. Dick was right behind him, and again, a few dozen yards back, there were Frank and the Sherpas. Ershler kept pushing, picking up the pace, only to see, every time he turned, that Frank held his position. Finally Ershler stopped, turned to Dick and shook his head. Frank was still coming on strongly. Ershler noted that he was, as usual, a little awkward, but there was no doubting his determination and there was no doubting he could make it easily through the Icefall in a single day.

"Well, so much for that idea," Ershler said to Dick. "But now what am I going to do with him?"

CAMP TWO: 21,600 FEET

On April 24 Peter Pilafian, the ABC cameraman, and I were on the final day of the walk to base camp. Before arriving we took the one-hour detour to the Kala Patar overlook to shoot an update of the expedition's progress. Holding a mike with the ABC logo on the handle, and the summit of Everest framed over my shoulder, I filed this report:

"The route is now through the notoriously dangerous Khumbu Icefall. It has taken the team nine days, fifty-one ladder sections, seventy-five ice screws, and six thousand feet of rope to fix the passage through the jumble of ice blocks. And today an advance team reached the site of camp two, at 21,200 feet, under the enormous southwest face of Everest. From here, the expedition will now alternate lead teams who will each day climb higher up the Lhotse Face, a four-thousand-foot-high expanse of ice that leads to the South Col, the saddle between Everest and its satellite peak, Lhotse. So far the expedition is on schedule, and if progress continues at this rate, the first team could be in position for a summit attempt in less than two weeks."

When we arrived in base camp Frank and Dick were out to greet us, and after introductions to those of the team we didn't already know we unpacked and pitched our tent on a platform of flat rocks prepared in advance by the Sherpas. Base camp was positioned in more or less the same locale we had used in 1976; even though the bumps and cracks in the glacial ice change each year, the position of base camp relative to the surrounding peaks remains more or less the same, and because there is always at least one expedition using the campsite each climbing season (before and after the monsoon), base camp has a kind of de facto geographic charter that has put it on several maps spelled with capital letters.

Pilafian and I decided to spend four days in base camp to acclimatize before ascending to camp 2, where we would remain for the rest of the climb. Frank and Dick said they would come up to camp 2 sometime later, after the ropes had been fixed to the South Col (since these ropes would all be fixed by the lead climbers, there wasn't any reason for them to be in camp 2 eating supplies that had to be carried up there).

Those of us on the ABC crew planned to use our time in base camp completing interviews and working on last-minute modifications to our video equipment, including the tiny modified home-type camera and accompanying two-pound microwave transmitter the summit team was to take with them to the top. We had the idea also to take an on-camera tour of base camp, with me pointing out the various tents, introducing the Sherpas, and explaining everyone's jobs. We started at the altar, with its overview of camp.

"There are fifty-one people on this expedition: nine climbers, including Frank Wells and Dick Bass, an expedition leader, a base camp manager, a government liaison officer, a climbing representative of the Nepal Police, twenty-five climbing Sherpas, five Sherpa cooks and their assistants, four cameramen or TV people, and a mail-runner who shuttles between here and the air strip, a four-day hike away. It takes twenty-one tents in base camp to hold everyone, plus a cook tent, two mess tents, and an equipment storage tent."

We then moved to the equipment storage, a rock-walled enclosure with a plastic sheet roof. Inside were the reels of climbing rope, dozens of aluminum snap links, ice screws, aluminum stakes, and other gear needed to fix ropes on the mountain. There was also the food.

"High altitude often creates a loss of appetite, and correct food can be one of the most important ingredients in a successful Everest expedition. Now this might not sound that appetizing, even at sea level, but some of the things in this tent include fifty pounds of canned salmon and tuna, twenty-five pounds of macaroni and cheese mix, fifty cans of meatballs with sauce, fifty gallons of dried soup mixes, seventy-five pounds of saltine crackers, forty-five pounds of cookies, one hundred pounds of cheese, one hundred fifty pounds of potatoes, two hundred pounds of rice . . . the list goes on."

We entered the cook tent—another rock-walled enclosure—to the smell of curry sauce and steaming potatoes, and the head Sherpa cook insisted we sit down and drink tea. He had 3 two-foot-diameter aluminum pots over large kerosene stoves. One pot was used only to melt ice, and in a moment an assistant cookboy maybe twelve years old came in with an iceblock that weighed more than he did lashed to his packframe. A transistor radio was tuned to the abrasive keening of Indian music while at the same time the cook was singing a discordant Sherpa tune. Before we finished tea, two Sherpanis (female Sherpas) showed up. They both had braided black hair, colored aprons, and red cheeks, and giggled when they saw us. They had herded from Namche Bazar two yaks loaded with fresh cabbage and potatoes, and wanted a glass of tea before reversing their journey.

There were two mess tents—one for Sherpas, one for Sahibs—and both had standing headroom. In the Sahib tent there were a dozen small woven bamboo stools along both sides of a table made from butted cardboard boxes, and also two folding aluminum chairs brought from the States. These aluminum chairs were first come/first served, and at the moment Frank had one and was taking his morning in leisure finishing his mountaineering history of Everest. We heard from the nearby cook tent the clanking of an oversize spoon on an empty pot: the lunch bell. In a moment the Sherpa cookboy brought in a pot of steaming curried potatoes.

"It's easy to get used to climbing with these Sherpas," Frank said, serving himself.

"Easy to get lazy, too," Dick chided.

"I'm saving myself," Frank replied. "Last year on the other side of this mountain I carried loads thirty days in a row and look what happened. I got pneumonia. Well, maybe not pneumonia, but it sounds better calling it that. Anyway, I had to go down and recover. And it was all because of that macho thing, everybody having to carry their own weight and the only way I could feel good was trying to prove myself. I've learned a lot, Bass. I've learned I'm of no use fixing the route through the Icefall or up the Lhotse Face. We'd both just get in the way. So we may as well enjoy ourselves here and wait to go up when things are ready."

"Well, if it's any consolaltion, you've definitely converted—or should I say—subverted me. But still, this sittin' around base camp is no good. We've got to do something."

"Dick, there's plenty to do. Go practice ice climbing on that serac some more, or hike up Kala Patar. Did you finish that letter you're working on, the one your wife is going to xerox to all your friends and family?"

"No, I've been busy on my Snowbird blueprints."

"See what I mean. You're saying there's nothing to do and you can't even finish the things you've got planned. Dick, you're always this way. Did I ever tell you how David Rockefeller did it? Each December he would gather his family and closest advisers around him and review the year, study his date book, see how he divided his time between running Chase Manhattan, six city boards, five business boards, adviser to the president, and everything else—and then knowing he couldn't do everything at once, plan the next year figuring what he could and could not do. That's what you need, Dick. A plan."

"I've got a plan. I'm planning on getting some exercise. I'm going to go for a hike, Wells, down towards Namche. Visit with some of these trekkers, meet some folks."

"You can't do that, Dick. That's going the wrong way: we're supposed to gain altitude, not lose it. You've got to gain some respect for this mountain. This is Everest! I'm telling you, people get into trouble up there. It's not that easy."

"Frank, you're always courting trouble by anticipating it. That's probably from being a lawyer—you're trained to look at all the potential negatives so you can anticipate ways to protect your client. But this is a mountain, not a courtroom. I'm gonna just take the problems as they come. Since there are no problems to deal with for the time being, I'm heading down-valley and have some good leg-stretching and sight-seeing."

"Dick, you just can't be so cavalier."

"Sure I can. As soon as they get those ropes in up there, and it's my turn, I'm going to start right up this mountain and not stop till I get to the top."

The rest of the team were eating their meal, smiling at this latest episode of what everyone was now calling the Frank and Dick Show. The two had spent enough time together on expeditions that they now knew each other like brothers, and as often as brothers they were getting into verbal scrapes. It was always friendly badinage, though, done in a spirit of good fun—although at times Frank was truly exacerbated with Dick's seeming casualness about Everest. Frank realized, though, he had no hope of dissuading Dick from making his down-valley foray. After lunch Dick shouldered his backpack, and with a wave like a pony express rider off into the sunset, he disappeared down the glacier.

"What bugs me most," Frank said when Dick was gone, "is that he's probably right. He *will* come back here and just march up the mountain to the summit. Doncha' just love it!"

Base camp seemed subdued with Dick gone. The fifteen Sherpas who that day had each carried forty-pound loads through the Icefall to camp 1 had now returned. Five more Sherpas had gone up to stay in camp 1 to begin shuttling the same forty-pound loads up to camp 2 the next day.

Frank now had his tent to himself, and as everyone usually did, he crawled in shortly after it got dark. Inside there was no headroom—he had to remain seated—but still plenty of space. It is important to be organized when living in such a small space as a tent, and Frank had all his belongings in a series of nylon sacks alongside his sleeping bag. The bag itself was spread atop an inch-thick air mattress that was on another layer of foam rubber: this helped both to cushion the rocks under the tent floor and also—especially when he would be higher, camped on snow—to insulate against cold. Frank stripped to his long-john underwear and crawled in his bag. At first it was cold, but in a few minutes he was cozy.

Across camp occasional laughter came from the Sherpas' tents: they often stayed awake past nine or ten, telling stories. From behind the cook tent, in the area where the garbage was thrown, two dogs were in a fight: they were the mangy but friendly mutts that had tailed the expedition up to base camp, and everyone had the impression they were in the habit of doing this with every climbing group that came through their village. Then it was quiet until on the moraine behind camp a single rock tumbled, perhaps loosened by some slight shift in the glacial ice.

In the middle of the night Frank woke, pulled on his down booties, and crawled outside to pee. The night sky was cloudless, and a sickle moon left black shadows between the rocks that covered the glacial ice. He was still in his long johns, so as soon as he finished he was quickly back in his bag. There was no wind, no sound in camp, and soon he was back asleep.

He dreamed he was in a tent, high on a mountain, waiting on a storm. The wind was blowing outside, and thunder rolled across the range, getting louder and louder. . . . He awoke, startled. The thunder was still there, still growing louder. What . . . ? Then he realized what it was: an avalanche off the west shoulder of Everest! He grabbed the tent door and pulled it open. Below the hanging glacier under the west shoulder he saw the avalanche halfway down the face, approaching the Icefall. It was like an upside-down high-speed cumulus cloud, belching huge white billows as it gained speed. He knew that avalanches off this shoulder have on past expeditions been big enough for the wind-cloud to carry across the glacier and flatten tents at base camp. This one hit the base of the Icefall, and then raced on the flat toward the camp. For a beat he wondered if he should get out and run for a rock to hide behind. Then the roar began to drop, and the billows slowed and then sank back into the now static wind-cloud. It had stopped several hundred yards from camp. He pulled his head back in.

Now he lay awake, pondering the quiet, until on the moraine another lone rock tumbled. Then again the quiet, a silence that his mind began to fill with thoughts of the climb, of his and Dick's chances, and inevitably, of the Icefall, of the towering precarious ice towers that now and again shift and tumble and crush. And then he had the thought everyone on the climb who is scheduled to go through the Icefall has, wondering if up there one of those ice towers already had his name on it.

For Frank Wells, his sojourn at base camp was the first time in his life since a summer break after his last year as an undergraduate at Pomona College that he had had two unstructured weeks in which he could do whatever he pleased. When he finished reading Unsworth's mountaineering history of Everest, he started an 800-page biography of Lyndon Johnson. Somewhat to his surprise he found there was always something to do. When he wasn't reading he could work on calculating how much oxygen and other supplies he would need for his own summit attempt. There was the daily radio call to Katmandu. And best of all was the day once a week when a runner arrived with the mailbag.

On a long expedition receiving mail can be one of the great joys, and often climbers who otherwise never in their lives have such inclinations find themselves writing long letters. Frank had never had time in his business life to write personal letters, but now he found himself putting on paper to his wife and two sons his most intimate thoughts, telling them how much he missed them, how much he loved them.

On April 29, Larry Nielson descended to base camp for a few days rest before his summit attempt. He had announced he was going to try to climb Everest without bottled oxygen. He knew it would be extraordinarily difficult—only six people had ever managed it—and also much riskier, with increased chance of frostbite, pulmonary problems, and even brain damage. Wondering just why he wanted to take the risks, the ABC crew interviewed him the morning he came down.

"All the climbing I've done to now has been without oxygen, and it just seems the way to do it. It's like after someone has climbed a section of a mountain free, without using artificial aids, it doesn't seem right to come along later and then hang on pitons or other anchors to get over it; you're better to develop the skill to do it in the same best style in which it's already been done. I'm not saying everybody should try to climb Everest without oxygen, but it's right for me."

Nielson spoke softly, almost too softly, as though to mask the ambition you knew had to be hidden somewhere behind his light blue eyes. He was of Scottish ancestry, five foot eight, lean and sinewy. His resting pulse was thirty-seven, as low as the best world-class athletes.

"Then you feel you're physically capable?"

"Except for my toe," Nielson said, removing his boot and then a foam rubber sleeve that covered his second toe. "As you know, I lost the end of the toe last year, on the North Wall climb when I got frostbite trying to make a solo push to the summit. It still bothers me."

The camera zoomed in to this toe. There was a nasty hole at the end of the stub and the bone was visible.

"Ed Hixson says I'm going to risk further damage to the toe, especially without oxygen. But that's one of the chances you take, I guess. I don't think I would do it if it were any other mountain. But this is Everest."

The next day Pilafian and I left base camp and climbed through the Icefall to camp 1, where we overnighted, and the following morn-

ing completed the long walk up the Western Cwm to camp 2 at 21,600
feet. This camp was located under the 7,500-foot southwest face of
Everest. In addition to the tents our team had pitched, there was a
white tent the size of a small trailer made of an insulated synthetic
batting stretched over a heavy-duty aluminum frame left the season
before by the Canadian expedition. The Sherpas had commandeered
it as the cook tent, and it was so well insulated they could all crowd
in stripped to their shirtsleeves and drink tea. Across from this was
a caravan tent pitched by our expedition large enough for us sahibs
to use as our mess. Then sprinkled around the periphery were eight
smaller yellow and tan paneled dome sleeping tents that looked like
futuristic modules set in an extraterrestrial icescape. The whole place
brought to mind those illustrations on the front of science fiction
novels showing lost cities on distant planets.

The next day Pilafian taped me standing in the middle of camp as
I filed my ABC report:

"We're at camp two, advanced base camp, altitude 21,600 feet,
higher than the tallest mountain in North America. This is where the
action is, where the climbing on the upper mountain begins. Right
now the lead climbers and some of the Sherpas are hard at work on
the Lhotse Face that rises just behind me. They have placed camp
three halfway up this face, at 24,000 feet, and the lead climbers are
now busy fixing more ropes toward the South Col, at 26,200 feet.
There is a chance they will reach the Col later today. But it's a nasty
day up there right now. It was five below zero in camp here last night,
and it's safe to say it was much colder in the upper camp. The wind
is blowing, too, making the apparent temperature even lower. On top
of that, in order to conserve supplies the lead climbers are working
without using bottled oxygen. They are optimistic that in a week or
two at least a few of them are going to be standing on the roof of the
world."

Just as we finished, the Sherpa cookboy rang the lunch bell—a
big spoon against a pot—and we gathered in the mess tent. First
course was packaged onion soup, followed by stew made with yak
meat. The cookboy was the same who had brought tea to Frank in
base camp, and now he served our meal with the same spunk. He
had also organized our mess tent, fitting stones into benches and
stacking the cardboard shipping boxes as backrests. Some of our
food, such as cereals, had been in flimsy boxes damaged in shipping
and he had transferred these into aluminum pots. To help us know

what was in each pot he had taken a marking pen and labeled the pots, copying the writing off the cereal boxes. One pot was labeled "Save 10¢" and the other "Special Offer."

"Care for any Special Offer this morning?"

"No thanks. I'm going for the Save Ten Cents."

After lunch it was time for the radio call with the lead climbers.

"Hello camp two. Do you read?"

"We got you Jim," Ershler answered. "How did you two do?"

"You've got your camp four. We reached the South Col."

There was a big cheer from our tent and when word made it to the Sherpas another cheer from their tent.

"That's great, Jim," Ershler told States. "Now get your asses down here for a rest so you can get ready for your summit bid."

"I'm going down to base tomorrow," Ershler said when the radio call was over, "to make sure the Sherpas are organized with the final loads that need to come up to two. Larry is coming back up here tomorrow so that means all of the first team will be in place to begin their bid on May fifth, which will put them on top the seventh. I guess we'd better radio down to Wells and have him start up so he can begin acclimatizing. And Bass, if he ever comes back. Any word from him?"

"He sent a note up with a trekker and said he'll be back in base camp in a couple more days."

"I'm not worried about him, anyway. He can catch up to Frank. But let's get Wells started up. He'll need all the advantage he can get."

The morning of his departure Frank awoke at 5:00, and base camp was still in cold shadow when he left at 6:00. The previous day two friends had trekked into Camp—Bill Sarnoff, an executive at Warner Communications, and his wife, Pam—and now they were up to send him off. It meant a lot to Frank to have them there: going through the Icefall might be old hat to these lead climbers but to Frank it was a major crux of his entire Seven Summits odyssey, and it was comforting having two friends who could appreciate the contrast of a climb through the Khumbu Icefall with a stroll down Rodeo Drive.

At the altar the Sherpas had the juniper incense burning and Frank stopped to breathe the smoke. Then making sure to leave the altar on his right he started toward the Icefall. Two Sherpas were with him. He had no pack—the Sherpas were carrying his gear—and he thought how the previous Everest climb he would have been chagrined to have someone else carry his weight. But now it was okay; now he didn't have to prove anything.

For the first half hour the route was easy walking, then they entered the seracs and the angle steepened. Soon they were weaving among the ice towers, following the yellow polypropylene rope as it wove from one anchor to the next. At the first ladder sections Frank tepidly tested the rungs with his crampons. Even without a pack he felt awkward, but at least he was protected by his waist harness attached to a fixed line and which he used both as balance and safety.

It was a clear morning, and shadow light gave a blue softness to the ice that made it easy to forget you were in a dangerous place. Then, passing under a towering block, Frank was reminded that it was only a question of when the block would tumble, only a question of statistics that it wouldn't let go at that moment.

An hour and a half above base camp Frank was at the entrance to the Interconnect. This was the most chaotic section of the Icefall, and here the ice looked different. Above this section Frank could see the blocks were huge and tinged a light blue. Here, though, the ice was broken in smaller pieces that were fresh white from recent cleavage. For some reason this area was unusually active, and every couple of days a Sherpa crew had to come through it to replace ropes and ladders that had been snapped or crunched by the shifting ice blocks. As Frank climbed into the Interconnect he could see fragments of ladders and ropes from past expeditions sticking out of the ice like bones in a bulldozed graveyard.

To make 100 feet of direct line progress it was necessary to weave and wind 300. Frank felt he was moving well, though, and in a half hour he was through the Interconnect and into a zone of house-sized blocks just below camp 1. He felt good. Sunlight was inching down toward the Icefall, but he knew by the time it reached his path he would be most of the way up. In the still morning the only sound was his boots crunching snow and his forced breathing. Even the Sherpas were quiet, foregoing their usual chants: Maybe they sensed, as he did, that danger was behind, that all would be safe to camp 1.

His strength seemed to match his high spirits, and he kept an even, steady pace. He stopped once to look around. He thought, What an extraordinary place, to be so dangerous and at the same time so beautiful. To his right was an ice arch shaped like one of those sandstone structures in the American Southwest. Everywhere the blocks gleamed light blue. It was a fairyland place, not quite real, the land at the bottom of Alice's hole. One two-story block had a four-section ladder leaning against it. On top he balanced along a block that was like scaling the backbone of a sleeping dinosaur. Another ladder spanned a narrow chasm that appeared bottomless: looking down revealed nothing but black. Then the sun broke above the neighboring ridge and he lowered his goggles. In a half hour he could see just ahead the two tents at camp 1, and behind them his first view of the Western Cwm, the highest valley of its size on earth.

Frank was through the Icefall. He dumped his load in front of a tent and felt like giving out a shout.

Too bad Bass isn't here, he thought. This deserves a Tarzan call.

Looking in one of the tents he found a radio and managed to get Ershler down at base.

"Phil, I made it. I'm in camp one. Three hours flat! And I feel great. This may be my greatest day of climbing yet."

Frank thought, That should take care of those who wondered whether I could get through the Icefall.

Frank peeked inside the tents to see if there was a place to spread his bag. Both tents were a mess: dirty pots, stained floors, soiled tea bags, spilled rice; the Sherpas were not good housekeepers. Frank pushed aside some soiled clothing to make room for his sleeping bag and pad, then lay down to read. He only finished one paragraph, though, when he set the book on his chest and considered the aluminum pot next to his head; it was half-full of some kind of brown gruel. Next to it was a spoon with the dried remains of the same concoction, and under the spoon a damp wool sock Frank guessed was an easy month past last washing.

He smiled, picked up his book and thought, This is probably as far as you can get from Beverly Hills.

But that wasn't a complaint. All in all, he wouldn't have traded that day for anything, anywhere.

While Frank was relaxing in camp 1 the first summit team made final preparations to depart the next morning to begin their ascent. They would first climb to camp 3, the next day to camp 4—the South Col—then in the predawn of May 7 begin the final climb to the summit. Our ABC high altitude cameraman David Breashears was planning to accompany the team to the South Col camp and perhaps even a short distance farther.

While Breashears, at age twenty-seven, was the youngest sahib on the expedition, he was also the most accomplished technical climber. He made his reputation while still a teenager when he showed up one day at the Boulder, Colorado, climbing cliffs while some locals were attempting unsuccessfully to scale what was considered the single most difficult route in the Rockies. The Kloberdanz Roof was a ten-foot wide overhanging ceiling that had then only been climbed once, and only when the climber had made a desperate but lucky lunge at a key hold. Some thought the route would never be repeated.

"It looks like there is a hold on the edge of the lip you could use," Breashears said to one of the locals.

"Then why don't you give it a try, kid."

Breashears climbed up the vertical wall to the roof, then hanging upside down like a fly on a ceiling made a series of smooth moves, reaching the key hold without lunging.

"Who is that kid?" one of the locals asked.

"Never seen him."

So Breashears was given his nickname, the Kloberdanz Kid.

Breashears was also a very accomplished ice climber, and a highly skilled cameraman. He had been on Everest the year before filming a team attempting the then unscaled East Face. The expedition failed to reach the top, but Breashears later won an Emmy for his efforts.

While Breashears made last-minute adjustments to his camera, Pilafian and I were at camp 2 busy getting final interviews with the summit team. Roach said he felt confident he was about to make good his resolution after his 1976 failure and "finally get this Everest thing out of my blood." Nielson too was ready to give it all he had even though without oxygen he knew his chances were reduced. What he didn't tell us, though (and what we wouldn't find out until later), was that for two days he had suffered nausea and dysentery. Still, he decided not to say anything for fear of missing his chance, and incredibly he still intended to try it without oxygen.

The summit team left camp 2 on schedule and made good time up the lower part of the Lhotse Face. Frank had called earlier that morning saying he was waiting for Dick, who was at that moment en route up from base camp, and if Dick felt up to it, they would continue together to camp 2.

"That is if Dick is up to a double carry," Frank said on the radio. "Otherwise we'll spend another night here and see you tomorrow."

Although he didn't tell anyone, secretly Frank was hoping Dick wouldn't be up to it. Not that he didn't feel like going to camp 2 himself, but there just had to be a limit to how much Dick could do. Frank had of course long ago accepted the fact that Dick could far outperform him, but still enough was enough.

Frank was lying on his sleeping bag reading when he heard the call:

"Aah-eah-eaahhh!"

He looked at his watch: 9:00 A.M.

"That s.o.b. made it in two hours," Frank muttered.

He looked out the tent door and there was Dick with his wide grin and a full pack that probably weighed a good fifty pounds.

"Pancho, get your buns out of that tent, boy. We gotta get on up to camp 2. Like John Wayne used to say, 'We're burnin' daylight.' "

"Dick, you're probably exhausted. We can stay here an extra day so you can rest."

Dick was a little puzzled by Frank's uncustomary concern for his welfare. "I appreciate your thoughtfulness, Frank, but I feel like I've got a tiger in my tank. Let's get moving."

Frank knew he was in a no-win position but he decided it would even be worse if he didn't at least carry a full load up to camp 2. He stuffed his backpack with all his personal belongings—forty pounds tops—and soon he and Dick were off into the Western Cwm.

They could see how a quarter mile ahead the huge walls of the valley bottlenecked, and the glacier floor, compressed through the narrow, began to split into transverse crevasses. Soon they were zigzagging, paralleling one crevasse until they came to a natural snow bridge, then reversing direction to the next crossing. Then they came to a wide chasm with no natural bridge, and here the lead climbers had rigged a ladder span. There were three sections bolted together—24 feet spanning a split in the ice maybe 200 feet deep —and even though there was a handline for balance that supposedly doubled as a safety rope, it was easy to figure that if you slipped and fell, the rope probably wouldn't stay secured with so much weight on it. Even if it held, you'd be hanging over the chasm like laundry on a line strung between high-rise buildings.

The Sherpas who had left camp 1 with Dick and Frank walked across first with hardly a change in stride. Dick went next. He had a length of nylon webbing tied to his harness with a carabiner snap link at its end which he clipped into the safety line. Then he stepped carefully, reminding himself to place his crampon spikes properly so they straddled the ladder rungs and he wouldn't skate off into space.

He moved his next foot, and looked over: about 200 feet down the blue-white ice walls constricted to a black bottomless pit. He made another combination of steps and felt the ladder start to sway and decided he had better keep moving.

"You're halfway," Frank called, trying to sound encouraging despite his growing anxiety about his own attempt.

"This wouldn't be so bad if you didn't have a pack on," Dick called back.

Frank felt his own pack suddenly gain twenty pounds. Dick made another two steps and was on the other side.

"Okay, Pancho, your turn."

Frank timidly tested the first rung with his boot. He stepped back, studied the ladder for a moment, then said "This isn't going to look too dignified, but what the hell." He then got down on all fours and crawled across.

"You've just got to know how to do these things," Frank said with a sly grin when he reached the other side.

They crossed two more big ladder sections and several smaller ones to gain the top of the bottleneck. The morning had been cool, but now they were in direct sun. "Let's take a break," Frank said. The Sherpas, always courteous, agreed to stop. One of them pointed up the Cwm to a spot on the Lhotse Face and said, "First team maybe two hours from South Col." Frank and Dick studied the huge ice slope and finally spotted five dots moving in a line.

"Gives you perspective on the size of this mountain," Dick said.

"And an idea how far we have to go," Frank added, removing his pack and setting it in the snow to use it as a seat. Both of them shed their nylon shell parkas. Dick smeared sunblock on his arms and face, and passed the lotion to Frank. They were both perspiring.

Dick got out his water bottle to take a drink, and Frank noticed it was doctored with lemonade mix.

"Dick, how about a packet of lemonade mix for your buddy here?"

"Frank, I swear, all you think I am is a walking grocery shelf where you can get whatever you want, whenever you want."

"I forgot to bring any, Dick."

Shaking his head, Dick rummaged in his pack until he found his standby packet. Frank poured it in his bottle. They both sat quietly for a few minutes, feeling the lethargy seep in.

"You sure get lazy fast when you stop moving. Must be the altitude combined with the heat," Frank mused.

"We wait here any longer, we'll never be able to get up."

Dick groaned as he hefted his pack to his shoulders; it was turning into a long day since he had left from base camp early that morning, and he was feeling each of those fifty pounds on his back. Frank was feeling his pack too, and with ski poles as walking sticks and a rope between them in case one should fall in a hidden crevasse they slowly followed the tracks in the snow toward the back of the Western Cwm.

Now they could see for the first time the huge southwest face of Everest. There were evaporation clouds beginning to form over the summit, but they were too small to shield the sun and in the direct rays sweat dropped from their foreheads. They stripped to their long johns and would have removed these except they didn't dare risk baring skin to the intense ultraviolet rays at high altitude. They were now close to 21,000 feet.

Their pace slowed.

Small bamboo wands with orange tags marked the trail every 200-odd feet, and Frank played a game of picking a wand as a goal and convincing himself he could keep going until he reached it. When he got to it he would look for the next.

Dick, too, was reaching into his bag of tricks and he pulled out his favorite—Kipling's poem "If"—and started through the litany that worked so well to get his mind off his aching body.

"Let's take another break," Frank said.

They dropped their packs and pulled out their water bottles; both had only a few sips left. They felt like the caricature of the ragged man crawling through the desert dying of thirst, only this was a desert of ice. The Sherpas, stopped a few yards ahead, were pointing up the valley.

"Camp two tents, sahib."

"Where?"

"On rocks at end of snow."

"I still don't see them. Do you, Dick? Wait a minute. You mean those tiny colored dots way up there?"

"Lord have mercy," Dick said.

Frank looked back over to the Lhotse Face to see how the other dots were doing. The guys were closer to the South Col, and would be there in an hour or less.

"They're really small," Frank marveled, pointing to the Lhotse Face.

Again Frank considered how tiny the dots of the climbers were and how huge the mountain was.

He thought, If I'm having this much trouble down here, how can I ever make it that far? Maybe with oxygen . . .

But Frank knew oxygen wasn't a magic elixir; at best it would make an apparent change in the altitude of a few thousand feet. No, there was no getting around it: if he was slow down here, he would be slow up there. Now he worried that he might hold up Dick if they were to go on the same summit team.

Frank thought, Maybe I should see if I could set up another team separate from Dick. That way Dick and his Sherpas could be the third summit team, and I could follow as a fourth team with my own group of Sherpas. And I wouldn't hold him back.

Frank made a mental note to talk about it with Ershler. But before he could talk to anybody he needed to get to camp.

"Guess we'd better keep moving," he said.

A half-hour later they stopped again and finished their water. It was 2:00, and it felt as though the sun was at maximum strength. If someone had told them in advance they would suffer possible heat prostration at 21,000 feet on Everest they would have laughed. The Sherpas had now gone ahead to dump their loads and get back to camp 1.

Dick thought, Man alive, this is about as tired as I've ever been on a climb.

It was as though he had been drugged, as though some kind of unnatural lethargy had polluted his body so that it was nearly impossible to take another step.

Dick knew he had to mine deep into his inner resources. He recited a few more lines from "If," but it was no good. His mind drifted, and he felt his strength start to go. He could see the tents ahead—they weren't really that far—and then he imagined he could see something else, actually not some*thing* but some*one*, right in front of him. He smiled: it was Marty Hoey.

This was a game Dick had learned recently, a game his mind tended to play whenever he really needed to find inner strength, whenever he really needed to get his mind off his aching body. It had happened a few months before on Aconcagua, just below the summit. He had decided it must have been a combination of fatigue and lack of oxygen, but as he neared the top and had to find the strength to keep going Marty had appeared right in front of him, and he just started following her, just like he used to when she was alive. She could goad him by sheer example into pushing himself to the top of anything.

And now that he needed her again, there she was. Dick just made one step after another, following in her bootmarks, keeping her step-step-step pace. She glanced back at him and smiled. Dick felt good, almost good enough to keep going indefinitely.

"Thought you two might appreciate someone to carry your packs the last hundred yards."

Startled, Dick looked up. It was Gary Neptune and Jim States, coming to give them a hand into camp.

"Why howdy to you all, and thanks a million," Dick said, shaking their hands.

Dick took off his pack and handed it to Neptune, and Frank gave his to States. In a few minutes they were on the edge of camp 2. And there was that Sherpa cookboy, once again carrying that tray with two cups of steaming tea, and even though Frank and Dick were still a little overheated they accepted the cup with a smile and a warm regard for the graciousness of this young kid.

EVEREST: LIVE FROM THE TOP

A sharp crack from somewhere deep in the ice brought me quickly awake. My tent shuddered, and with ear close to the ice I heard the rifle report sound down the deep crevasses, like a hammer blow on a long steel beam, reminding me I was pitched on living ice that was growing, expanding, sometimes cracking.

Then it was quiet. I burrowed in my bag, my eyes open. I could see with gray vagueness the gear around me—boots, climbing equipment, cassette recorder, journal, notebook. I realized it must be nearing dawn. I looked at my watch: 5:30 A.M., May 7.

I thought, Today's the big day. The summit team should already be on their way, weather permitting.

I unzipped the tent door and peeked out. No wind, clear sky, perfect day for climbing Everest. I found the walkie-talkie, turned it on and placed it in my bag between my legs to warm the batteries. It was probably too early for a call but the previous evening I had told Breashears I would monitor beginning at dawn. At that time Breashears had reported everyone at camp 4, the South Col, was getting to bed early, confident of a predawn start. He added that he was planning to climb with the team a short way above the Col to test the microwave and give final instructions before handing the camera gear off to the others as they continued, we hoped, to the summit.

I dozed again until I heard the Sherpa cookboy outside my tent. "Good morning, sahib. Would you like tea?" I opened the flap and handed out my metal cup and he filled it with steaming milk tea. I wrapped my fingers around the warm cup wondering what those guys up there would give this moment for such luxury.

I dressed and walked to the mess tent. Ershler was there, and Frank came a moment later. "Still no word," I said.

"Let's try to call them," Ershler suggested. I tried the walkie-talkie again but had no luck.

"They're busy climbing," Ershler said. "I'm sure they'll call when they take a rest break."

Now Dick and the others arrived, and we waited. By 9:00 clouds rose in scattered puffs around the Lhotse Face, and we crossed our fingers the weather would hold long enough for them to reach the top and get back down. About 9:30 the radio crackled.

"Breashears calling camp two. Does anybody copy?"

"Dave, this is camp two. Where are you?"

"About 27,000," Breashears said, breathing hard.

"Where are the others?"

"Right here. We're taking a break. Everything's fine. We're making good progress. It's a nice day although some clouds are starting to build below. I've got the microwave transmitter and camera."

"Are you going higher?"

"I hope all the way. The camera's too heavy for Gerry and Peter, and Larry is going without oxygen. So the Sherpa and I are lugging it up. We've got to go now. I'll call from our next rest, and try to send some pictures."

A half hour later Larry Nielson called down, and I handed the walkie-talkie to Ershler.

"How you doing, Larry?"

"A little slow, but still keeping up. We're at a rest break, maybe 27,400. Dave's got his camera out to try this microwave thing. I need to reach the engineers at Everest View. Hello Everest View. Anybody copy?"

"Got you loud and clear." It was the voice of the engineer at the receiving dish twenty miles away.

"The camera's on. See anything?"

"Point the microwave toward us. Yeah, there. It's coming in. Move it just a hair. Hold it. There. Incredible. You guys look great! Perfect pictures."

"There's the top of Lhotse," Nielson continued. "See it?"

"Yeah, perfect."

Breashears completed a panoramic shot, and turned the camera off. Nielson said they had to keep moving, and would call next stop. Down at camp 2 we waited patiently, watching the growing clouds obscure the South Col and the lower flanks of Everest. We estimated it would take them another three hours to reach the top. Would the weather hold? In a half hour the first snow flakes dusted our tents; soon they were falling thickly. We only hoped that the bad weather was local, that at higher elevations the sky was still clear. Another half hour and Breashears called.

"What's the weather at camp two?" he asked.

"Socked in," I said, "and snowing. What's it like up there?"

"Snowing. Not blowing hard, but we're concerned about visibility. We're going to sit here and think about it. We've got about three hours left on the route. Wouldn't want to be up here if things get real bad."

"We've got our fingers crossed. Camp two standing by."

In five minutes Breashears came back on. "Due to a downgrading of conditions, I'm turning back. The other four are continuing up. They're not taking the camera. I've got to go. Over and out."

The morning's elation suddenly drained, replaced by doubt and concern. We knew it was a tough decision for all of them: Breashears turning his back on a chance to reach the top, to make his microwave transmission, but deciding the weather wasn't worth the risk; the others deciding to take the risk, knowing there was a chance visibility would drop, possibly trapping them near the summit, where their chances of surviving a storm would be close to zero.

I knew why the summit climbers hadn't taken the camera with them. In questionable conditions, they didn't want to be slowed by any extra weight. To all of us on the film crew, it was a bitter disappointment. Without the summit footage, the show would be emasculated. I thought too of the ABC producer, John Wilcox, sitting in Katmandu. He had $750,000 squeezed from his annual budget riding on that summit shot, and if he returned home without it he might as well go straight to the unemployment office.

Ershler had other things on his mind. He paced in the snow next to the mess tent. "Larry's really sticking his neck out," he said. "Without oxygen, he'll be much more susceptible to cold."

The snow continued at camp 2, sticking to the tent flies, sticking to our hair and jackets, seeming to weight us with a growing depression. Then the radio crackled.

"Breashears calling. Do you read?" His voice was excited.

"Yes, Dave. What's happening?"

"I was . . . going down when . . . weather improved." He was out of breath. "So I turned around . . . I'm going back up . . . heavy pack, all camera equipment . . . going fast to catch up."

Everyone cheered. It was now 11:30, still early in the day. Another half hour and Breashears was on again. "We've reached the South Summit. The weather is still okay. Larry is a little behind, without oxygen. So is the Sherpa Ang Rita, also without oxygen. We have maybe one hour more to the summit. Call you from there."

At camp 2 the clouds began to break, and we could see the upper mountain. Although the climbers had been hidden from our view all morning behind the bulk of Everest, I knew that just beyond the South Summit was a short section where we might glimpse them, so we trained our camera with a 1,000-mm lens on the spot.

"I've got one! Just below the Hillary Step. There's another, and a third . . . and the fourth."

Even through the telescope they were small figures, shimmering as they slowly climbed through the field of the lens. A minute later they disappeared, and we knew we wouldn't see them again until they were descending. But where was the fifth? Perhaps Nielson was still behind, going slowly without oxygen.

Ten minutes passed, fifteen. We took turns on the telescope.

"I've got him. A blue parka—that's Nielson. Moving very, very slowly."

In a few minutes he too disappeared. A half hour passed, then forty-five minutes. We knew they should be close.

"Calling camp two. Breashears here."

"Got you loud and clear, Dave."

"We've got a problem. Better put Ershler on."

All of us stared at one another. What could be wrong? We all knew that near the summit of Everest there is little margin for error, little chance to survive a mistake.

"Ershler here. What's the problem?"

"Phil, this is Gerry. The problem is we don't have anywhere else to climb. We're on top of this mother!"

We exploded in backslapping cheer. Frank's face beamed. "They did it," he said. "Those guys did it."

We went silent as Roach's voice came back on. "And by the way, Phil. Happy thirty-second birthday."

"Gerry, I couldn't have asked for a better present. Now where's Nielson?"

"Maybe twenty minutes below us. Moving slow, but he'll make it."

Now we waited for Breashears to unpack the camera, connect the microwave, and try for the first electronic broadcast from the top of the world.

"Breashears calling the engineers at Everest View. You guys got a picture down there?"

"Move the microwave," one of the engineers said excitedly. "There, coming in, better, better. Unbelievable. Great pictures. I can see all you guys standing there on the summit!"

With the ability to run continuously for several hours, the camera remained on while Breashears made pans, zooms, static shots. The engineers, all the while preserving the pictures on their large broadcast quality video cassette recorders, confirmed over the radio a close-up of Roach's ice-encrusted beard and broad smile. Then to Jamieson with an equally wide grin: even though there was no sound the engineers watching the screen could see clearly as he looked at the camera and said, "Hi Mom." Roach and Jamieson unfurled the American flag, then Frank and Dick's Seven Summits banner. Finally Breashears pointed the camera downhill to a lone figure making one slow step at a time. Nielson had maybe thirty such steps to go, thirty steps to become the first American to climb Everest without oxygen.

In a few minutes Roach's voice came on. "Nielson has five more steps." We waited. "Three steps . . . two . . . one . . . he's on the summit."

More cheers at camp 2, more bear hugs. Ershler took the radio, "Summit, this is Ershler. Put Larry on."

"Ersh, Nielson here." His voice was strained, his breathing fast. "I made it."

"Congratulations buddy."

Frank took the radio and said, "Congratulations from Bass and Wells, Larry. We've never had such a great moment. Hold on. Bass wants to say something."

"Nielson, you're an animal!" Dick shouted, the same kudos Marty Hoey had given him after he'd climbed McKinley.

"Thanks everyone . . . now I've just got . . . to get down."

• • •

After the summit transmission camp 2 didn't hear anything until 10:00 that night when Breashears made a very brief one-way radio call. "Everyone's down. Call in the morning."

It was terse, but sounded as though they were okay. Next morning Breashears called early.

"Larry and I dragged in about two hours after dark on the last energy we had. The others made it a few hours later in a storm. I had a flashlight, the others didn't, they just made it somehow. Kind of incredible. Over."

Breashears sounded fatigued, as though he had barely enough strength to talk.

"Is everybody okay?" we asked.

"Larry's had a hard night. He's frostbitten and throwing up blood. His tongue is swollen, cracked, and bleeding. Coughing badly, too. We really had a tough time descending last night. He had to hold to the back of my pack coming down. He's partially blind."

Our team doctor Ed Hixson was alarmed and wanted Nielson to get down as quick as possible, on oxygen if necessary. We watched that morning as the figures left the South Col and slowly descended the rope that laced down and across the Lhotse Face. They reached camp 3—mid-point on the face—and then we saw only four of them continue; one was still behind, perhaps resting in one of the tents. By mid-afternoon Breashears reached camp 2. (Roach and Ang Rita were still fifteen minutes from camp, and Jamieson was another fifteen minutes behind them.)

"Where's Nielson?" Ershler immediately asked Breashears.

"Apparently he's staying in camp three."

"Why did they let him stay there?"

"I don't know. I thought he was coming down with Jamieson, but for some reason he decided to stay in camp three."

"Somebody should have stayed with him."

Without hesitation Ershler said he was going up to camp 3, and Hixson said he would go too. Ershler appointed two Sherpas to accompany them, and in a few minutes they were off. Roach and Ang Rita were just getting into camp, but they too had no idea why Nielson was staying in camp 3. Then minutes later Ershler passed Jamieson, who said Nielson had told him just below the South Col he wanted to stay in camp 3 because he was moving too slowly and was too weak to get down in one push.

"I couldn't talk him out of it, and there was no way I could stay up there myself in my condition. I'm sure relieved you're going up.

There's no lighter at camp three, no way for Larry to start a stove and make drinks. Plus he has no sleeping bag."

As darkness fell we at camp 2 watched the figures of Ershler, Hixson, and the Sherpas, no more than specks against the shining ice, ascend the ropes. The weather was deteriorating fast; sweeps of snowy spindrift scudded across the figures. With last daylight gone Ershler radioed he had reached camp 3 and was making soup for Nielson, who appeared stable. Ershler said he was now worried about Hixson, who was still several hundred feet below, moving slowly up the ropes in the dark.

"I told the Sherpas to stay with Hixson," Ershler said, "or I would kill them. I think they got the message."

Hixson finally reached camp at 11:00 P.M. The group crowded in the tent and, without sleeping bags, huddled through the night. With the hot soup Nielson was regaining a little strength, and in the morning was able to descend most of the way under his own power. Near camp 2, though, Ershler and Hixson had to support him, one under each arm; as an interlocked trio they made the last distance to the tents and to a warm homecoming.

Nielson was laid in his tent, and Hixson, completing an exam, reported he had probably suffered a pulmonary embolism and was lucky to be alive. In addition, his extreme coughing had broken several ribs. His partial blindness was related to dehydration and hypoxia, and on that count at least he was already feeling better.

After hot soup and rest Nielson felt up to joining us that evening in the mess tent, where he related his story.

"I was sick when I came back up to camp two for the summit attempt," he explained, his voice hoarse and weak. "Nauseous, throwing up, some kind of bug. I couldn't hold anything down, including water."

Some of us glanced at one another in astonishment; this meant that he was sick at least three days before the summit attempt, but didn't tell anyone.

"I think it was the dehydration that really got me on the summit day," he continued. "I had an awful night at the South Col. I had a bad cough, bad enough that I broke a couple of my ribs. I remember looking over and seeing Roach in his oxygen mask sawing logs, and if I had had a mask with me I would have chucked my no oxygen commitment right then.

"In the morning I still couldn't hold anything down, but I decided to go through with it: I had put too much effort in at that point not to give it my all. For a while we were roped together, then we got to this deep snow, and I couldn't keep up. We unroped, and I fell behind. I kept plodding as well as I could, and got to the South Summit in time to see the others get over the Hillary Step, then disappear above. When I got to the Step I started up a fixed rope and got about ten moves when suddenly I got dizzy. I threw up, and it was blood. I was worried, but decided that if whatever I had was going to kill me, it would kill me whether I made the last distance to the top or not. The wind was now blowing, and I couldn't see any tracks or signs of the others. I got up one pinnacle and looked beyond to the next. No sign. Your mind starts to play games. I thought, Did I go the wrong way? Did those guys fall through a cornice? On top of the next pinnacle I still couldn't see anyone. I climbed the next one, then I saw them, on the summit.

"I don't remember much of the last part except I kept thinking of my wife and kids, and how they would be proud of me, and that kept me pushing. Then I was on top. What a relief it was to know everything from there was downhill. But the descent turned into an ordeal. The dehydration hit me hard and my tongue swelled so much it split in several places and was bleeding badly. So were my lips. Then I started seeing double, and as it got dark I had to hold on to Dave's pack. Dave would say, 'Here's a crevasse. Step.' A couple of times I started to fall in and he said, 'Bigger step.' And so on until we reached camp four, and then next day camp three. It was a godsend to have Ershler come up there and make soup for me. It was one of those things you never forget."

Although never openly discussed, there was a strong feeling of criticism in camp over the fact that Nielson had been left behind in camp 3. Ershler and Hixson were sharply critical of the others for what they thought was abandonment of a fellow climber in distress, while Roach and the others on the first team countered that they thought all the time Nielson was planning on coming down. Only Jamieson knew differently, and he wasn't in condition to help anybody. Furthermore, Roach and the others let it be known around camp they felt Nielson had used bad judgment both in pushing, despite his illness, with no oxygen, and in not telling anyone he was sick. They felt that by increasing the chance he would need rescue he had placed everyone in jeopardy, and consequently had mitigated their own responsibility to risk their lives for him. Fortunately with everyone down safe there had been a happy ending, and what otherwise might have developed into bitter controversy was overshadowed by the success as well as by the need to concentrate on the next summit bids.

Frank and Dick felt they were ready. Frank had been successful in his effort to create his own summit team separate from Dick's. Dick's team, now consisting of Ed Hixson, Yogendra Thapa (the Nepalese police officer whom Dick and Frank had invited to join the expedition), three Sherpas, and himself, would follow the second team, and then Frank's group would go fourth.

"I'll go last," Frank had told Ershler, "and I don't want any of the climbers with me, because I don't want to feel responsible for holding anyone back. So number one, I want three strong Sherpas."

"Three!" Ershler had said. "I need every one for hauling loads now. How can I hold three in reserve?"

Ignoring Ershler's rejoinder, Frank continued, "Second, I definitely need a high camp above camp four. Otherwise it's too far for me to go in one day."

"That means hauling a tent, sleeping bags, stoves, fuel, food, sleeping oxygen, all the way to 27,500!"

"Third, I need eight bottles of oxygen: one to sleep on at three, one to climb to four, one to sleep on at four, one to climb to five, one to sleep on at five, two to go to the summit, and one in reserve for descent."

"Frank, it would be a waste of the Sherpas' efforts to haul all that crap up there before we even know if you are strong enough to get to the Col."

"You worry about getting the equipment up there, I'll worry about myself."

"I tell you what, then. In the morning why don't you and Dick go up to camp three, and let's see how you do."

It was a repeat of Ershler's earlier strategy when he had tested Frank by having him climb through the Icefall, only this time he was certain Frank would have trouble. The next morning Frank and Dick were up at dawn, intending an early start. But the Sherpa cook was late with breakfast, and it was nearly 8:00 when they finally got away. For the first hour the climbing was similar to the stage between camps 1 and 2, following a trail through the glacier snow from one marker wand to the next, heading toward the back of the cul-de-sac Western Cwm. At the base of the Lhotse Face they had to cross a crevasse where the glacier floor separated from the face. This bergshrund was offset so the lip on the face side was much higher than the glacier side, and the lead climbers had propped a ladder over it. Dick was first. At the top of the ladder he took his jumar clamp and clipped it to the fixed rope that led up, then disappeared around a bulge of ice. One step above the ladder and he was on the Lhotse Face proper. He felt his crampon points bite the hard ice. He splayed his feet in a duck walk, moving one foot, then the next, then sliding his jumar clamp up, feeling it lock when he pulled back on it, then moving his feet again. In a minute he was around the bulge. Looking up he could see the entire face sweeping to the summit of Lhotse 5,000 feet directly above his head. The yellow rope lay on the gleaming ice in a line from one anchor to the next, nearly 2,000 feet connecting him eventually to the tents at camp 3. He couldn't see the tents—they were hidden behind the snow ledge on which they perched—but he knew their approximate location.

Dick had about thirty pounds of supplies in his pack; he had decided that as long as he was going to camp 3, he might as well do something useful. The wind that had blown most of the night was now abated, and under clear skies he soon had to stop to shed his parka. He carefully removed his pack; if he dropped it here, it would rocket down the steep ice several hundred feet and then no doubt toboggan across the glacier for a few hundred more. When he had the parka stuffed, he put the pack back on. Now he felt he had just the right amount of clothing. This was important to Dick; if he was dressed too warmly, or if some piece of gear was out of adjustment, it created a nagging distraction, one of those negative thoughts that drained him and hampered him from reaching maximum performance.

He slipped into a steady pace, moving one foot, the other, then sliding the jumar, reciting Kipling and Service. Looking down he could see Frank several hundred feet below, moving slowly.

Considering how little time he had to acclimatize since leaving base camp, Dick was climbing amazingly fast. Soon, though, he began to feel the telltale fatigue of hypoxia, but he was confident he would reach camp 3 with no problem. He wasn't so sure about his partner, as Frank was dropping further behind.

About 1:00 in the afternoon Dick saw the tops of the two tents at camp 3, and in a few minutes he stepped onto the snow bulge that formed a small flat area on the otherwise steep face. He unshouldered his pack, unzipped a tent and sat in the doorway. This was a room with a view: from his aerie he gazed down the length of the Western Cwm, Everest on the right, Nuptse on the left. Past the mouth of the Cwm he looked down on the summit of Pumori, and beyond, several

The first adventure: Africa, 1955. The plane didn't make it, but Frank (right) and his Oxford classmate did climb Kilimanjaro, where Frank first had the seven summits dream. (*Credit: Frank Wells collection*)

Dick Bass, Aconcagua 1983. (*Credit: Rick Ridgeway*)

Frank on the first Everest attempt, 1982. (*Credit: Jim Wickwire*)

Marty Hoey with a guanaco friend, Aconcagua, 1982.
(*Credit: Jim Wickwire*)

The memorial cairn to Marty,
under Everest's North Wall.
(*Credit: Jim Wickwire*)

Lou Whittaker evacuates a frostbitten
Larry Nielson following the unsuccessful
summit bid. (*Credit: Jim Wickwire*)

Aconcagua, 22,834 feet, highest peak in South America.
(*Credit: Jim Wickwire*)

At the start of the big year, Frank signs
his will while his wife Luanne watches.
(*Credit: Rick Ridgeway*)

Battered, bloodied and breathing hard:
an out-of-shape Frank Wells following
his near-fatal slip above the Vacas
River. (*Credit: Dick Bass*)

The indefatigable
Steve Marts,
cinematographer on
all seven summits.
(*Credit: Rick Ridgeway*)

Rick Ridgeway (left)
and Frank still have
trouble with swollen
rivers even on the
easier 'ruta normal.'
Aconcagua 1983.
(*Credit: Dick Bass*)

Ice-climbing seminar. Yvon Chouinard (left) coaches Dick on proper ice-climbing technique near base camp, Aconcagua '83. (*Credit: Rick Ridgeway*)

Taking five at 16,200 feet, Camp 1 on Aconcagua. (left to right) Dan Emmett, Frank Wells, Rick Ridgeway, Gary Neptune. (*Credit: Dick Bass*)

Days end as seen from Camp 1 on Aconcagua, 16,200 feet. (*Credit: Dick Bass*)

Dawn light at 20,500 feet, Aconcagua. Dick and Frank (left)
take a break on the first summit bid.
(*Credit: Rick Ridgeway*)

Almost there: Gary Neptune (yellow) and Yvon Chouinard
near Aconcagua's summit. (*Credit: Dick Bass*)

Success at last! Aconcagua, Dick and Frank's first summit
as a team. (*Credit: Dick Bass*)

The big one. Everest, 29,028 feet. (*Credit: Galen Rowell/High and Wild Photo*)

The '83 Everest team: (bottom) Rodney Korich; (first row, left to right), Jim States, Steve Marts, Peter Jamieson, Yogendra Thapa, Ed Hixson; (second row, left to right) Dick Bass, Phil Ershler, Larry Nielson, Gary Neptune, Frank Wells; (rear) Gerry Roach. (*Credit: Jim States*)

Trekking to Base Camp, just beyond Tengboche Monastery.
(Credit: Dick Bass)

Chorten memorials to Sherpas
killed in the Icefall on
previous expeditions.
(*Credit: Dick Bass*)

Sherpa cook prepares dinner
at the '84 Everest base camp.
(*Credit: Dick Bass*)

Ice-climbing practice near Everest Base Camp.
Frank rests on top of a large serac.
(*Credit: Rodney Korich*)

ABC cameraman David Breashears with his 25-pound
video camera-recorder. (*Credit: Ed Hixson*)

The Sherpa puja ceremony at Base Camp,
to guarantee "good luck" on the climb.
(*Credit: Dick Bass*)

In the Khumbu Icefall: Dick Bass (red pack) crossing a ladder. *(Credit: Harold Knutson)*

Crossing a crevasse in the Western Cwm at a little over 20,000 feet.
(*Credit: Rick Ridgeway*)

Ascending the fixed ropes
on the Lhotse Face
with the Western Cwm
in the background.
(*Credit: Jim States*)

Color commentator Rick
Ridgeway gets Frank's
reaction on learning
the first team made
Everest's summit.
(*Credit: Ed Hixson*)

South Col Sunrise: second team heading for the summit.
(*Credit: Gary Neptune*)

Mt. McKinley—Denali—20,320 feet, The West Buttress on the right skyline.
(*Credit: Dick Bass*)

Arrival at
the Kahiltna
International,
McKinley.
(*Credit:
Robie Vaughn*)

With Steve Marts on board, Susan Butcher mushes up the Kahiltna Glacier.
(*Credit: Dick Bass*)

An evening break in the storm
at the 17,200 foot camp.
(*Credit: Dick Bass*)

Postholing through deep snow
at 18,000 feet on summit day,
McKinley.
(*Credit: Dick Bass*)

The summit ridge of McKinley. (*Credit: Dick Bass*)

The highest point
in North America,
Frank and Dick on
the summit of McKinley,
20,320 feet.
(*Credit: Robie Vaughn*)

Kilimanjaro, 19,340 feet, highest peak in Africa.
(*Credit: Leo LeBon/Mountain Travel*)

Roughing it in the proper British tradition. (*Credit: Dick Bass*)

Dick and Marian Bass. (*Credit: Kevin Wells*)

Safari lunch, a pleasant interlude before returning to rock and ice. (*Credit: Dick Bass*)

Kilimanjaro Approach: The climb starts in equatorial forest and ends in perennial snow. (*Credit: Dick Bass*)

Frank in front of Kilimanjaro. (*Credit: Dick Bass*)

Scrambling on the Machame Route, approaching the crater rim. (*Credit: Dick Bass*)

Where the dream was born. Nearly 30 years later, Frank (left) returns to the summit of Kilimanjaro, with Dick (center) and Danny Bass (right). (*Credit: Dick Bass*)

The highest point in Europe, Mt. Elbrus, 18,510 feet, in Russia's Caucasus Mountains. (*Photo: Norman Benton/Peter Arnold*)

The inimitable Peter Jennings and his nurse, Dr. Olga, only partially recovered. (*Credit: Dick Bass*)

Frank and Luanne Wells with Elbrus in the background. (*Credit: Dick Bass*)

Five down, two to go. Lenin and comrades on top of Elbrus. (*Credit: Frank Morgan*)

Vinson Massif, Antarctica, 16,863 feet (by the old measurement).
(*Credit: Dick Bass*)

TOP LEFT: The man who made it possible, Giles Kershaw. (*Photo: Rick Ridgeway*)

TOP RIGHT: Refueling the Tri Turbo at Rothera Base. The drums were dropped
by parachute from a Chilean C130. (*Credit: Dick Bass*)

The Vinson Team (left to right) Chris Bonington, Sandy Bredin, Rick Mason,
Captain Frias, Rick Ridgeway, Giles Kershaw, Frank Wells, Steve Marts,
Yuichiro Miura, Dick Bass, Tae Maeda. (*Credit: Chris Bonington*)

All business class aboard
the DC3 Tri Turbo.
(*Credit: Chris Bonington*)

At the landing site near Vinson, it's warmer to set up tents than sleep in the plane. (*Credit: Chris Bonington*)

Dick Bass (left) and Frank begin the steep gully above base camp, Vinson.
(*Credit: Rick Ridgeway*)

Temperature 30 below, wind 40 knots. Frank nursing a frostbitten nose, just before turning back on the first attempt at Vinson's summit. (*Credit: Rick Ridgeway*)

Rick Ridgeway digs the "bolt hole," the snow cave they will bolt to in case high wind should demolish the tents. (*Credit: Rick Ridgeway collection*)

Premier British climber and expedition leader Chris Bonington. (*Credit: Rick Ridgeway*)

The modern-day samurai.
"The Man Who Skied Down Everest,"
Yuichiro Miura, prepares
to ski down Vinson.
(*Credit: Rick Ridgeway*)

The third time works the charm. Dick on top of Vinson Massif,
highest point in Antarctica. (*Credit: Rick Ridgeway*)

Dick Bass trickle-charging shortly
after take-off from Vinson.
(*Credit: Rick Ridgeway*)

35 feet under ice. Frank emerges
from the catacombs of Siple Station,
Antarctica. (*Credit: Rick Ridgeway*)

A long way from the presidential office at Warner Bros. Frank's shining moment, the summit of Vinson. (*Credit: Steve Marts*)

A walk in the park, the stroll to the top of Kosciusko, Australia. (*Credit: Dick Bass*)

On top down under. Dick (left) and Frank on the summit of Kosciusko, 7,310 feet. (*Credit: Dick Bass collection*)

"To strive, to seek . . ." David Breashears (in the lead) and Sherpa Ang Phurba leave the South Summit toward the Hillary Step. (*Credit: Dick Bass*)

"To find . . ." Breashears in the Hillary Step, elevation 28,800 feet. (*Credit: Dick Bass*)

"... and not to yield." Seven Summits fulfilled, Dick Bass on top of Everest April 30, 1985. (*Credit: David Breashears*)

Safely back in Base Camp, the Icefall behind, Dick and Breashears toast to success. (*Credit: Dick Bass collection*)

Dick follows through his promise to throw a no-holds-barred bash. Snowbird, August 1985. (*Credit: Rick Ridgeway*)

Victory is sweetest to those who have tasted defeat. (*Credit: Rick Ridgeway*) (*Mickey Mouse Character ©Walt Disney Productions*)

The Impossible Dream. (*Credit: Rick Ridgeway*)

valleys removed, the massive Cho Oyo, the world's eighth-highest peak.

He found a packet of powdered lemonade to doctor his water bottle, then looked around the tent for lunch. One plastic food bag produced a packet of M&M's and a granola bar, another a handful of mixed nuts, Rye Krisp crackers, and a can of tuna. It wasn't caviar, but to Dick it was a king's feast. With lunch finished, he lay back and took a nap, waking about a half hour later. He looked out, but no sign of Frank. It was time to head back. He strapped on his empty pack, clipped a safety link to the fixed rope, wrapped the rope around his arm and behind his back to brake his descent, walked to the edge of the platform bulge, and lowered down the forty-five-degree slope.

A hundred yards below camp he met Frank coming up the rope.

"You're not far now, Pancho."

"Don't think I can make it. Too tired. I'm turning back."

Frank rested his arms on his knees. He was breathing deeply and rapidly, and Dick could see the red scarf around his neck was soaked with sweat. Frank had pushed himself as far as he could go.

"Don't worry about it, Frank. We'll just consider this an acclimatization exercise. Next time you'll zoom right up."

"Hope you're right."

At camp 2 Phil Ershler had followed through the telescope Frank's snail's pace up the ropes, and his failure to reach camp 3.

"Two things bother me," Ershler told those standing around the telescope. "First, if we go to the trouble of putting in another high camp, Frank will never get that high to use it. Second, if somehow he does get that high, there's a good chance he's going to kill himself."

"He really has no business going above the South Col," one of the others said.

"But I can't tell him he can't go. We all agreed everyone gets a chance on this climb," Ershler answered.

"At least we're obligated to tell him how we feel. Maybe we can even talk him out of it."

"I guess it's worth a try," Ershler said. "Let's have a meeting tonight."

Frank and Dick returned late that afternoon, and although Frank was obviously pooped, after a couple hours' rest he seemed recovered, even feisty. Ershler announced a meeting after dinner. Following the meal, then, everyone stayed in the mess tent waiting for Ershler to open the discussion. Looking around, it was easy to spot those on the team who had just returned from the summit. Cracked lips, chapped cheeks, drained faces. Nielson was the worst. In addition to his general fatigue and his cracked ribs, he had sustained further damage to his already frostbitten feet, so he was planning on descending the next day to base camp. The others on the first team were planning on going down, too.

"Let me start by saying you guys turned in a poor performance today," Ershler told Frank and Dick. "You didn't even get out of camp here until after eight."

"How could we leave on time when the cook sleeps in?" Frank countered. "That one's hardly our fault."

"Okay, but the fact remains you couldn't get to camp three, and I don't think it makes sense to ask our Sherpas to carry supplies to a camp five if you can't get up there to use them. And that's only half of it. Even more, and I think all the others in the tent here agree with me, if you guys go above the South Col, there's a good chance you won't come back. Look at these other guys. Nielson's half-dead, Roach and Jamieson hardly have the strength to get from their tent to here. And these are tough hombres."

Dick winced. He was being included in this critique even though he was sure it was Frank that the criticism was directed at. He decided it would be more politic, though, not to say anything, at least for now.

Frank was also quiet, staring at the makeshift table littered with dinner leftovers, not angry but pensive.

When Ershler was finished Frank looked up, and in a calm voice said, "Fellas, you may not fully understand what this climb means to me. I've sacrificed a lot for this, in terms of money, job, the strain on my family. But I've figured it was worth it all because it was a dream I've carried now for thirty years. A lifetime dream, to reach the top of Everest, to climb the highest mountain in the world. Now it's even more, it's a double lifetime dream because it's part of the whole Seven Summits. So you fellas have got to keep that in mind, you've got to know that I only want one thing from you, and that's my fair shot at the summit. And now that we've got this far, you just can't pull the rug out. We made a deal at Snowbird. I've volunteered to go last, without any other climbers than the Sherpas."

There was a silence, then Ershler said, "We're not trying to make it easier on ourselves. We're saying these things out of a concern for you two. We're saying, Here are two guys who have been very good to us, and we don't want to see them get hurt."

"It's our duty to make you aware just how dangerous it is up there," Nielson added. "If something went wrong, if a storm came, or you ran out of oxygen, you don't have those years of experience that lets you instinctually get out of a tight spot. And we're afraid if you try to go above the Col, that might happen. We don't want to take your dream away, but we want you to know how risky it is up there."

"I know it's risky," Frank said, "but I've already considered that. If there's a one in thirty chance I might not come back, I'm willing to accept those numbers."

"I'd say the odds are worse than one in thirty," Ershler said.

Then Ed Hixson spoke: "There's another point, Frank. It's not just yours and Dick's neck, but if either of you do get in trouble, then those who have to go up and attempt a rescue are also at great risk. So there's an overall responsibility here."

"Now we're getting to the heart of the matter," I said, "whether a climber is justified in taking risks when he might be risking the lives of those who have to rescue him should anything go wrong."

This question also happened to be at the heart of the controversy surrounding Nielson's decision to push to the summit in spite of illness. Now, perhaps sensing the common ground, Nielson was the first to offer his views in regard to Frank and Dick's case.

"I've already said I feel it's our obligation to make Frank and Dick aware of the dangers, but having done that, I would also say it's their right to take the risks if they choose. After all, it's that right that draws most of us to the mountains—the right to make our own decisions, draw our own lines."

"I agree with that too," Gary Neptune added. "I might be reluctant to go with Frank on his rope, but we all have the right to take our own risks. That's what climbing's about."

To this, everyone nodded agreement. For this, everyone in the tent was drawn to mountaineering. Because of this, everyone found the freedom to measure against the indifferent peaks a personal standard that was theirs and theirs alone.

"Just promise me you'll be careful," Ershler concluded.

"And know we're saying these things because we love you guys," Nielson added. "And we want you to come back."

Later that evening Frank and Dick were snug in their sleeping bags, talking about the meeting.

"At first," Dick said, "I thought everybody not wanting us to go above the South Col was really everybody not wanting you to go, but

I figured nobody wanted to come out and say it that way because they didn't want to hurt your feelings. But then as we were leaving the tent Ed Hixson got me aside and said he was not going on our summit attempt because ours was such a weak group. Now I know he wasn't referring to the Sherpas, or Yogendra Thapa, because they have a lot of experience, so what he's saying is the weak link on the team is me."

"I can't understand why Hixson would say that," Frank said.

"I can't either," Dick said. "Especially after he saw me last year on Everest carrying those heavy loads all the way to camp five. He knows I'm strong."

It wasn't Dick's strength, however, that Hixson questioned as much as his experience. Even before the meeting Hixson had discussed his worries with some of the others.

"I know Dick has lots of guts and really good endurance," he had said. "And Yogendra is supposed to have good experience, and so do the Sherpas, but nobody else, including myself, has much technical mountaineering ability. I'm afraid that if we were to get in trouble up there we wouldn't have anybody to know how to get us out. I bet if you look through the records you'd find we are the weakest, most inexperienced team that has gone up against Everest."

Hixson went on to say he felt Dick lacked respect for the difficulties at extreme altitude, and after the first team had returned he was quick to point out that they were all haggard, despite being in superb physical condition. But his criticisms notwithstanding, Hixson never again brought up, beyond his short conversation with Dick, the possibility of dropping out of the third team, and Dick concluded that Hixson's yearning to get a chance at the top of Everest was stronger than his reservations about the strength of the team.

For the next week the climbing schedule unfolded as originally planned. The second summit team—Neptune, States, Ershler, and a Sherpa—departed camp 2, and two days later left from the South Col in the predawn of what promised to be a good summit day. This time those of us at camp 2 had no way to follow their progress; they had left the radio at the Col, and they had no video camera. Midmorning, though, we unexpectedly received a radio call.

"Camp two, this is Ershler. I'm back at the South Col. I got very cold going up and knew I would risk frostbite if I continued."

Ershler had tried to repeat Nielson's no-oxygen ascent, and we guessed that without the warming effect of the gas he had become more susceptible to the cold.

"The others are going up," he continued. "I got a glimpse of them a few minutes ago, and they should be close to the South Summit."

We mounted our telescope with hope of spotting them at the same place we had seen the previous team, but now clouds blocked our view. There was nothing to do but wait for Ershler's reports. He radioed that the clouds had blocked his view as well. Early evening we had his final report: States, Neptune, and their Sherpa had all reached the summit and were back safe at camp 4.

The expedition had now placed eight climbers on top, more than all but two previous expeditions in Everest's history. Now it was time for Frank's and Dick's attempts. Frank was feeling he was as ready as he could be. The day before he had carried a load to camp 3 and felt much stronger. In addition he had been successful in convincing Ershler to establish an additional high camp above the South Col, and the Sherpas had been freighting the necessary gear to a cache at 27,500 feet.

With everything in place, on May 15 Dick and his group were ready to leave camp 2. Frank gave him a bear hug, and the Sherpas cheered for their good luck as they tied together on a rope for their passage over the crevassed region at the back of the Cwm leading to the Lhotse Face. The weather looked stable: no wind, no clouds.

Dick made good time up the fixed ropes to camp 3, feeling much stronger than he had twelve days before. Arriving in camp, he squeezed in a tent with Hixson and Yogendra, and spread his sleeping bag. Then he arranged his personal gear of extra socks, extra underwear, two types of sun lotion, lip cream, vitamins, personal salves and medicines, a sewing repair kit, backup mittens and goggles, extra hat and hood, Xerox sheets of his favorite poems. We were always chiding Dick about the amount of gear he hauled with him, but he was quick to return our ribbing whenever any of us asked to borrow something from him.

They woke early next morning to start the long task of melting snow for tea water. Hixson called camp 2: "Hello Phil. Everyone had a good night's rest, and we'll be leaving in an hour. We'll call from the South Col."

"Frank wants to talk to Dick," Ershler said. Hixson handed the radio to Dick.

"Dick, this is Frank. How are you feeling?"

"Like a bull elk smelling the rut. I'm going to charge right to the top of this mother."

"We're all rooting like crazy for you. Remember, if you get this one we'll not only have the Seven Summits but you'll be the oldest man ever to have climbed Everest."

"I'm pushing for all I've got."

Dick finished dressing, then loaded his backpack. Hixson was watching and said, "Dick, you've got too much crap. You'll slow us all down."

"Well, I think I know what I can handle," Dick said.

As he finished packing he thought, I'm going to show this guy once and for all I'm not the weak sister of this group.

Outside the tent Dick clamped his jumar on the fixed rope and left camp, setting a determined pace. It didn't bother him that he had more weight on his back than even the Sherpas; he had convinced himself that a heavy pack was good for his conditioning. Anyway, he planned on summit day to leave most of the extra weight at the South Col; he figured that then his pack, even with the oxygen bottle, would be so much lighter he would feel like he had wings on his heels.

He was almost flying now. Each time he glanced back the distance to the others had increased. For about an hour he lost himself first with thoughts about Snowbird, then with stanzas from "The Cremation of Sam Magee" and "The Shooting of Dan McGrew."

Soon he was sliding his jumar clamp up the rope as it ascended a rocky outcrop named the Geneva Spur. The grade steepened to over fifty degrees near the top of the Spur. The altitude was 26,000 feet. Even though he wasn't using any supplemental oxygen, he felt great.

Dick thought, I really am made for this kind of work. If I'd gotten into mountaineering as a young man I might have been world-class with a whole big list of first ascents. But that might have been at the cost of other things, like Snowbird. But if I do make it up tomorrow, it will be like having my cake and eating it too.

He slid the clamp and pulled back to tighten it on the rope as a balance while he moved his feet. One boot up, scrape the rock to find a foothold, step, move the other foot, balance, slide the clamp, pull tight, move the feet again. The slope eased and he looked up to see an easy snow traverse leading to the South Col. And there, tantalizingly close and awesome, was the upper mass of Everest.

In thirty minutes Dick was at the Col gazing from the saddle across the plateau of Tibet, arid and brown and extending to the horizon. What a vaulted world—to his right the ridge climbed to the summit of Lhotse, to his left to the summit of Everest. He stood transfixed for a moment until he felt the chill of the first afternoon breeze, then he moved his pack into one of the three tents at camp 4. In an hour he heard the crunch-crunch footsteps of the others, and stuck his head out to greet them.

"Howdy you all!"

"We're late because we dropped behind to get photographs," Hixson said.

Dick thought, Heck, I took pictures too. Why doesn't he just accept the fact he took longer to get here? People are always doubting my ability to be able to do what I set out to do. I'll show them all tomorrow.

Hixson moved into the next tent, and soon they were all busy melting snow, preparing drinks and dinner so they could get to bed early; they hoped to leave camp about 2:30 next morning. Dick slept restlessly, not so much because of the altitude, he felt, as the anxiety over the task that lay before him. He tried to bolster his confidence by telling himself he had done very well on Everest the year before, and he had done very well so far this year. But at the same time he couldn't help wondering if things would suddenly change when he hit 27,000, or 28,000 feet. Would it be like a marathoner's "wall" that either you had to break through or it broke you?

Man can take bad news, Dick told himself as he rolled and tossed, but he can't stand uncertainty.

At 1:30 A.M. Dick heard the Sherpa light the small butane stove, and opening his eyes could see the blue flame like a waning moon cast a steel-gray light over his sleeping bag and other gear in the tent.

Well, Bass, he told himself, let's get your tail in gear and have at it.

In this halflight Dick searched for his clothes to dress. He had slept in his long john underwear, and now over this he pulled quilted down pants and a pile fabric jacket. Then over the quilted down, another pair of pants made of nylon to protect against wind and a down parka over the pile jacket. He had slept in one pair of socks, and over these he pulled another, thicker pair.

By now his fingers were numb, and he welcomed the metal cup of hot tea, wrapping his hands around it, sighing with the first sip. Then he finished dressing. He held his boots over the stove, kneading the tongues until he could force his feet in; it took another ten minutes for his toes to overcome the cold-boot shock and regain feeling. Next he pulled on knee-high nylon overboots. He was breathing hard; even something like getting dressed, when at 26,200 feet, can be a major

effort. Although he wasn't hungry—another effect of high altitude—
he forced down some cereal mush. Then he crawled out of the tent
to strap on his crampons.

It appeared their luck with the weather would last. There was no
wind, and the stars through the rarefied night sky lit the snowfields
so brightly they would be able to navigate without headlamps. One
of the Sherpas led the rope, and Dick was second. As they climbed
out of the Col the slope abruptly steepened. Soon there was loose
snow that sloughed with each step so it was necessary, especially for
the first two people, to kick in each foothold. Still, they made good
progress and before long Dick was lost in the rhythm of pressure-
breathing and rest-stepping so that it came as a surprise when he
realized the star-lit snow was growing a brighter, pale pink.

The lead Sherpa began to slow, so he switched places with the
Sherpa on the back of the first rope. Dick remained second. An hour
past dawn they stopped for their first rest. Dick could now look over
the Lhotse-Nuptse ridge that had for so many weeks fenced his view.
The giants of the earth were now before him: Lhotse, Makalu, Kanchenjunga, Cho Oyo. There was still no wind, no clouds, everything
promised a perfect summit day. Hixson, last on the second rope,
arrived and sat down.

"How do you feel?" he asked Dick.

"Tired, but I'm all right."

"Well, I feel great."

Dick thought, You should, being sixth on the ropes. You ought to
try breaking trail in second position.

He looked away from Hixson, then stared across the sea of peaks.
Nearly all the summits were now below him, and soon even the two
or three that appeared eye level would be below. All of them, every
one across the surface of the planet, would be below. The thought
fortified him, helped him put things in perspective. He decided it
was foolish to continue letting Hixson upset him. It was only producing
negative thoughts that would drain his energy—no, more than that
—detract from the joy of what he was about to achieve.

Feeling better, he looked out again over the remote fastness of
Tibet, down on the glaciers like flows of frozen lava spilling from the
peaks and onto the sere, umber earth. Then the corner of his eye
caught something closer at hand, about thirty feet away. It was faded
orange and red.

"What in the world?"

The others turned.

"My God," Hixson exclaimed.

"It looks like a body."

"It's gotta be Mrs. Schmatz."

They had all heard the story. Mrs. Schmatz had been the wife of the leader of a German expedition in 1979. Up to the time of the tragedy their climb had been a notable success, having in only thirty-two days placed all team members on top, including Mrs. Schmatz. She and three others, one of whom was Ray Genet, the foremost guide on McKinley and a legend in his own time, plus two Sherpas, were the second group to reach the summit. On their descent, about halfway back to high camp, she and Genet decided to bivouac without sleeping bags or tent because she was so tired. It became a bitterly cold night, and when dawn finally broke, Genet was dead. One of the Sherpas returned to them from the South Col, tried to get her moving, but she managed only a few steps when she too collapsed and died. That Sherpa, Sungdare, seriously frostbitten, continued down alone. He lost several toes, but since then has gone on to climb Everest three more times—more than anyone else.

Now they stared at her, frozen in the place where she had died if the body hadn't fallen. She was lying face-down, her head turned away from them. Dick could see she was half in the ice; her clothes, a parka and windpants, were sunbleached but intact.

"I sure don't feel like going over and having a close look."

"Me neither. Let's go."

They shouldered their packs, and were about to start when Dick spoke up. "What do you say I trade this second position with someone. I'm afraid I might burn out before we get to the top."

Dick still felt good, but he was concerned, having heard the stories about how easy it is to drain your energy at this altitude. He was now much higher than he had ever been, and he didn't want to take any unnecessary chances. One of the Sherpas took his second position on the lead rope while he tied to the rear of the second rope, with Yogendra and Hixson. Soon they passed the equipment cache that Frank would use to establish a high camp on his ascent; that meant they were at about 27,300 feet. A rope length above the cache the snow started to deepen, and their pace slowed. It was a minor nuisance for Dick and the other two on his rope, but for the Sherpas up front it was a strenuous task: the lead man had to lift each foot as high on the slope as he could, then pack it until the snow supported his weight—usually not until after he had sunk to his thigh—then lift the other leg out of its hole and strain to place it as high as possible. At high altitude such postholing, in order to keep after it hour upon hour, requires an undistracted lust for the summit.

Now each Sherpa could lead only for a little distance before rotating the lead to the one behind. Looking up, Dick could see the Sherpas had reached the crest of the southeast ridge and were sitting together, resting. Dick still felt strong. For the last two hours he had been climbing on only one liter a minute oxygen flow; he was confident he now had gas reserves sufficient to reach the top. As he approached the crest he could feel the wind start to build; they were high enough to begin losing the shelter of the lee. But the wind wasn't bad. There were a few clouds building too, but again they didn't seem bad. Everything looked good; he was confident they would make the top.

Yogendra reached the Sherpas, and sat down next to them; Dick could see they were discussing something. Then Hixson joined the discussion. Dick couldn't make out what they were saying while he continued climbing toward them. When he was within twenty feet Hixson turned toward him and said, "Well Bass, this is as far as we go."

"What are you talking about?"

"The Sherpas have had it. They don't want to go any higher."

"What should we do?"

"Go back down."

"Back down?"

"If we go on we'll slow down even more and I'm afraid we'll run out of oxygen. And with this group, we're very dependent on it. Plus it's steep here, the snow is unconsolidated, and if one of us slips, I don't think the other could hold him."

There he goes again, Dick thought. What he means is, if he slips, *I* won't have the ability to hold *him*.

"But we're so close," Dick said.

"I'm worried if we tried to push on we might get stuck on the way down in the dark."

"Well, hold on a minute. Let me think." Dick hunkered over his ice axe, then looked up. Above and to the right was the summit. They were almost at the 28,000-foot level, only 1,000 vertical feet and less than a mile distant from the top. Dick knew he had the strength to make it. More than enough strength. In fact, he felt great. Should he go alone, then?

He looked down. The clouds below were building and the wind was picking up.

He thought, It'd be my luck to take the gamble and then have the weather trap me up there so I'd end up like Mrs. Schmatz.

Dick had promised his family he would above all be prudent, and not take any foolish risks. To go alone was definitely contrary to that promise.

If only I had someone strong, Dick thought. A good rope leader with the background experience to get up and down this thing in one piece.

So what to do? He recalled how Frank had always said that if he himself couldn't make it his first attempt, he wanted to have the supplies necessary to try again. Dick considered the possibility: there was still oxygen at the South Col, and these Sherpas had with them right here three full bottles that they could cache at this spot. That would be more oxygen than he would need. Why couldn't he follow Frank's backup strategy, then? Especially since he felt so strong. It would be a little more work to go down and come back up, but at least this initial effort wouldn't be a complete waste: first, they had this oxygen up here, and second—and much more important—this would be valuable experience. The second time he would know what it is like at 28,000 feet; he would know it would be within his physical strength. That mental comfort alone was worth the effort of this first attempt.

Dick thought, So I'll go down to camp two, get a fresh Sherpa group together, come back up and climb this beauty.

"Okay," he said to Hixson, "I guess you're right. Let's go down."

Dick watched the Sherpas cache their extra oxygen in the snow so he could use it for his next attempt. While taking the extra bottles out of the Sherpas' packs, though, they discovered that one of them, Ang Dali, had failed to open the control knob. No wonder he had been so slow: he had been climbing all morning without supplemental oxygen, trying to breathe through a useless mask and as a consequence rebreathing his own spent air while carrying two bottles weighing seventeen pounds each. This Sherpa, throughout the expedition, had been very strong, always carrying the heaviest loads, but now, as they started the descent, he was completely spent and near useless.

Hixson, ever-more worried that if one of them slipped he might pull the others off the slope, insisted they belay their descent. After an hour of this, though, it became obvious it was not really necessary and was taking far too much time. It took them nearly four hours to get down to camp 4, everyone except Hixson. He obviously was feeling very tired, and he sat down for nearly an hour before crossing the Col to camp. Dick figured Hixson's high anxiety level up above had drained him. When he finally joined them, they called camp 2.

"What's going on? Where are you?" Ershler inquired intently.

"South Col. We turned back at the Southeast Ridge," Dick said.

"Why?" Ershler shot back, having seen the weather look good from below.

Dick couldn't hide his deep frustration and disappointment. "The team quit me. The Sherpas were worn out from postholing and Ed didn't want to chance it without them. Yogendra was noncommittal."

"Will you try again in the morning?"

"How can I? I certainly can't go alone, and this bunch has had it. I'm coming down to get some fresh Sherpas and try again in a few days, after Frank's team."

"How's Hixson? Will he go back up with you?"

"I'm not sure. You talk to him."

"Hello camp two, this is Ed Hixson."

"Ed, will you go back up with Dick?"

"No, I'm very tired. I don't intend to try again. Dick is apparently feeling much better and should try again. We'll be down tomorrow."

The next morning Dick woke early, but there was no reason to get up right away since it would take no more than a few hours to get down to camp 2. So he lay in his bag, thinking about his plan to come back up. Then Hixson called from the neighboring tent.

"Dick, are you dressed?"

"Not yet."

"When you are, could you come over."

"Be there in a few minutes."

Dick leaned over and started the stove. He thought, This next attempt is going to be a pleasure since I won't have a lot of anxiety over the unknown. I still have that Hillary Step ahead of me, but I'm sure I can handle it. Then it's just a stroll along the ridge to the summit, and I'll have this one in the bag.

He made tea, then sat up in his bag and wrapped his fingers around the warm mug.

"Dick, can you come over here?" Hixson called again.

"I'm sorry, Ed. I got sidetracked. Just a minute, I'll put my clothes on."

Yogendra had come over from his tent to join Dick for breakfast, so he was already dressed and left the tent to see what Hixson wanted. In a minute Yogendra called back, "Dick, come here quick."

Dick, half in his clothes, bolted out and over to Hixson's tent. He stuck his head in and saw Hixson in his sleeping bag, his face waxen.

"Ed, what's wrong?"

"I think I've had a stroke."

"What! You've got to be kidding."

"I woke up and couldn't move my right arm. At first I thought I'd slept on it wrong. It was warm to the touch but totally paralyzed. Then I realized the right side of my neck was numb, and down through part of my trunk."

"Good Lord. What should we do?"

"Don't know if we can get help from below in time. My legs are okay, though. Maybe I can get down myself."

"Well let's pack and get out of here immediately."

Dick hurried back to his tent and started throwing his gear together. Now guilt swept him. He thought, Thank heaven I didn't berate Hixson into going higher. This must be God's way of chastising me for having had ill thoughts about Ed.

In minutes Dick was packed, and then he was over to help Hixson, who was now out of his tent, being helped by Ang Dali. He could stand on his feet, but he was off-balance, obviously weak and faint. They strapped his crampons on.

"I just can't believe you've had a stroke, Ed." Dick said.

"It sometimes happens at high altitude. Caused by the thick blood you get living in thin air for a long time. Now I'm worried if there's a clot I might have another stroke as we start moving."

It was only a few hundred yards to where the fixed rope started, but to get there they decided to rope Hixson to the Sherpas; they would have more strength and skill in arresting a fall if Hixson were to slip. They started down the slope, which at first traversed gently, then steepened as it approached the Lhotse Face. Just before the steep part of the route, Hixson crumpled.

Oh, my God, Dick thought, he's going to die.

When Dick caught up to him, Hixson was already on the radio to camp 2: "My right side seems to be partially paralyzed. Probably a stroke."

"Where's Bass? Let me talk to him," Ershler urgently demanded.

Hixson handed Dick the radio.

"Ersh, this is Bass."

"Is Hixson on oxygen?" Ershler asked.

"Oh no, I didn't even think of that," Dick exclaimed. He looked up; they were now some distance below camp. "It'll take over a half hour to climb up and get a bottle."

"Oxygen is at Japanese camp," one of the Sherpas said pointing downhill a hundred yards to ruins of two tents where a Japanese team had placed a camp last year.

"But we don't have a regulator."

"I have one in my pack," the Sherpa said.

"Let's pray it fits."

They helped Hixson to his feet. He still had partial use of his right leg and managed to hobble. As soon as they reached the campsite, Hixson rested while the Sherpas dug with their ice axes in the snow. They found a bottle and quickly turned the valve: empty. Then another: empty. Dick, waiting with Yogendra on the trail a little above in case they had to return to the South Col for oxygen, watched in disbelief. Three bottles, four, five—all empty.

Dick thought, Hixson will die because I didn't even think to get him on oxygen while we had some at camp four.

Then one of the Sherpas found another bottle, and pulled it out. Dick held his breath as they cracked the valve. Empty.

Dick slumped. He thought, I should climb back to camp right now as fast as I can. It will take time, though, without oxygen. Lord, it will take time.

He closed his eyes, took a deep breath, and steeled himself to the task of going back up. Then he heard a noise, a loud hiss. He turned. One of the Sherpas, holding a tank, was quickly closing its valve. With a big smile the Sherpa carried the full tank to Hixson, secured the regulator, which thankfully fit, and held the mask over Hixson's mouth.

Five minutes later Hixson said, "I'm feeling much better. Getting warm, and I can feel my leg coming back." He stood, then said, "Okay, let's go."

They started slowly, but as Hixson continued to breathe the oxygen at maximum flow their pace quickened and soon they were descending at full speed. As they neared camp 3 Dick could see five people in front of the tents. Soon he could distinguish Frank and Steve Marts with several of the Sherpas; he remembered Frank was on the way up for his summit attempt. At the camp they had hot soup ready for Hixson, who soon left to continue the descent to camp 2. Dick stayed awhile to tell Frank about his summit attempt and Hixson's calamity that morning.

"And when are you coming back up?" Frank asked.

"As soon as I get back to camp 2 and put another group of Sherpas together. Good luck on your attempt. We'll probably cross on the ropes."

Dick then left Frank and sped down the fixed ropes, arriving in camp 2 feeling frustrated, but strong and confident he would make it on a second try—and ever so thankful Hixson had sided with the Sherpas on stopping their summit effort after what had transpired earlier that morning.

That evening in the mess tent, over hot tea and cookies, Dick told us about his experiences high on the mountain, and as we listened I watched his bright eyes and animated hands and it occurred to me that in my experiences on several mountain climbing trips to the Himalaya I had never seen anyone come down who, after having been above the 8,000-meter mark, looked as spunky as Dick Bass. And I'd certainly never seen anybody who was fifty-three years old and was absolutely convinced that on the second time he would waltz right to the summit.

Dick finished his story and then said, "Now I've got to go canvass these Sherpas and see who's willing to go back up."

"I don't know where you find the energy to go up twice," one of the other climbers said.

"It's not so hard now that I know what's up there," Dick said. "And besides, I'm excited that it'll mean more to me this way." Dick took another sip of tea, and with his trademark grin added, "Because what we gain too easily, we esteem too lightly."

The next morning Frank Wells adjusted his oxygen regulator to two liters a minute, strapped on his face mask, and left camp 3 to start the long upward traverse across the Lhotse Face. Other than his oxygen bottle he was carrying no weight—the Sherpas ahead of him had the equipment—but he was still moving slowly, feeling the enervation of high altitude. It took two hours to gain a point where the rope turned upward in a more direct line to the South Col. Looking up, Frank could see the Sherpas a hundred yards above, moving one slow step at a time. He looked at his oxygen tank's dial; the bottle was three-quarters full.

He took the regulator knob and turned it to three liters a minute.

What a difference. With the extra liter a minute he felt like his afterburner had kicked in. He caught the Sherpas and passed them. The fixed rope continued upward in a direct line paralleling the Geneva Spur, which lay to Frank's left, obscuring his view of the summit pyramid of Everest. Then the rope angled across the Spur. Frank was surprised at how strong he felt as the slope steepened. As he approached the crest he glanced up. The view caught him by surprise; he wasn't expecting it to look so close. But there was the giant pyramid of snow-laced rock, the plume cloud boiling in a long banner off to leeward. The summit. If only tomorrow he could find the strength he now felt, then maybe, just maybe . . . He told himself he'd better stop daydreaming, and finish the job at hand.

In fifteen minutes he reached the Col. He looked at his watch: four hours and fifteen minutes from camp 3. He thought, Maybe I really do have a chance of making the top.

The thought thrilled him, put him in a buoyant mood. Just to see what would happen, he adjusted his regulator to its highest setting —eight liters a minute—and took a walk around the flat Col. For a few minutes he didn't notice anything until he realized he was speeding effortlessly from one side of the saddle to the other. Just like taking a walk around the block in Beverly Hills, he thought.

But at the same time what an antipodal contrast to Beverly Hills. And how delightfully improbable, Frank thought, that a movie executive in his fifties who only two years before had hardly done anything beyond fantasizing about mountain climbing was now by himself waltzing around at the 8,000-meter mark of Mount Everest.

Frank was ecstatic: reaching the South Col had been a goal in itself, a dream and fantasy that only a few months before had seemed as elusive as the summit.

Even if I don't get any higher, he told himself, this feels pretty good.

With a light gait he walked back to the tents, and took his pack off. Even without the oxygen he was surprised how strong he felt. The Sherpas still hadn't arrived, so he crawled into the tent feeling so good he thought he might even try to figure out how to start one of the stoves and make himself some hot chocolate. Then he decided that might be going too far; he would wait for the Sherpas.

They arrived about ten minutes later. With the stoves going, and a hot brew in him, he lay back to relax. A moment later the first breath of wind caused the tent to give a slight flutter. Then it was quiet, but soon the fabric walls again ruffled, only this time they didn't stop. Ten minutes later there was a solid fifteen-mile-an-hour breeze, and by nightfall it had increased to what Frank guessed was hurricane force.

"Are the tents holding up?" Ershler asked over the radio.

"So far," Frank yelled, raising his voice above the staccato snapping of the tent fabric.

"What's it like outside?" Ershler asked. Frank could tell Ershler was quizzing him to determine just how strong the wind was.

"I can't stand up. Have to crawl to get to the next tent."

"What do the Sherpas think?"

"That we can't go anywhere. Have to stay here."

The next day conditions were even worse. The tents still held, but it was clear to Ershler and everyone else there could be no summit bid until the wind abated. Frank spent the time in his sleeping bag, happy he had decided on the extra weight of the paperback *King Rat*. He was also, in a way, happy to have an excuse to postpone the summit attempt. While half of him still daydreamed about reaching the top now that he was this close, the other half realized this last section would nevertheless be the most physically demanding undertaking of his life. It was a funny thing that he couldn't seem to overcome, this sort of dual pull between giving it his all versus giving in, and he realized he would actually be relieved to have an excuse to go down, as long as it was for some reason beyond his control, as long as he could tell himself later he really had stuck with it as long as possible.

While Frank was pinned at the South Col, Ed Hixson spent one day in camp 2, sleeping on oxygen, and then descended on his own power to base camp. He appeared to be getting better although he complained of being oppressively tired. The next day he slept, getting up only to walk to the mess tent for meals. He was having trouble keeping his balance but attributed it to fatigue and thought another night's sleep would help. When he awoke, though, and sat up in his sleeping bag, he was so dizzy it made him nauseous. He couldn't hold food or water, and by noon was too weak to crawl. He could still think clearly enough to deduce that his stroke was moving into his cerebellum, affecting his motor control. He knew the only antidote was to get immediately to lower altitude.

But how? He couldn't walk. If he had himself tied to the back of a yak the jostling might make things worse. There was no one in camp with the strength to carry a litter that far. The only solution might be the Nepal air force, which had a helicopter capable of landing at 18,000 feet. A few minutes later when Gerhard Lenser came to Hixson's tent to check on him, Hixson was so weak all he could muster was a few words in a strained voice: "Radio Katmandu for helicopter. Must get out or I won't make it."

Luanne Wells and Marian Bass had come to Katmandu the week before expecting to join their husbands as they came off the mountain and together take a few extra days on the way home and enjoy themselves in Hong Kong. Now they learned that Dick had made one attempt and was planning another, and that Frank had been pinned by high winds for three days at 26,200 feet waiting his chance. Worse, they heard that nearly all the other team members (everyone except Ershler and Neptune) had quit the mountain and were heading down.

Nielson and Jamieson had been the first out. After the ABC honchos had received the microwaved videotape of Nielson making the summit, they fed it via the Katmandu earth station to New York, where it was on *Good Morning America* about four hours after the group left the summit. Then the network editors began working furiously to edit the show and have the one-hour special ready for broadcast in less than a week, even while the subsequent teams were on the mountain making their attempts. Meanwhile, though, since the first summit team had returned to base camp the ABC producer John Wilcox had the idea to send a helicopter to base camp to fetch Nielson and bring him to Katmandu where Bob Beattie would then interview him live.

The chopper had room for one extra person and since Jamieson had minor frostbite he got the nod to join Nielson. With those two gone, Roach decided he was going to leave, and after the second summit team got off the mountain States decided he too would go home.

To Luanne and Marian it looked like rats jumping a sinking ship. Without the full team it seemed to them the expedition should be called off and that Frank and Dick should come down. Even the ABC crew was packing up. The associate producer who had each day monitored the radio for calls from base camp, Mary Jo Kinser, had taken a day off to go sightseeing, but had told Luanne and Marian they were welcome to come to the Sheraton where all the television gear was housed and monitor the radio at call times in case there was any news. She showed Luanne how to work the radio.

It was Saturday morning when Luanne and Marian got the key from the desk and went up to the now deserted ABC room to see if anything was coming in on the 9:00 A.M. call. They heard the radio crackling as they worked the door to get it open and ran to the transmitter. It was the pidgin voice of the Nepalese who monitored the radio link at the Everest View Hotel.

"Hello Katmandu, this is Everest View. Does anyone monitor? Repeat, does anyone monitor? This is an emergency."

"Oh, my God," Luanne said, unable to speak what she feared.

"Hello. This is Katmandu. What is wrong?"

"We have a report from base camp that Dr. Ed Hixson is gravely ill. He must have a helicopter to evacuate him immediately or he will die."

"Yes, yes. We understand. We will get a helicopter as soon as possible."

The radio operator at Everest View said he would stand by.

Luanne looked at Marian. "Where are we going to get a helicopter?" she said.

"Look here at this piece of paper," Marian said, indicating a list of numbers next to the radio. One said "helicopter pilot." They went down to the lobby and phoned the number. It was a colonel in the Nepal air force who was their chief chopper pilot.

"Yes, we can fly. But first you must pay."

"What do you mean?"

"We only fly if the helicopter time is paid in advance. The round trip to base camp costs nineteen hundred dollars U.S."

"We'll be right over and write you a check."

"I am sorry. It must be cash."

The clerk at the hotel lobby wouldn't cash a personal check, and as it was Saturday the banks were closed. Then they saw Mary Jo, the ABC person, coming in from her sightseeing trip. She was also the production purser, and quickly cashed Luanne's check.

With the cash in hand Luanne, Marian, and Mary Jo caught a cab and raced to the airport, where the colonel took the money but told them he couldn't fly as it was Saturday and the co-pilot was away from his house and couldn't be found.

"Our Panasonic camera engineer was a chopper pilot in Vietnam," Mary Jo said. "Let's get him."

They located the engineer, Alan Wechsler, and after quizzing him the colonel agreed to go. "Except that the weather is bad at base camp. I can't go until things improve."

The Everest View Hotel radio operator relayed a report from base camp that the area was partially covered by broken clouds. Conditions were improving, but Hixson was rapidly worsening and might die before the day was out. In Katmandu the women waited nervously by the radio. The next report said the bad weather was holding. An hour passed, then two. Finally the report said there was a temporary hole in the clouds at base camp; they immediately called the colonel at the airport.

"Okay, we'll try it," the colonel said.

They flew the chopper through the building clouds, poking from one hole to the next. They followed the Khumbu Glacier, and the colonel kept an alert hand on the stick as he felt the lifting power of the rotors wane—the thin air at 18,000 feet is considered about the limit for a helicopter of this type to land and take off.

When they reached base camp the colonel cautiously eased one skid onto a rock, balancing the ship while Wechsler delicately eased off and ran over to help Hixson. Lenser came up and threw Hixson's pack in the chopper, but the pilot angrily motioned him to throw it back off—he wanted minimum weight for takeoff, and that meant only Hixson.

Unable to walk on his own, Hixson was muscled by Wechsler into the chopper, and the colonel carefully lifted the skid off the rock. The helicopter was on the edge of its ability. When he had a few feet clearance he eased the ship forward, and was safely airborne.

Two hours later Hixson was in the Katmandu hospital. Luanne and Marian decided it made sense to wait and visit him in the morning after he had rested. Exhausted themselves, they went to the Sheraton bar to have a drink, worried sick about their husbands.

The next morning she and Marian went to the hospital to find Hixson. They walked the labyrinthine hallways on floors that were by western standards filthy. Finally they found his room. He was lying on his back, staring at the ceiling.

"Excuse me. Are you Dr. Hixson?"

They watched in horror as he tried to sit up. He was paralyzed on one side, so half of him hung limply as the other half struggled to overcome the deadweight. He looked at them, then slowly raised his hand and covered one eye; he was seeing double and that was the only way he could focus.

With slurred speech he said, "Am I glad to see you guys." Then he collapsed back in bed.

Luanne stared at him, thanking God he was at least alive, but at the same time wondering that if in seeing Hixson in this condition she was also seeing her husband a week from now. That is, if she ever saw her husband alive again.

The day that Luanne and Marian visited Hixson in the hospital was the fourth day for Frank at the South Col. His situation was tenuous. One of his Sherpas was sick, and he had to promise the other a 1,000-rupee-per-day bonus (about $100 U.S.) to keep him from turning back down. There was only one day of food remaining, and as little oxygen for sleeping. Even if the Sherpas had been more enthusiastic, even if there had been more supplies, Frank knew that each hour he spent languishing at 26,200 feet his body, from breathing the thin air, was growing gradually weaker. He knew his time had run out.

"I'm coming down," he told Ershler over the radio.

"That's the most sensible thing I've heard out of you all trip," Ershler said. "But keep an eye out for Bass. You'll pass him coming down—he's on the way back up for another go with Yogendra."

At camp 2 Dick had offered a 1,000-rupee bonus to any Sherpas willing to accompany him and Yogendra on another summit bid. Two had accepted, and with this new team Dick left for the South Col, and passed Frank on the ropes just above camp 3.

"Goddamnit, Dick, why don't you have any oxygen on," Frank scolded, raising his voice above the wind.

"I didn't use any the first time to camp four. Besides there's only a few bottles left and I want to conserve them."

"Don't you realize by now you need every advantage you can get?"

"But I don't need any oxygen just to get to the Col. It's only 26,200 feet."

Frank shook his head, wondering where Dick managed to find his unlimited optimism and stamina.

They carefully passed on the fixed rope, encouraging each other with a shoulder slap. As Dick neared the Col the wind increased, and in the stronger gusts he had to lean to stay upright, then move quickly to catch his balance when the gust eased. He started to get cold. When they had left camp 3 that morning conditions were milder, and now he found himself underdressed. But it was blowing so hard he didn't dare take off his outer parka to put on an extra inner layer. It was also snowing, and driven by wind, rime built on his parka and pants. Although protected by gloves inside mittens, his fingers, always squeezing the jumar clamp, were going numb, and now he felt the cold down his back and in his legs and feet.

Last time up the Lhotse Face it had taken him thirty minutes to climb the final section into the South Col; now, slowed by wind and fresh snow, it took him an hour and a half. Arriving in camp, he unzipped the tent, plunged in and lay there for ten minutes before getting enough willpower to unpack and sort his gear. Yogendra arrived and looked equally haggard. Once in their bags they had to fight the temptation to eat only a few snacks and go to sleep. It was of tantamount importance in order to prevent dehydration to start the stove and melt snow for drinks.

Through the night the wind blew, making the tent walls snap like a loose jib sail in a strong headwind. In the morning there was no letup. This was now the fifth day of the wind storm, and Dick wondered if it would ever stop.

"It'd be impossible to make an attempt in this wind," Dick told Frank over the radio.

"In a way I'm glad to hear you say that," Frank said. "At least I know I wasn't being a wimp turning back."

"You did the right thing, but I'm not sure I did."

Dick was getting depressed. Normally he could successfully counter depression by daydreaming, but now his thoughts kept returning to their diminishing oxygen supply, to how little time they had to wait out the bad weather.

He thought, I've done everything I'm supposed to do, yet here I am with my chances dropping by the hour. I should have gone alone the last time when I was so close.

His spirits sank lower, and to make matters worse he now had to go to the bathroom. If it had only been a matter of peeing, it would have been easy: he had a plastic bottle he used for that, emptying it from the tent door at arm's length. This was another matter. He crawled out. Spindrift scudded over the hard snow, and he shielded his face against its stinging bite. There was a small rock not far from the tent; it wouldn't really offer any protection from the wind, but somehow it made him feel better to be next to it. The wind was too strong to stand up, so he crawled toward the rock. There he squatted, dropped his pants, pulled down his long johns, and immediately felt the sting of windblown ice.

He thought, What indignity will I have to endure next?

In a second he found out: without the usual warning symptoms, he had diarrhea, and before he could control himself he had made a mess on both pant legs.

"This has to be the nadir of my existence," Dick mumbled aloud.

He had to take off his heavy mittens and gloves to handle his toilet paper, and his fingers immediately started freezing. But his privates were freezing too, so abandoning concern about his hands, he finished wiping, pulled his underwear and pants up, and started the demoralizing job of cleaning off his pants and boot covers. No sooner did he swipe at the mess with his toilet paper than it flaked off, frozen, and blew away in the wind. A few brushing passes and his clothing was as clean as if it had just returned from the dry cleaners.

Now that's what I call cold! he thought, as he laughingly jammed his hands into his mittens as quickly as he could, not messing with the gloves first since his fingers felt like they had knives being stuck up them and were very near to becoming numb and frostbitten.

"Hallelujah," Dick said, as he crawled on his knees back to the tent, still laughing at the thought of being miraculously saved from such an ignominious situation. It was just what he needed: some humor, albeit bizarre, to lift his spirits.

Back in the tent, he found Yogendra sitting cross-legged, rocking back and forth, mumbling incoherently some chant.

"You okay, Yogendra?"

"It will not quit blowing. We will have to go down tomorrow."

"I know," Dick said, admitting what he had tried not to think about. "I'm thinking the same." He felt the depression start to creep back.

"But I tell you," Yogendra said as he stopped rocking, "in Katmandu I will get the Inspector General of Police to help us get a permit or on some other expedition. You, me, and Frank too. We will come back and climb Everest together."

"You've got to be kidding. You can do that?"

"We'll make a joint American–Nepalese police expedition."

"When could we do it?"

"Next year hopefully."

"Yogendra, I feel like Lazarus rising from the dead."

They spent the rest of the afternoon enthusiastically discussing logistics, equipment, personnel. Dick thought how he and Frank had missed their chance to do the Seven Summits in one year, but that was a small matter as long as they finally did them.

When they awoke next morning the tent walls were still snapping, and they were nearly out of oxygen, so after breakfast they dressed as warmly as they could and descended to camp 2. There Dick explained his plan to come back next year, but Frank wanted to make sure they had definitely used up all the options available to them while they were there, that there was no chance they couldn't make one more attempt.

"Let's put it this way," Ershler said. "All the lead climbers save for me and Neptune have left the mountain, so if anything goes wrong up there, nobody is here with the strength to help. Then there's only one oxygen bottle left at camp four and none left here at two. Even if there were, the Sherpas say they've had it. Also, it's May twenty-fourth, and the monsoon will arrive any day. Finally, the Icefall is shifting, the ladders and ropes are snapping each day, and soon our retreat out of here will be cut off."

"If the truth be known," Frank said, "I guess I'm not too sad to hear that. We've been here nearly three months, and I'm getting burned out. I just need an excuse at this point, somebody to tell me it's impossible to go on."

"Well, it's impossible," Ershler declared, with a glint in his eye, knowing he'd finally checkmated Frank.

That evening they radioed base camp that the expedition was over. The next day they dismantled camp 2, and loaded the Sherpas with tents, stoves, and pots and pans until they looked like Asian counterparts of dustbowl refugees. When the last man was through the Icefall everyone sighed with relief. It had been a very successful expedition. No one killed (Hixson was recovering satisfactorily in Katmandu), eight to the summit, the first American to climb Everest without supplemental oxygen, the first microwave transmission from the top.

Frank and Dick didn't miss a beat getting on with their plans for the rest of the Seven Summits. As they hiked out they reviewed logistics for McKinley with Ershler, whom by now they had retained as guide and leader of that expedition. And they made plans for their return to Everest.

"I'm going to talk to Luanne about it as soon as we get out," Frank said. "Dick, I bet we can pull it off the next try. I found out one thing on this climb that I never really believed. And that is, with a break in the weather, I really have a chance of making it to the top."

McKINLEY:
TWO DOWN

"**I** really think Dick and I might have
a chance this next time. Especially Dick. If you could just see how
strong he is up there, darling. All we need is a shot at it. Yogendra's
not positive he can arrange permission for this coming spring, but
he thinks he can get it for the fall of eighty-four. What do you think?"

Luanne didn't answer immediately, but stared out the plane's window. They were en route from Hong Kong on a flight back to Los
Angeles.

After a moment she said, "Frank, when you started this mountain
climbing business you said it would be two years and no more. You
promised."

"I know, darling, but this is Everest."

Luanne again turned to the window and didn't answer. Her lips
were firmly closed, face resolute. While Frank could see it was
obvious she wasn't overly enthusiastic about the idea, he didn't fully
realize just how opposed she was.

And this was because he didn't fully realize just how hard the
Seven Summits had been on her. He knew it had been tough, of
course, especially when Marty had been killed, but he didn't know
how tough. He didn't know that she had not only been forced to accept
the fact that it might be him next, but also to start thinking in a very

practical way just how she might get along if he were next. And he didn't know that from these inner searchings Luanne had discovered and developed in herself strengths she had never known existed.

And these included the strength to firmly draw the line on what she saw as Frank's near desertion of her and her children in order to pursue his mountain climbing.

But she decided, at least for the moment, not to say anything. It made more sense to wait and see if first they actually got the permit for this next attempt. Otherwise she would only be causing an unnecessary brouhaha, and again she knew that the Seven Summits meant so much to Frank she didn't want to spoil the remainder of it for him if she could help it. After all, regardless of how she felt about his climbing these mountains, she did love him and wanted to be a supportive wife.

She continued to stare in silence, and Frank decided it would be best to drop the subject for the time being. He thought, It's still a long ways down the road. And besides, I'd do better to spend my time thinking first how we're going to get to the tops of the rest of the summits.

It was June 10 when they arrived back in Los Angeles, less than two weeks before they were to leave for McKinley. Fortunately most of the work organizing McKinley would be done by Ershler, and the big decisions, such as who would be on the team, had already been made back in early March, before they had left for Everest.

March had been a tough month, what with the pressures of putting the Everest trip together while at the same time continuing to work on the other climbs, especially Antarctica; but in his indomitable fashion Frank had juggled all the pins, or rather phone calls, without dropping any.

Even though Dick had been too busy to help much ("I'd love to but I'm just spinning on life's merry-go-round, grabbing at the rings trying to catch up before we go away again"), Frank had managed nevertheless to include him in all important decisions. In one of their phone calls, for example, Frank had discussed with Dick who they might include on their McKinley team.

"How about that girl who's the dog musher in Alaska," Frank had suggested. "The one Chouinard told us to get ahold of."

"Susan Butcher?"

"That's right. She goes each year on that thousand-mile dog sledding race that's like the America's Cup of Alaska. Beats the Eskimos, everybody."

"She'd be a boost for our movie, that's for sure," Dick agreed. "Fits in with that idea we had to have something distinctive and indigenous for each segment. You know, we had the gauchos on Aconcagua, and we'll have the Sherpas on Everest and that photo safari before Kilimanjaro."

"And Alaska will be dog mushing. I'll call her right now."

But that was easier said than done. While Susan had never actually won the Iditarod—the 1,200-mile dog sled race from Anchorage to Nome—twice she had finished second out of a field of rugged male sourdoughs and Eskimos, and in Alaska she was close to being the national hero. She had also become a sweetheart of the media, and as a result of being constantly hounded by newspaper, magazine, and television people she had secluded herself and her dogs—all seventy-five of them—in a cabin cum kennels twenty-five miles from the nearest town (population sixty). She had no electricity, no water, and no telephone, and to get a message to her you had to go through the nearest neighbor, who had been instructed to ignore calls from anyone who sounded like a New York or Los Angeles media type.

"Hello, will you please hold for a call from Mr. Frank Wells," Frank's secretary said to Susan's telephone contact.

"Hi, this is Frank Wells calling from Los Angeles. I'm going to be climbing Mount McKinley later this year. We're filming it, and I'd like to have Susan join our trip. Susan and her dogs. Can you get a message to her?"

Eight calls later Frank was still getting nowhere. On the ninth call he decided to try a different tactic. "Let me explain," he said. "I'm president of Warner Brothers Studios, and my partner and I are very serious about this climb. Perhaps I didn't mention it, but we are willing to pay Susan a fee for doing this."

Frank got a call from Susan later that day, and after he had explained the Seven Summits, Susan said it sounded like fun and to count her in.

"Have you done any climbing?" Frank asked.

"I've been up McKinley."

"Perfect. Now what we had in mind is maybe the dog team helping us freight our equipment up the glacier. Do you think they can travel on a glacier?"

"They've already been on McKinley."

"They have? How far did they go?"

"All the way to the summit." There was a short pause, then Susan added, "With the sled."

Susan said she didn't want to go through that again, but agreed it would be fun to have the dogs on the lower part of the climb. With her and the dogs now on the team, Frank and Dick then decided to ask Phil Ershler to be the leader and guide.

So, when Frank and Dick asked Ershler to be the McKinley climbing leader, they mentioned Susan and her dog team to him. Phil didn't like the idea but said he would be cooperative. Frank also told Ershler, "I want this climb to be first cabin," he said. "So, if you think you need any more people to help you, get them."

"I'll bring two more guides from the Rainier Service."

"Fine. Second, we want the best food you can get. No more emphasis on granola bars and M&M's."

"No problem," Ershler said. "Just one thing. On McKinley there are no Sherpas, and even though you'll be with guides, when you're with me you do your share of the work: you haul loads, you help set up camp, pitch tents, build snow walls."

"That's the way I want it," Frank replied. "Except for one thing. I won't cook. I hate to cook. I've never cooked in my life, and now that I'm past fifty I'd like to maintain my record."

Back in the U.S. Ershler took charge of final preparations, adding to the team three more Rainier guides: Andy Politz, Ed Viesturs, and David Stelling. In addition Frank and Dick extended invitations on a pay-your-own-way basis to other climbers they knew who might like to come, and four accepted: Chuck Goldmark (who had been on that first Aconcagua climb in 1982), Jeff Haley (a lawyer friend of Goldmark's), Robie Vaughn, and Bill Neale (the last two being friends of Dick's children). There was nothing for Frank and Dick to do beyond catching up with their business lives. That was a handful, though, especially for Dick, who was now working to find a way to finance his next building at Snowbird despite the fact he was still, as usual, struggling to meet his bimonthly payroll and quarterly loan payments.

At least now Dick didn't have to spend any of his time packing. Other than taking out his socks, long johns, and windsuit for laundering, he left his backpack and bags packed after Everest, ready for the turnaround to McKinley. Still, Snowbird and other business kept him hopping, and the day he left home, he had been without sleep for two straight nights.

At the Anchorage airport Ershler had made arrangements for a van to drive them the hundred miles north to Talkeetna, the springboard for bush flights into McKinley. In front of the van was another vehicle that looked more at home on Alaska's potholed highways: a 1978

Chevy one-ton truck—with a built-in kennel sufficient to haul thirty-six dogs and a sled—and a large sign on the side that read SUSAN BUTCHER'S IDITAROD TEAM. Susan introduced herself and her friend Dave Munson, who was going on the climb to help with the dogs, and also to bring the dogs down once they reached the end of the glacier (so Susan would be free to continue the climb). She was about five-six, with dark hair parted in the middle and done in two long braids. She had bright eyes, rosy cheeks, and looked to be in good shape. As soon as the luggage rolled down the conveyor, she grabbed two of the bags and Dick noticed the well-delineated muscles on her forearms.

"Let's load the gear in my truck," she said. "No room in that thing you've got."

"I'll ride with you and Dave," Dick said to Susan.

"Me too," Frank chimed in.

Out of Anchorage they followed the Susitna River north on the Fairbanks highway.

"I'm twenty-nine years old, born and raised in Cambridge, Mass.," Susan said, answering Frank and Dick's questions. "My family had a summer place in Maine, but my sister and I had to go back to Cambridge every year for school. It was totally against my blood. Maine was for me. I tried Nova Scotia when I was sixteen, then Colorado for a couple of years, studying to be a vet technician. I had two Siberian huskies, and on my seventeenth birthday, I got a sled. With a few more dogs I started racing, but at first I didn't like it so much, I guess because it was a sport, a weekend thing. I didn't want any part-time mushing: I wanted it to be total. I wanted to be some-place where they needed dogs for *transportation*, so I came to Alaska.

"When I got here I had to learn mushing all over. I still didn't like racing—I was mushing for the adventure of it—but I was also going broke, so I entered the Iditarod because there was fifty-grand prize money. That was in seventy-eight, and I was surprised how much I actually got into the racing. For the next three or four years I worked summers in the fish camps to support my dogs and me, until I could make it from the kennels alone. And somewhere in there I took the dogs to the top of McKinley. Took forty-four days to get them up."

"Susan, I can't believe it," Dick said. "You're a carbon copy of this young lady Frank and I knew, who more than anyone taught me how to climb. Did you ever hear of Marty Hoey? She was the only female guide on McKinley."

Susan hadn't. Dick told her the story of Marty's death, as well as their recently completed South Col expedition.

"So you were with this Phil Ershler both times on Everest, and now McKinley?"

"That's right," Dick said. "And I got to admit, he's a little uptight on this one. He didn't have much time to get it ready, and to be candid, he was a little upset about you coming. Well, not you, but your dogs. He's a guide on McKinley every summer, and he thinks if the dogs raise hell and crap all over the glacier it'll give him a bad name."

"That's understandable. But you watch, everything will work out."

Dick was certain everything would work out; he was pleased to have someone on the team of such obvious confidence and ability. But he was a little apprehensive wondering if Susan, as the only woman on the team, might feel out of place. That had never been a problem with Marty, but then it was one of Marty's strengths to fit naturally in an all-male group. Dick hoped Susan would be the same, but he made a mental note to at least be careful with his mountaineering language until they knew each other better.

Talkeetna, the only town of size along the upper Susitna, has only a couple hundred permanent residents, but in climbing season, especially after a spell of bad weather, the number of mountaineers waiting to fly to the base of their climbs can nearly match the local population.

"Weather looks stable, though," their pilot Doug Geeting told them. "Should be okay to get out of here tomorrow."

In the morning they decided Frank, Dick, and Steve Marts would go in the first flight. The rest of the team would follow, with Susan and her dogs coming last. They handed their gear to Geeting, who loaded the ski-equipped, single-engine Cessna. It was obvious this thirty-one-year-old pilot was a man who enjoyed his work. Gregarious and showing telltale signs of Alaska's unofficial state sport—beer drinking—he loaded the plane with boyish enthusiasm, as though it were his first flight to the mountain.

Frank and Dick sat in the back, on top of all the gear, and when they were airborne Frank leaned forward and yelled above the engines, "How long have you been flying in Alaska?"

"Nine years. I'm originally from L.A. myself. Used to fly a Cessna towing those advertising banners up and down the beaches."

"Do you climb?"

"Nope. But I love working with climbers. All kinds of characters up here, from all over. You wouldn't believe how many nationalities."

Excited to have an interested audience, Geeting turned around, leaving his left hand on the wheel so he could talk directly to Frank and Dick. Apparently he had made this flight so many times he could literally do it blind.

"Russians, Chinese, Japanese, Italians," Geeting continued, speaking loudly above the plane's engine. "Mexicans, Czechoslovakians, Poles, Koreans—sometimes we have eight or nine nationalities at a time on the glacier, all speaking different languages."

Geeting was still turned backward, and Frank and Dick listened attentively, glancing from Geeting to the compass to the altimeter.

"But you know, climbing is a common link to everybody who's up there. Even if you don't know somebody, you still know them. Know what I mean? It's a real friendly atmosphere, a real healthy one."

Geeting nodded his head and broke into a reminiscing smile. He still faced backward.

"I'll tell you, when you see that many people from different places getting along, it makes you feel pretty good inside."

Dick glanced at the compass.

"Then you see these people come off the mountain, and they're back in Talkeetna at the Fairview bar, drinking beer and singing songs together, people from all over the world, and it makes you wonder."

Geeting shook his head, which was still facing the wrong way.

"You wonder why, if things can work so good here in Talkeetna, why in the hell is it that the rest of the world can be so screwed up."

Geeting shook his head again to acknowledge the irony of it all, then turned around and continued toward McKinley without having to make even the slightest correction to his heading. Below them the wide Susitna, broken into dozens of small channels, braided over gray gravel bars. The sky above was peppered with fair weather cumulus that each floated at exactly the same altitude so it felt as though they were covered with a white and blue quilt. In the distance, at the edge of the green forest, they could see the white peaks of the Alaska range, and highest and most massive of all, McKinley, or as most Alaskans and climbers call it, Denali—Indian for the Great One.

Approaching the range they picked up the long Kahiltna Glacier where it spilled for several miles onto the forested flood plain. They followed it into the white heart of the mountains. To their left was the great snow massif of Mount Foraker. They banked right, following a subsidiary glacier, and could see through the cockpit window the dozen tents and the black-flagged wands marking the landing zone.

"The Kahiltna International," Geeting said as he throttled back and made his line up. In a few minutes they were down, and as soon as they unloaded, Geeting was off for the next shuttle.

There was another group camped a few yards away busy sorting their food and equipment before starting up the glacier. While they waited for Geeting, Dick walked over.

"Howdy. My name's Dick Bass."

"We're a Sierra Club group," the leader said. He introduced his wife, and she added, "This is the first time on McKinley for most of us, and we're pretty excited."

Dick told them about the Seven Summits project, then the Everest climb, then in a few minutes he was encouraging everyone to "come ski the Bird." Frank was sitting nearby on their piled gear, shaking his head.

"We got three square miles of skiable terrain now, but someday we'll have twenty-four," Frank overheard Dick saying. "Thirty-one hundred vertical now, and we'll have forty-two hundred when it's done. That'll be bigger than anything in the U.S. Plus we got the greatest snow, not like that Eastern boilerplate or Sierra cement. Ours is light, dry, and fluffy."

On those last words Dick's face got that faraway look it did when he read a Kipling poem. He continued to chat with the Sierra Club folks until down the glacier he heard the drone of Geeting's Cessna. Soon the plane set down, off-loading Ershler and the others, then was off again to get Susan and the dogs. When it landed again, Susan jumped off, pulled her dogs out and leashed them to a long cable staked in the snow. With that done she next set a metal dog dish in front of each one, and gave them water.

Dick noted how she moved between her pile of gear and the dogs quickly, with firm steps, planting her feet with authority. She had her long braids tied together at the end with a ribbon, and wore navy blue long johns with the shirt sleeves pushed up exposing those strong forearms. Without showing any strain, she picked up a sixty-pound sack of dog food and loaded it in her sled.

Ershler came over to help. "What's this one's name?" he asked, scratching one of the dogs.

"That's Co-Pilot. She's shy. At first I was going to leave her, but her replacement got sick. A shy one is better than a sick one."

"What do they eat?"

"Seal meat."

"No kidding. Where do you get it?"

"Pribilof Islands. Go out each year on a hunt with the Eskimos."

Susan grabbed a duffel, while Ershler reached to pick up a pack. Susan said, "Now are you and I going to be enemies on this trip?"

"What do you mean?"

"Heard you might be worried about my dogs."

"Well, no. I mean, yeah, I was a little worried. In fact, I still am."

"I don't blame you. You've probably never been around dogs. Don't worry about them, though. That's my job, and I promise they won't get in your way or cause any embarrassment."

Susan stacked the case, then said, "And another thing. I don't know too much about climbing, so I was hoping you could show me a few things."

"My pleasure," Ershler said. "Actually I'm a little concerned about getting this sled and you safely through the crevasse fields. When you climbed this mountain before, it was earlier in the season so the crevasses weren't as open as they are now. If you're walking next to this sled you won't be able to tie in with us, and if you happen to step on a hidden crevasse, you might go in. So we have to figure some way to secure you."

With help from Chuck Goldmark, they worked a system whereby Susan could safely tie into the sled in case she went in a crevasse, yet release herself should the sled go in one. Susan finished loading her sled. Ershler was at the same time relieved and impressed; relieved that Susan promised the dogs would behave, impressed that by all appearances she was hard-working, strong, and competent. He liked her straightforward style.

Two hours after arriving they were ready to get underway. The Sierra Club group, who had been there nearly two days doing the same thing, were impressed.

"It's not that you're doing anything wrong," Ershler told them. "But this is my sixth year in a row here, and if I don't know how to do this quickly by now, I'd better get another job."

"We're almost ready ourselves," they said. "We'll be right behind you."

Ershler led his team out of camp. Most were towing additional gear on plastic sleds, and everyone had heavy packs weighing sixty pounds and more. Even Susan was carrying a heavy pack despite the extra work she had mushing the dogs. Everyone except Susan wore skis, to support them in the soft afternoon snow, with bindings that adapted to their climbing boots and skins on the bottoms that allowed them to climb slopes with ease. Susan, because she had to move quickly from one side of the sled to the other and occasionally hop over the reins to tend a dog, was wearing only boots on her feet, and under the weight of her pack she sank with each step. Still, she managed to keep the same fast pace as her dogs.

With no wind, and direct sun reflecting off the snow into everyone's faces, they had to take care to coat themselves with sunscreen lotion. On a glacier the reflective sun can be so intense that as you walk huffing and puffing you can suffer sunburn on your tongue and on the roof of your mouth. The climbers were stripped to their long johns, and Dick, with a bandana draped from under his billed cap to protect his neck, looked like a bedouin nomad crossing a glacial desert.

Dick was having trouble with the sled he was pulling. Until they got to the main glacier the gradient was slightly downhill and the sled, connected to his waist with a piece of line, was constantly gliding forward over the back of his skis and clipping him. He was losing patience, and Frank wasn't helping by laughing and constantly yelling to Marts, "Steve, did you get a shot of Dick falling."

The sled tripped him again and this time Dick went facedown in the slushy surface.

"That son-of-a-bitch . . ." He continued cussing until he saw Susan mush by, then he self-consciously shut up.

"Susan, I apologize for that language."

But Susan wasn't paying attention to Dick; she had her hands full with the dogs: "You four-legged sons-a-bitches, if you don't get off your asses and start pulling I'm gonna . . ."

And that was the last Dick worried about Susan fitting in as one of the guys.

An hour past the landing zone the tributary glacier on which they had been traveling joined the larger Kahiltna Glacier, and turning the corner they started the slow trudge up the gentle gradient. Each person had a sling of nylon webbing over his shoulder holding a few aluminum snap link carabiners, and either a pair of jumar ascenders or loops of rope called prussiks; these would be used to climb back up the rope should anyone fall in a hidden crevasse. When traveling on a glacier there is usually no great risk crossing open crevasses— you walk alongside until the crevasse either narrows so you can jump it, or you find a snow bridge. It is the hidden crevasses—those that have widened while the snow lids covering them, fed by wind-blown snow, have remained intact, blending with the surrounding snow— that demand vigilance, as they are trap doors for the unwary.

They had gone about three hours up the glacier when Ershler raised his hand, calling a halt.

"What's up?" Frank asked.

"Smells like a crevasse."

Frank couldn't see anything, but Ershler, looking right, then left, sensed in the snow a depression running in a long transverse line. Moving cautiously, he approached the edge of the suspect zone, and bending forward probed with his ski pole. So far, so good. He moved forward on his skis another two feet, and probed again. Suddenly his ski pole broke through, leaving a dinner-plate size hole, black against white.

"Looks like a granddaddy. Keep the slack out of the rope."

Working his ski pole, he opened the hole until he could judge the width of the crevasse. It was a wide one, six feet or more. He moved along the side of the crevasse until he found what seemed like a solid snow bridge.

"It might hold with skis," Ershler said, referring to the advantage of spreading your weight over the larger surface of the skis. "Keep the slack out."

He slid his ski forward, delicately transferred his weight, then moved the other ski. Another step and he was across.

"Okay, now you guys follow in my *exact* tracks."

Frank and Dick crossed, then the others. Everyone waited until Susan and the dogsled were safe on the other side. Ten minutes later they looked back and could see the Sierra Club group a half mile behind, approaching the crevasse. Then they climbed a small rise, leveled out on the other side, and lost visual contact.

In a few more hours Ershler called another halt, saying they would camp for the night. They divided jobs setting up tents, digging a cook pit with a windbreak, and digging a latrine. With these tasks done they started the stoves and when the first tea was ready they called an end to a good first day. Everyone but Susan, that is. While the others relaxed she attended to her dogs, melting snow for drinking water, cooking seal meat, shoveling excrement down crevasses. She inspected their paws to make sure none were cracked. Only when she finished with the dogs did she eat her own meal. She did not begrudge the others their leisure, though; on the contrary, she did her chores with an ardor that suggested the others were the ones who should be envious. And if Ershler had at the beginning of the trip been skeptical about taking the dogs up the glacier, seeing Susan clean up after them dissolved any hesitation.

There was no wind, all clouds had cleared from the sky, and the sun, behind the surrounding peaks but still a few hours from its short pass below the horizon, cast a soft Arctic pink on the snowfields above them. Sitting on their foam pads lining their sunken outdoor dining booth, they finished their meal, drank tea, and swapped stories.

"Susan, tell us what the Iditarod is like."

Susan, cradling her tea in both hands, breathed the steam and said, "That's a tall request, but I'll try."

"They have the race in March," she began. "That's exciting because it's the first month when you feel warmth from the sun, and each day is noticeably longer. Still, maybe sixty percent of the time you're in the dark—I don't remember one race when there was a full moon. But there's enough light, especially when the stars are out. You race along hour after hour, and all you see are the shadows, and you hear the sled's runners swooshing through the snow, and the owls in the trees and in the distance a wolf. Then there's this long section where you break into big, sweeping valleys, and then open tundra. In the Arctic dawn you can see the trail disappearing like a ribbon into the distance, and it's just you and the dogs and no hint of anyone else in the universe. You race through the short day and into the long night, and it gets colder. Then you're on the Bering Sea, mushing over the sea ice, and you can see the village ahead, the lights just twinkling; even though it's fifty miles away, somehow the light bends over the clear, straight horizon. Then the aurora starts to dance overhead, and you can feel its energy. It comes down in curtains of red and green mostly, and you stop the sled and stand out on the sea ice by yourself with nothing in any direction. Then everything gets quiet. The dogs go still, the sled is still, the sky is still, and you can hear it, in the sky, the aurora, making this barely perceptible noise. You have to listen carefully, so carefully, but it's there, this whooosh, whooosh, whooosh . . ."

• • •

Dick opened his eyes, and seeing the bright yellow and tan panels of the tent, guessed that the morning sun had peeked above the surrounding ice ridges. Outside he could hear the purring of the stoves and the chatter of the early risers. Glancing to his side he saw Frank still in his sleeping bag, reading a book.

"Frank, you ever stop to figure how many days out of this year we'll be living in tents?"

"Good question. Let's see, about three weeks on Aconcagua, then about ten on Everest. Then two or maybe three weeks here, say one on Kilimanjaro, then Elbrus will be huts, so it doesn't count. Maybe two more on Vinson, and Kosciusko again is a day hike. That's nineteen weeks, or, let me figure it, a hundred thirty-three days."

"That's a lot of camping out for a couple of businessmen in their fifties."

Dick sat up on one elbow and surveyed the stuff sacks lined neatly along his sleeping bag, looking for the one that held his vitamins. Then he picked up the one with his powdered-energy-drink packets and mixed one with his bottle of water. After taking his vitamins, he then looked for the sack with his bottle of Absorbine, Jr., to rub on a sore leg muscle. Next it was the sack that had the sunscreen and lip protection for his face.

"Dick, I bet you've got a sack for each part of the body."

"Now don't go ridiculing me again, Wells. I don't hear you complaining when you need to borrow something, which seems to be at least twice a day."

"As a matter of fact, I was going to ask if you had any ointment for a cracked lip."

Dick muttered and handed Frank a small tube. When Dick had finished all his ablutions he slipped out of his bag to dress. It was already warm enough so he wouldn't need any more than long johns, which he was already wearing. Putting his boots on, and his overboot gaiters, he crawled out, pulling with him his sleeping bag, which he hung to air over his skis planted upright in front of the tent. He put his goggles on, and looking down the glacier he could see in the sky over the distant flatlands a thin haze, but it seemed innocuous; overhead there was nothing but cerulean sky.

The glacier here was wide, perhaps a half mile or more, with McKinley on one side and Foraker on the other, and everywhere there was thick ice, lying over the mountains like frosting that had dried and cracked into hundreds of crevasses. Here and there, exposed in naked patches on the sides of the peaks, were rocks too steep for the ice to adhere to, and along the tops of these cliffs the thick ice, always creeping downward, sometimes would break off in big blocks that would pulverize when they hit below and with great thunder kick huge billowing white clouds in the air.

Dick joined the others in the cookpit sipping their morning brews. Susan was with them, and Dick, knowing that since she was drinking her tea she must already have completed her chores attending to the dogs, guessed she had been up at least an hour. A few minutes later Frank arrived and sat next to Dick.

"What's for breakfast?" Dick asked the others.

"We haven't made anything yet."

"Well, if you need some help, let me know."

Frank elbowed Dick and whispered, "We cook one meal, and we'll be cooking from here on."

"I'm just trying to help."

"Listen, we'll carry anything they ask us to, we'll pitch the tents, dig the cook pit, even dig the latrine. Anything but cook."

"Okay," Dick whispered. "I don't really want to cook, anyway."

After breakfast they broke camp. There was a lot of gear to carry: food for two weeks, ten gallons of stove fuel, cooking pots, three tents, everyone's personal gear. With only backpacks it would have been impossible to haul it all without shuttling, but with some of the gear on Susan's dogsled, and more on the smaller sleds the others took turns pulling, they were able to progress up the gradual slope of the glacier in one slow-moving stage. They had lost track of the Sierra Club group, and they hadn't seen any others until later that morning when a group heading downhill, sitting on top of their gear piled on their sleds, rocketed by waving and hollering as they passed. An hour later three climbers, each towing their extra gear in makeshift sleds made of big plastic bags tied to a line, crossed their path.

"We all got to the top," they said.

"Congratulations. Are there many other parties ahead?"

"Yeah. There have been several days of good weather, so all the groups that were holed up waiting to go to the top are now on their way down. There's more on their way up, too. An all-woman team just ahead of you, staying at the next camp, and a guided group further up. There are also a couple of park rangers coming down."

"Sounds like that circus on Aconcagua," Dick said. McKinley was in some ways a mirror reflection of the South American peak. In fact McKinley was probably more popular than Aconcagua. To date nearly

4,000 people have reached its summit, and at least three times that many have tried and failed.

It took another seven hours to reach the day's campsite at the 11,200-foot level, where the west buttress of McKinley rises from the head of the Kahiltna Glacier. This was a standard campsite, and they saw that the all-female group had pitched their tents nearby. Later that evening the two climbing rangers passed through camp on their way down.

"Did you guys leave the airstrip the same time as that Sierra Club group?" one of the Rangers asked.

"They started just behind us, but we lost track of them."

"So you haven't heard. We got a report on our radio yesterday. Sounds like they were on the lower part of the main Kahiltna Glacier where they ran into a big hidden crevasse."

"We know the one. We took our time getting over it."

"They didn't do as well. Apparently the leader's wife was crossing when the snow lid broke, and she went in. She was pulling a sled, and somehow it pressured her waist. It took them quite awhile to get her out. By then she was dead."

"We were just talking to her yesterday," Dick said incredulously. "That's hard to believe."

They pressed the rangers for more information, but the pair didn't know anything beyond the brief radio report.

The rangers left, and Frank and Dick were quiet, both thinking about that big crevasse, both feeling that nervous flush that sweeps you when you learn of a death that could easily have been yours— that unease when you're forced to acknowledge your own vulnerability.

"Thank God we've got Ershler," Frank said after the rangers had left.

"Thank God we've got the best there is on all these climbs," Dick agreed.

As planned, the next morning Susan's friend Dave Munson readied the dogs for the trip back to the airstrip. He would take them home while Susan stayed to finish the climb. She gave each of the dogs a big hug.

"Stay out of trouble until I get home," she chided them.

"And you stay out of trouble too," Ershler told Munson. "If that big crevasse looks too gnarly, wait until someone comes along to rope you over."

With the dogs gone the camp suddenly seemed deserted. Ershler broke the silence, "Let's get on with the day's work."

That would be shuttling loads to the next campsite, at 12,700 feet. To get there they followed a moderate-angled gully alongside the West Buttress, and as they were now off the relatively flat glacier it was best to abandon the man-haul sleds and, still wearing skis, carry all of the gear on their backs. After reaching the campsite, they cached their loads, then clamped the heel locks on their ski bindings for the downhill run back to the 11,200-foot camp.

"It's June twenty-third and look at this snow!" Dick yelled as he stopped halfway down. He let out a Tarzan call, then made a series of parallel turns the rest of the way to camp. Next day they moved up to occupy the 12,700-foot camp. The weather was clear, and Dick wore only his long john underwear, leaving his wind suit in his pack.

"Wells," he said, "at this rate we'll be on top in a week."

"Home for the Fourth of July."

As usual, Dick had an abundance of personal gear, and his pack was so heavy—around sixty pounds—that he started to fall behind even Frank. The wind began to fill, and with them still a half hour away from camp, it was blowing twenty miles an hour. Dick was getting cold quickly, but he was now close enough that he didn't want to stop his rhythm and take off his backpack to get his windsuit on. Airborne spindrift plastered on his underwear making him look like a frosted Christmas ornament. It was a repeat of the day he went to the South Col, little more than a month before, when he had started out dressed for a fair day only to be freezing by the time he reached camp—but then he at least had on his windsuit.

Ahead he could see the others setting up tents. He was shivering and worried about frostbite, not on his feet or hands but, because he had only the one layer of underwear, he had lost all feeling on the end of his "dinkie," as he called it.

"It's going to freeze and fall off for sure," he muttered.

He tried to move quickly, but the weight of the pack kept him to a snail's pace. He walked in a penguin waddle, with his gloved hand like a fig leaf over his privates. Twenty-five yards ahead he could see Frank sitting on his pack—fully dressed for the cold weather—eating a candy bar. Susan was pitching a tent, and the others were busy constructing camp.

As he reached the edge of camp Frank looked up and said, "What's wrong Dick? Have to pee?"

"Pancho, the wind's going right through this underwear. I'm afraid my dinkie is frostbitten."

"Bass," Susan spoke up with a wide grin, "what are you looking for—a blow job?"

When he could finally get a word between everyone's guffawing all he could say was, "And when we started this trip I was concerned that you might be one of those prudish New England types."

"Too many years in Alaska, I guess," Susan said.

Still laughing Dick crawled in his tent to examine himself but was relieved there was no apparent damage.

In the morning Ershler explained the next stage of the ascent.

"We climb up and out of this gully, then around Windy Corner and into the basin at 14,000. The campsite is on a wide flat at the base of the summit pyramid."

The following day was clear, and although there was no indication Windy Corner would live up to its name, Dick nevertheless opted to wear his wind suit. Everyone continued on skis, zigzagging up the thirty-five-degree slope, kick-turning at each switchback. Frank had never done this kind of ski mountaineering, and now he was toppling every dozen yards. He didn't complain, though, nor did he suggest he carry any less than the others. He might not have been willing to do his share of cooking, but he was determined to do his share of load hauling.

When they reached the basin at 14,000 feet they cached their loads and skied down, returning next morning with the rest of their gear. Rounding Windy Corner they climbed into a stiff headwind, with building clouds portending storm. Pitching their tents in the wide, flat basin, they cut snow blocks to build windbreaks. The all-female team arrived, and Dick invited them to set up their tents alongside but they moved on a hundred yards to the site of several snow caves dug by some previous group.

"They act like we've got B.O. or something," Dick said.

It was snowing by the time they had the tents up and stoves started. They crawled in one of the tents to eat, and the steaming water had the inside warmed to a comfortable room temperature.

"I don't know about this younger generation," Dick said to the others. "Here we are with a whole expedition of pretty girls down the way and you guys sitting here with us old bucks sipping tea. If I was young I know where I'd be."

The tent was warm inside, and there was that warm feeling that comes from sharing stories with your buddies. Outside the wind had let up, and it was quiet. If they listened carefully they could just hear the big snowflakes on the fly tent as they landed and then gently slid off to the snowbank growing around the base as the storm settled in.

For three days it snowed, and finally on the fourth it cleared.

"Too much avalanche danger to move up," Ershler warned. "We'll wait and see how it looks tomorrow."

Next morning Ershler judged it safe to move.

"We'll carry a load to the 17,200-foot camp, come back down here, then move up and occupy the camp tomorrow."

Remnant clouds from the storm hung above the slope as they climbed out of the basin, following a fixed rope placed by some earlier party. The slope rose nearly 2,000 feet above the basin, although in the persistent clouds their view was obscured. It was the wearisome task now so familiar to Frank and Dick, the placing of one foot before the other in the rest-step fashion, the sliding forward of the jumar, the heavy, rhythmic breathing. Toward midday they could glimpse the crest of the ridge through the clouds. Frank decided to make it his goal.

Soon one of the climbers disappeared over the crest, then reappeared and yelled down, "Wait till you see this view." Frank was puzzled, as all he could see was more clouds, but when he reached the crest he discovered why the others were so excited. For some reason the ridge was the dividing line between good weather and bad, and all of a sudden the world opened and it seemed he could see across the breadth of Alaska. In front of him the great white sweep of the northern glaciers flowed to the foothills, and through clear air he could see 14,000 feet below the tongues of white ice spilling onto the vast carpets of green forest that then extended to the horizon. He stared and felt the warm Arctic sun glow on his face, giving his skin a soft orange complexion.

He stared as though the scene were a physical addiction he couldn't turn away from. And as he stared, his thoughts became reflective. He thought how most of his friends and acquaintances back home, the people he knew in Los Angeles and New York in the movie business, would pass their lives never knowing that scenes like this even exist in the world. It made him a little sad to realize, but at the same time all the more pleased he had decided to take the year out of his life to discover such things himself.

They continued up a snow-and-rock ridge to the campsite at 17,200, cached their load and returned to the lower camp. The next morning they moved back up to occupy the camp. Residual clouds clung to the basin, giving the feel that the weather was still unstable. But now they were at least above that basin, above the ridges and faces that until then had always enclosed them. Now for the first time on the climb they were following a ridge crest so that there was nothing surrounding them, and the only thing higher was the goal ahead, the summit. There was exhilaration, a feeling of being near the summit-day push, a feeling of being above human barriers, being free to go for it.

The ridge ended at a wide bench with a backdrop slope leading toward the summit. This was their high camp. Dick had fallen behind Ershler and a couple of the others, but ahead he could see another party camped in the middle of the flat. He guessed they were the guided party they had heard about, and went over to introduce himself.

"Say, you all haven't seen the rest of my group, have you?" Dick asked.

"They went that way."

Dick walked across the flat until he spotted Ershler and the others. They were below the lip of the flat.

"What are you doing down here?"

"This is out of the wind."

"But when I climbed this mountain before we camped back up there, where the other group is."

"Guess they don't know what they're doing."

Dick shrugged his shoulders; it didn't matter that much to him. But when they got the tents set up Ershler walked back toward the other group, and soon returned with the news he had found a snowcave perfect for a kitchen. Now Dick was upset. He grabbed his cup and spoon and walked fifty yards uphill to the "kitchen," knowing each time they had a meal he was going to have to repeat the hike. Dick knew he shouldn't let some small thing like that bother him, but at the same time he couldn't help it. It was an example of how high altitude and cold weather can cause someone to lose patience.

It snowed through the short night, and in the morning it was obvious they would have to wait for better weather. By McKinley's standards it wasn't cold, never much below zero, and the snowfall wasn't heavy, either, but it was like a head cold that wouldn't go away, that was just bad enough to keep you bedridden.

"It'll be a close call whether we get home for the Fourth," Frank said.

Through the day, as the snow continued, Dick kept reminding himself that since he already had climbed McKinley two years before he was going through all this just to climb the Seven Summits within a year. And even that was out the window now that they had missed Everest.

"What's got me worried is the food," Frank said. "We've got maybe two days' rations. There's another two days down at fourteen, and maybe two more at eleven, but we'd eat that much bringing it up to here."

"Yeah, Pancho, and here we are two grown men able to afford the best hotels and restaurants in the world, and we're sitting up on a snowheap in the middle of Alaska freezing our buns off, eating food unfit for convicts. Sometimes I think I need my head examined."

"There's no way we can *not* climb this mountain," Frank said, ignoring Dick. "If this storm continues I'll have to think of something."

Next day the snow continued.

"How about a helicopter," Frank said to Ershler. "We'll have a load of groceries delivered from Talkeetna."

"You can't do that."

"Why not?"

"It's the ethics. You might as well have the chopper take you to the summit."

The third day the snow continued. They were on their last day's rations, and if it didn't clear in the morning they would have no choice but to descend.

"Even if it's clear tomorrow," Ershler said, "We may have to wait a day for the slopes to slough."

With the other two guides Ershler decided to climb a short distance above camp, to judge the snow conditions at the base of one slope he was particularly worried about. While they were gone Frank lay in his sleeping bag considering options. Maybe there was someone below who had more food than they needed. Maybe there was a food cache somewhere that someone had left behind. Maybe he would ignore Ershler and get a helicopter anyway.

Maybe none of these things would work out, the storm would continue, and they would fail.

He hated the thought but had to acknowledge the possibility. Failing on Everest had been disappointing, but really not a surprise; actually he was pleased to have done as well as he had. Everest notwithstanding, the Seven Summits would still be a great success . . . if they managed to get to Antarctica . . . if they managed to get to the top of McKinley . . . if, if, if.

While Frank mulled over these thoughts, Dick lay in his bag reading his *Complete Works of Robert Service.* Despite the grim logistics of their circumstance Dick's mood was improving. First, he had told himself there was no sense fretting about their food shortage because he knew if there was anything to be done about it, Ershler and Frank would figure it out. Second, he had realized that feeling sorry for himself only made things worse. So he had looked around for something positive to do, and had landed on the idea of re-reading Service cover to cover, and rating each poem one to four stars. Now in the middle of that project he was reasonably content.

Ershler returned and said the snow was deep but apparently not layered. If it cleared in the morning it might be safe to make a last-ditch effort.

"It'll be hard work postholing in that soft snow, but there's no other way," he said.

That evening it didn't take long to make dinner, as all they had were a few candy bars. When everyone finished Susan said, "For breakfast we've got one packet of soup and one packet of cocoa each. That ought to get us to the top."

Frank and Dick were asleep when Ershler called from the neighboring tent.

"We haven't got all day. Let's get going."

Dick opened the tent door and looked out. In the morning half-light he could see to the west the summit of Mount Foraker eye-level with their position. There were a few clouds hanging round it, and above, at extremely high altitudes, a few thin wisps. It was definitely clear enough to climb.

"Let's get this mother behind us," Dick said excitedly to Frank as he started to get dressed.

With only their one packet of soup and cocoa, they didn't have to be concerned about lingering too long over breakfast, especially with the temperature several degrees below zero. In the cold shadows they left camp and began the slow plod up the slope toward Denali Pass. In line ahead of them were the eight climbers from the guided expedition. It was quite a procession, like those old black and white photos of gold rush miners struggling through the deep snows of the Chilkoot Pass on their way to the Yukon.

As they turned a corner and started going straight up the slope, they took the lead from the other group who were very tired from breaking trail. The snow was so deep that for a while Ershler had to dig a trail with a snow shovel. The other two guides alternated this job with Ershler, and Dick maintained the second-place position. It was a tough task as Dick's legs postholed into the half-packed trail and each step required several stomps with his boot. After an hour their progress was so slow Dick wondered how they could ever expect to make the top. There would be no second chance, either, not with their total food supply nearly gone. As he continued to stomp steps in the amorphous snow his morning elation ebbed and once again he had to hold back his "negative thoughts."

It took over two hours to get near the top of the slope. Looking down Dick could see they were not that far above their camp.

"I hate to admit it but I'm having doubts we'll make it."

"Maybe the snow will be firm once we get on top of this slope," Ershler said.

Ershler's hope came true an hour later at Denali Pass—a saddle between McKinley's two summits—where they found that the snow, exposed to constant wind, was hard enough to support them on the surface. Dick's and Frank's spirits rose with their quickened pace. There was a growing wind building out of the west and the high cirrus was congealing. They had fingers crossed that the weather would hold long enough to reach the top, now only several hours away.

In spite of the thinner air at the increasing altitude, Frank and Dick continued to move smartly, no doubt still enjoying the benefits of their acclimatization on Everest.

Below the final summit slope everyone took a break to give Steve Marts time to work ahead so he could film their arrival on top. Ershler sat on his pack, next to Frank.

"You did your share on this climb," he said. "I made no effort to make it easier for you. You had the same loads as everyone."

"Thanks Phil. That means a lot to me. You don't know how much."

"In fact," Phil said, "I can't even believe you're the same guy I was with that first trip to Everest a year ago. You've come a long way."

Frank was beaming as he stood to follow Ershler. It might have seemed odd for the former president of a large movie studio to relish a compliment from a mountain climbing guide, but movie making and mountain climbing were two separate worlds and here Ershler was in a sense the president, with full authority. Frank had worked at this mountain climbing as hard as he had on any project in his life, and it felt good to have the effort recognized by his leader.

Not everyone was feeling as fit as Frank, however. After a few minutes Ershler paused to examine the snow at his feet; there, next to the footsteps, was someone's red spittle.

"Hold up. Who's spitting blood?"

"It's me," Susan called. "I think it's just this cough. Caused my throat to bleed."

Bloody spittle can be a sign of pulmonary edema, a potentially fatal bleeding in the lungs caused by high altitude. Ershler put his ear to Susan's back, but couldn't hear the telltale gurgling sometimes associated with edema.

"I'm okay," she said. "It's just the leftovers from a cold I had when we started."

"Okay, but don't do anything foolish."

Susan turned and kept climbing. She was breathing hard, coughing, obviously straining with each step, but not about to give up.

Dick thought, Boy, that's just what old Marty Hoey would be doing in her place.

Dick knew they were close to the top. Fifty yards ahead the ridge they were on seemed to stop. He could see another ridge from the south coming up in a way that gave the feeling the summit was just ahead. Then he saw the top of Marts's head, and then Marts waved. This was it.

Twenty yards from the top, Marts yelled down for them to stop. The camera wasn't ready.

Five minutes later they were still waiting.

"It's freezing here," Dick yelled.

Ten minutes later Marts yelled for them to come up. Anticlimactic though it was, Frank and Dick were both fired up when they reached a small wooden sign that said DENALI SUMMIT 20,320'.

As Marts rolled the camera Dick and Frank bear-hugged and Dick said, "Pancho, two down and five to go."

"That was okay," Marts said, "but could you please go down and come up again."

"Marts, I don't believe you," Dick groused. "Here we are on the roof of North America with storm clouds on the horizon, and you're doing a Cecil B. DeMille retake number."

"I've got to get another angle from over here."

The guided team was now just reaching the top and they looked puzzled as Dick and Frank climbed down and then back up.

"Once again, please," Marts said. "This time when you get to the top I want you to look like you're gazing across all of Alaska. Then we'll make a dissolve into another scene where you're gazing across Africa, and we'll be right into the next segment."

"Lord, I can't even celebrate one and I've got to think about the next," Dick said.

Now the all-woman team arrived, and about twenty people stood on top of the highest peak in North America watching Frank and Dick climb up and down.

"Pancho," Dick said, "I don't know about you, but I feel like an idiot."

It was crowded, and Frank and Dick had trouble squeezing onto the top so no one else would be in the frame.

"This shot had better be it," Dick yelled at Marts, "because you just saw me summit this thing for the last time."

"I don't like the looks of that cloud," Ershler said. "Let's get the hell out of here."

He pointed to a sinister hammerhead cumulus rising to the northwest. Still concerned Susan might have a pulmonary edema condition, Ershler tried to set a fast pace but Frank was lagging. Ershler then had the good idea to put Frank in the lead, where it would be easier to prod him, and that seemed to work. The pace picked up, and Frank maintained a steady momentum. It was just getting dark when they reached camp, and after a few cups of hot water Frank and Dick crawled into their tent, exhausted. It had been a long day: sixteen hours since they had set out that morning.

Susan was sharing her tent, so Ershler came in to listen to her lungs. She had a pain in her chest, but there was still no gurgling.

"I think it's just my diaphragm, sore from breathing hard and coughing."

"Probably, but we'll still watch it."

In the morning Susan said she felt better. It had snowed off and on through the night, and now they were anxious to move down before another storm trapped them. At the 14,000-foot site they camped briefly, digging into their cached rations for their first full meal in three days. By now they were all losing weight and dreaming of their first meal when they got out.

"Once we're back to our skis," Ershler said, "we'll beeline to the airstrip and fly straight to the Latitude 62 Bar and Grill in good old downtown Talkeetna."

They had a great ski down the glacier until a heavy fog set in and they had to use a compass to navigate. The next day it cleared and they reached the Kahiltna International, where the radio operator called Geeting to come get them. When he got there Geeting said it would take four flights to get everybody out.

"Let's draw cards."

Frank got the Two of Clubs, so he had the next to the last flight. While he was waiting, he asked the radio operator how late the Latitude 62 stayed open.

"Closes at eleven."

"What time is it now?"

"Ten."

"Then we have to call them. Right now."

Frank, with a twinkle in his eye, picked up the receiver. He was now back in his familiar world, holding the tool of his trade. With an ice axe in his hand he might still be a stumblebum, but with a phone he was king.

"Hello, this is Frank Wells calling from Kahiltna Glacier, on McKinley."

Frank explained the situation, asking if he could make arrangements for them to stay open late.

"Sorry, mister. We're on fixed salaries here. Everyone goes home at eleven."

"Please, let me explain. We've been on this climb up McKinley and we've been out of food for several days—"

"Mister, half the people come in here have just been on McKinley and they're *all* starving."

"But you don't understand. We're willing to pay extra. A lot extra. Listen, there are eight of us. I'll give you fifty bucks a head. That's four hundred bucks."

"I don't know."

"Five hundred."

"I'm not sure the cook will stay that late."

"Six hundred."

"And the dishwasher, too. It's late, mister . . ."

"Seven hundred."

"Mister, like I said . . ."

"Eight hundred."

"Like I said, we'll be waiting when you get down."

KILIMANJARO
AND ELBRUS:
THREE TO GO

Of the seven mountains on their list, Kilimanjaro was the one that for Frank held a special meaning. It was the mountain he had climbed almost thirty years before during that spring break from Oxford, where on descent he first had the notion to someday try to climb the highest peak on each of the other six continents.

Now he was returning, and it was as though this great snow-capped volcano rising 16,000 vertical feet above the acacia-studded African savanna to an altitude of 19,340 feet above sea level was a talisman of his life's direction, a great physical presence that had sent him on his way those three decades before, and only now to have him back again. There had been a lot of water under a lot of bridges, but he had held on to his dream, and the mountain represented that faith. Kilimanjaro was like a pole marker rising at both ends of his adult life.

In addition to this kind of spiritual affinity, Frank was returning to Kilimanjaro looking for something very real: the summit register he had signed in 1954. Wouldn't it be incredible if it were still there cached among the rocks, that small booklet with his name in it? He imagined opening that old can, leafing through the fragile pages and finding his name. Then he would sign again, the new signature under the old.

Kilimanjaro, then, would be special. It was also going to be the one expedition where both Frank and Dick could bring their wives. Not that the women would climb the mountain, but Frank and Dick had the idea to precede the climb with a photo safari to the big game parks of Kenya, something everybody could share and enjoy.

"And maybe I'll invite my kids," Dick said during the planning. "I think Dan at least will be able to make it."

"And I'll have mine come too," Frank replied. "I could even bring my mother."

"Let's invite everyone who's been on any of the Seven Summits," Dick said zealously. "We'll have a great big party, Pancho. This'll be fantastic."

Frank hesitated, knowing as he did Dick's penchant to host the world to good times. "Okay, but they have to pay their way."

Most of the climbers who had been with Frank and Dick couldn't afford a big game safari, especially in the style Frank and Dick were proposing, but one did sign up. Dan Emmett, who had been on the Aconcagua climb, not only said he would come, but wanted to bring his wife, Rae, and their two eldest children, Daniel, thirteen, and Roz, twelve. Not just for the safari, either. Emmett explained that he and his wife had climbed the mountain nineteen years before and now they wondered if Frank and Dick would mind if they tried again, with their kids.

Frank and Dick were thrilled. They had gotten to know Emmett on Aconcagua, and since then Frank had seen Emmett fairly regularly because they both lived in the Los Angeles area. Of all the delightful people he had met on these Seven Summits climbs Emmett was (other than Dick, of course) perhaps his favorite. Frank admired the priorities Emmett had set for himself. Foremost was his family. Then came his business, a real estate development company that had become one of the biggest in West Los Angeles. Then came his avocations, like kayaking, running, trekking, and climbing. Frank considered Emmett the consummate amateur adventurer, and he often said, "Call Emmett at three in the afternoon and ask him to show up at the airport at six for a six-week adventure—don't tell him what or where—and I'll guarantee you he'll be there." Frank could have added that likely as not Emmett would also show up with his family.

• • •

With the team chosen, the Kilimanjaro group rendezvoused in Nairobi, where they were met by safari guide Alan Earnshaw and his petite and spunky wife Moira. Earnshaw was typical of many safari guides. Born in Kenya to farming parents, he was schooled at Cambridge and probably would have continued the family business, but with national independence and expropriation of his parents' farm, he had decided rather than leave Kenya to stay and work in the guide business.

They traveled to the Masai Mara, Lake Baringo, Aberdare. This was the season of the big mammal migrations, and they saw zebra and wildebeest by the tens of thousands marching to their instinctive grazing regions and perennial watering holes. They camped among great herds of eland, waterbuck, reedbuck; Emmett said he felt like he had gone back to the beginning of the world, when all land in all directions was wild.

If they were going back to the beginnings of time, however, they were going in style.

"I don't want you to get the impression," Dick said to his wife, "that this is the way Frank and I have been living on all our climbs."

Indeed, the tent campsites that the native African staff erected made Everest base camp seem like the Hoovertown that it was. Here standards were inspired by the best traditions of British colonial bush living. Each couple had their own large private tent with sleeping cots, mosquito netting, rugs on the floor and an extra anteroom for hanging clothes and tidying up. Here the day started when one of the staff brought hot wash water to your portable basin in your tent for the morning's toilet, and each twosome also had their own portable potty tent and separate shower tent behind. There were always between twenty-five and thirty native Africans in camp to assist should you need anything additional. Breakfast was served in the mess tent on a long table covered by a red-checkered cloth: fresh fruit, fresh-brewed Kenya coffee, eggs, sausage, ham, bacon. After breakfast they loaded in the four-wheel-drive vehicles, standing through the sun roofs for a better view as they searched for game with "white hunter" guides. Then back to camp for lunch, out again for the evening animal movement, back for cocktail hour and, if you liked, a shower in your personal tent stall complete with hot water poured by one of the native staff into a reservoir mounted above the spigot.

Here Dick Bass drew the line.

"Since I've been climbing I'm just used to going without bathing or shaving. And I wouldn't want to get weakened or spoiled, not until we finish these Seven Summits, anyway."

The safari lasted nearly two weeks. Everyone left with indelible images of the largest congregations of mammals on earth—of the herding wildebeest which stretched from horizon to horizon moving in large oceanic swells, of the giraffe munching the leaves of the flat-topped acacia fifteen feet off the ground. For Frank, though, the most lasting image came on a day he overheard Dick talking to a tribal Masai:

"And the snow is this light powdery stuff that I'm telling you gets waist deep and deeper. So if you ever get a chance to visit, there's no place in the world like the Bird. Come ski me."

The Masai, whose tribal warriors were among history's bravest, stood tall and proud. This one, dressed in a homespun cape and holding his long herder's spear, which he used if lions got too tempted by the cattle he was herding in his bare feet, politely nodded his head.

The summit of Kilimanjaro is less than twenty miles inside the Tanzanian border from Kenya, and since 1886, when Queen Victoria deeded the mountain as a birthday gift to her German grandson, there has been a border dispute. For the Seven Summits team it meant that instead of crossing directly into Tanzania, which was only a three-hour drive south of Nairobi, they had to fly first to Ruanda, then back to Tanzania.

Alan Earnshaw and his wife Moira had accepted Frank and Dick's invitation to join the climb. Earnshaw was new to climbing but Moira had been up Kilimanjaro several times, as a guide for the Outward Bound school. The team, then, consisted of Frank and Dick, Dan Bass, Dan and Rae Emmett and their two kids, Daniel and Roz, Steve Marts the cinematographer, and the two Earnshaws.

After landing in Tanzania they proceeded directly to the hotel at the base of the peak. The next day they loaded their gear in an open truck and drove toward the roadhead. The weather was stable and clear, and the mass of Kilimanjaro with its snow glaciers descending like frozen lava from the old volcano rim seemed to float unconnected above the acacia plain. They were headed for the less-frequented westerly flank of the mountain with the idea of trying a route different from the so-called tourist trail that Frank had followed thirty years ago.

This plan had been suggested by a local climbing guide named

Ian Allen, who knew Kilimanjaro perhaps better than anyone. They had met Allen in Nairobi and hosted him to an evening of drinking, and Frank had regaled him with tales of Everest, Aconcagua, and McKinley. Probably thinking he was with some Himalayan hotshots Allen had said, "You two don't want to take the tourist Kibo route. You'd enjoy it much more going up something more interesting, say the Machame."

"But we've got Emmett's wife and kids."

"They'll have no problem," Allen assured. "Only a little rock scrambling near the top. Don't even need a rope."

Frank, emboldened with a half dozen silver bullets (martinis), had agreed.

Now they were keen on this more remote western side of the mountain. Their buses left the main tarmac and continued on a rough back road that passed through banana groves, then ended at a few ramshackle huts. There fifteen native porters, people of the Chagga tribe, unloaded the vehicles of their supplies, which had been pre-packed in trussed bundles for balancing on their heads, and set out through the thick forest. The team hefted their own backpacks, loaded with personal gear, and following the porters, started the four-day walk to the point where the climbing began.

Kilimanjaro is only two degrees south of the equator, but as a climber ascends its flanks he passes through five climatic zones that are roughly parallel to the vegetation zones you might encounter traveling from the equator north or south toward the poles. Only roughly parallel, however, because many of the plants in the biological bands that girdle the mountain are unique to Kilimanjaro and other high peaks of East Africa.

This first stage was through equatorial forest. The ground was carpeted in ferns and vines, the sixty-foot African rosewoods swathed in hanging moss, and the canopy dense to the point it allowed only occasional rays of sun to penetrate to the ground. It was damp and dark. Along a faint trail they followed the porters with their loads balanced on their heads. Just like in the Johnny Weismuller Tarzan movies, Dick thought. Without any extraordinary imagination you could see yourself some early explorer such as Burton or Speke, venturing for the first time into some hitherto unseen, unknown place. Especially for the Emmetts' two kids, Roz and Daniel, this was big-time adventure, and they stuck close to the heels of Moira Earnshaw, the one person of the expedition who knew best the mysteries of Kilimanjaro.

The trail made a gradual ascent, and by late afternoon they climbed above the forest zone, and at about 9,500 feet entered the region of giant heather, trees up to forty feet high draped with gossamer strands of the mosslike lichen known as old man's beard. These trees were in stands between meadows of tough scrub, and they camped under open sky, the porters getting a meal going while the team set up their climbing tents. The food was first-class, and after supper the porters collected plates and cleaned pots while the climbers enjoyed a cup of tea. The afternoon clouds had dissipated, the temperature was mild, and best of all, there were no pestiferous insects.

"We deserve a comfortable one after all those weeks of snow and ice," Frank said.

They hiked about five hours a day, gaining between 1,500 and 2,500 vertical feet each stage, passing through the Heather Zone into the Moorlands, a cloud-level stratum that is home to the giant groundsel, a bizarre plant rising twenty feet on a naked, rubbery stalk capped with a rosette of wide, waxy leaves that at night fold against the diurnal cold. Above the Moorlands they gained the open expanse of the Shira Plateau. This was the Alpine Zone, and now they trekked over miles of packed volcanic gravel peppered with football-sized pumice rocks. The only plant life was occasional tufts of tenacious grass tucked between the black rocks. Before them, imperceptibly closer with each step, was the great mountain. Kilimanjaro was different than any of the other peaks they had attempted: there were no surrounding summits, no deep valleys to conceal the goal, only the singular massive mountain that each hour revealed itself in greater detail. Now they could see the individual contours of the Western Glaciers, and they knew somewhere in the dark lava cliffs adjacent to the glaciers, through a notch called the Western Breach, lay the route known as the Machame.

On the fourth day they awoke at daybreak to the porters singing a mellifluous hybrid of tribal chants and Lutheran hymns. They broke camp and were on the trail by 9:30. Behind them all they could see was the pyramidal summit of Meru floating thirty miles in the distance above a sea of clouds that otherwise obscured the Africa plain. This was the final Summit Zone, and although devoid of all plant life save for the ancient lichen, they did see track of eland, the migratory antelope that venture to higher elevations in search of soda salt. It was in this zone, too, where in the 1920's hikers on the regular route found the frozen carcass of a stray leopard, and the enigma of why this animal had climbed to such a desolate place set the mood in the opening of Hemingway's celebrated short story, "The Snows of Kilimanjaro."

Early that afternoon they pitched high camp at 15,800 feet near the tongue of the Arrow Glacier. Their plan was to get an early start, leaving all the porters except the three native guides who would go with them to the top. The porters would break camp and make a girdling carry to the regular Kibo route, where all would reunite late that afternoon as the climbers descended from their traverse of the mountain. It was a good plan except that it assumed everyone would be able to make it up the climb, because otherwise there was no camp to come back to. And looking up the steep rock cliff above them, some of the team were apprehensive.

"How are we supposed to climb *that*?" Rae Emmett asked.

There was no discernible way, and Dan Emmett asked the guides to point out the route.

"Maybe over to the left side, bwana," said the first.

"No, route stays up straight to rim," said the second.

"No, no, no, right side goes all the way," said the third.

While they argued Emmett looked through his binoculars and decided he would treat tomorrow as though they were on a first ascent, and scout the way as they went. One thing for sure, it would take all day to climb the cliff, traverse the summit crater to the highest point, then descend to their rendezvous with the porters. And that meant they wouldn't have any time for much filmmaking, so Steve Marts suggested they spend the remainder of that afternoon shooting on the glacier near camp.

"Just one thing," Dick said to Marts. "No more of that cockamamie repetition like you put us through on the summit of McKinley."

"I've been meaning to tell you about that," Marts said. "Some of it didn't come out too well."

"What do you mean?" Frank asked.

"Well, the magazine must have been jammed or something, and I didn't know it. Anyway, only a little of the summit footage came out."

"You mean to tell me," Dick said, "we were marching up and down that summit umpteen times in front of all those females on that all-woman expedition making fools of ourselves for nothing!"

Dick was still berating Marts as they hiked over to the nearby glacier. It was kind of a pecking order that had evolved: Frank to Dick and Dick to Marts. Unfortunately, Marts didn't have anyone to vent on. As the most tenured climber of the bunch, Emmett drew short straw to lead a 30-degree pitch where he could then belay the rope while Marts filmed Frank and Dick climbing. Emmett had to chuckle watching Frank. Even with all the expeditions he had now been on he was still awkward. Emmett held the rope snug, certain Frank would slip. He was right—a second later Frank caught his crampon on his pant leg, but he slid only a couple of feet before Emmett had the rope tight.

"Did you get that Steve?" Frank asked.

"No, Frank, how am I going to make you look like a folk hero if I record how clumsy you are?" Marts rejoined.

Emmett had to laugh. If Marts managed to turn Frank into a classical hero, it would only be by some incredible cinematic legerdemain. But even without old-fashioned heroes, Emmett knew Seven Summits was a good story. His favorite part was how the Seven Summits odyssey had changed Frank and Dick, and especially Frank. Dick knew at the outset what he was getting into (mainly because of McKinley), and if Dick had learned things from the climbs, it was probably more in the way of underscoring what he'd already done. But Frank really had changed since the beginning. Emmett felt that change started on the second Aconcagua climb, when Frank achieved his first summit. And although it was an important achievement for him, Frank realized there were other parts of the trip that were even more meaningful. There were the memories of the storm-bound story tellings, the sense of shared uncertainties and adventure, the new friends. He realized that now, by the time of the Kilimanjaro trip, for him the goal of the Seven Summits had changed from having a big challenge to having a good time with his newfound mountaineering companions. Frank had started the project motivated by achieving things that could be measured objectively, but now had learned that the real goal was to achieve subjective things that couldn't be measured finitely at all.

That evening they finished dinner early, since they would need to get up before dawn to get an early start on the summit. Before they turned in Frank said, "Bass, we haven't had a new poem for a couple of days. What have you got in that stack?"

Dick pulled the photocopied poems from his pack and leafed through the Kipling and Service.

"Have I layed on ya Robert Service's 'The Rolling Stone'?"

"Haven't heard that one yet."

"Well get ready. This is one of the best."

Dick hardly had to read this one—he could recite most of it from memory. Everyone listened attentively:

> *"To scorn all strife, and to view all life*
> *With the curious eyes of a child.*
> *From the plangent sea to the prairie,*
> *From the slum to the heart of the Wild.*
> *From the red-rimmed star to the speck of sand,*
> *From the vast to the greatly small;*
> *For I know that the whole for the good is planned,*
> *And I want to see it all."*

"Stop," Frank said. "Recite that stanza again."

"What are you talking about?"

"Just recite it, Bass, and listen to what it says."

Dick recited it again, and Frank said, "That's it."

"That's what?"

"That explains it. I've been trying to find some way of telling people how I feel about these expeditions, about quitting my job, about taking a year out of my life. And that says it right there: 'And I want to see it all.' "

The loose scree broke under each person's step, tinkling like shifting shards of glass, the only noise in the cold predawn. There was just enough light from a waning moon to see their way up the talus above their campsite. There was no wind, and the stars shown brightly in the clear sky.

For being so close to the equator it was surprisingly cold, only a little above zero. Kilimanjaro is one of the only places in the world, other than perhaps the volcanoes of the equatorial Andes, where you can go from rain forest to Arctic conditions in such a short distance.

They moved off the scree and onto a long rib of broken rock that angled about forty degrees to the crater rim. Finally the sun broke above the rim and it warmed quickly. This endless freezing and thawing had fractured the rocks into rectangular blocks that in places looked like the crumbling construction of some ancient civilization. Although the rock rib fell away steeply on both sides, it was easy scrambling and the only danger was one climber knocking a rock on another.

Near the top, however, the exposure increased, and although the climbing was still relatively straightforward, Emmett decided it prudent to rope his wife and kids past the worst difficulties. Frank and Dick seemed to be doing fine, even though Dick, as he was always wont to do, carried a heavy pack with a full assortment of "emergency" gear. Dan Bass, too, was keeping the pace and feeling strong. Both Rae Emmett and Alan Earnshaw suffered acrophobia, but they seemed to have learned quickly never to look down. Nevertheless, it was with no small relief to the two when just before noon they crested the crater rim.

The summit crater of Kilimanjaro is huge, nearly two miles wide, and feels Martian. Looking across the burnt expanse of raw lava, they could see another inner crater, and within that a hollow brown and black pit. To their left, like an iceberg floating in a sea of black rock, was the northern glacier. This remnant of ice is slowly diminishing, perhaps victim of some as yet unmeasured global weather trend; sitting solitary with the hot black rocks on three sides, it had the look of a doomed species. Opposite this glacier, across the crater to their right, was Gilman's Point, where the tourist route joined the rim. And 700 vertical feet above that was Uhuru Peak, the high point along the crater rim, the true summit.

They started across. Through a faultless sky the high-altitude sun bore down with equatorial intensity and young Daniel Emmett, following Dick's example, hung his bandana from behind his hat Lawrence of Arabia style. Their feet sank in soft sand. With anticipation they approached a snow patch, but when they started across they found a field of short ice pinnacles more difficult to walk on than the sand.

Everyone was feeling the effect of the heat and high altitude, but the Emmett kids were still walking sprightly and Frank went to great pains to conceal how tired he was. It took nearly two hours to cross the crater.

Everyone was exhausted when they reached Gilman's Point. They now had been climbing nine hours above 16,000 feet. Frank and Dick, of course, as well as Marts, were planning on hiking the remaining distance to the highest point, but Emmett said he was happy just to stay there with his family and wait for the others to return.

"Come on, Emmett. You're not getting off that easy," Frank said, still concealing his fatigue. Then, without further ado, Frank stood and started up the trail.

"Pancho here has summit fever," Dick said, and he got up to follow Frank.

"I can't believe this is the same guy I watched agonize up each step on Aconcagua eight months ago," Emmett said as he too stood and followed Frank. Dan Bass was also in with the rest of them as they started toward the summit.

Frank was anxious to get to the top. He was thinking about that summit register, wondering if after all these years it was still there. Now, for the first time on the climb, he was on the same trail he had followed thirty years before. Nothing looked familiar, however, although that could have been a result of the passage of time and the fact he was throwing up every ten minutes at this stage that first climb. Now, even though tired from the heat, he had plenty of reserve strength. What a difference from when he had been twenty-two years old; now he was fifty-one.

The trail followed the crater rim. To one side they saw the caldera of the volcano, looking like a devil's punchbowl of brown and sulfur lava rock, crater cones, and steaming fumaroles, to the other side the African savanna 15,000 feet below. Frank had his ski pole in hand for balance, and was breathing with his practiced huff-huff—style pressure-breathing that was now so habitual as to be nearly involuntary.

The summit is still a ways, Frank thought, so I'd better be careful to pace myself.

Even through their tinted glacier goggles the equatorial sun seemed to bleach all the color from the dry hot rock. The white light burned out textures, while dark shadows were like holes to the middle of the earth. It was a black and white world colored amber through heavy sunglasses.

They were out of water, and each step seemed to wring from their bodies another measure of the little moisture that remained. Mouths felt dry from forced breathing of dry air, and, as they had now experienced several times on previous climbs, the thin atmosphere gave to their task a dreamy gloss so that the crunch of their steps in the lava trail seemed to come from a distance, like the soundtrack of a movie in which they were not the players but rather the audience, watching themselves in this slow plod.

Keep the pace, Frank told himself. Step, breath, breath, step.

Then he wondered, How much further?

Step, breath, breath, step.

And he thought, The register? Will it still be there?

Step, breath, breath, step.

What's that just ahead? A marker? And who's that? Dan Bass and Steve Marts? Good old Marts, there again with his camera filming Dick and me getting up another of the seven.

Step, breath, breath, step.

"Okay, wave your arms," Marts yelled. "You're on the summit. Look excited!"

Frank grabbed Dick and gave him a bear hug. Emmett had already summitted earlier and passed them on his hurried way down, wanting to rejoin his family, who had forgone the last little section. Then Frank sat down to catch his breath. He was there.

"What a difference thirty years can make," he told Dick when his breathing had slowed. "Damn, I feel great and last time I was here I was puking my guts out."

"Yeah, Pancho, you're definitely getting stronger as you get older. Kind of doing things backwards."

"But at least I'm doing them. That's what counts."

Then he thought about the register. There was a small concrete block with a plaque on it, and he looked there first. There was no register but the plaque read:

"We the people of Tanzania would like to light a candle and put it on top of Mount Kilimanjaro to show beyond our borders, giving hope where was despair, love where was hate, and dignity where before there was only humiliation. Mwalimu Julius K. Nyerere."

Frank thought how it was a beautifully poetic marker to find on a summit, but tragically ironic in view of the poverty and political chaos they had observed in Moshi and Arusha.

But where was the register?

Frank scouted the summit area, looking under rocks. There was nothing.

"I didn't need it anyway," he said to the others. "It's just as good as a memory."

And what a memory.

Frank sat down again and scanned the savanna that stretched to the sky.

I never could have imagined, he thought to himself, when I was here last time. Never imagined all the stuff that's gone under the bridge these intervening years. All the great stuff.

The descent of the tourist track, or Kibo trail, was an easy but long plunge-step routine down wide slopes of volcanic sand. The

Emmett kids made a game of it by racing ahead and reaching the base hut well before the adults. Word had preceded their arrival that a large group with two kids had climbed the Machame route, and now several of the hikers they encountered congratulated them.

Emmett, pausing to consider the age range and the inexperience of their party, said, "You know, it *was* a hell of an accomplishment."

Back at the Kibo hotel they had a celebration dinner and discussed their next plan. They would fly back to Nairobi, from where part of the group, including Emmett's family and Dan Bass, had to return home. The rest of them—Frank, Dick, Marts, Emmett, Luanne, Marian—would fly to Copenhagen, where they would rendezvous with two additional team members, Frank Morgan and Peter Jennings, both friends of Emmett's. From there, as a complete team, they would continue to Moscow and then on to Elbrus.

Once again because of politics, to get out of Tanzania they flew a circuitous route to Addis Ababa, then back south to Nairobi, where they reunited with Luanne and Marian. In the Nairobi terminal Frank glimpsed a newspaper headline: "Russians down KAL 747, 269 feared dead." The story had just broken and the report was brief, so in Copenhagen they asked their cab driver what he knew.

"Everybody knows it was one of your CIA planes. So the Russians shot it down. What do you expect?"

The hotel desk clerk said more or less the same thing. Next morning they rendezvoused with their other two teammates, Morgan and Jennings, and together discussed what to do. The *International Herald Tribune* made it clear it was not a spy plane, so now they were concerned a world boycott might cancel flights to Russia. They contacted the U.S. Embassy which, as usual, equivocated. They dialed the British Embassy and a counsular officer said they were advising their subjects not to travel to Russia. "Several flights have been canceled, and if you go, there is a good chance you will be stuck trying to get out." Then they dialed the Russian Embassy and were connected to some gruff-sounding official with a two-pack-a-day voice.

"You have visa?"

"Yes."

"You have plane ticket?"

"Yes."

"Ahh, then, you go Russia!"

They were still uncertain if they should take the risk.

"Pancho, I'm glad you picked Elbrus for that first practice climb," Dick said.

"That's easy for you to say. You climbed it. We jolly well *have to* go back."

The women were less certain. As it was they were coming on the expedition knowing they would have to spend most of it waiting in the hotel at the base of Elbrus, but adding to that an indefinite extension in Moscow was too much to contemplate.

"Darling, I have only one consideration to add," Luanne said to Frank, "and that is if we should get stuck in Moscow, you'll never hear the end of it."

Morgan and Jennings said they didn't mind waiting an extra day in Copenhagen to see what happened. "We've got some shopping to do, anyway." But Frank was adamant they should get to Moscow, and finally he swayed everyone to his way. They would leave the next day.

"Which means we better get our shopping done," Morgan said to Jennings with a mischievous grin.

"What do you guys need to buy?"

"Lingerie."

"What?"

"Brassieres and negligees," Morgan said.

"And don't forget the black panties," Jennings added with a demonic gleam. Luanne and Marian glanced at each other with the same look of dismay.

"What in the world?"

"For gifts," Jennings said. "You know, the women in Russia have to be *starving* for that kind of stuff. I mean, they'll go *bananas* when they see it. I can just picture their sweet young faces now."

"We'll be in like Flynn," Morgan added wistfully.

Frank Morgan and Peter Jennings, both bachelors in their early forties, lived in Jakarta, where Morgan ran a law firm assisting foreign companies doing business in Southeast Asia and Jennings headed up Fluor Corporation's Indonesian operations. Any resemblance the pair might have had to normal business types, however, ended with their job descriptions. The two lived Somerset Maugham lives like in a South Seas idyll. They each had beautiful homes with full staffs (Morgan even had one servant whose only duty was to care for his parrot) and they shared a weekend pad in Bali on the sand at an exclusive stretch along Kuta Beach (where the young French tourist girls were always sunbathing topless) that was so exquisite it had been featured in *Architectural Digest*.

Emmett had known Morgan since they were roommates at Harvard Law School, and it was there these two best friends had made a pact that every year or two they would try to get together for some kind of adventure. They had been impressively faithful to their resolution; in the last fifteen years they had been on two climbing expeditions to the Himalaya (including the Bicentennial Everest Expedition in 1976, where I had come to know both of them), ski trips to the Arctic, jungle mountaineering in New Guinea, and white water rafting on uncharted rivers in Borneo. When Emmett had been invited on Frank and Dick's Russia climb, then, he had asked if Morgan could come along, and Morgan had brought his partner-in-crime, Jennings.

When Morgan and Jennings returned from their shopping spree Emmett became concerned that the over $500 worth of lingerie the pair were trying to jam into their already stuffed backpacks might not make it through Moscow customs. In addition to the assortment of black lace panties and bras Emmett spotted something that looked like a deflated flesh-colored beach ball.

"What's this?"

"Our life-sized blow-up doll. Isn't she cute?"

She was also very X-rated.

"What are you going to do with her?"

"She's our climbing partner," Jennings said. "We're going to leave her on the summit of Elbrus. It'll blow the Russians' minds. Can you imagine the next group that comes up after us and sees her sitting there?"

Emmett could also imagine the Moscow customs getting ahold of her, so as much as he hated to dampen the fun he felt obligated to draw the line: lingerie, yes; blow-up doll, no.

He need not have worried, though. Just like in 1981, they were whisked through customs, and also like in 1981 they were greeted by the stainless-steel-toothed smile of Mikail Monastersky, the affable, vodka-loving head of the mountaineering division of the Soviet Union's All-Sports Federation, the same man who had hosted Frank and Dick on the last trip.

They loaded in a microbus for the drive to the hotel. On the way Frank leaned forward and asked Monastersky, "Do you have any news about the KAL disaster?"

"What is this?"

"The Korean airliner you guys shot down."

"Oh, that. No, problem. Everything's okay."

"Okay? The world is up in arms!"

Dick kicked Frank in the shin, but Frank wouldn't ease up.

"There's going to be a boycott of flights in and out of Russia. We might get stuck here!"

Waving his arm Monastersky said, "Oh, that will not happen." Then, changing to what he seemed genuinely to believe was a more important topic, said, "Mr. Wells, we have everything taken care of for you. We are so happy you have returned to the Soviet Union, with so many of your friends. For this, we have decided to pay for all your expenses."

Monastersky waited for the translator to finish, then using his own limited English said, "You climb in Soviet Union free!" He broke into a wide steel grin, wrinkling his already grizzled face. He lit another cigarette, and concluded, "So tonight eat dinner, make party, drink vodka!"

True to his word, the following day Monastersky had everything arranged. They toured Red Square, followed by an evening at the fabulous Moscow Circus. Part-way through the performance Jennings complained that an earache from an infection he had contracted two weeks earlier during an expedition in the interior of Borneo was hurting so bad he would have to excuse himself and go back to the hotel. (This was an expedition that I had organized and led to make the first direct coast-to-coast crossing of Borneo. We had started it only a few weeks after I had returned from Everest, and Jennings wasn't the only one who got sick; I nearly died from a severe bout of typhoid fever.) The interpreter who was accompanying them thought it might be better if they went to the hospital.

Jennings told the others he would see them back at the hotel, then followed the interpreter as they left for the hospital. It turned out to be a depressingly drab building with bare bulbs lighting gray-green walls. An elder heavyweight nurse escorted them to a room, and soon a doctor came in and made a lengthy examination, asking Jennings for particulars about Borneo. He left, and Jennings was transferred to a gurney.

"What did the doctor say?"

"He said they will have to make a cut in your ear to clean it. But it will be only a small operation."

Another heavyweight Russian woman wearing a babushka then wheeled the gurney to a bare-walled room with a concrete floor, and left. Jennings was alone, and worried. He knew he was within walking distance of the hotel. He got up and went to the window. It looked like he was up maybe three or four floors. The window opened.

Thank God, he said to himself. A fire escape.

Meanwhile the others had returned to the hotel with no idea of when or where they would next see Jennings. They were still awake when he walked in with a big grin, telling everyone about The Great Moscow Hospital Escape, and that he would be quite happy to put up with his earache, confident the best strategy was to let it heal itself.

It took some patient diplomacy to calm the interpreter as well as the hospital staff the next day, but with everything in order they caught the flight to Mineral Vody, where they began the drive familiar to Frank and Dick up the Baxan Valley to the base of Elbrus.

As was the case in Moscow, their itinerary was planned down to the least minutia. They met their guides as well as a distinguished gray-haired Moscow physician who was in charge of the Elbrus summer camp sports programs to which the Seven Summits group was assigned. He gave them a briefing:

"This morning you will first have your physical examinations. Then in the afternoon you carry your equipment on the ski lift, then hike a short distance to the hut. There you will leave your gear and return to sleep here. This will help your acclimatization."

With raised eyebrows Emmett glanced at Morgan. Formulized mountain climbing was something new to them, but the Russians really were doing it all in a concern for their safety.

"Then the following day you return to the hut and sleep. The next day you spend at the hut to acclimatize, and the next you start early and climb to the summit."

Emmett thought it made a very long summit day but again the Russians were so polite it seemed out of place to suggest anything contrary. Besides, Emmett rationalized, they probably had some residual acclimatization from Kilimanjaro, that is other than Morgan and Jennings. But then Jennings' earache was still bad, so he was probably sidelined from the climb anyway. That meant only Morgan would have to gut it out. None of them felt too bad for Jennings, however, who had been assigned a personal female doctor to look after him. She was an attractive, big-bosomed woman, but at the same time rather serious and professional.

"We'll get her turned around in no time," Jennings grinned. "Wait till I lay a couple of black lace bras on her."

Luanne accompanied them when they left next morning on a short bus ride to the small, rickety aerial tramway that took them from 7,500 to 10,500 feet; then a single-chair ski lift took them all to 11,500, the summer snow line. Now they continued on foot, hiking up moderate snow slopes for about 1,800 vertical feet to the metal-sheathed hut, the one they recognized from their previous climb and which looked like a huge Airstream trailer. Here they saw the Russian Olympic ski team at their summer practice. Luanne, wearing pink on white tennis shoes, stepped out smartly, staying up with Frank, who was huff-huffing with his habitual pressure-breathing. When they got to the hut at 13,300 feet, she said, "So that's all there is to this mountain climbing business? Big deal!"

The next day they returned to the hut although Luanne, as planned, remained at the lower hotel with Marian.

"One day is all I need to get a taste of mountain climbing," she said, "Besides, staying down here watching Jennings is sure to be more entertaining."

At the hut they were scheduled to have an additional acclimatization day, so Steve Marts, knowing that the actual climb of Elbrus was for the most part a boring slog up a long snow slope, took advantage of the "rest day" to film a climbing sequence on a steep, rocky serac on the glacier near the hut. As had happened on Kilimanjaro, Emmett would lead the hard section, with Frank and Dick following. And again, Dick got up okay, but Frank slipped and was held by Emmett's belay. Morgan stood on the sidelines, watching.

"What kind of documentary is this?" Morgan asked.

"A new genre," Emmett answered sarcastically, "called a ficumentary."

They got to bed early that night, as their guides promised a predawn start. True to their word, they woke everyone at 3:00 A.M., and they were on the trail by 4:00.

It was cold, close to zero. There was wind, but the predawn sky was cloudless and promised good weather for the job. For nearly two hours they followed the trail, moving between rock and snow patch until they reached the base of a continuous snow slope where the guides motioned they should fasten their crampons. This was much lower than where Frank remembered putting on crampons that first climb, but this year there was more snow.

As he fastened the crampon straps over his boots Frank remembered how on the first climb he had been too exhausted even to do this simple chore. How things had changed. Frank felt like the ninety-eight-pound weakling who gets sand kicked in his eyes, disappears to lift weights, and comes back to take care of the bully.

Frank felt great and made good time up the slope. The guides, apparently assuming everyone was climbing well enough not to need assistance, made even better time and soon pulled ahead. Marts and Emmett were also ahead although not quite as far, when they came to the only steep part of the ascent, a back-and-forth traverse up an exposed snow slope. Marts climbed it, showing skill and agility despite his pack full of heavy camera gear. Then it was Emmett's turn. He felt confident, but moved carefully. His crampons squeaked as they bit the hard snow. This was perfect snow for cramponing, as long as you didn't pull a "Wells" and catch your pant leg and trip. Emmett looked down. It was well over a thousand feet until the slope started to ease. A slip here, unroped as they were, would be fatal.

Emmett reached the safety of a rock outcrop at the top of the section, and sat to wait for the others. Marts was perched above him, setting up his camera.

We'd better rope those guys over this, Emmett thought.

Then he realized the Russian guides had all the ropes. He looked up but they had disappeared over the rise. He yelled; no answer. All he could do was talk the guys up, and cross his fingers.

Dick came across first. Emmett noted he was in balance and seemed to climb with confidence. Then he also noted all he had in each hand was a ski pole.

"Bass, where's your ice axe?"

"Don't have one."

"Don't have one?"

"Frank loaned his to one of the guides, so I let him have mine. Besides, we didn't take such a steep, exposed route last time."

Emmett guessed it had been warmer when Dick climbed this face two years ago, but now with the snow this hard Emmett knew Dick's only chance of surviving a slip would be to make an arrest with an ice axe. And without an ice axe, his only chance was not to slip.

Emmett also realized the worst thing would be to make Dick nervous.

"Don't worry about it. You'll be all right."

Emmett tensed as he watched Dick. Marts had his camera on. Dick looked good, though, and made it smoothly. Morgan was next. He was much more experienced, and had his ice axe, but he was also feeling bad, from his lack of acclimatization.

I'll be glad when this section is behind us, Emmett thought.

Morgan got across, and now it was Frank's turn. Again, Emmett figured the best strategy was to sound encouraging.

"Slow and easy, Frank. We're in no hurry."

Frank knew the consequences of a slip, and the unlikelihood of his being able to stop himself even though he did have Dick's ice axe. He moved as carefully as he could.

Emmett sat motionless, trying to look nonchalant but with his eyes glued on Frank's feet.

"Make sure you clear your crampons around your pant leg with each step," Emmett said, trying to sound encouraging.

"I know," Frank answered curtly.

Fifteen more feet . . . ten more feet.

Then Marts said, "Frank, could you climb over about five feet. The view below you is incredible."

Frank snapped. "Goddamnit it, Marts, I'm trying to get across this alive and you want me to—"

"Hold on," Emmett interrupted. "Don't start yelling, just concentrate on getting across. Steve didn't mean any harm."

Five more feet . . . Frank was across.

Emmett grabbed Frank's arm, eased him up to the rock platform, and thought, It's amazing how Frank is only as good as he needs to be. The only time during all these climbs he ever falls is when he can afford to.

Still, Emmett was going to breathe a lot easier when they were not only down from this climb, but when Frank and Dick were finished with the whole project.

Above the rock platform the slope eased and now everyone could relax. Morgan was getting worse, stopping twice to throw up, but insisting he could make the top. Emmett was concerned for his buddy. Morgan's face was ashen, and he was definitely suffering acute mountain sickness. Still, they were close, and Emmett judged if they got up and back down quickly, Morgan would be okay.

Frank was feeling good and strong, an incredible difference from his condition two years earlier. Soon they could see the heads of their Russian guides above them. It looked like they were sitting. A few more feet they could make out a rock cairn next to them. It was the top. With fifty more feet to go, Frank caught up to Dick and put his arm around him.

"We're doing this one together," Frank said.

"Marts," Dick yelled, "get your butt up there and get Pancho and me coming in on this one arm-in-arm. And this time the footage better be good."

They headed for the top, arms over each other's shoulders.

"Pancho, this deserves a poem."

" 'Gunga Din,' " Frank said. "Let's do it together."

> *"Now in Injia's sunny clime*
> *Where I used to spend my time . . ."*

Twenty more steps

> *"A-servin' of 'Er Majesty the Queen . . ."*

Ten more steps

> *"Of all them blackfaced crew*
> *The finest man I knew . . ."*

Five more steps

> *"Was our regimental bhisti, Gunga Din."*

The others cheered as Frank and Dick, still arm-in-arm, reached the summit and bear-hugged. With the camera rolling, they waved their ice axes, then hugged again.

"Damnit, Dick, I can't tell you how great I feel," Frank said. "It's just so great."

Frank was on the edge of tears. He stood on the very top, and looked around the compass. The valleys were filled with noontime clouds, the lesser peaks like snow islands in the fluffy sea. Next to him, on the rock cairn, was a small bronze bust of Lenin. It was a great summit, not as high as some of the others but great nonetheless. Again he thought how this was the first of the Seven Summits he had attempted, the first of what became a long string of failures. He had come back to have his day.

"And it's not like I just barely got up here, either," he told Dick. "Because I feel absolutely fantastic."

The only concern now was Morgan. He still hadn't reached the top, but he only had about twenty feet to go. He hunkered over his ice axe, and the others cheered, trying to encourage him. He made ten more feet, and hunkered again.

"You got it. Come on, buddy."

Morgan was unsteady, but he reached the top. The others gave him hugs, then he sat half-collapsed next to the bust of Lenin and threw up. Then he smiled.

They had all made it. Dick gave out with his summit trademark. "Aah-eah-eaahhh!"

Morgan looked up. "The only thing wrong," he said, "is poor Lenin here. He's going to be a lonely boy. We should have brought the inflatable doll, Emmett. Where's the inflatable doll?"

Then Morgan puked again, laughed, and got up to start down.

Back at the hotel they walked into Jennings's room and found the Russian nurse sitting on his lap, draped in black lingerie and wearing a multicolored party hat. A half-finished bottle of Vodka decorated the nightstand.

"Hi, boys," Jennings grinned. "How was the climb?"

"We made it. Looks like you did too."

"I'm happy to announce my ear infection is cured."

They had a celebration dinner that night and after two more days of relaxation started home. Now their only concern was getting out of Russia. While waiting at the airport in Mineral Vody they met an interesting British engineer who had been living for several years in Russia helping install western technology in Russian factories.

"It's been terrible," he said. "No flights out of Moscow and thousands stranded. I haven't heard any news for a few days, but I doubt it has improved."

"You won't hear the end of this," Luanne said to Frank.

Eight hours later they arrived in Moscow, and there was the affable Monastersky, attentively waiting to take them to their hotel.

"Mikail, we understand there is a serious problem with the airline boycott."

"Problem? Who told you this?"

"An Englishman we met in Mineral Vody."

"Problem? Oh, yes. He is right. Big problem. No more flights now, maybe never." Monastersky took his time to light a cigarette, letting the information sink in. Then he said, "You spend rest of your life in Soviet Union!"

The women went ashen, and Frank and Dick felt their stomachs tighten. Then Monastersky gave them a big stainless steel smile and said, "Good joke, huh?"

Actually the boycott was still in full swing, but there were a few flights out to less-frequented destinations, and Monastersky as usual had taken care of everything, booking the necessary connections. Jennings left via Helsinki, Morgan was out to India by way of Tashkent, and the rest made a connection through Vienna.

Five expeditions down and two to go.

Just as Frank and Dick had decided to combine Kilimanjaro and Elbrus in one trip, Pat Morrow had also made a similar plan, only in reverse. In July of 1983 he had climbed Elbrus and then had traveled directly to Kilimanjaro, where, he learned later, he missed Frank and Dick by only a few days.

After strolling to the top of Kilimanjaro, he returned home by way of Australia and was on the summit of Kosciusko about the time Frank and Dick were beginning their climb up Elbrus.

All he had left was Vinson in Antarctica. He wasn't sure how he was going to get there, but by this time he had seen an article in *Fortune* magazine describing Frank and Dick's Seven Summits odyssey, and he intended to call them as soon as he got back and chat with them about how *they* were planning on getting there.

He knew enough about Antarctica to know it wasn't going to be easy. But he also felt that with enough work, enough perseverance, enough creative thinking, and enough luck, he could figure out how to do it. After all, he was too close to realizing his dream to give the effort anything less.

Pat Morrow had six summits down, and one to go.

THE ICE DESERT

"**Y**ou've got a call from a mountain climber named Pat Morrow," Frank's secretary said over the intercom. "He says he is also trying to climb the seven summits, and would like to talk to you."

It was mid-September, about a week after Frank had returned from Russia, and he was working in the office Warner's had given him while he continued his position as consultant.

"What's he want to talk about?"

"He says he has now climbed six of the seven peaks, including Everest."

"What?"

"He says the only thing he has left is to figure a way to get to Antarctica."

"Put him on."

Morrow introduced himself and explained to Frank how he had come up with the idea of climbing the seven summits, and how he had now done all of them but Vinson.

"I've seen the *Fortune* article about you and Dick and I wondered if I might ask how you two are planning to get to Antarctica?"

"Do you have $200,000?" Frank asked.

"No."

"Well, that's what it takes."

Frank then told Morrow about the Tri-Turbo, and all the difficulties he had overcome in chartering it. Morrow thanked him for the information and for his time, and wished him good luck climbing Vinson. When the conversation was finished, Frank called Dick.

"He sounds like a very nice guy," Frank said, "but he didn't have the money to charter the plane, and who knows if he can come up with it. One thing's for sure, he won't be able to charter it this year, since we've already got it, and even if he does figure out a way to come up with the money, he wouldn't be able to make the attempt on Vinson until next year, and that would be after we have another shot at Everest. Speaking of which, heard anything from Katmandu?"

"I just talked to Yogendra yesterday," Dick said. "He says he's been in contact with the Indian team which has an Everest permit on the South Col route for next spring. The Indian Ambassador to Nepal is a good friend of Yogendra's boss—the Inspector General of Police—and he has approached the Ambassador about our being able to join their expedition. Seems like the Ambassador is acting as a sponsor for this climb, so we should have a good chance."

Frank was ecstatic. That evening he once again broached with Luanne the subject of going back to Everest, and as had been the case on that plane ride back from Nepal, she once again said very little. A couple of days later, though, she was ready to speak her mind.

"Frank," she said, "I want to have a meeting with you."

Frank was surprised. In their twenty-seven years of marriage they had had hundreds of discussions, but they had never had a "meeting."

"Sounds serious," he said.

"It is."

They went upstairs to Luanne's dressing room, where they knew they would not be disturbed.

"I've talked it over with the boys," she said, "and they support me. I've also talked to your mother. Frank, I'm not saying you can't go. I'd never do that, never say no to something you want to do. But we *did* have a deal, and I've made a decision. If you go back to Everest again, and are lucky enough to get home alive, I won't be here."

Frank sat with his hands clasped, arms on his knees, staring down.

"You mean it, don't you?"

"Yes."

They were silent, then she said, "Frank, the boys and I understand how much you want this. Kevin and Briant, they like to achieve things, too; they like to excel; they understand. But you don't know how hard it's been on us, darling. I've tried to have faith, to convince myself nothing is going to happen to you. But that doesn't work all the time. Oh, in a way it's not as hard now as it was that first year. But that's just because now I'm numb. I guess if I've learned anything from this it's just how durable human beings are, how they learn to accommodate pain."

Learning to accommodate pain had been a new experience for Luanne, and one that had changed her in subtle ways she didn't think Frank was aware of. She had just told him the first year had been the hardest, but she hadn't told him that the reason it was hardest was because she couldn't come to grips with the possibility that he might die. She hadn't told him, either, that by the second year, even before she fully realized she was doing it, she had begun to account for the possible event of his death. She had his power of attorney, and she began to make decisions about family financial matters. She took over the job of paying bills, besides running the household. She began to imagine how she would deal with the boys in the years to come if there was no one else to help counsel them.

She realized she was changing, and not necessarily for the better—that depended on how you saw things—for she was no longer just the graceful angel. Those days were forever behind her, and she found herself gaining a certain firmness. She realized, for the first time in her life, she could be as strong as she needed to be.

She realized, too, there was an irony to it, that it had taken the Seven Summits to give her the strength and confidence to tell Frank that she would leave him if he were to continue the Seven Summits.

Frank continued to sit arms on knees, considering what Luanne had just said. He knew as soon as she had spoken her ultimatum there was really no choice. Alongside his wife and two sons—everything he had worked for and valued all his life—the chance to go back to Everest had no comparison. Furthermore, he knew she was more than justified in her position. She had been patient the first time he went to Everest, and she had been tolerant the second time, especially in light of Marty's death when there was no longer any way to mask the danger of the undertaking.

He was of course deeply disappointed he wouldn't be able to return with Dick, that he would no longer be able to hold the dream, no matter how remote the real possibility, of making the Seven Summits himself. But Frank was not a man to feel sorry for himself. He accepted Luanne's judgment, he made the obvious decision, and in the next breath he told himself the Seven Summits had already been such a resounding success he could in no way be disappointed. Besides, he still had the most adventurous of the seven climbs yet to do.

"Well, it's pretty clear what to do, then," Frank said.

Luanne was silent.

"It's clear I'll just have to be content with six summits instead of seven."

Dick was naturally disappointed Frank wouldn't be able to return to Everest, but it was clear to both of them that Dick shouldn't hesitate a moment to continue plans even without Frank.

"But I'm going to feel guilty as heck going back without you," Dick said.

"Nonsense," Frank replied. "You've always had the best chance at it anyway, and I would probably only hold you back. Besides, it's not like we're never going to climb with each other again. We've still got Antarctica and Kosciusko."

And on the subject of Antarctica, things were looking good, too; for the first time in two years plans were on track. So much so, in fact, that with a fat six weeks before they were to depart Frank found himself, for the first time in years, with what could reasonably be called free time.

Not a great deal of free time—he still had his consultant job at Warner's, and there were the day-to-day chores to attend to preparing Antarctica—but compared to the hectic pace he had been keeping, it was the first time since he had started the Seven Summits he had an occasional moment to sit back, take a deep breath, and think about things.

And not surprisingly, the thing he thought about most was what he was going to do with the rest of his life after the Seven Summits was over in December, especially now that he wouldn't be going back to Everest. Up to then, Frank had done a good job forcing himself *not* to think about the future. When he had quit his job as president of Warner's he had made a pact with himself not to dwell on it because he knew there would be no better way to spoil the joy of his adventure than to be standing on the tops of the peaks fretting about what he might do when the climbs were over. There had been occasional lapses, of course, but all in all, the demands of planning for the Seven Summits had pre-empted any time he might have otherwise spent brooding.

Now, though, he began to wonder. It wasn't a stress-producing worry that kept him up nights, or even a nervous preoccupation, but more a conscious consideration of the possibilities.

The easy way out would be to keep the consulting job with Warner's. It would last several more years, if he wanted it, but it wasn't a clearly defined position and, moreover, having left as president there was a certain awkwardness in continuing as consultant. He considered public service work. In some ways it seemed a natural, considering his interest in politics, but he knew it would also mean probable relocation to Washington, and a readjustment learning to work with special-interest groups and bureaucracies, both less responsive than the kind of people he was used to in the business world. He could, perhaps, return to business, to the entertainment industry (in something more than his present consulting job), but that might not be easy. When you have been president of one of the biggest film studios in Hollywood you don't exactly scan the want ads for a job.

"Don't worry," a good friend of Frank's, who had been in a similar position, told him. "When you're ready to work again, you won't believe what will come in over the transom."

Frank tried to take his friend's advice to heart and again push his preoccupation out of his mind until the climbs were over. His friend was probably right. Things would come up he couldn't even imagine now. So he might as well take advantage of these few weeks before they were to leave for Antarctica and relax.

Frank didn't have long to enjoy his free time, however. Once again the Antarctica project started to unravel.

For the first two weeks after returning from Russia, everything seemed in place. The DC-3 Tri-Turbo had completed its season flying logistics for the navy in the high Arctic, and was back at its home base in Santa Barbara. Clay Lacy was on board as pilot, Giles Kershaw as co-pilot. While not quite finalized, it seemed the insurance coverage from Lloyds would go through. There was a green light on the Chileans parachuting the crucial refueling cache halfway down the Antarctic Peninsula, at their Rothera base on Adelaide Island. Yuichiro Miura, the Man Who Skied Down Everest, was eager to come and fund half the expedition's $250,000 cost. The other two lead climbers, Chris Bonington and I, were both ready to go.

Now in early October the plans began to come apart. The first problem was Lloyds, which couldn't find all the underwriters required to insure the project.

"It's eighty-five percent in place," Frank told Dick over the phone. "But the owner of the plane says a hundred percent or no go. I don't know what else I can do but keep pressuring Lloyds to contact everybody they can think of."

A few days later Frank called Dick again: "Insurance is looking okay, but now we've got another wrench in the gears. Clay Lacy is having health problems and just dropped out."

Frank knew this had the potential of a death blow, as the plane's owner had said he would allow the aircraft to go only if Lacy were pilot. Frank called the owner to ask if there was any conceivable replacement.

"What about Giles Kershaw? He has more hours in the Antarctic than anybody. Let's make him pilot."

The owner agreed, if a suitable co-pilot could be found. With only ten days before the plane was to depart, they had to find someone qualified who could also, on such short notice, get away for a month and a half. They finally located Sandy Bredin, a United pilot who also operated a charter service to Southern California's primitive Channel Islands and was used to wilderness flying.

Eight days before the plane was to begin the five-day trip from California to Chile Frank again called Dick:

"Unbelievable. One of the engines on the plane just blew. A bearing or some damn thing; the entire engine has to be taken apart. It'll take a week at least to fix."

The plane's owner agreed to rebuild the turboprop as quick as possible, a $90,000 job. They were halfway through the task when Frank called Dick with yet another hurdle.

"Just got a call from Chile. They're having trouble down there finding enough money to keep the country going. The price of copper is so low they may scrap their whole Antarctica program. If that goes, our fuel drop goes, and if the fuel drop goes, we don't go."

Frank decided he should leave for Chile a couple of days early to do what he could to guarantee the fuel drop. The engine rebuild was completed and the aircraft was ready, barring any new problems. Just when things seemed in place, though, the next problem developed.

"We've got some kind of trouble getting clearance to fly over Peru," Frank told Dick. "It's because Giles is British and the Peruvians are still mad about the Falklands war. Apparently they just forced two British Antarctic Survey planes to land and held them under arrest."

Giles Kershaw told Frank not to worry. "We won't let something like this stop us. We're taking off tomorrow regardless, and if by the time we get there we still don't have clearance I'll refuel in Ecuador and fly out to sea around the place."

This solution was typical Kershaw. After eight continuous seasons flying in the Antarctic he was used to operating with no international boundaries, no traffic control towers, no flight clearances. Antarctica was the last true land frontier on earth and Giles Kershaw was in every sense one of its pioneers, a man used to surviving by his wits, not by the strictures of bureaucrats.

Shortly before midnight on November 7, Kershaw, co-pilot Sandy Bredin, engineer Rick Mason, and Beverly Johnson—a well-known climber and adventurer hitching a ride to Patagonia—took off from Van Nuys airport near Los Angeles and shuttled to Palm Springs where they waited for dawn. On a crisp morning under clear skies over the California high desert they took off on a five-day trip that would average 130 miles an hour. Their hopscotching itinerary included stops in Texas and the tiny Caribbean island of San Andres. Then Panama and Guayaquil. There they learned they had gained clearance to fly over Peru, and after a short stop in Lima they made it to Arica, then Antofagasto. In several places they made short layovers to spread their sleeping bags in the fuselage and get a few hours sleep.

Meanwhile Frank caught a Pan Am flight to Santiago to press the generals on the question of the fuel drop. During the last phone call before he left his contact in Chile said the drop was still questionable, but added he was nevertheless optimistic. When Frank arrived his contact, General Lopotegui, met him at the airport.

"Things look good," the General said. "The C-130 should make the airdrop in two or three days."

"We just may pull this thing off yet," Frank said in a weary voice, tired but relieved.

Next day the Tri-Turbo arrived, and by the following day all team members were in Santiago. I flew down with Dick. Bonington, who had arrived the day before from London, met us at the airport. From there we shuttled to a nearby military airport where the Tri-Turbo was parked. We found Frank and Steve Marts at the officer's club, eating lunch on a veranda overlooking a palm-lined swimming pool.

"Here's the plan," Frank said. "The Tri-Turbo leaves for Punta Arenas day after tomorrow. Any of us can go down on it, or catch a commercial flight, your choice. Right now we're organizing climbing gear in the hangar, so we'll finish that and load the plane tomorrow."

Frank introduced us to a Chilean air force officer, Captain Frias, who had been appointed to accompany us on the expedition. As we walked toward the hangar Frank explained that the Chileans were interested in the possibility of chartering the Tri-Turbo in the future for their own Antarctic operations, and as part of the deal to give us a fuel drop they asked we take Captain Frias, who would file a report on the plane's performance.

"What an irony," Sandy Bredin said, "spending three weeks parked in subzero weather at the base of Vinson with some Latin American military air jock named Captain Cold."

In the hangar I met Yuichiro Miura and his cameraman Tae Maeda. Miura was sorting his gear, which was spread around the hangar. He had extremely well-muscled legs and a handsome, sun-weathered face. He looked in his late thirties, perhaps early forties. (I was impressed to learn later he was fifty.) With the austral summer temperature in the mid-eighties, he was bare-chested and wore jogging trunks and, incongruously, large leather climbing boots.

"New boots," he said smiling. "Better to break them in early."

His cameraman filmed while he sorted his gear, adjusted his ski bindings, and packed his rucksack. Miura's plan was still to ski from the top of Vinson, and to complete a one and a half hour show on the adventure for Japanese television. Miura was a modern-day samurai, unflinchingly facing danger on skis; a folk hero so well known in Japan that he had once been besieged in a Tokyo restaurant by a gang of young women who ripped his shirt off and wrote their names with marker pens on his chest.

I sorted my gear, then went to work mounting the traces on our sledges. Before leaving, Frank had put me in charge of food and equipment, but with a hectic schedule I had had little time to take care of it all so now I wanted to double-check to make sure we had everything. A quick survey revealed we were short two ropes, but there was a store in town that sold mountaineering gear.

"How about the first aid kit?" Bonington asked.

"First aid?" I had forgotten all about it.

"The plane has one," Giles said. "Let's see what's in it."

We pulled it from under a seat and opened it: Band-Aids, tape, compresses, and several sacks that looked like bean bags.

"What are those?"

"Says here, 'Chemical Ice Packs.' "

"Hmm, wouldn't want to go to Antarctica without plenty of those."

I spent the next morning shopping for first aid supplies while the others readied the plane. Frank, dressed conservatively in dark suit and tie, waited for a delegation of Chilean air force brass who wanted to inspect the plane, as part of their interest in it for their own Antarctic operations. Several colonels arrived, and while they waited for the commanding general, Frank chatted with them; they all spoke reasonably good English. Steve Marts was standing by to film the scene. The general's car appeared on the tarmac, and when he spotted it Frank yelled over to Marts, "Get ready to shoot the general." Two of the colonels suddenly whipped around, reached for their pistols, and started toward Marts.

"No, no," Frank said, raising his arms to stop the colonels. "I mean *film* the general. You know, shoot film."

With the colonels called off, the inspection was completed, and shortly after midday we took off. It was a clear day, and the snow peaks of the Andes extended north and south like backbone vertebrae of some mesozoic creature. Two hours south we approached the white cone of Osorno volcano, the Fuji of Chile. Kershaw flew directly toward it until the cockpit window filled side to side with crevasses and snow fields; he banked right, corrected, then dipped sharply left under the smoking summit, all the while wearing a mischievous grin. Over Patagonia the prevailing westerlies packed clouds against the peaks, smothering them from our view, and we climbed to 17,000 to insure we were well above the highest of them, Fitzroy. With no cabin pressurization we were all feeling giddy, and our Chilean friend Captain Frias was turning an odd shade of pale blue.

"We've got some oxygen up here for us to sniff," Kershaw yelled aft, "but I'm afraid you mountaineering types will just have to get some preacclimatization."

Captain Cold had the queasy countenance indicative of imminent nausea, when a half hour from Punta Arenas we entered a rare calm. The clouds disappeared, Kershaw brought the plane down to 10,000, and ahead we could see the fabled spires of the Torres de Paine.

"I've flown by here maybe twenty times," Kershaw said, "and never seen it this clear. Let's take a close peek."

With that same mischievous grin Kershaw banked the plane sharply.

We were glued to the windows. We winged by 4,000-foot granite towers orange in the golden light of a low afternoon sun. Cameras clicked like the paparazzi's. Kershaw flew between two spires so that out every window of the plane all we could see was orange granite. The sharp tip of the great Central Tower passed by; our own Chris Bonington had been the first to climb it, twenty years before, and only two parties since had ever done the same.

Kershaw banked sharply again, and we bounced in an updraft.

"Okay, Giles," Frank yelled forward, "we've had our show."

Kershaw looked aft and winked. "One more pass," he said, and the Tri-Turbo banked again while the rest of us gaped as the great sheets of granite sped by.

We corrected and resumed coarse toward Punta Arenas. The sharp peaks gave way to low hills carpeted with dense southern beech. Areas of open range marked the great sheep estancias of Patagonia, and to the west the afternoon sun glistened off deep-fingered fjords. Through the cockpit we could see a stretch of water cutting the land east to west. This was the Straits of Magellan, and on its shore, the city of Punta Arenas.

When Bonington was here twenty years before, Punta Arenas had been a small town, but now an oil boom supported several hotels, a supermarket, a fleet of taxis, and at least one whorehouse. After landing and buttoning down the plane, we took a taxi in and chose one of the modern hotels near downtown.

Our original plan was to overnight here and next day cross the Drake Passage to the Antarctic Peninsula, but now several things developed to cause at least an extra day layover. One of the plane's radios went down, and there was a delay with the C-130 scheduled to airdrop our fuel cache. Even if these things had been in order, a low pressure system now moving across the Drake sealed any chance of immediate departure.

The next day Bonington and I purchased perishables such as butter and cheese, then caught a taxi to the airport where the crew was busy fixing the radio. We loaded the supplies into the open fuselage, adding them to a long pile of gear that we then secured with cargo straps. The inside of the Tri-Turbo was all business. This cargo section took up two thirds of the plane, and the only passenger accommodation was a stateroom aft of the cockpit with four seats on one side and a bolted-down couch on the other that looked like a refugee from a Volunteers of America thrift store. There were hydraulic lines and wires exposed everywhere so that the plane looked like a cross between an auto repair shop and a warehouse. I was reminded of the hotrods I used to build in high school, and I also remembered how often my jalopies used to break down. But an engine konk-out on the Golden State between L.A. and Santa Ana is a little different than one over the Drake between Cape Horn and Antarctica.

Kershaw was in the cockpit at the radio controls while Mason, the engineer, was buried in the instrument rack adjusting the electronics.

"Try it now," Mason said.

"Still nothing."

"We'll get it right," Kershaw said to me. "If not, the Chilean air force here may have a spare. Besides, we're really not losing time anyway, since we can't leave until the weather report from the Peninsula is better."

"Because you need clear skies for the landing?"

"That's part of it. But more important, we don't have any de-icing equipment."

"I thought this plane was made to fly in the Arctic."

"It is. But up there conditions are dry-cold, so icing's not a problem. Actually, it's the same in the Antarctic, but not over the Drake. There it's wet-cold, the worst."

Kershaw must have noticed my furrowed brow.

"But don't worry," he said. "This plane is superb, and it would take a hell of a lot of ice to force it down."

He gave the bulkhead a good whap, and following his hand I noticed a greening I.D. plaque that read: "Douglas DC-3, built March 1942."

Seven years older than me, I thought, and I'm not feeling so hot myself.

Back at the hotel, Frank reported the C-130 was ready to parachute our fuel drums into Rothera. The radio was fixed, and Giles confirmed the weather was improving, so with luck we might get away the following day.

The morning weather report indicated a high center moving across the Drake, so we quickly checked out of the hotel. Crossing the airport tarmac to the plane, we had to lean into the ubiquitous Patagonian wind, but apparently it was no indication of conditions over the Drake; Kershaw told us it was a "go."

"Before we take off, though, I'd better give you instructions on using the life raft," he said. We all gathered aft as he muscled the raft into position.

"It inflates automatically when you pull this cord. It has a canopy, a few survival rations and whatnot, but there is one problem. It only holds eight, and there are eleven of us on the flight. So if we should go down, just remember to stay calm, and follow me out the door."

Kershaw started the engines and we buckled into our seats, such as they were. We taxied into position for takeoff.

"I bet the weather comes in and forces us to land at Marsh, the Chilean base on the northern end of the Peninsula," Frank said. "We probably won't even get to Rothera."

"Damn it, Pancho," Dick said, "there you go again, being pessimistic."

"Something will go wrong, you just watch. This whole thing has been so incredibly complicated, it's just about taken the fun out of it."

Frank spoke quickly, with a curtness that revealed not only exhaustion from all the work he put into this project to get to this moment, but also a tension now that the moment had arrived. Dick leaned back in his seat, staring out the window as the tarmac sped by and we lifted off. Although he didn't indicate it, Dick was nervous too. It was Kershaw's life raft joke that had done it, that had made him fully realize what a dangerous adventure this really was.

Through breaks in clouds we glimpsed the glaciers on the islands of Tierra del Fuego. The clouds thinned and below we spotted the final land's end, Cape Horn. Beyond was open ocean, and even from 10,000 feet we could see the pitched graybeards whitecap under the howl of the Furious Fifties. Kershaw, wearing his pear-shaped aviator sunglasses, took the plane to 15,000 to fly above the building clouds, and once leveled-out turned aft to give us a thumbs-up.

Kershaw was deceptively at ease. I would learn later (in talking to him) that while he had made this flight too many times to be nervous, he was also too smart to be complacent. He had developed his easy-going style because he knew that was the best way to inspire calm in both crew and passengers. He knew the worst thing on a plane is a captain with a furrowed brow nervously shuffling charts, twisting dials, tapping gauges.

"Rick Mason," Kershaw yelled aft. "Would you please turn on the windshield de-icing. It's starting to get a bit frosty."

We watched Mason search under the pilot's seat until he produced one of those small scrapers that are made to clear ice from automobile windows. Then, buttoning his parka and putting on his big fur-lined

Alaskan mittens, Mason opened the window next to Kershaw, and while Kershaw held him by the belt he wormed out into the freezing air and scraped the front windshield clear.

"Thanks Rick," Kershaw said when Mason was back in. "That'll do for now. You can turn off de-icing."

"Sixty-two south," Kershaw yelled aft. "If the weather was clear you would see the end of the Antarctic Peninsula."

A glance out the window, however, revealed only clouds. Worse, I noticed a white coating building on the leading edge of the black wing.

"Don't worry," Rick Mason said. "It'll take several inches before there's danger. Even that won't bring us down."

"What will?"

"If the engines ice up."

"How can you tell when that's going to happen?"

"You can't. It just happens."

Mason smiled, his Camel cigarette hanging loosely from the corner of his mouth. As the plane bucked in the turbulence he braced against a bulkhead while pouring hydraulic fluid into a funnel stuck into an opened line, his head cocked back so his cigarette ash wouldn't fall into the funnel.

"Got a leak somewhere," he said, shrugging his shoulders as the plane lurched violently.

"Taking her to sixteen," Giles bellowed.

The plane climbed into blue sky, and at least for the time being the icing stopped. We were now beyond the point of return: too far from Punta Arenas to go back, committed to Rothera and to the assumption it would be clear enough to land.

"Rothera reports broken clouds," Kershaw said when he made radio contact. "So we should be able to find a hole to get down."

The view below, however, was solid cloud. Kershaw had the aeronautical chart spread on his lap, transferring to it the coordinates from the inertial navigation.

"Mount Frances should be abeam. It's over 10,000 feet, so I was hoping we could see it."

We peered through the windows, straining to discern any glacial ice camouflaged in the white and gray clouds.

"I think I see the edge of a peak," Bonington said. "There."

It was difficult to tell with certainty. Then a small hole opened, and we saw an unmistakable mix of rock and ice. Forty-five minutes later Kershaw nosed the plane through another hole. Flying low over a berg-choked bay, Kershaw lined up on a saddle along a steep icy ridge rising out of the water. It was hard to figure what he was doing. Then we flew through the saddle only a hundred feet off the ice, and suddenly we were over a long bench of smooth snow. It was the Rothera landing zone, a down-sloping stretch of crevasse-free ice marked with fuel drums painted black. In a second we touched down smoothly and taxied toward a group of tents pitched on the edge of the landing zone. That would be the Chileans' camp. Nearby were two Twin Otters painted international orange and marked "British Antarctic Survey." We knew the British base was less than a quarter mile away, and it looked like several of their people, as well as a group of Chileans, were out to greet us.

Mason opened the plane's door, and Frank jumped out onto the Frozen Continent holding his clinched fists skyward as though he had the theme music from *Rocky* playing in his head. Then Dick hopped out.

"Welcome to Antarctica," Frank yelled to Dick as he grabbed him in a tight hug.

"I told you not to worry," Dick said. "We're on a roll, Pancho, and our luck's going to hold all the way to the top of Vinson."

The Chileans and British walked over to say hello.

"Howdy you all. Name's Bass. Dick Bass. Glad to meet you."

The Brits invited us to visit their camp, and loading in a snow cat we made the short drive. Rothera Base consisted of five buildings, including a two-story central structure that housed most of the base's thirty or so summertime inhabitants. After a hearty meal we returned to the airstrip and the Chileans' camp, which was nothing more than a dozen small nylon tents pitched alongside the landing zone. We pitched our own tents nearby, and when we awoke the Chileans were nice enough not only to host us to coffee and breakfast, but also to fire up their French Alouette helicopter and collect the fuel drums that lay scattered in the area where they had descended by parachute from the C-130 drop. Mason oversaw the refueling, using a small gas engine pump to empty each drum. The plane was loaded to capacity, and Kershaw told us the upcoming takeoff, with the plane at maximum weight and the strip coated with wet snow, would probably be the most critical moment during our entire expedition.

But nearly as critical was Kershaw's estimate of weather conditions at Vinson. If we took off and flew to Vinson only to find the mountain socked in—and then have to return to Rothera—there would not be enough fuel to make another attempt. And if we returned to Rothera to find this base also socked in so that we couldn't land, we would be in even bigger trouble as our on-board fuel supply would then be near empty.

The nearest base to Vinson was the American Siple Station, and when we had first arrived Kershaw radioed there and was told the weather was cloudy and uncertain. There was no question but that we wait for better conditions. Now the next morning Siple reported improving but still questionable conditions. Two hours later they reported good weather.

"What say we pack up and get out of here," Kershaw said in his unruffled manner.

His equanimity was impressive, especially considering his responsibility. He had to judge the weather correctly, he had to make a tricky takeoff, a tricky landing. He had to look after the plane once we were at Vinson, too, and make sure it didn't get damaged if a wind storm were to come up. Besides all this, there were other pressures on him as well. Just by agreeing to fly for our expedition he had burned bridges with the Americans as well as the British, since both were so vehemently opposed to private expeditions in the Antarctic. They would probably refuse Kershaw any future employment as a result of his association. But Kershaw didn't care; he was hopeful, anyway, that if the Chileans did indeed want to charter the Tri-Turbo next season for their Antarctic work, he would fly for them. Then, too, he had already worked a deal with the plane's owner to fly it in the Arctic during its summer sojourn there. For Kershaw, that possibility sounded like a dream come true, flying the Arctic during the northern summer and the Antarctic during the southern summer. But all this assumed he got the airplane back in one piece.

"Yes, I do feel a little pressure," Kershaw admitted when I asked him. "If I screw up a decision, or make a bad landing, that would be my last chance. I mean, aside from cracking up the plane and losing my future job, or even getting stranded and starving to death, or simply getting killed, what really worries me is cracking up and then having to get rescued. That would be the worst thing. You know, the ignominy of it."

It's probably accurate to say the rest of us would have gladly chosen ignominy over death, but whatever his motivation we were all glad to have Kershaw behind the plane's controls. I had been curious to learn more of his background, and while in Punta Arenas I had gotten him to tell me some of his personal history, and how he came to spend so much time in the Antarctic.

"I was born on a rubber and tea plantation in southwestern India," he had said. "It was very remote, and my friends were the servant's kids. Our house was on top of a hill, and about a mile away from a thick jungle, and we could wander there all we wanted as long as we were back for dinner. There were no roads, no fences, no signs telling you where you could and couldn't go. Only the stillness of the jungle, and I loved it.

"One day that stillness was broken by a clattering that steadily grew louder until suddenly appeared a helicopter, there to spray the rubber trees. This was really innovative of my father, as no one else had ever tried it. The chopper pilot took me for a ride, and then and there I decided that what I wanted to do was fly.

"The helicopter came back every year, and stayed for two weeks. Our plantation was one of the best run in the region, but despite that I knew things weren't going right. I was born in 1949, two years after partition, and I could sense, in the whispered talk around the house, the coming end. Finally it happened, our plantation was expropriated. I was the fifth generation of our family in India, and still we chose to move to England.

"I hated it in England. Everything seemed gray and lifeless compared to India. But I had an uncle who worked at a flying club, and at fourteen I got my first instruction. Eventually I got my license, then my instructor's rating, and one day I answered an ad to fly for the British Antarctic Survey. I'll never forget that first season on the ice. All of a sudden I was in a place that gave me that same sense of freedom I knew as a kid. In the Antarctic there was no one telling me anything, no control towers, no traffic, no restrictions. It was incredible, like I had found once more that jungle of my childhood."

Kershaw taxied the DC-3 up the gently inclined snow slope to its very end so he would have maximum takeoff distance. We were all silent. He turned the plane, and for a moment it sat poised like a black and yellow wasp looking down the glacier. Then Kershaw pushed forward on the throttles and the turbos screamed. For a hundred yards the plane lumbered in heavy snow, slowly gaining speed. Halfway down the runway the plane still seemed stuck in the wet snow. We bounced heavily. What had Kershaw chosen as the abort mark? The end of the runway was a fifty-foot ice cliff that dropped into the ocean. We bounced again, went airborne, dropped back to the snow. Kershaw pulled back once more, and the old DC-3 gently lifted off.

"Aah-eah-eaahhh," Dick yelled, and Kershaw looked aft with a thumbs-up.

We climbed above King George VI Sound, the smooth sea ice veined with leads and channels. Ahead through the cockpit window we saw a small range of jagged peaks. The weather cleared, and under a cloudless sky we approached the great ice cap of the Antarctic proper. There was flat ice as far as we could see, and we could see several hundred miles.

"Whenever I fly this route," Kershaw told me as I leaned over his shoulder, gazing through the cockpit window, "I think of Lincoln Ellsworth, when he made the first transantarctic flight, more or less over this same terrain. Only then he had no idea what was here. These mountains below, he named them: Faith, Hope, Charity. No one had ever seen them. He had some bad weather, and had to land three times to wait for it to clear. You see, he had no idea what mountains might be in the area. Even if he could have gone to 30,000 feet he wouldn't have been sure there didn't exist some peak higher than Everest. Think about that. I mean really think about it. It was only fifty years ago, and as he flew along he wondered if he would discover a mountain higher than Everest.

"And there they are," Kershaw said, pointing ahead. "Just like he first saw them. The Ellsworth Mountains."

Ahead I could make out the jagged interruption on the horizon, the long line of great peaks rising like islands in a frozen sea. Among them was Vinson.

Kershaw gazed ahead with a placid smile that gave his face a confident composure. He was back in his childhood jungle.

VINSON:
TWO TO GO

"**T**hat must be the summit of Vinson there. That peak in the middle of the massif."

"I think the route goes up the plateau, then follows that right-hand ridge of the actual summit pyramid."

"Looks like a piece of cake."

Kershaw piloted the Tri-Turbo above a col between Vinson and its neighboring peak, Shinn, then banked right while we scrambled to the other side of the plane to view the western escarpment. This vantage was dominated by Mount Tyree—at 16,290 feet the second highest peak in Antarctica. Tyree was only 570 feet shorter than Vinson, at least according to the rough field survey done in the early 1960's, and it was a good thing it wasn't the highest. If Vinson was a moderate slope with few if any technical climbing difficulties, Tyree was something else again, steep and rocky on all sides. Bonington and I had discussed the possibility of attempting to climb it after we knocked off Vinson.

"It's quite impressive, isn't it?" Bonington said with studied understatement. Then, casting aside British reserve he exclaimed, "That West Face has got to be one of the greatest unclimbed faces in the world."

As he lost altitude Kershaw doubled back toward Vinson. Now our attention changed from mountaineering challenges to the more immediate problem of getting the plane down in one piece. We knew the primary factor Kershaw had to consider in choosing a landing was wind. Not just ground wind, but he had to think about the wind the plane would be exposed to while parked. He knew that if he picked a landing too far from the protection of the mountain's lee the aircraft would be exposed to the full force of the fierce Antarctic winds that blow across the icecap. On the other hand, if he parked too close the plane might be buffeted by gusts coming from unpredictable directions. This latter concern was a very real hazard, as Kershaw knew from the experience of friends of his in the British Antarctic Survey. Two years before, this other group had landed a Twin Otter at a field camp and tied the wings to anchors, with the plane's nose facing into the wind. Then they went in the hut for a rest, and while they were asleep the wind suddenly changed direction, hitting the plane broadside. When they came out they found the plane's wings still tied in place to the anchors, but the fuselage twisted upside down.

In addition to wind Kershaw had to consider the sand dune–shaped formations on the flat ice cap called sastrugi. Standing sometimes two or more feet, these wind-tortured formations can trip a plane's skis when it's landing, sending the aircraft's nose augering into the hard snow. The trick is to determine from the air the direction of the prevailing wind and then land with the lay of the sastrugi.

Kershaw eyed a section of the icecap a few miles from the base of the west side of Vinson. He circled his candidate landing zone, banking the plane while Mason opened the fuselage door and tossed a smoke grenade. On the ice the red smoke rose lazily.

"Negligible ground wind," Mason said. He lit another Camel then returned forward, got final instructions from Kershaw, and turned back to us.

"Fasten your seat belts. We're bringing this bucket of bolts down."

Faces that moments before were exuberantly glued to the windows were now intently somber, and I thought once again how the nearest human habitation, the nearest source of support, was 180 miles away across a flat, trackless ice desert. If the plane were to crack up on landing, that would be a helluva long way to ski.

Kershaw made his line-up and came in. Out the window the shadow-lined sastrugi, well defined by the low Antarctic sun, came up to meet us. The plane gently settled, then hit hard. I felt an adrenaline surge as Kershaw applied full throttle and the screaming turbos lifted us up and we went round for another pass.

"Just testing the surface," Kershaw yelled to us above the turbos.

We again made the same line-up. The peaks of the mountain range—Shinn, Epperly, Tyree, Gardner—rose in a great wall filling the plane's windows. We slowly came back down, gently losing altitude, then made contact. We glided smoothly for a few seconds, then came a heavy whump! as we clipped a sastrugi formation. We rose, came down, bounced hard, rose and came down again. Another bounce, and we had full contact. I stayed tensed, ready to tuck into a survival roll in case the skis tripped. We bounced again, then slowed and came to a stop.

"Aah-eah-eaahhh," Dick called.

We all cheered, and Kershaw turned with a wide grin and another thumbs-up.

Mason, with the Camel still hanging from his lips, opened the plane door and the cold air rudely swept in.

"What a place," I said to him. "There's nothing else to compare in the world."

"Maybe," he replied. "But when you've seen one piece of ice, you've seen 'em all."

Steve Marts was down first to film the rest of us jumping out. Frank was next, then Dick, then Bonington.

"Say something about the climb," Marts yelled while the camera continued to roll.

"I bet Vinson's only a mile or two away," Frank said.

"Yes, it seems," Bonington added. "And I think that left-hand route on the whole is probably best. A bit smoother, and of course the other guys went that way on the first ascent, didn't they?"

With binoculars Bonington scrutinized the route. Everything suggested a straightforward climb, a four- or five-day enterprise. Conditions seemed perfect: no clouds, no wind, daylight twenty-four hours.

Dick, however, was thinking otherwise.

Gazing up at Vinson rising 9,000 feet above our plane, he thought, It might be a walk in the park, but it sure as heck looks like a long and cold one to me.

He was about to say something, but then told himself that those of us who were seasoned climbers were so much more experienced he'd better keep his mouth shut.

It was too bad he didn't speak up, as it might have given Bonington and me pause. For in our exuberance we were overlooking a few key considerations. First, we were forgetting that because the air in Antarctica has no water vapor, no dust, no anything, you can see for hundreds of miles, and consequently distances and sizes are very deceptive. Then, too, we were forgetting that even if the slopes on Vinson were moderate, they were still at an altitude of nearly 17,000 feet at a latitude only 700 miles from the South Pole, and that far south, that altitude—because the atmospheric envelope gets thinner toward the poles—is equal to 20,000 feet in the Himalaya. We were forgetting that, in fact, the summit of Vinson is the highest point on earth at such an extreme latitude.

Knowing it would be warmer sleeping in tents than on the metal floor of the plane, we pitched camp next to the aircraft. While we constructed snow block walls as windbreaks around the tents, the plane's crew dug pits under the wings to bury anchors to tie down the plane. It was midnight, with the Antarctic sun approaching its lowest dip as it circled the horizon—but still well above setting—when we finished dinner and crawled in our sleeping bags.

Bonington was awake at 5:00 A.M., and we were still bathed in sunlight.

"We should get going and take advantage of this good weather," he said.

Already I could feel the effect of perpetual daylight, a kind of mild disorientation, like jet lag. I crawled outside to help with the cook stove, which we had set up alongside the tent. I bent over the billy and felt the back of my neck glow in the warmth of sun while at the same time my face stung in the cold of shadow. I melted snow, made hot drinks, then prepared a cereal mush mixed with a quarter pound of butter. A mountaineer's diet in the high Arctic or Antarctic is different than at high altitude such as the Himalaya. There the lack of oxygen makes it difficult for your body to digest animal fats. But here, at comparatively lower elevations but even colder temperatures, you crave the energy provided by something like butter, and in the days ahead it would be a staple in our diet.

Following breakfast it took several hours to make final adjustments to our equipment and then load each of our two sleds with about 250 pounds of gear each. We then harnessed three men already loaded with their own heavy backpacks to each sledge and began the trudge to the base of Vinson. Since the day before when Bonington and I had casually guessed the distance to be a mile or two, Giles had pulled out his chart and, triangulating our position, showed us it was more like five miles. That's when we realized that through the crystalline air distances were deceiving.

Even though it was only a gentle incline, the combination of backpacks and sleds made for tough work.

"This in a small way is what Scott and his men must have gone through," Bonington said.

Whenever the fiberglass sled caught under the sastrugi we had to bear our full weight against the traces to pull it over, and after five hours our stomach and leg muscles were feeling the strain.

At the head of a shallow cirque between Vinson and neighboring Mount Shinn we set up camp. It took several hours to cut blocks from the brick-hard snow for a windbreak, but we judged the task essential: the potential this land held for extreme weather was a constant background threat that influenced our every decision. I had been to Antarctica once before (on an adventure to the Peninsula in 1979) and I remembered a day returning to camp when a storm suddenly blew in, and before we reached our tent the wind strength forced us to belly crawl the remaining distance. We were almost to the tent when we heard a strange noise, like a giant engine running at top speed about to explode. It was a super gust approaching, and when it hit we had to hold on to the shafts of our ice axes while our bodies flapped like flags on the flat surface.

With the windbreak finished we drank hot soup while we studied the features of a snow and ice gully at the back of the cirque. This was the route we would follow in the "morning," and both Bonington and I were surprised to see that up close it looked longer and steeper than we had guessed.

"Still, our view from here is foreshortened, so it probably looks steeper than it really is," Bonington said optimistically.

The sun passed behind the ridge bordering our little cirque, and the temperature instantly dropped to thirty below. After a quick dinner of dehydrated chili mixed with the requisite butter we scrambled to our tents and were in our sleeping bags by midnight. When we woke at 6:00 the cirque was still in shadow and we waited until the sun broke once again into the open before we lazily made breakfast. It was 11:00 by the time we were ready to go.

Our plan was to carry mostly food supplies up the gully, continuing toward the main peak of Vinson until we found a good location for our next camp. There we would cache our loads, go back down and return next day with tents, bags, and stoves to occupy this next camp, which we would call camp 1.

As we left base camp our crampons squeaked in the snow, and in places the flat surface was so hard that even with body weight and full packs, the steel points would only penetrate the wind-hardened snow a quarter inch.

A short distance beyond our tents the slope began to steepen, and soon we were following Bonington's steps as he made a zigzag up the ever-steepening gully. An hour later we could see our tents below like small colored dots decorating the base of the cirque, and I realized if someone were to slip here, and drop their ice axe or otherwise fail to arrest themselves, they probably would be dead by the time they skidded to a halt.

"I must say," Bonington noted, apparently sharing my thought, "this is a bit steep going, isn't it. Perhaps we should take the extra time to rig a belay."

Looking down toward Frank and Dick, I agreed heartily. Although Frank's climbing technique was much improved from when we had been on that similarly exposed slope on Aconcagua eleven months before, I could only too vividly imagine him catching his crampon point on a pant leg.

In fact we were all sharing the same thought because about then Frank yelled up, "Don't you think it's time to put a rope on?"

Instead of taking the time to belay each climber we decided it would be faster if we tied our climbing ropes together and Bonington and I took turns leading the length up and fixing it, so the others could follow with their mechanical jumar ascenders. This technique worked well and by 5:00 we were at the top of the gully. It had taken us six hours.

"I'm beginning to realize this mountain may take a bit more time than we first guessed," Bonington said.

From the top of the gully we surveyed the next stage: a walk across a broad basin, then a climb up a small icefall to gain the col between Vinson and Shinn. We made it across the basin in less than an hour, and on the far side we decided it was time to search out a camp spot.

"It's absolutely essential we find a place to dig a solid bolt hole," Bonington cautioned.

Bolt hole was British for snowcave, meaning a secure shelter we could bolt to in case a windstorm came up that was too strong for our tents. Usually it's no problem building a snowcave; you simply start digging. But here the snow was so hard it was difficult to cut even with snow saws, and we knew the only way to get a cave without hours of labor was to find a hidden crevasse we could modify into a shelter. A little probing in the area soon revealed what we were looking for. We tunneled in from the side, cached our food in it, then headed back to base camp.

The basin was still in full sun as we hiked toward the top of the gully. We were now high enough to see the great ice cap stretching to the horizon. A small peak in the distance rose like a singular island in an expansive sea; this was Welcome Nunatak, and although it looked close we knew from the maps it was forty miles away. Again, the clear air, the deceptive distances. How far away then was the horizon, which seemed far beyond Welcome Nunatak. One hundred fifty miles? Two hundred fifty? We looked at the long horizontal line, so clear there was a fine distinction between the ice and the sky. So clear that staring at it we realized you could actually tell it curved from one end to the other. We guessed this had to be perhaps the only place on earth where you could see this phenomenon. And we realized that if the ancients had been witness to this view they would have known the earth was round.

We paused a moment to absorb the panorama.

"Kind of hits you when you realize the place doesn't belong to anybody," I said.

"The last true wilderness on earth," Frank added.

Even beyond wilderness, it was as close on earth as you can come to being on another planet.

A good adventure needs to combine some risk-taking, some unvisited, untracked, or unexplored territory, and some physical challenge. In Antarctica, we had all three. And we had them to a degree that we couldn't help but compare this to other trips we had been on. Between us, that was quite a range of territory in nearly every corner of every continent on earth. But looking out over this frozen frontier, we all were in agreement those other places paled in comparison, that for all of us—including the globe-trotting Bonington— this was the most unusual and exciting adventure we'd ever had.

"You two have come a long way toward developing your climbing skills," Bonington said to Frank and Dick, "but to be seasoned mountaineers, there remains one thing. You must learn to cook."

Frank moaned. It was the morning after we had returned to base camp, and we were just ready to begin preparing our meal before moving up to occupy camp 1. Bonnington was unaware of Frank's aversion to cooking.

"Now I don't mind cooking," Dick said, "but Pancho here has told me that because we're paying for this, we shouldn't have to cook if we don't feel like it. And if he isn't going to, I'm not going to cook for him. I've been wet-nursing him enough on these climbs."

"Wait a minute," Frank retorted. "I never said any such thing. You know we've decided to be equals with the other climbers whether we're paying for it or not."

"But on McKinley I was going to offer to cook, and you said, 'No, don't tell anyone that or we'll be cookin' from here on.' "

"But I never said I don't have to cook because I'm paying for the trip," Frank insisted.

"Not in those exact words, but that's what you meant."

"But it's the crassness of putting it that way."

"Now that's the trouble with you liberal Democrats," Dick said. "Never call a spade a spade. Listen, I'm happy to cook, but if you don't, well, I'm paying for this odyssey too, and I don't want to feel like a second-class partner."

While this latest episode of the Dick and Frank Show was under way, Steve Marts, shaking his head and smiling, had quietly assembled the stove and started cooking.

We ate our morning mush the morning after we returned to base camp while we swapped stories about past and future adventures. Bonington told us his next trip was back to Everest.

"I'm joining a team of Norwegian friends," he explained, "and this time my goal is to get to the summit myself before I get too old."

"I can sympathize with that," Dick said. "I hope I can get a shot at it before I'm over the hill."

"We'll keep in touch," Bonington replied. "If you can't get on with that Indian team, there might be a way to get you with this Norwegian group."

After breakfast, Kershaw made the announcement he was giving up his ambition to climb Vinson, and would return to the plane.

"Chris and I had a long talk about it, and it's clear to me now my responsibilities lie with the safety of the aircraft. As much as I would love to be with you, and love to climb this mountain, we'd all be in deep shit if a storm came up and something happened to that plane."

As Kershaw disappeared in the distance toward the plane, Bonington said, "One of the things I like best about these trips is meeting new people. I've a feeling Giles and I will become good friends."

Leaving one of our tents at base camp, we loaded our backpacks and set off once more up the gully. Once again Bonington and I fixed the climbing ropes and the others followed. All except for Marts, who, as he often did, was climbing off on his own, at the sides of the gully, to get the best camera angles. He was indefatigable at his task, climbing quickly ahead of everyone, setting up his camera and shooting, then breaking down, packing, and once more scurrying to get ahead, climbing confidently without a rope.

Our two Japanese teammates, Yuichiro Miura and his cameraman Tae Maeda, were also climbing strongly. Miura had perhaps the heaviest pack of anyone, as he was also carrying his downhill ski equipment for his planned descent off the top of Vinson. By now all of us realized how lucky we were to have Miura and Maeda on the trip, for they were both even-tempered, hard-working, and companionable. Fortunately, too, they both spoke good English although Dick was always practicing his traveler's Japanese.

We made better time up the gully, and soon we were across the basin and at the site for camp 1. We pitched tents, then crawled in our snowcave to fetch the food bags cached the previous day. It was 3:00 A.M. in the sunlit Antarctic night when we finally had dinner and brews finished. Before turning in I crawled out to pee, and Bonington called out to ask if I could guess when the sun would break above the ridge crest above camp.

"Looks like a half hour or so."

Then I realized I was miscalculating the direction the sun was moving. It wasn't really rising and setting, but rather making a sideways crab-crawl above the horizon.

"Make that two or three hours. We won't see sun until it moves sideways into that col over there."

"Let's get a few hours sleep, then get up and finish the bolt hole," Bonington said. "There's really no sense going any higher until we see what this sky brings, anyway."

The faultless clear sky had been replaced by a portentous veneer of thin cirrus, and when we awoke at 10:00 the next morning the sun was backlighting a glitter of sprinkling snow, the kind mountaineers call angel's dust. After breakfast we finished the snowcave, and by mid-afternoon conditions were the same.

"I wish it would either storm or clear," Bonington said. "This is frustrating."

"But not so bad," Miura added. "I think maybe okay to climb to next camp."

We considered Miura's suggestion. With the comfort of knowing we had a bombproof snowcave in the neighborhood should a storm move in, we agreed it made sense to risk moving up. At six in the evening we were packed and ready to leave. What a great treat it was to be able to ignore the clock and climb at whatever time of the day we felt like moving.

We were all optimistic that in another twenty or thirty hours we would be on top. Our plan now was to carry everything we would need to make the next camp, and there pitch our tents, sleep a few hours, then continue without packs to the summit. That would put us back down to the plane only six days after arriving, not far off our original estimate. There might even be enough time for Bonington and me to attempt Mount Tyree, or perhaps a climb up nearby Epperly Peak, which we guessed to be the highest unclimbed mountain in Antarctica.

Above camp 1 we negotiated a short icefall, scouting a route between several seracs, some the size of small houses. Above this the slope lay back as we approached the broad, flat col between Shinn and Vinson. The sun inched behind Vinson. As we climbed into shadow a slight breeze blew out of the col, and the combination was suddenly numbing. Stopping to put on another layer of clothing, the cold penetrated my torso and I was anxious to keep moving. We now turned and climbed toward Vinson, following a slope that was only moderately angled but riddled with hidden crevasses. I was leading, and it took vigilance to sniff out the crevasses and steer around them. I was getting colder, and it occurred to me that this temperature— at least thirty below—was cold enough to be dangerous. If I were to pop in a crevasse, and had to jumar out, I might freeze up before I could complete a self-rescue. It was a sobering thought, and I was all the more careful to keep a watchful eye for the telltale depressions in the snow's surface that pinpointed the black chasms.

We climbed back into sunlight, and things cheered up. Soon we arrived at an inviting flat bench just below the edge where the slope dropped away down the steep west side of Vinson.

"Good-looking campsite," I said.

"Except it's bloody exposed if a storm brews up," Bonington countered.

"Well I think everything's going to be just fine," Dick said. "The clouds seem to be clearing."

The worrisome high clouds did seem to be dissipating. By the time we had camp pitched and dinner finished it was 2:00 A.M., and we were all confident we were only hours from success. We awoke at 6:00, and by 9:00 we were off, carrying only extra clothing and a few candy bars. The sky was clear, there was no wind, conditions seemed perfect. We climbed a steepening slope above the tents, and on top we followed the ridgeline that bordered the steep west face so we had a grand view of the ice cap 8,000 feet below. Behind us we could see the other peaks of the Ellsworth Range running in a line like an island archipelago frozen in an otherworldly icescape. Certainly there could be no similar or comparable vista on earth.

"This has to be the most fantastic day of my whole climbing career," Bonington said.

Coming from perhaps the most experienced expedition mountaineer alive, that judgment put the austere beauty of Vinson in perspective.

We now left the ridgeline and traversed into a long, open basin that led to the summit pyramid; ahead we could see a notch on the right side of the pyramid from where it appeared we could follow the ridge to the top. The air was cold, but in direct sun, and with no wind, it was warm enough while climbing so that we wore only two thin layers of clothing under our parka shells. I took the lead from Bonington, careful to take a traversing line that would lead us at an even gait into the col. I was confident we would be on top in two or three hours.

Then I felt the first wind. It was only a breath, but enough to give the cold air a biting sting. It calmed for a moment, then puffed again. This time the puff, like an ominous portent, did not die. I raised the hood on my windsuit.

The wind built quickly, and soon we called a halt in order to pull heavy down parkas from our packs, and cover our exposed faces with masks. The gusts were coming at us through the col, hitting twenty, thirty, then forty miles an hour. We hunched over into the headwind, looking up only to verify our course. One gust hit hard, knocking me off balance, and I guessed that it was getting close to fifty miles an hour. We only had a few hundred more yards to the col, but then what? There we would be exposed to the full force of the wind, and if it were to increase any more, we might be forced back. I glanced around at the others and saw their figures blurred through the spindrift now scudding across the hard snow.

Dick was cursing to himself that he hadn't brought his face mask. With the clear skies and calm air of the morning, he hadn't thought to stick it in his pack when we left camp. Now he was forced to climb holding a mittened hand over his nose and mouth, careful not to direct his breath upward where it would instantly ice his goggles. Frank too was having trouble. He had his face mask, but it wasn't adequate to keep the wind from biting his cheeks and nose. He raised his mitten to hold over his face, and realized there was no feeling in his nose. It was the first time this had ever happened to him, and unsure whether it was any cause for alarm, decided not to say anything.

I was leading, and stopped to fasten the chin snap on my parka hood. I couldn't seem to get the two parts to match, and I motioned Bonington to give me a hand. By the time he had it secured the others had caught up, and for a moment we rested. It was so cold we couldn't sit so we walked in little circles, stomping our feet and swinging our arms to force blood into our numbing fingertips. We looked like a band of parka-clad primitives doing some kind of tribal dance.

Frank lowered his face mask to clean his goggles.

"Let me look at your nose," Bonington yelled above the wind to Frank.

"What's it look like?" Frank asked.

"Completely white. First stage frostbite. You've got to go down immediately."

Frank digested this news. If he went down, and the others continued and made it, that for sure left him without anyone to go with for another attempt. On the other hand, Dick would make it, so at least one of them would be successful. And obviously it wasn't worth losing his nose.

"Okay, I'll go back."

"Someone has to go with you. How about Steve?"

Marts immediately agreed, and Frank realized he had a chance for another attempt.

Then Miura and Maeda said they would go back, too, and accompany Frank on another attempt when the weather improved. It was unclear whether they were making their decision because the weather was bad, or because they were such polite men they wanted to help Frank. We suspected the latter.

"If they're going back, I'm going too," Dick yelled.

"What do you mean?" Bonington asked incredulously.

"I'm in this with Pancho here, and I'd like to get that movie footage of us together on top of this mother. So I'll wait for better weather and we'll go back up together."

Now Frank stepped back in. "What are you talking about? We may not get another chance. We're doing this together, all right, and that's why you've got to go up. So at least one of us will have made it."

"He who fights and runs away," Dick yelled, quoting Falstaff, "lives to fight another day, but he who in the battle is slain, will never rise to fight again."

"Dick, don't be so flippant," Frank yelled.

"Hell's bells," Dick yelled back, "you're the one always saying you have more than one chance on these climbs. I want that picture of us together on this mountain."

"I'm sure as hell not going to pass up the summit for a bloody movie," Bonington yelled.

We were quite a sight, all of us stomping around, swinging our arms, yelling at one another above the wind.

Up to now I hadn't said anything, but suddenly I found myself in a quandary. I agreed with Bonington in that when you're on a climb, and you want more than anything to succeed, you have to take advantage of every opportunity. There was certainly no guarantee if we were to go down now the weather would improve in time to allow us another try. On the other hand, I felt an allegiance to Frank and Dick, who had put their pocketbook, their time, and their dreams into this climb. To increase their chances, I should stay with them.

"I'll go down too," I said.

"Don't be silly," Frank yelled. "You're going with Bonington, and that's it. The rest of us will head back, although I still think Dick's crazy."

No one said anything. Frank spoke with such final authority things seemed settled. So Frank, Dick, and the others turned downwind while Bonington and I lowered our heads and continued toward the summit.

An hour later Bonington and I reached the col and felt the full blast of the wind. Now my goggles were iced so badly that to navigate I was forced to stay on Bonington's heels, following the fuzzy form of his boots making one step, then another as we angled up a steepening slope. To save time we had agreed to unrope; there was an unspoken understanding each man was on his own.

Bonington braced as another gust blasted us. Temperatures were probably thirty below, and the gusts now approached sixty. That made the wind chill, what? One hundred below zero? Whatever it was, it was brutal.

Bonington stopped and turned back to me, "These have to be the worst conditions I've ever climbed in."

I reminded him later that this judgment followed his earlier one —that it was the most fantastic day he had ever climbed in—by about four hours.

Bonington kept a strong pace, though, and soon I found I was having trouble not only with my goggles, but with my strength. What was it? Perhaps residual effects from the typhoid fever I had contracted in Borneo three months earlier? The body shock of going from equator to South Pole?

Bonington pulled ahead. I couldn't keep up. Then he disappeared, but I couldn't see enough through my iced goggles to know where. I took the goggles off, and squinting against the spindrift I saw he was traversing what looked like a picket fence of rocky towers. It was steep on both sides. I decided to go without goggles. I pulled the case for the goggles from my pocket, but it slipped from my mittens and fell on the slope. I reached for it and was about to grab it when a gust plucked it off the slope and hurled it straight up and out of sight.

I grabbed my ice axe and climbed to the first rock tower. I moved slowly but deliberately, placing my boots carefully on the footholds, testing each handhold. It was no good. My head was swimming; I was off-balance. I looked down. It was a several-hundred-foot drop on both sides. I hunkered in the lee of a rock, and tried to think.

I realized in my condition there was a good chance I might make a fatal slip. That settled it. I tried to signal Bonington, but he was once again out of sight. I turned and started back, glancing around after a few dozen yards. Now I could see him, past the rocky traverse, approaching the final slope to the summit. I waved, but he wasn't looking my way. I continued down, and past the col I stopped once more to study the summit block. Where was he? Then I saw him, a lone red dot. He was on the summit, perched on top the highest mountain in Antarctica. I smiled. At least the expedition was now a success.

The others were in the tents asleep when I arrived back at camp 2. Feeling completely exhausted, I dropped my pack next to my tent, and sat on it to take my crampons off.

"Who's there?" It was Dick's voice from inside his tent.

"Me. Rick."

"Well, tell us." He poked his head out the tent door.

"I didn't make it. Too weak and dizzy, and my goggles were iced badly. But Chris pulled it off. I saw him on top. He should be down soon."

I crawled in my sleeping bag, and in an hour heard the telltale squeak of crampons biting hard snow; it's amazing how that sound carries through the snow, especially when you're lying with your ear close to the surface. As Bonington walked into camp we all cheered.

"Fantastic!" Dick said.

"Job well done!" Frank added.

Bonington looked exhausted. We fixed him tea, but there was so much ice in his beard he couldn't get the cup to his mouth, so we had to cut out the chunks with a Swiss Army knife. With the brew in him, he perked up.

"Fabulous view up there, but I was also able to see off toward the Weddell Sea. There are some very sinister-looking clouds moving our way. I think we have no choice but to pack up and get out of here immediately. Down to our bolt hole."

"What about our next attempt?" Frank asked. "We would have to come all the way back."

"I'd rather have you do that than risk getting caught here in a big blow. This camp is exposed, man, and if a fierce wind blew these tents apart, you might not be able to find your way down."

There was silence; then Bonington, a bit reflectively but in dead earnest, added, "This mountaineering is a serious game. Believe me, Frank, I know."

Once more, I recalled that wind storm I had experienced on the Antarctic Peninsula a few years before, and how our heavy-duty tent had started to rip, and how we were able to collapse it and pile ice blocks on top, then escape to the safety of a hut down on the coast and wait for it to blow over. Here, though, we might not be so lucky.

"I think Chris is right," I said. "We shouldn't risk it."

"I don't agree," Frank said, "but I suppose I'll have to defer."

"Well, I'll just go along with our leaders," Dick said. "I'm sure we'll still get our chance."

Frank wasn't so confident. Despite the belief he had come to on Everest that if a climber sticks with it he usually gets more than one shot at a summit, he now sank in a funk believing that after all the months and months of work, after the cost, neither he nor Dick might reach the summit of Vinson, the one achievement that would had added a unique feather to their Seven Summits cap.

Maybe it was a sign of his exhaustion and fatigue that he was unable to lift himself out of his depression. But as we packed up and started downhill Frank was, other than the day Marty died, now at his lowest moment at any time during the Seven Summits expeditions.

By the time we got down to camp 1 it was midnight, and after a quick meal we turned in and didn't wake up until noon the next day. The hurricane winds that Bonington had feared never materialized, but it was still a good feeling to be near the snowcave. The sky was clouded, and it was windy enough up high that it would have been uncomfortable at camp 2. Until things improved, we had to stay put.

After breakfast Frank called a meeting, and right away it was evident that after a good night's sleep he was back to his old positive self:

"I'm sure everyone here would agree," he said, "that for as long as we have food and fuel we keep trying for the summit. Now, Chris, I know after having already summitted you might not be up for another try, but I would like to make it clear that as soon as this weather clears we would more than welcome you coming back up with us."

"To be honest," Bonington replied, "I'm not sure I would have the energy. But I tell you what. We only have about three days' food left here, and if this storm lasts longer than that you'll need more supplies. What if I were to go down, rest a day, and come back up with more food?"

Everyone heartily agreed to the plan, and a few hours later Bonington descended.

"That clears up whatever black thought I might have had about Bonington," Frank said.

"What do you mean?"

"I'm embarrassed to admit it, but yesterday up at camp two when he ordered us to go down, I actually wondered if he was doing it so none of the rest of us got to the summit, so he could have all the glory. Obviously, I couldn't have been more off-base."

Frank realized just how much fatigue and high altitude combined could hamper his ability to judge people and situations, and he remained chagrined he could have held such a dark thought about Bonington.

We spent the rest of the day sitting in the tent, tearing apart our only paperback novel and passing it around in installments. Dick kept himself busy with his poetry and Snowbird blueprints.

Though we had now been on Vinson a week we were still not used to the perpetual daylight, and it remained an odd feeling to go to sleep with light and wake up with light. It was about 10:00 P.M. when we dozed off on the twenty-fourth, and noon on the twenty-fifth when we finally awoke. The weather looked about the same, and we passed the next twelve hours sitting in the tent swapping stories until finally, around midnight, we got drowsy enough once more to go to sleep.

It was nearly noon again the next day when we awoke, and now the clouds were thinning, and up higher it looked like the wind was dying.

"Let's wait awhile and make sure it's a solid spell," Frank said.

"We might as well wait until about three A.M. or so," Dick added. "That way we would be making most of the climb during the highest sun."

Even with the twenty-four-hour daylight we had noticed that during the early morning hours the sun made a detectable dip closer to the horizon, and at the same time it passed behind Vinson so that most of our climbing route fell in shadow. It was noticeably warmer, then, during the "daytime" part of the twenty-four-hour cycle, and consequently we decided to wait for these warmer hours and then try to climb directly from camp 1 to the summit, bypassing camp 2. We felt that if the good weather were short-lived this strategy would be our best hope for success.

We crawled into our sleeping bags, and before falling asleep someone noticed a lone figure down in the basin. That would be Bonington, up with our additional food. We lay back in our bags and soon heard the crunch-crunch of crampons outside the tent.

"Hello Chris," Frank said through the tent wall. "How was the climb up?"

There was no answer but the tent door started to open just as a voice said, "Not bad as long as I didn't look down."

It wasn't Chris's voice! Frank and Dick bolted upright in their bags as Kershaw stuck his ice-encrusted face through the tent door.

"What . . . where's Bonington?" Frank asked incredulously.

"He was too fagged to make it up the gully, so he's waiting in base camp while I'm delivering your groceries."

"You mean you climbed the gully solo?"

"It's really not that bad, you know. Just one foot in front of the other kind of thing."

Frank couldn't believe it. Here was this 130-pound absolute neophyte climber carrying what was easily a fifty-pound load unroped up an icy gully a good 1,500 feet high. It was testimony to Kershaw's natural athletic ability that Bonington had judged him able to do it at all.

"Just the same, I don't think you should go back alone," Frank said.

"What, stay here?"

"Sure. Look, the weather is getting better so why not catch a few hours sleep, then go with us to the summit."

Kershaw beamed. Here was a chance to see his dream through.

Dick and Marts zippered their bags together, and the three jammed in for a cozy nap, with Dick in the middle. We knew Bonington would be waiting for Kershaw at base camp, but we guessed that after a while he would climb up to see what had happened.

We were asleep when Bonington arrived. He agreed it was sensible keeping Kershaw from returning alone down the gully, but he still insisted it was not the best idea for him to go to the summit.

"His first duty is with the safety of the aircraft," Bonington said, making the type of dispassionate analysis that had made him the world's preeminent expedition leader.

"You're probably right," Dick agreed, "but I sure hate to lose half of my sleeping bag warming team."

Then, quoting the "Cremation of Sam McGee," Dick recited, " 'Since I left PlumTree, down in Tennessee, it's the first time I've been warm.' "

As he had before, Kershaw was quick to agree with Bonington's assessment, and following a cup of tea the two returned to the plane.

We used the few hours remaining before our planned departure to catch a little more sleep. We awoke at 3:00 A.M., but now the clouds were scudding over the ridge above camp, indicating wind above. By 6:00 it had eased, and although it was still cloudy we decided to chance it.

We made good time now that we knew the best way to weave around the seracs, the best route to skirt the crevasses. We all felt strong, and climbed at a good pace. But with each step forward, the clouds seemed to close an increment inward, and by the time we reached

the site where before we had set up camp 2 we knew our luck was
out. I was worried we might get into white-out conditions that would
make it difficult to find our way back to our tents. And if that happened, and if the wind were to come up even more . . . again, there
was that omnipresent potential for danger that this frozen, inorganic,
austere place had, like a feeling that some sort of shadowy, undefined
concern was always following at our heels.

"We better throw in the towel," I said.

So we returned once again to camp 1, silently retracing our steps.

The next "morning" Steve Marts opened the tent door. "Well,
Frank," he said, holding the door open so the others could see outside,
"what do you think?"

"I can't tell," Frank said, staying in his sleeping bag while he
propped up on one arm, "whether that's steam from our stove I'm
looking at, or reality."

"I'm afraid it's reality," Marts said, zipping the tent door back up
as he placed another snow chunk in the pot of boiling water positioned
next to the door. Indeed, conditions outside appeared about as soupy
as the steam rising from the pot, and our thermometer indicated 35
below.

"But I'm confident we'll get our break," Frank said. "Remember,
it's springtime down here, with the good weather still to come. We
just have to wait for it."

"I'm glad to see you're thinking positive again, Pancho," Dick
said. "I'm telling you, we'll get it this next time. I've got this thing
where the third time always works the charm. Just like when I got
to the top of the Matterhorn with my kids on the third try. You watch,
it'll be the same here."

As the storm continued for another day and a half we spent the
time sleeping, eating, or sitting in Frank and Dick's tent telling
stories, listening to Dick recite poetry, or singing songs.

We still planned on our next attempt to try to climb directly from
this camp to the summit—over 5,000 feet of vertical—again rea-
soning that if we only had a short window of good weather, this strategy
would be more likely to succeed. But now Miura and Maeda had a
different thought.

"Frank is maybe not strong enough to go all the way at once. Maybe
it would be better if we carry up and make camp two again, rest
there, then go to top."

"But it will take longer," I countered.

"I have an idea," Frank said. "What if Steve and I stay at camp two, and the rest of you go in one push?"

There was wisdom in the proposal. It would maximize our chances if the good weather were only brief, and yet, if the good weather lasted, Frank would have a better shot at the top. I only had one concern.

"The thing is safety," I said. "If the weather comes in, it would be just the two of you up there. You'd have to make certain your decisions were conservative, and not take any unnecessary risk."

"If I take any risk, it'll be calculated," Frank said.

"What do you mean?"

"Well, Bonington said the risk of staying at camp two was the one-in-thirty storm. I've been thinking about that, and Vinson is important enough to me that those numbers seem okay."

I remembered that conversation earlier in the year, with the Everest team at advanced base camp just after the first summit team had returned, when we all had agreed that the heart of mountaineering was the freedom for every man to choose his own odds. That still seemed fair enough, but my concern was the same as it had been then: that Frank be careful enough to make sure he stacked those numbers as much as possible in his favor. It wasn't enough to rely only on luck, though admittedly that played a part. I had noticed Frank still had around his neck the sacred red string from the lama at Tengboche that the Sherpas had given him during the blessing ceremony at Everest base camp before going into the Icefall.

We agreed to the plan, then a short time later Miura and Maeda were back in the big tent saying they had decided they would go with Frank and Steve, and also stay over in camp 2. Just as they had opted to turn back with Frank on the first summit attempt, we suspected their motivations this time were based on their wish to help Frank get to the top.

So it would be just Dick and me on the first attempt. We left the tent, Miura and Maeda returning to their shelter, me to the small tent I had been sharing with Bonington. I fell asleep to the sound of spindrift spattering the tent. When I awoke I checked my watch: a ten-hour sleep. I recalled my dream, and thought how for me the expedition had just turned a corner, as my dreams had changed from sex to food. One thing about mountaineering, it does order your priorities.

I also noticed my tent had nearly collapsed. I zipped open the entrance, and instead of sky and mountain all I saw was an amorphous gray wall. I was buried in snow, with no shovel to dig out.

"Anybody awake? Can you hear me?"

In a moment Frank was over digging me out. When finally I could peer out I saw the weather wasn't nearly as bad as my burial suggested; in fact the clouds were thinning and the wind had died. After "breakfast" (it was 1:00 in the afternoon) we made the decision. Dick and I would leave in a couple of hours, carrying some of Frank's gear to camp 2 en route on our summit effort. The others would wait a few more hours after we left in the hopes that Bonington would arrive with another load of food. We were now so short there was only enough for two meals, and we knew that even with more provisions up here our food supply back at the plane was so low that this was most likely our final chance.

It was 4:00 in the afternoon when Dick and I got away. We realized that for the last half of our climb we would be in the coldest part of the twenty-four-hour cycle, but since this calm weather could be brief, we had to take advantage of it while it lasted.

For the first several hours we were in sun and quite comfortable. We made good time back to the site of camp 2, and stopped to unload Frank's gear. Then the sun moved in its sidewise crawl behind Vinson and we entered shadow. There was no wind, but for some reason it was far colder than anything we had yet experienced. We didn't have a thermometer with us, but certainly it was 40 below and probably colder. We climbed slowly but very steadily. At one point, after we had been moving for six hours without stop, Dick motioned he wanted to rest. He pulled his water bottle from his pack, and even though he had it encased in an insulated cover it was frozen solid. My candy bar was frozen too, and biting on it was like chomping down on a bar of steel.

We had stopped for perhaps a minute when I realized we were quickly losing body heat.

"My toes are starting to go on me," Dick said, "and my fingers, too. Lord, but it's a cold mother."

We were doing a little war dance, walking in circles stamping our feet and swinging our arms.

Then Dick got poetic:

" 'Talk of your cold/through the parka's fold/it stabbed like a driven nail.' "

"Dan McGrew?"

"No, Sam McGee. You know, I always enjoyed *reading* it, but *living* it is something else."

"I think I'm getting more worn out from this rest than from climbing," I said. "Let's get moving."

As we continued upward, we stomped our feet with each step to force blood to our toes. We had constantly to switch our ice axes from hand to hand as the steel conducted cold through our double-layer mittens. My goggles were beginning to ice again, and I made the mistake of pushing them up on my forehead. When I brought them down again they had cooled so quickly away from the heat of my face that the plastic lens had buckled and they were now useless. As we were still in shadow, and there was no wind, I decided to go without them, although that meant with no covering I had to be careful to keep my face mask hitched over my nose. Without protection, it would have frozen in minutes.

I had an idea that we could avoid the technical rock "picket fence" section where I had turned around on my attempt with Bonington by traversing further around the backside of the summit pyramid, then climbing up. Doing this, we also climbed into a very welcome stretch of sunlight. It was still brutally cold, but our progress was steady and soon we were climbing a steepening slope that led to the ridge just below the final summit rise. Dick was behind me, following my footsteps. We were unroped, as there was no way in this cold to stop and make the belays that would have justified using a rope.

Although he didn't say anything, Dick grew apprehensive; a slip here could be big trouble. Even if you only sprained an ankle, in these temperatures you could die before anyone could get back to help.

Dick said to himself, Remember what Marian told you, "Never let your guard down, remember how much you have to come home to, I love you." So place your footsteps carefully, keep in balance, don't make any foolish mistakes.

Dick was incredible. With only a couple of years of any real climbing experience, here he was scaling unroped a steep slope in the heart of Antarctica. It was almost midnight; we had been climbing with only two brief stops for nearly eight hours. And at fifty-three, Dick showed no sign of fatigue.

We made it up the steep slope, then across the short ridge connecting the final summit rise. Dick was about forty feet behind me.

Ahead I could see the top of a ski pole sticking above the slope. It was maybe thirty feet away. I knew that the previous party who had climbed the mountain (a German, a Russian, and an American from a scientific party who made the second ascent in 1979) had left a ski pole buried on the top, but I was surprised to see it still there. I made the last few steps to the ridge crest: there was the summit, an easy ten steps away. Dick was a few feet below me, still unable to see the pole.

"Dick, you've got maybe thirty feet before you're standing on the highest point on the coldest continent."

"Rick, are you pulling my leg?"

"No, Dick, we've got it!"

Dick crested the ridge, and arm-in-arm we marched the last steps to the top. Then we bear-hugged. It was a good, solid, long-lasting hug, and I wasn't sure whether it was for joy or because we were freezing to death. I decided it must be joy because I had tears in my eyes. That presented a new problem when the tears quickly froze and glued my eyelashes together.

" 'When our eyes we'd close/then the lashes froze/'til sometimes we couldn't see.' "

"Dan McGrew?" I asked.

"Still Sam McGee."

The sky was faultless, there was no wind, and we commanded a view down the backbone of the Ellsworth Range, across the ice cap that stretched like a great frozen plain uninterrupted for the 700 miles between us and the South Pole.

"Let me take your picture," I said.

Dick posed on top with a Snowbird banner while I tried to take the shot. My eyelashes were so frozen that I had trouble seeing through the camera, so I had to yank a few out before I could get the shot. Then I ran out of film. I pulled out one of those small black film containers but the plastic was steel-hard and the cap wouldn't come off. I set it on a rock and beat it open with my ice axe.

With the camera reloaded I gave it to Dick to get a picture of me. He removed his bulky mittens and exposed his bare hands; by mistake he had opted to start out without glove liners and it soon became too cold to try to get them out of his pack. It was another mistake when he grabbed my camera, for instantly his skin stuck to the metal and we had to carefully peel his hand away to keep from leaving some of it behind.

"Where the careless feel/of a bit of steel/burns like a red hot spit."

"Sam McGee?" I asked.

"No, Blasphemous Bill."

Below, the huge Nimitz Glacier inched implacably over an underlying shelf that split the deep ice cover into hundreds of parallel crevasses. We gazed over the expanse, and again we had the impression of the ice cap as frozen ocean, the mountains as otherworldly islands, and we as voyagers in an alien icescape.

"What's that peak down the range there?" Dick asked. "That big one."

"Must be Tyree," I answered.

"Gosh, it looks higher than this one."

I gazed downrange and could see that while Tyree wasn't necessarily higher than Vinson, it did certainly appear to be at least as high.

"I don't know," I said. "The survey of these peaks was done a while back, and the National Science Foundation does admit it wasn't too accurate."

"Can you imagine," Dick said, "all the way down here, and we climb the wrong mountain."

"Naw, this has got to be the highest peak," I said.

We stared downrange for a few more minutes, trying to convince ourselves. Then I noticed we were both starting to shiver uncontrollably.

"Time to get the hell out of here," I said.

Dick agreed. So it was, in the best tradition of mountaineering, having worked our asses off to get there, we were more than happy when it was time, as Dick put it, "to put this mother behind us."

Meanwhile Frank and the others had waited a few hours in camp 1, but with no sign of Bonington they went ahead and packed what food they had and started for camp 2. Frank made very good time, no doubt in part because Miura, despite the extra weight of his downhill skis on his pack, had insisted on taking part of Frank's load, as we had helped with the rest. If we considered Dick Bass a physical dynamo, then this self-effacing, handsome Japanese ski hero at age fifty was a superman, and Frank said he'd never forget his generosity. In fact, in months ahead Frank would constantly refer to Miura as having the single greatest character of any person he had ever met.

At the camp 2 site they erected their tents and crawled in their bags to wait for us. Frank was just waking up when he heard a faint squeak-squeak of approaching crampons.

"We'll know in just a second if they made it," Frank said to Marts.

A few seconds later they heard it:

"Aah-eah-eaahhh!"

"They got it," Frank said, his whisker-stubbled, frostbitten face breaking into a wide grin. "Goddamn, they got it."

Frank was out of his tent to give Dick a big hug. Dick and I were by then very tired, having climbed for twelve hours straight, and we wasted no time playing musical sleeping bags, switching places with Marts and Frank as they dressed and then left, with Miura and Maeda, for their attempt. The weather appeared to be holding, and even better it was 5:00 in the morning, which meant they would be climbing in direct sunlight for most of the day.

It took nearly eight hours to reach the steep slope below the final summit rise, and by then Frank was exhausted to the point of losing motivation. He vomited twice, just minutes apart.

He thought, Please, Steve, tell me I'm going too slow, that I'm too sick. Tell me I've got to turn back.

Marts judged it would be a good idea to rope up for this next section. Still in direct sun, the temperature was now only about 20 below zero, warm enough to make it easier to accommodate the delay caused by rope handling. They divided into two rope teams—Marts with Frank, Miura with Maeda. They scaled the steep slope at an agonizingly slow pace, and Marts knew, having memorized the geography of the peak from a distance, that from there they only had a few hundred more feet to reach the top. But Frank was unaware of this. He was sure it would be another one of those mountains where you had to climb one rise after another to get to the true summit. He was also sure, if that were the case, he wouldn't be able to make it.

Marts figured the exposed climbing was now behind them so he had Frank untie from the rope and leave it at the top of the steep slope. What Marts didn't know was that Frank was now pushing himself to his limit, that he felt like a drunkard in a world divorced from reality. Marts pulled ahead until the distance between the two men was 300 feet; Miura and Maeda were another 300 or so feet behind Frank. Ahead Frank saw Marts reach a ridge crest with nothing behind it but blue sky.

"Where's the top?" Frank called.

"Over there." Then Marts disappeared. Frank was certain that by "over there" he had meant, "Over several more humps."

Frank told himself, I can't make it much further.

Then he threw up again.

He recovered and convinced himself he could make it to the ridge crest, anyway. It was now only thirty steps higher. He started counting them . . . four, five, six. He made ten feet, then twenty. He made another step and was just a foot short of the crest when suddenly his foot skidded from under him. He shifted weight and like a shot the other foot popped out.

My God, I'm starting to fall.

In an instant he began picking up speed. He fumbled for his ice axe, trying to remember how to stop himself. Fifty feet, seventy-five feet . . . he was going faster, faster . . . one hundred feet down . . . the slope steepened below, then it seemed to drop off, down toward the basin to only God knew where.

Get the ice axe, get the ice axe, where is it? Where's that damn thing . . . ?

It was gone, out of his hands. He had dropped it.

There, below him, some rocks were sticking out.

The slope started to lay back. Frank slowed, then grabbed for a rock. It popped from his hands. He grabbed another. It started to pull through his mittens—then it held. He stopped.

Panting, he looked up. He had gone maybe 200 feet. He could see Marts' face peering down from the ridge crest.

"What happened?" Marts called.

"Never mind what happened, did you get it on film?"

Marts had missed seeing it, much less filming it, and disappointed he again didn't have his high-action footage, Frank steeled himself to the task he knew he had to face, and slowly started climbing back toward Marts, picking up his ice axe on the way.

Once again he wondered how far he could get.

He thought, I dare not slip again because this is the last bit of energy I've got.

He threw up again.

He recovered, and thought, And if the summit is still a distance away—I'll never make it.

He had three more steps to reach Marts and the top of the ridge crest when he looked over and saw the tip of the ski pole sticking up.

"What's that?"

"The top."

"You mean I'm going to make it?"

Suddenly the fatigue left his body and he quickly made the last steps to the ski pole. Then, with one leg forward on the summit he pounded his ice axe into the slope once, twice, three times, venting all the frustration, the anxiety, the physical pain it had taken to get where he was. Then he held his ice axe outward in the snow, like a sword planted at a rakish angle away from him, so he looked like Washington crossing the Delaware.

He gazed across the white panorama, feeling different than he had on the tops of the other peaks he had achieved. This one was really special, truly unique. He thought how his team was only the third that had ever stood in this rarefied place, and the first to have done so completely with private financing and organization, without military equipment and support personnel.

That last point made Frank feel better than anything. He knew the main reason they had achieved success was because of his effort. If there was a flesh and blood example of how his modus operandi of tenacity and unrelenting hard work could pay off, then standing there on the highest real estate in Antarctica was it.

Frank knew that if you considered the whole project, climbing Vinson was in many ways every bit the achievement of getting to the top of Everest. They had missed the Big E, all right, but by God they had pulled off Antarctica. It might have taken fifteen days—over twice as long as they had anticipated—but they had hung in there and got it. And with Kosciusko in Australia a sure bet, what the hell, six out of seven wasn't too bad in anybody's book.

Especially for somebody who two years before hadn't even been able to hike to the top of Mauna Loa in Hawaii without falling and bloodying his nose.

Dick Bass had often called Yuichiro Miura a modern-day samurai. "Those old samurai used to train themselves to the highest proficiency with weapons, and develop their courage to the ultimate degree. Miura's doing the same thing on skis, facing extreme danger, even death, unflinchingly."

We had all seen Miura's movie *The Man Who Skied Down Everest*, where he showed that skill and bravery skiing down the Lhotse Face with a parachute to brake his descent. Even with the chute, he had hit speeds close to one hundred miles an hour, and when he finally lost control he rolled, tumbled, and slid for several hundred yards before coming to a stop just above the bergshrund at the bottom of the face. Going into that crevasse definitely would have killed him.

That was in 1970, and since then Miura had been working on skiing down the flanks of the other highest peaks on each continent, and now that he was positioned to knock off Vinson, he would have only Elbrus and Aconcagua left on his list. (He still wouldn't be the first to *climb* the Seven Summits, however, as he had never actually gone to the summit of Everest.)

The slope immediately below the summit of Vinson was mostly rock, so Miura downclimbed it before putting on his skis. With both Marts and Maeda filming, he then skied the several miles back to camp 2 over the ice-hard snow.

Dick and I were out to greet Miura as he skied into camp 2. It took a couple more hours for Frank and the others to get down. Frank was slowed because his glacier glasses had fogged so badly he had to take them off. Worried about snow blindness, he had then descended the rest of the way to camp by opening his eyes, memorizing the terrain right in front of him, closing them again and making six steps, then doing the same thing over.

With everyone in camp we again played musical sleeping bags because Frank wanted to rest a few hours before continuing nonstop down to the plane. Dick and I told them we would see them below, and left. After a short sleep, they got up, prepared a meal, and then again Miura stepped into his skis.

Frank, accustomed as he was to the movie business, figured Miura's plan was to ski only part of the terrain between them and camp 1. After all, this section contained the crevassed icefall with its towering seracs. Frank guessed Miura, like a trueblood filmmaker, would find a few photogenic positions and ski them several times to get all his angles. But he was wrong.

"Miura skied from the tents at camp two to the doorstep at camp one," Frank later told us. "Jumping crevasses, weaving around the seracs, leaping off blocks. It was the most incredible skiing I've ever seen."

Just as important for Miura, the good weather held and Maeda and Marts got the entire performance on film. Now we were a complete success. All the climbing team had reached the summit, and we had the film in the can.

Bonington was up at camp 1 to help us freight everything down, and the plane's crew was out to help us pull the sleds the final distance from our base camp to the aircraft.

As soon as we arrived Kershaw said, "I'm in touch with Rothera (where we had to go to refuel), and they report building clouds. I've also talked to Siple, and we have an invite to stop there. Now I'd like to get the hell out here if there's a storm brewing because I'm still apprehensive about gusting winds coming off these slopes. So I suggest flying to Siple, getting an update from Rothera, then continuing if things look right."

Siple was that American station a little less than 200 miles from us, and Frank and Dick were also anxious to get messages out that we were down and safe. We were a week overdue, and Frank knew Luanne—who by original plan was in Australia waiting to meet them for the Kosciusko climb—would no doubt be pacing the floor.

"So let's get out of here right now," Kershaw said, "while the weather's right."

We loaded our gear, closed the fuselage door, then crossed our fingers. Would the turboprops kick over? Kershaw flicked switches, and the low rpm whine started. Number one kicked in, then two and three. Now, as long as we didn't catch the ski tips on the sastrugi . . .

With the engines warmed, Kershaw throttled the turbos to near full power to break the skis out of their settled positions. Then he spun the plane, and we started to gain speed. We bounced once, then delicately lifted off. Out the window we watched the shadow of the plane grow smaller on the sculpted snow.

Kershaw made a wide bank left and then we gathered on the starboard windows as he dipped the wing in a farewell salute to Vinson. With the radio headset over his ears, he turned aft and yelled, "I've got Siple on now. They say they've got the beer iced down."

KOSCIUSKO:
A WALK IN
THE PARK

Luanne Wells sat in her room
on the twenty-sixth floor of Sydney's exclusive Regency Hotel. It was
one of the best rooms, overlooking the scenic harbor, on what was
called the "butler's floor," meaning there was a butler stationed at
the door of every room; all she had to do was push a button and a
well-groomed strapping Australian appeared and said, "Ma'am, what
can I do for you?"

But she wasn't enjoying it. This was her eighth day in Australia
waiting for Frank and Dick. They were a week overdue. She had no
idea where they were—on the mountain, back at base camp, en route
home. Or somewhere between, crashed in that airplane? She tried to
push the thought from her mind.

She stared at the phone. When would the call come? She had been
afraid to leave her room for more than an hour at any one time in
fear of missing it. She had a friend with her, Betty Borman (Marian
Bass had been unable to come), and they had done a couple of things
the last week—an afternoon at the horse races, a cricket match—
but each time Luanne had left word at the desk how to reach her,
and each time she had called back for messages.

The phone rang.

She stepped toward it, reached for it, hesitated, then picked it up.

269

"Hello, Mom?"

"Kevin, is that you?"

It was her eldest son. Why would he be calling? Had he heard something? Was anything wrong . . .

"Have you heard from Dad?"

"Yeah. I just got a call from some ham radio operator in the Midwest. He said he had made contact with an American base in Antarctica called Siple Station, and that Dad, Dick, and the others are caught there in a storm and can't fly out. They're all okay, but they don't know when they'll be able to leave."

The news was good and bad. At least they were off the peak safely, but now they still had to fly in that god-awful airplane over a thousand miles to get out of Antarctica. For Luanne, that held as many potential hazards as the climb. She had been on board the plane once, at Van Nuys airport a few hours before Kershaw and the crew had left. She remembered climbing up the rickety aluminum ladder through the side fuselage door, past the gear strapped in piles, to the "stateroom" with its thrift-store couch, to the cockpit with its exposed wires and lines. For Luanne, with nothing to compare but commercial carriers, the DC-3 had to her looked held together with tape and baling wire, and left her quite literally sick to her stomach.

Now she spent the next few days thinking about that plane flying over some white wasteland she could hardly imagine. She received another message from Frank (again passed on by a ham radio patch) that the storm was not letting up. Four days passed, five, then six. There was nothing to do but wait, and stare at the telephone.

It had taken an hour and a half to fly from Vinson to Siple. Once we left the Ellsworth Mountains all we could see ahead was the flat and trackless ice cap. Siple appeared suddenly: an emergency Jamesway hut, three tall antennas, and a flag pole with the stars and stripes coloring the otherwise featureless landscape. Everything else, the living quarters and the research stations, was under ice, housed in a long single story building inside an under-ice cavern thirty feet high. The twenty-nine men and women who manned the base were out to greet us, and that evening we were treated to "Independence Cocktails" made with ice from the strata of a core sampling that the scientists on base said was laid down in the snowfall of 1776. Drinks were followed by a memorable steak and baked potato dinner with fresh salad and watermelon flown from New Zealand.

We had hoped to leave shortly after dinner, but Giles radioed Rothera and they reported the weather conditions seemed to be worsening. "It's a bit risky going there in anything but perfect conditions," Giles explained, "as we'll have no extra fuel to go elsewhere if we can't land."

A few hours later we exited topside to check on the plane and saw the storm had moved in on us. The plane had half-disappeared above the wind-driven spindrift that obscured the ice cap like a streaking ground fog. In the sky the scudding clouds had reduced visibility to a few hundred feet. It was obvious we had no choice but to wait.

And we waited—four days. We marked time watching movies on the base's VCR. And we ate. Each of us had lost ten to twenty pounds on the climb, and we couldn't seem to eat enough. Each meal we swept the buffet table like vacuum cleaners sucking up every crumb. Then in the early morning hours, between classics like *Bridge on the River Kwai* and *Deliverance*, we raided the refrigerator. Even Frank learned how to heat leftovers in the microwave.

"Bass, can you believe this? Me in a kitchen, cooking."

"Cooking! Heck, Pancho, all you're doing is pushing buttons."

The base personnel at Siple had seemed as happy as we were when Rothera radioed improving weather conditions. We spent an hour digging the DC-3's skis from the drifted snow, then took off with the entire base waving us good-bye, like townfolks in some Western.

Much of the route toward Rothera was still clouded, although on occasion we would see through a breach in the cover the edge of a peak or a piece of coastline, and Kershaw would identify the landmarks from memory, saying things like, "There's the Ronne Entrance to the Bach Ice Shelf on the south side of Alexander Island."

Then it clouded in completely.

"Rothera reports building clouds," Kershaw reported. "They say visibility is now too low to land."

"My God, what are we going to do?" Frank said, voicing for all our immediate reaction.

"Oh, not to worry. I have contingencies for this sort of thing. You know, alternative landing spots."

Arriving over Rothera our fears materialized when all we could see was solid cloud over the landing zone.

"There's another crevasse-free area on the other side of the island," Kershaw said. "When it's cloudy here it's almost always clear there. So don't worry, we'll fly over there and land, then when they tell us by radio it's clear, we'll come back."

Kershaw changed course while the rest of us kept vigil out the plane's windows. The clouds remained unbroken.

"How much further to this other place?" Frank yelled forward to Kershaw.

"We're over it."

"But it's socked in!"

"Yes, I can see that."

"Well what are you going to do?"

"Fly around until I find someplace clear."

We knew that was a tall order. We also knew there were jagged peaks on all sides—we could see many of their summits sticking above the clouds. And we knew there was less than an hour's fuel remaining.

"There's one more place I know of not far from here," Kershaw said. "I flew over it several years ago, and filed it away as a possibility for some circumstance like this."

Kershaw spotted a hole in the clouds and we dipped below the cloud layer, flying about a hundred feet above ice-free water. We skirted a long calving ice cliff edging the sea, then passed a spit of land that was home to several hundred penguins that waddled around hurriedly as we buzzed over. The clouds above started to break, and in a moment we were in a small clearing.

"I hope and pray Kershaw's spot is up there where it's clear," Frank said.

A moment later Kershaw turned aft and yelled, "There's the landing. It's good and clear."

"Thank God," Frank said.

In a few minutes we were safely landed on the crevasse-free glacier.

"Now we simply wait for Rothera to open," Kershaw said with British nonchalance.

Six hours later it did. Kershaw fired up the turbos and in a few minutes we were at Rothera and welcomed by the several dozen British and Chileans. It took a few hours to refuel the plane, and when we received a favorable weather report for the Drake Passage, we climbed aboard and bid farewell to the frozen continent.

It was a six-hour flight back to Punta Arenas. The rest of the Antarctic Peninsula was clouded, so for the second time we missed the spectacular view of the sharp ice-encrusted mountains that rise from the ocean the length of the peninsula. But it was clear over the Drake, and we were spared the threat of icing that had added such an element of anxiety and excitement on our trip over.

"I guess we've earned an easy one," Dick said. "I'm looking forward to Punta Arenas and soaking in a big bathtub of hot water."

"Yeah, and I'm anxious to get to a phone," Frank added. "I know Luanne must be worried sick."

In her Sydney hotel room, the phone finally rang.

"We're in Punta Arenas, at the tip of Chile, darling," Frank said, his voice raised to make the long-distance connection. "Tomorrow we catch a flight back to Santiago, and then in the quickest way we can, we're going to Sydney. See you in two days or so."

That night, for the first time in over a year, Luanne went to bed without feeling the emptiness next to her, without considering if possibly that emptiness was something she was going to have to get used to for the rest of her life. It was the first night in over a year she slept all the way through without waking and wondering.

In Santiago, Frank and Dick hoped to catch a flight to Easter Island and on to Tahiti, where they could connect to Sydney, but the once-a-week Lan Chile flight had just left so their best alternative was to return to Los Angeles, then connect to Sydney. In three days they went from Antarctica to Patagonia to Los Angeles to Australia, and it was a very jet-lagged pair of mountaineers that Luanne picked up at the Sydney airport.

Jet-lagged, perhaps, but phlegmatic, never. Frank was like a little kid telling Luanne his Antarctic adventures.

". . . and then we took off from Vinson and got to Siple, and you wouldn't believe how the people there live under the ice. But they did have a cassette machine for movies, and even better a kitchen stocked with goodies. You would have been proud of me, darling, cooking my own meals. Well, not really cooking them, but they had this microwave thing that was incredible. Just push a button and presto! Darling, we've got to get one."

"Frank, we've had one for twelve years."

Luanne could hardly believe how haggard Frank looked. His frostbitten nose was now covered with a black scab in places cracked and bleeding. On the one hand she had a hard time looking at him, but on the other had never been so glad to see him.

She had originally planned a big party in Australia. Dick's earlier idea to end the film with a tuxedo and champagne banquet on top of Kosciusko had evaporated when they failed to get to the summit of Everest (we'll have it at Snowbird instead, Dick had said, after I make Everest on the next expedition), but Luanne still wanted to celebrate with champagne on top of Kosciusko followed by a gala dinner at a nearby inn. She had bought a case of the best champagne she could find, and made the dinner reservations. The Emmetts had flown down, and Morgan and Jennings were going to come in from Indonesia. With the delay, however, everything was cancelled.

"But we still have the champagne," Luanne said. "And Betty and I are taking a bottle to the top to help you guys celebrate."

They took a ski lift from a parking area near the base of Kosciusko to the beginning of the trail. There were already several dozen tourists in front of them, out for a weekend walk to the top of the mountain.

"Maybe we should hike up off to the side," Marts suggested. "Over by those boulders. We could do some rock scrambling that way. Look a lot better on film."

Frank and Dick started to argue the merits of Marts' suggestion.

"I think the trail will look just fine," Dick said in a pleading and frustrated voice. "It'll be terrific humor, the juxtaposition of the incongruous—all these months of misery and privation living and climbing on rock, snow, and ice, and here we end it like a stroll in the park."

"Too boring," Frank said. "Marts is right, we need more action."

"Wells, I swear, you might be a Hollywood hotshot and all that, but you don't have any sensitivity for the nuances of this moviemaking stuff. Now close your eyes and let me tell you what it will look like . . ."

Meanwhile Marts had started hiking up his proposed alternate route.

"Marts, get back here," Dick yelled.

But Marts kept going.

"Guess we have no choice," Frank said with a sly grin.

"See you mountain climbers on top," Luanne said as she started up the tourist trail.

Dick reluctantly followed Frank, who followed Marts. An hour later Marts stopped to film a scene of Frank and Dick scrambling up some big boulders. Dick was in the lead, trying to get up a ten-foot rock, scraping his boot as he searched for a toehold. Frank reached up and gave him a boost.

"Damnit, Wells, Marts has got the camera going. What are you trying to do, make me look like I can't get up this on my own?"

"I'm just trying to help you."

"Well, I don't need it. Besides, we're supposed to look proficient. I mean, otherwise how are we going to be folk heroes?"

It had started as such a beautiful day they wore only T-shirts, and Frank was in shorts, but now a cold south wind started to fill and

Dick took off his pack and pulled out his parka. Frank stood by with goose bumps growing on his bare arms and legs. He had no pack at all, and of course no extra clothing.

"Dick, you wouldn't happen to have an extra windbreaker or anything?"

"Wellsie, seven climbs later and you're still not able to take care of yourself. What are you going to do when you don't have me anymore?"

"Fortunately I have another indulging roommate to take over—my wife."

Dick handed Frank an extra wind suit he had thought might be needed under just such a circumstance. They continued up the boulder-studded slope. The country was open and barren save for a tough tussock grass sprouting between boulders. Below them the treeless brown and green Kosciusko Plateau, reminiscent of the Scottish Highlands, spread to the horizon. To their right they could see the wide trail with a long line of tourists on their weekend stroll. Frank and Dick estimated they had about a half hour to the top.

"Dick, did you bring any sunscreen?"

Despite the chilly breeze, the sky was still clear and Frank was concerned about sunburn.

"Frank, I just don't understand you. Why can't you remember to bring your own stuff?"

"You let me borrow your toothbrush in Punta Arenas, so what's wrong with letting me borrow your sunscreen on Kosciusko?"

"What's wrong is, one, it's a pain in the rear for me having you think you can borrow all the time, and two, it's making you *weak*, Frank. The worst thing in the world you can do is weaken your fellow man by waiting on him all the time. You have that bleeding-heart, social-welfare attitude of yours that makes you feel justified in leaning on your fellow man unconscionably—"

"Dick," Frank interrupted, "let's not get off on that one again. All I want is some sunscreen," Frank said impishly.

"Well, here it is. Anything else?"

"Got any chapstick?"

Dick sighed as he dug in his pack. Then they were on their way, Frank with a smile, knowing he was going to miss not having his buddy to badger anymore, Dick shaking his head over Frank's lack of embarrassment, almost glee, in acting so helpless at times. They were now only a few minutes from the top, but as he was about to achieve the final summit of this fantastic year, Frank's emotions were a curious mix of jubilation and melancholy.

"Dick, let's just sit here for a minute and contemplate it before we walk over there, because there's some part of me that doesn't want to finish," Frank said.

"Yeah, I know what you mean."

"We're never going to repeat this year. There will never be another one like it."

"I guess it is kind of sad," Dick said. "But you have to admit, Pancho, it's been one unbelievable adventure."

"A lot more than I ever guessed when we started," Frank agreed. "You know, I just had a thought a moment ago, about what we could call our movie. How about *The Eighth Summit.*"

"What's the eighth?"

"What we've learned from the other seven: that there's a wide world out there most people don't even begin to know about. And that thank God we took the time out of our lives to see it."

"Like Auntie Mame said when talking about how so many people are only marking time and just existing," Dick said. " 'Life's meant to be a banquet, but most poor bastards are starving to death.' "

They looked toward the summit fifty yards away. Luanne was leaning against the small obelisk summit marker in a kind of what's-taking-you-so-long attitude, motioning them to hurry up.

They stood and walked together toward the obelisk.

"As T. S. Eliot said," Frank mused aloud, " 'Not with a bang, but a whimper.' "

They strolled to the top and bear-hugged.

"Six and a half down and none to go."

"Aah-eah-eaahhh!"

Marts had the camera rolling, and with clasped hands they raised their arms while Luanne popped the champagne. Frank took a swig out of the bottle, choked and spit foam.

"Let's try another take of that," Marts suggested.

Frank choked again, this time with foam running from his nose.

"Take three," Marts said.

Now he got a full swig down and handed off to Dick.

"Frank, we've come a long way in one year," Dick said. "From Budweiser on top of Aconcagua to champagne on top of Kosciusko."

"I wonder how I would have felt if we had made Everest," Frank said, again melancholy. "If this really were number seven. Maybe in some way we learned more from not making Everest. I don't know, it's going to take awhile to think about."

" 'Men are made strong not by winning easy battles,' " Dick said, " 'but by losing hard-fought ones.' "

"You're right. But I just can't help wonder for me anyway what's going to happen next. If there will be another adventure. At least you've got Everest."

"Yeah, I'm going home from here by way of Katmandu, to talk with Yogendra and try to get on with the Indian expedition."

"Maybe I'll go in search of the world's seven greatest beaches," Frank said.

"When I get Everest behind me, I'm going to get a big boat and sail the seven seas," Dick said. "Why heck, Pancho, let's *sail* the Seven Seas in search of the seven beaches."

"You're on, partner."

Both men were now a little maudlin, a combination of the wistful melancholy from finalizing their goal and the buzz from drinking champagne at 7,316 feet.

"You're great company," Dick said with a twinkle. "One in a million."

"I feel the same about you."

"I couldn't have asked for a better partner."

"Me neither."

"I just hope one thing, though," Dick said.

"What's that?"

"I just hope, now that this is over, you're able to go home and find yourself a job."

As they descended from the summit, the shallow ponds that dotted the gentle Kosciusko slopes reflected the late afternoon alpenglow. Their feet padded softly through ankle-high grass, and Frank kept a slow pace because he didn't want it to end.

It'll never be the same, he told himself.

He felt a growing apprehension about what he was going to do when ge got home. Would he be able to get another job? A meaningful, fulfilling job? He had no idea.

For over two years he had managed to keep that question out of his mind. He had managed not to spoil the adventures by fretting about the future.

But now the future was here.

Well, almost here. He still had an hour or two left before this climb was finished. The thought gave him a smile, and his face glowed in the warmly tinted light of day's end.

EVEREST: HUMAN BARRIERS

When they got off Kosciusko Frank and Dick headed back to Sydney and went separate ways. Dick returned home by way of Katmandu, where Yogendra told him that unfortunately the Indians had turned down his request to join their expedition. As soon as he got back to the States he called Frank to tell him the news.

"They said they have some twenty-odd members—including several women—and they just felt adding us would be the straw that broke the camel's back."

"Can't you explain that your group would be self-sufficient?" Frank asked in his typically imperative way. "Emphasize that Breashears and Neptune would be terrific help putting in the Ice Fall and fixing the Lhotse Face."

"Frank, Yogendra's already explained that. But they've said no, and he says that's that. Anyway, let me explain that Yogendra also told me that a Dutch national team has the permit for the South Col route next fall. I'm going to call their expedition leader in the morning."

"Why wait. Call him now."

"Look, it's the middle of the night there now."

"Well, that way you'd be sure to catch him."

"Frank, you're still talking like you're a corporate executive with big company muscle to beat people over the head with. But I'm telling you, now that you're on your own you're going to have to learn to be more patient and considerate. Especially when you're the one doing the asking."

"Dick, you're always dillydallying."

"B.S., I'm just more circumspect."

"Damnit, will you please just call the bastard?"

Dick did—the next morning. The leader of the Dutch team, Hermann Plugge, was not at all receptive, however, and the more Dick tried to explain the merits of having his group along, the more he realized the only chance would be to meet the team face-to-face in Holland.

So, several weeks later, in early January 1984, Dick traveled to Amsterdam and had an initial lunch meeting with Plugge and Han Timmers, the climbing leader. As usual, Dick did all the talking, but no matter how personable he tried to come across, the Dutch pair remained poker-faced. They agreed to have a follow-up dinner meeting that evening, but the two Dutch leaders failed to show. Instead, they sent the team photographer, who could only talk about how much they needed money. Not only was Dick's sense of common decency offended, but he now surmised he could probably join the Dutch climb only if he was willing to contribute enough—like pay for their whole expedition.

From Holland Dick again went home the long way, via Katmandu, to talk once more to Yogendra.

"And I can't afford to underwrite them all the way," Dick explained to Yogendra. "So I don't see any hope pursuing it further."

"There must be another expedition we can join," Yogendra said. "I'll check and see who has permits for the next couple of years. We will find someone."

When Dick got back to the States he called Frank again to fill him in.

"Now I have to wait for Yogendra to get back with a list of possible teams we can approach. Then I guess I'll do my song and dance and see if I can talk someone else into taking me on."

"Let me know if there's anything I can do," Frank said.

"Thanks, Pancho. I'll keep you posted."

Then, with an ironic laugh, Frank added, "After all, I've got plenty of free time."

• • •

To most people what Frank called free time would be full-time work. He still had his consultant job with Warner Bros., and he was busy assisting them in the divestiture of the parent company's Panavision division, and he had been asked to make an analysis of studio operations on the Burbank lot to see if they might be run more efficiently.

The work was challenging, certainly, but to Frank it was less than fulfilling. The reason was simple: he was now on the sidelines waiting to be asked to do things instead of calling the shots and aggressively moving forward on his own.

He knew if he was going to be satisfied, he would have to find another job where he was at the helm.

But how? He was still playing in his venture capital schemes, but he wasn't sure that would lead to anything. He kept reminding himself of what his friend had told him several months before, that "You won't believe what will come in over the transom."

Frank just hoped he didn't have to wait too long for something to wash aboard. Not that he wasn't enjoying his relative hiatus. It was great to be able to spend an occasional weekend with friends, or get away with Luanne for several days of skiing.

"Why don't you and Luanne come out to Snowbird," Dick offered. "In fact, why don't we get Emmett and his family. And Ridgeway and Chouinard, and their families. Why heck, Pancho, let's get everybody who was on the Seven Summits. I mean we'll still have that big banquet once I climb Everest, and that'll still be the end to our film, but meanwhile let's have a kind of pre-reunion reunion."

Dick invited everyone who had been on any of the Seven Summits expeditions, and over fifty RSVPed yes. Bonington and Kershaw would fly in from London, Jennings from Jakarta. Even one of the two Alaskans we had met on Aconcagua said he would fly down from Anchorage.

With so many coming from all directions, Dick realized it was a perfect opportunity to fulfill the obligation he felt toward Marty. He well remembered that conversation with her on Aconcagua, back in January 1982, when she had said that if she should make a big mistake on Everest, she didn't want any tearful ceremony. She wanted an Irish wake with everyone partying into the wee hours.

So in addition to the Seven Summits crowd he invited Marty's mother and father, and all her friends at Snowbird. Dick opened the party with an introductory speech about how his mentor Marty was responsible for whatever success he had achieved on the Seven Summits. Then the drinking and dancing started and lasted late into the evening. At sunrise all the group, along with the ski patrol, rode the aerial tram to Hidden Peak at 11,000 feet—the high point overlooking the resort—and fired a twenty-one-round salute with the 75mm gun used for avalanche and slide control.

For the next four days we skied all day, showed slides and movies of the Seven Summits climbs in the late afternoon, and socialized into the night. As will always happen with a gathering of mountaineers, there were endless stories. The Alaskan from the Aconcagua climb had one none of us had heard:

"Remember that Korean who disappeared after he had reached the summit," he told us. "The one we all thought was dead? Well, they found him—alive. Seems he took a wrong turn coming off the summit and descended into this uninhabited valley and had to walk out. He was still wearing his street shoes when some peasant farmers found him eight days later wandering, jabbering incoherently."

The Alaskan paused, then concluded, "Boy, you sure meet some weirdos down there."

The reunion lasted five days. We hated to see it end, but as Dick promised, there would be an even bigger party when he got back from Everest.

Now all he needed was another chance.

In mid-March, about a month after the reunion, Dick heard back from Yogendra.

"I have a new plan," Yogendra explained long-distance. "For several years now some of us in the Nepal police have wanted to organize a clean-up expedition on Everest. We would go up the mountain and clear off all the litter and oxygen bottles, and then go to the summit. If you could support us with money and equipment, maybe we could make such an expedition this fall. We should have a good chance with the permit."

Dick immediately grasped the possibilities. Not only was this another chance at Everest, but equally as important, supporting a clean-up of the mountain would be good exposure and publicity for the mountaineering school and center he was planning for Snowbird.

"Heck yes I'll help you!"

As soon as he was off the phone with Yogendra, Dick called Frank.

"Yogendra says we'll clean all the way to the South Col," Dick told Frank, "and from there we'll go up to get Mrs. Schmatz down. And as long as we're that high, we might as well go ahead and nail the summit."

"And there's no problem being there the same time as the Dutch?"

"Evidently not."

"Sounds good," Frank said. "Just one thing, though. You'd better get it this time. I just got news from Giles Kershaw that this Pat Morrow fellow is chartering the Tri-Turbo to go to Vinson in November this year."

"How's he paying for it?"

"Sounds like he has somebody with a lot of bucks who is underwriting in exchange for a ride to Antarctica."

"Well, I'll still get up Everest before he gets up Vinson."

"But only by two or three weeks."

"That'll be perfect."

"Perfect?"

"It'll make a race out of it, Pancho, with me crossing the finish line just ahead of him. Why, think of how it will spice up our movie. I'm telling you, we're going to have a blockbuster."

Dick was excited. All the pieces were fitting together. Well, almost all the pieces. There was still one piece missing—Frank.

But there had been no change in Luanne's view and as much as Frank would have loved to go with Dick, he knew it was only fair to Luanne not to push the issue. She had certainly fulfilled her half of the deal by enduring her lonesome vigils those eleven months out of the last twenty-four or so that he had been away on expeditions.

Frank did have one consolation, however. Luanne had no objection to an idea he had to hike into base camp and meet Dick as he came off the mountain. That way at least he could be with his buddy to celebrate that joyous moment when he walked out from the Icefall for the last time. It was an exciting prospect, and it gave Frank something to look forward to.

The rest of that spring of 1984 Frank kept himself busy dabbling in his venture capital projects, and also fund-raising for the Mondale campaign. Meanwhile, in May, I got the commission to write this book. I needed to spend several days interviewing Frank and Dick, and it was a challenge to get them in the same place at the same time. We met a few times in California, then the three of us got together again the first part of August in Snowbird for my last interview the day before Dick was to leave for Everest. That evening we had a pleasant farewell dinner at one of Snowbird's fine restaurants.

"Dick, there's one thing I've got to tell you before you leave," Frank said. "I got some intriguing news today. You know how I've been working on some venture capital deals lately, meeting all kinds of fascinating people along the way. Now something interesting has possibly come out of it. You know the Bass family out of Fort Worth has become heavily invested in Disney, and there have been all those upheavals there lately in upper management. Well, they are in touch with me and want to talk. It may lead to something."

"Like what?"

"Don't tell anybody, but they're talking about the presidency of Disney."

"Frank, that's absolutely fantastic," Dick said.

"The only bad thing is you know it'll mean I can't come to base camp to see you if it really happens."

"I know, Frank, but listen, this is far better. I mean, you don't need another hike to base camp. You need a big challenge, Pancho. Man, I'm telling you, if they really want to talk to you, why, we'll *both* have summits to ascend."

The next morning we drove down to the Salt Lake City airport and each caught flights in different directions. Frank took a plane east to meet with a top associate of the Fort Worth Bass family. I headed back to Los Angeles to work on the book, and Dick, joined by Breashears, Neptune, and fifteen friends of Dick's who were along for the trek to base camp, caught a plane to Seattle, where they connected for the long flight to Asia.

On arriving in Katmandu, they were met by Yogendra and told that most of the police cleaning-team was already in base camp acclimatizing and starting to gather litter from around the base of the Ice Fall. He would be involved leading an all-woman police team attempting nearby Lobuche Peak, but would proceed to Everest base camp as soon as he finished his obligation of overseeing their expedition.

"So everything is in order," Yogendra told Dick, "except for one small problem."

"What's that?"

"There may be a misunderstanding with the Dutch. They are complaining about our expedition."

"I thought you had received permission."

"We will take care of it, don't worry. But right now, because the Dutch have complained, the Ministry of Tourism has asked us to be off the mountain by September fifteenth."

"Good grief! We can't climb the mountain that fast," Dick protested.

"We will take care of it. So day after tomorrow you and your group fly to Lukla and proceed to base camp."

Because the monsoon rain had closed the dirt landing strip to fixed wing aircraft, Dick and his people flew out in two big Puma helicopters. From Lukla they trekked up the Khumbu and arrived in base camp on August 18. Now the plan was for Dick, Neptune, and Dick's trekking friends to spend a few days making a practice climb up 20,306-foot Island Peak while Breashears and a few top Sherpas began work on the Icefall.

Island Peak is located a little down the Khumbu, and after climbing it several days later Dick was on his way back to base camp when he met the Dutch team in the Sherpa village of Pheriche. He actually was glad to see them, thinking it would be a good chance to have a friendly chat and iron out whatever problems might be brewing. He found Plugge and Timmers in a Sherpa tea house looking tired from the long trek from Katmandu. Since their team was too big for helicopters, they had walked the 125-mile distance.

"Howdy, you all. Good to see you. How was the trek?"

"What are you doing here?" Plugge and Timmers said in unison.

"I'm here with the Nepal police cleaning expedition. You know that."

"This cleaning expedition is just an excuse to get you on Everest again. We have the permit and we don't want anyone else on our route until we're through."

Dick knew his best strategy was patience. He offered them a beer, but they both declined without even a thank you. Dick made a few more attempts to break the ice, but to no avail. Finally, he left, and as he resumed the walk back toward base camp, he could feel that all-too-familiar knot in his stomach.

Here I am going for Everest and still can't escape the human barriers, he thought.

At least back in base camp the news was better. The day after Dick arrived, Breashears and his Sherpa team completed the route through the Icefall, an impressive mountaineering achievement considering it only took them five days. Still, it was progress clouded by uncertainty over what the Dutch would do when they arrived.

The Dutch pulled into base camp two days later, setting up their tents a few hundred feet from the police cleaning expedition. They kept to themselves, and since things at least for the time being seemed peaceful, Dick decided he would keep to his original plan, which was to make a conditioning climb up the Icefall the next morning.

He left camp at 4:30, following in single file Breashears and Neptune. The millions of stars glowed brightly through the rarefied night sky. It was a crisp, clear dawn, and Dick was elated to be "back in the harness again," feeling stronger than he ever had at the beginning of a climb.

They reached camp 1 at the top of the Icefall, dumped their loads, and started down. The noontime sun shone with a vengeance, and his legs sometimes would posthole up to his crotch in the softening snow. Back in base camp Dick went to his tent to put on some fresh clothes, as Breashears and Neptune stopped by the mess tent where they found Plugge and Timmers waiting for them.

"How is the Icefall route?" Plugge asked Breashears in a pleasant tone.

"The Sherpas think we've got a good one. Should be easy to get supplies up to one."

Breashears was relieved that the Dutch seemed in a good mood. They chatted for a while, and then the Dutch got up to leave.

"Just one thing, though," Timmers said. "We want to make sure you know that you have to be off the mountain by September fifteenth."

No one said anything. Then Timmers added, "And since it doesn't make any sense for us to build a second route through the Icefall, we will use yours."

When the Dutch left, Breashears blew up.

"It'll be a cold day in hell before I let those bastards use our route," he said.

Dick was upset when he got to the mess tent and heard the news.

"Sounds like they're trying to be a steel fist in a velvet glove," he said. "Yogendra ought to be handling this. I'll head down to Lobuche in the morning and talk to him."

The base camp of the all-woman police team attempting nearby Lobuche Peak was about a day's walk down-valley.

"Don't worry," Yogendra said after Dick had located him. "We won't allow the Dutch to use our Icefall route unless they show us cooperation. Otherwise, they can put in their own route. Be patient. Things will work out."

Dick was not fully confident, yet he felt he had no choice but to put his faith in the police. Yogendra had gotten him into this, and Yogendra would have to get him out.

Dick returned to base camp disappointed that Yogendra would not come and get directly involved until the police women had finished Lobuche.

The Dutch opted for putting in their own Icefall route (probably to remain free of any police pressure), and things rolled along the next several days without any conflict as they completed their base camp and acclimatized.

On September 5 Dick and Breashears met them, however, supposedly establishing their own route through the Icefall. Instead of staying at least fifty feet away, as the police prescribed, the Dutch route was being laid out almost coincident and even criss-crossing the police route in places. Evidently, this first exposure to the Icefall dampened their nationalistic pride about putting in their own route all the way up the mountain, but it didn't dilute their intransigence about the police being off the mountain after September 15 and until the Dutch had finished summiting.

The police decided, therefore, to enforce their position in the matter by patrolling the lower entry to the police route with rifles slung over their shoulders.

That was too much for the Dutch to take. Bart Vos, reputedly their most experienced climber after Timmers, came to Dick's tent.

"This is ridiculous," Vos fumed. "In fact, your whole expedition is ridiculous. This mountain does not need cleaning. Everything gets covered by snow and what is here now will weather away in thirty years."

"That's just not true," Dick replied patiently. "You haven't seen it up there yet. There's garbage all over the place."

"Still, the whole thing is an excuse to get you up the mountain without a permit."

"Well, I admit I want to climb the peak, but this is truly a needed and worthwhile project."

"We insist once more that you and the police expedition be off this mountain by September fifteenth."

After Vos left, Dick sank into a funk. Here he was caught up in a soap opera of petty pride when all he wanted was a simple one-on-one chance at Everest. He lay in his sleeping bag, staring at the checkerboard pattern in the tent fabric. An hour later the Sherpa cookboy rang the dinner gong, and in a lackluster way he grabbed his cup and headed for the mess tent.

The others were in a similar mood. It was a sober meal, without conversation. Then partway through, one of the police officers on the team rushed in.

"I just received this message from Yogendra. He has been in touch with Katmandu, and they have ordered a new plan."

They read the message: The Dutch were to be allowed to use the police route through the Icefall and up to camp 2. In return the police could use the Dutch route up the South Col. The police team were not to go to the South Col or the summit, however, until after October 4.

"That's when the weather gets good anyway," Breashears said. "It's a great plan."

"Aah-eah-eaahhh!"

Everyone dug heartily into their meal, feeling like kings dining on ox-tail soup, canned barbecued beef, cottage fried potatoes, and sliced pears.

Dick was delighted. Now he could keep to his master plan, which was to go to camp 2 and spend at least a week acclimatizing, then descend down to base camp and head all the way back to Tengboche or Namche, where he could rest a few days at lower altitudes. Then, before his body had time to lose any of its invaluable acclimatization, he would march back to base camp, through the Icefall, up the Western Cwm, the Lhotse Face, and on to the summit.

They decided, then, to move in the morning to camp 2. Dick was so excited he awoke at 1:30, and sitting in his sleeping bag used his headlamp to sort through his dozen stuff sacks full of medical supplies, film, batteries, sun lotions, socks, glasses, gloves, sewing kit, and photocopied poems with the normal margins on the paper trimmed off to save weight. Everything was sorted by 3:00, and then with a small tape deck and earphones, he listened to music, putting on, as the finale, Richard Strauss's *Thus Spake Zarathustra*. He got dressed, and with the stirring kettle drums and French horns still sounding in his head, crawled out of the tent feeling ten feet tall, and thought to himself, Man alive! I'm ready for Everest or any other dragon standing in my path.

Dick made good time to camp 1, where he spent the night. Then next day continued to camp 2, at the base of Everest's southwest face. The advance party of the Dutch team arrived the following day, and Dick, Breashears, and Neptune were pleased to see that they apparently were satisfied with the new plan. The three of them helped the Dutch set up their large dome tent, then shared some of their canned, stateside food with them.

Things are finally on track, Dick thought. And I'm going to check this mountain off the list once and for all.

They had a pleasant dinner, then turned on the walkie-talkie for their evening call to base camp.

"We have just received another communication from Katmandu," the base camp manager said. "The Ministry of Tourism says that all American members of the police expedition are to descend the mountain at once because they do not have a proper permit. They can only go up after the Dutch have reached the summit."

"But I thought we had everything worked out," Dick said, incredulously. "Why are we being treated this way when we're trying to be helpful?"

"I don't understand it."

Once again, Dick felt that knot grab his stomach.

"Didn't Yogendra say the Inspector General of Police is due to fly in to Gorak Shep (a few hours below base camp) for an inspection tour?" Dick asked Breashears the next morning.

"I think so. Tomorrow or the next day."

"Then let's go down there and see him. Find out what's really going on."

Acclimatized as they were to 22,000 feet, they sped down to base camp, then on to Gorak Shep, only to learn the Inspector had cancelled his trip.

"Let's go ahead with our previous plan," Dick suggested, "and descend to Namche. Maybe we can get a chopper there and go back to Katmandu and straighten this thing out. Then come directly back and climb this mother."

In Namche they were told by police radio their requested helicopter would arrive September 20; but it never showed up. They radioed Katmandu and again were told it would come the next day. But again it didn't arrive, and now they were told it might not be available for yet another four or five days.

"Even if we wait until then there's nothing to guarantee it'll ever get here," Dick said dejectedly. "I guess the only thing is to return to base camp and wait for the Dutch to get up."

Arriving back at base camp on September 25, Dick found better news. With generally good weather for ten straight days the Dutch had made better progress than anyone had imagined, and now they were approaching the South Col and might actually be in position to make their first summit attempt in a week or so. In the meantime, Dick's Sherpa team was stocking supplies at camp 3 on the Lhotse Face and all the way to camp 4 at the South Col.

"You know, we might just pull this thing off yet," Dick told the others.

Although strictly speaking they weren't supposed to go back on the mountain until the Dutch summitted, everyone thought it would be okay to go up to camp 2 on October 1 and be in position to begin a summit bid as soon as the Dutch were down. Dick's optimism returned.

That afternoon a Sherpa runner came into camp with a cable for Dick that had been wired from the U.S. to Katmandu, flown to Lukla, then posted on foot to base camp:

DEAR DICK

WELL, GOOD NEWS AND BAD. THE GOOD IS YOUR OLD BUDDY BECAME PRESIDENT OF WALT DISNEY PROD. ON SEPT. 22 AND HAS HAD THE MOST EXCITING WEEK OF HIS LIFE IN HIS NEW JOB. BAD NEWS IS OF COURSE I WILL NOT BE ABLE TO COME BUT WILL AWAIT YOUR ARRIVAL HOME WITH OPEN ARMS AND A BIG HUG. THIS MESSAGE SHOULD REACH YOU AS YOU BEGIN YOUR ASCENT AND I HOPE WITH ALL MY HEART IT WILL GIVE YOU EVEN ADDITIONAL SUPPORT TO YOUR INCREDIBLE INNER STRENGTH IN THE DAYS AHEAD. I AM PACING THE FLOOR WAITING, AND I WILL KEEP PACING UNTIL THE JOYOUS NEWS ARRIVES. YOU KNOW HOW DEEPLY I CARE ABOUT YOU AND IF I GO ON ANY MORE I WILL CHOKE UP. SO I WILL SIMPLY CLOSE WITH . . .

LOVE, FRANK

Dick smiled as he folded the cable and put it in his pack. With Frank's words, and then of course good old Marty Hoey out there in front when the going really got tough, Dick knew he had all the carrots dangling in front of him he needed to find the inner strength required to get up Everest. Now all he needed was his chance.

• • •

On his 1983 Everest climb Dick had promised his wife Marian he would go through the Icefall only once. This time, however, Dick found himself without choice being yo-yoed up and down by the on-again, off-again status of their climbing permission. Now, as he made his fifth trip through the Icefall (seventh if you counted 1983), all he could do was place his faith in his creator that none of the dozens of precariously balanced house-sized ice blocks had his name on it.

At least there was consolation in the fact that each time through the Icefall he felt stronger. Climbing with Breashears and Neptune, even with a full load he reached camp 1 in two and a half hours and camp 2 three hours after that. This time, with temperatures noticeably cooler, it was actually pleasant walking up the Western Cwm.

"The only problem is, it means it's really cold up high," Breashears pointed out. "And it will be getting colder each day."

"I just hope those Dutch get their act together soon," Dick said.

But that was not to be the case. Two hours later Han Timmers and two Sherpas made their first bid for the top, but high winds kept them from going above the South Col. The next day another team joined Timmers for a second attempt, but their supply line was in disarray, with some of the food and equipment that should have been at the South Col still in camp 1. Worse, the Dutch seemed to lack any climbers with the mountaineering experience and discipline needed to get to the top.

This gave Breashears an idea. There was a young climber on the Dutch team whom Breashears and everyone else liked and had felt sorry for because he was not being included on any of the Dutch summit teams. What if they invited him to join their attempt? It would give the climber a chance and help improve relations between the two groups. Breashears approached Plugge with the proposition, and to everyone's delight the Dutch leader went along with the idea.

Plugge called base camp by walkie-talkie and requested a message be sent to Katmandu to get approval of this new plan. That afternoon they got the reply.

"Any agreement made between the Dutch and the police team is not valid," the message said. "The police team will be allowed above base camp only to clean the mountain. Foreign members of the police team are not allowed to go to the summit."

Dick felt his stomach knot as he realized that after all this time and money and energy, his dream was over. After the attempt in 1982, then in 1983, and now in 1984, he had spent, what? nine months on this mountain. Nine months of his life only to be turned back now because of some unknown problem in Katmandu, because someone or something he didn't know about evidently didn't want him on the summit.

All he had wanted was a chance, just a simple chance to test his strength and resolve against rock and snow and ice, but certainly not against some faceless bureaucratic barrier.

"Let's not give up yet," Breashears said. "Let's go down to base camp and call Katmandu ourselves. There's got to be some solution to this."

It was now October 7.

The following day they descended to base camp, but they had no luck trying to get a radio patch through to Katmandu.

"The solution is just to go climb the thing without telling anyone," Breashears said.

Dick knew there wasn't much time before the winter winds would arrive, precluding any chance of making the top with or without a permit. Still, there was something in him that definitely didn't like the idea of sneaking it. He didn't even want to think of doing things like that, and he knew that even if he did get up the mountain, the bad publicity he would generate would make it at best a Pyrrhic victory—especially since he was planning his Snowbird Mountaineering Center and definitely didn't want to jeopardize its future chances of conducting treks and climbs in Nepal.

But he also knew it would be his last chance, his last opportunity for the summit of Everest, and certainly his last hope to be first on the Seven Summits, since Pat Morrow was all set to go to Vinson.

"Okay, let's go back up in the morning," he told Breashears and Neptune. "Maybe by the time we are ready to go to the top the police will have come through with formal summit permission."

Once more they climbed through the Icefall to camp 1 and on to camp 2. They no more than settled into their tents, though, than they got another radio message.

"The Ministry of Tourism is furious that you've gone back up the mountain," Yogendra said from base camp. "They want us to dismantle the route through the Icefall."

"Go ahead and dismantle it," Breashears replied. Breashears was confident that even without the ropes and ladders they could get down okay. But first he planned on their going to the top.

"But you cannot go above camp two," Yogendra pleaded. "If you do, we will all lose our jobs. Please wait one more day, and we will try to get permission."

"Do you know the meaning of the term 'coitus interruptus'?" Breashears asked.

"No."

"Well, it's something you can only take so many times before it drives you crazy. We'll wait one more day, but that's it. Then we go to the top, with or without a permit."

Dick was still hesitant about going along with Breashears' plan, but next morning the decision was made for him. During the night a hurricane wind developed and gusted so hard it flattened the tent Dick and Neptune were in, and ripped loose Breashears' tent and blew it fifty feet through the air, with him in it. No one was hurt, but they had no choice except to abandon camp 2 and get down to the safe harbor of base camp.

Once more they descended and next day the windstorm abated.

"Let's tell everyone we need to go back up to camp two to collect our gear," Breashears said. "Then if the weather is good, we'll knock it off."

Dick was still torn, hating the idea of sneaking it, hating the thought of giving up his dream. The next day, on October 14, the three of them—Dick, Breashears, and Neptune—climbed once more to camp 2. Once more through the Icefall, up the Western Cwm, once more to camp 2, only again to receive more bad news in that evening's radio call.

"We have just received a new message from Katmandu," Yogendra said. "This time from the Inspector General of Police. He says the Americans are to come down off the mountain immediately or he will cancel the whole cleaning expedition. This is serious."

"Yogendra," Dick said, "Get Katmandu back on the line and order a helicopter for the sixteenth. I'm going to Katmandu to straighten this out, then fly right back and climb this mountain."

Dick was angry at Yogendra for misleading him all this time, for telling him not to worry, telling him things would work out. He was about to say something, but checked himself.

I'll just do what I should have done in the first place, he thought, and grab this thing by the horns.

Back in Katmandu, Dick went to the Ministry of Tourism and met with the undersecretary in charge of mountaineering permits. The official listened to Dick's case and told him he would take it to the Secretary of the Ministry.

"We will let you know the answer by this afternoon."

Dick was in his hotel room when he received the call.

"We are sorry we cannot grant you a permit. Regulations do not permit it at this late date. If this had been done months ago, it would have been possible. But now it is out of our control."

Dick lay on his bed, motionless. There was nothing else to do. This was it. The summit of Everest was not to be. The Seven Summits record was not to be—at least not for him.

"It wouldn't hurt so much if at least I'd been turned back by weather or by my own human frailties," Dick told Breashears and Neptune.

Dick still couldn't figure out what had gone wrong. Why the seeming brick-wall refusal of the Katmandu officials to grant his request? After all, wasn't he helping a very worthwhile project?

There's got to be more to this than I know about, Dick told himself.

For the next several days Dick made the rounds, visiting every official he could get in to see. But each time he was given the same answer: there was nothing anyone could do.

He had given up when he got a call from someone who said he couldn't give his name but could give Dick some insight into why he couldn't get the permit.

"Basically, the problem is that the Katmandu press, influenced greatly by initial interviews with the Dutch team in August, has run several articles saying that you have bought the police off in order to get a climbing opportunity. Even though this isn't true, the Ministry of Tourism cannot now grant you a permit because they would then be open to the same charges and they fear it might become a Nepalese-style Watergate."

Dick wasn't sure why this person was telling him this, but maybe he had been sent by some of the officials who were anxious to get him off their backs. Whatever the reason, it was clear there was no point in pressing any further for a permit.

"So I suggest you leave Nepal before you get any more bad publicity," the Nepalese said.

"But all I was trying to do was help clean up the mountain."

"I know that."

"Well at least I've got to clear my name."

"Then why don't you call a press conference."

"I can do that?"

"Certainly. It would thrill the press—give them more to write about. Just make sure you talk to them directly."

Then, as though to impress Dick with his command of English, he added, "In other words, don't beat around the bush."

"Don't worry about that."

Dick scheduled the press conference for the next day at his hotel, and when the reporters gathered he handed out a prepared statement. He wasn't sure anyone would read it, but at least the facts of the whole affair from his standpoint would be on record.

There were about a dozen reporters and all of them were reserved. Dick had already decided it was time to take the offensive.

He read his statement, which defended the Everest cleaning expedition and his participation in it, then added, "And as far as I can see, the only thing you guys seem to be interested in is creating sensationalism in order to sell newsprint. It was absolutely slanderous the way you characterized me as buying my way onto the expedition as though I were bribing people. I've never bought shortcuts on anything in my life. Furthermore, expeditions are always taking on people who help fund the climb. As you all know, that's what we did last year here on Everest on our German-American expedition and none of you said anything then."

One of the reporters raised his hand. "How much did you give to Yogendra?"

"Every rupee I contributed went exclusively for expedition expenses," Dick fired back. "And let me say this, too. That as long as I'm helping fund a climb, I'm much more proud to back one that's also doing some good besides just reaching the summit. How many of you have even been to your own mountains to see the litter? Go ahead, raise your hands. How many?"

No one raised his hand. In fact, some sank lower in their chairs.

"Two thirds of your economy is based on foreign aid, and not one penny of it goes to cleaning up the litter that is accumulating on your trekking routes and mountain slopes. Furthermore, much of your foreign exchange comes from tourists, and if you don't start cleaning up your own house, you'll find people will stop coming to visit you."

None of the reporters said anything, but clearly they were impressed by the passion of Dick's speech.

"I'm telling all of you, you ought to be hugging me instead of vilifying me."

That caused a smile.

There was a pause, then the reporter who had asked the question about Yogendra raised his hand again. "Mr. Dick, we know that you are a man who likes poetry. Could you recite us a poem before you leave?"

That caused another smile.

"Well, I don't know of a poem that fits this occasion, but I do know a suitable quote from Shakespeare. Do you know who he is?"

"Oh, certainly."

"Then here it is: 'Who steals my purse, steals trash. 'Twas mine, 'tis his, and has been slave to thousands. But he who filches from me my good name robs me of that which enriches him not, and makes me poor indeed.' " Dick paused so his audience could absorb the meaning, then he said, "And that's what you buggers have been doing to me!"

Immediately the reporters stood clapping, and several walked up and gave Dick a shoulder pat and a handshake.

"Don't worry Mr. Dick," one of them said. "We will get the story right this time."

Well, at least I got that off my chest, Dick thought.

Gathering his papers and jamming them into the tattered and stained leather satchel he always carried with him, Dick then thanked everyone for coming, and headed for the door. Just as he left the room he saw a police officer with a grave look on his face running toward him.

"Mr. Bass, Mr. Bass . . ."

"Yes, what is it?"

"I have some bad news."

"What's wrong . . . ?"

"From the mountain . . . Yogendra and one of the Sherpas, Ang Dorje," the policeman blurted between pants. "Evidently they have tried to bring down . . . Mrs. Schmatz' body . . . but this time they are without luck. They have fallen to their deaths."

It was just like when Dick had held those miffed feelings toward Ed Hixson, and then Hixson had suffered a stroke the next day. And now this with Yogendra.

Once again it's God's way, Dick thought, of telling me never to harbor ill will toward my fellow man. Things had turned out bad enough, but now this—Yogendra and Ang Dorje. How could something so well intended turn out so tragically?

Now Dick only wanted to leave Katmandu as soon as possible. He wanted to go home, to put some distance and time between himself and Chomolungma, the cleaning expedition, the suspicions and jealousies of the people he had been dealing with.

Seven Summits has been so fantastic up to now. Why does it have to end like this? he thought.

He needed time to sort things out, to put them in perspective. What he really needed, more than anything, was to talk to his buddy Frank.

He looked at his watch. It was 1:00 in the afternoon.

I'd better wait a few hours, Dick thought. I wouldn't want to pull a Wells and wake him up in the middle of the night.

"I guess my schedule for climbing Everest just wasn't God's schedule," Dick told Frank later that evening over the long distance satellite connection.

"At least you're still alive," Frank replied. "Poor Yogendra."

"You're right, Frank. I really don't have any problems by comparison."

The two chatted about what Dick might do next. Frank asked if Dick had any plans while he was in Katmandu to investigate who had the Everest permit for next year.

"I don't know, Frank. I just don't want to think about it now. I'll probably feel differently once I get home and rest for a few weeks. But right now I just need to put Everest out of my mind for a while. I don't even want to think about Seven Summits, especially since I imagine Pat Morrow has it in the bag."

"Sure looks that way," Frank answered. "He's got the DC-3 chartered, and they're scheduled to leave in less than a month. I don't see any way he can miss."

On November 14, 1984—only two weeks after Dick returned to the States from Everest—Giles Kershaw landed the DC-3 Tri-Turbo in Santiago to pick up the Canadian Pat Morrow's Antarctic team. Besides Morrow there were several non-climbing passengers who were helping underwrite the plane's charter. The logistics of the flight were about the same as Frank and Dick's trip, except for one difference. This time they had arranged with the Argentine government to supply the refueling depot. Unlike the Chileans, the Argentines were not charging for the fuel, but they were asking that the expedition take as passenger an army general in charge of their Antarctic operations.

Kershaw was asked to pick up the general at Argentina's Hope Bay base on the extreme northern end of the Antarctic Peninsula, but he was reluctant because the landing strip there was on a snow-covered ridge exposed to winds that frequently sweep the area.

"Can't he get over to Marambio?" Kershaw asked. (Marambio was another base with a much better landing field.)

"This is not possible," the Argentines replied.

"Then tell him to be standing at the landing zone with his kit bag ready. I don't want to stay there more than the time it takes to land and take off."

When they landed the general was waiting, but instead of parka and boots he was outfitted in his dress uniform complete with ribbons, stripes, and medals. Kershaw left the engines idling while one of the team members disembarked to find out why the general wasn't ready.

"He wants everyone to stay for a party," came the reply.

"Well tell the general to forget it. There's a storm on the way, and I'm not leaving this plane here."

The general was insistent, however, and when the passengers who had chartered the plane told Kershaw it was politically important to do what the general wanted, he threw his hands in the air and tied the plane down into what he guessed would be the prevailing wind. As an extra precaution he had the Argentines park two snow cats over his wing anchors to make sure they wouldn't pull out of the snow. With much misgiving, but judging he had done everything he could, he followed the others down the hill to the base.

The storm started about 3:00 A.M. There was nothing Kershaw could do but cross his fingers. By 9:00 next morning the base's anemometer indicated a wind speed of 70 miles an hour, and by noon 115 miles an hour. Kershaw stared out the window and saw a gust rip a rock from an outcrop and send it smashing into the side of one of the buildings. Any minute he expected to see windborne pieces of the aircraft.

The wind eased that afternoon but Kershaw, certain the plane was in pieces, couldn't bring himself to hike up to have a look, so the mechanic Rick Mason volunteered to go. Mason couldn't believe what he found. The winds had ripped the anchor plates right out of the old DC-3's wings. She had then apparently spun nose to wind, jumping over one of the snow cats as she turned, then skidded back into the cat and began pushing it downhill toward the cliff. The plane went about 300 feet when the snow cat somehow dug into the ice stopping the plane just short of certain destruction.

When he heard the plane was at least intact, Kershaw hiked over to inspect the damage. The inside of the plane was filled with snow, and there was a three-foot drift in the cockpit. They could clean that out, but there was also a big hole in the wing where it had chafed against the snow cat.

"I can jury rig it with some sheet metal," Mason said, lighting a Camel. "It'll get us back to South America, where we can make a better repair."

In South America they fixed the wing and decided to make another attempt. This time, however, they would obtain fuel from the Chileans, just as Frank and Dick had done. Once more they took off across the Drake Passage but now headed for Rothera. Knowing that at least the Chileans were reliable, Morrow was once again optimistic he would soon be wearing the Seven Summits crown.

Partway down Rick Mason noticed a drop in the oil pressure of the left-hand engine. The engine was nearly new, and while he wasn't alarmed he made a mental note to check it when they landed five hours later.

Once again the British and Chileans were out to greet the plane. While everyone stood chatting in the warm sun, Mason unbolted the engine cowling to make his inspection. In a few minutes he motioned Kershaw to come over.

"Bad news," Kershaw told the others when he came back. "Looks like the engine sucked in a piece of ice, probably from that storm at Hope Bay. Some blades are bent in the turbocharger. I'll make a radio call to Pratt and Whitney in Montreal to see what they recommend."

The next day Kershaw got his answer and made his decision. "I know we can take off here at sea level, but it's another story at 9,000 feet at the base of Vinson. I'm afraid there's no choice. There are fifty-one known plane wrecks in the Antarctic, and I don't want to become number fifty-two."

So they once more returned to South America. Without the funds necessary to pay for the major engine repair, Morrow and his team had no choice but to call off the expedition.

The Seven Summits record remained up for grabs.

THIRD TIME WORKS
THE CHARM

Even before word of Morrow's
defeat got back to the U.S., Dick Bass had made up his mind.

" 'To strive, to seek, to find, and not to yield,' " he told Frank
over the phone. "Even in the wake of my last fiasco, I've got too
much emotional investment in this Seven Summits dream to give up
now, Pancho, so I'm going to try Everest again whether Morrow makes
it up Vinson or not. At least I'll be the oldest person to make all of
them. Breashears is going to get in touch with the leader of a Norwegian team that has the permit for the South Col route this coming
spring."

"Wait a minute. Isn't that the team Bonington's on, the one he
told us about in Antarctica?"

"That's right, and he said he'd put in a good word for me. You
see, these Norwegians have already talked to Breashears about joining
the team because they want him to film. So I've got two spokesmen
lobbying for me, and I feel there's a fair chance."

"When will you know?"

"Maybe tomorrow. Breashears is going to call the expedition leader
and put it to him. Thought it might be better than me going to him
directly, since we don't know each other."

The next day Breashears called Arne Naess, a wealthy Norwegian businessman and the expedition's leader.

"Arne is willing to consider it," Breashears reported to Dick. "He said first, though, he has to sound out the other team members. He'll get back to us in a week or so."

While Dick was waiting to hear back from Naess, he got another call from Frank.

"This is unbelievable," Frank said, "but I just got news that Pat Morrow and his group have had all kinds of trouble trying to get to Vinson. One of the Tri-Turbo's engines konked out at Rothera, and they had no choice but to turn back."

"You've got to be kidding!"

"It looks like you may still be first on the Seven Summits."

"Man, I'm still in the game," Dick said, "but the price of poker is sure getting steep."

A few days later Breashears heard back from Naess.

"Arne says the other team members aren't sure they want any more climbers on the team," Breashears told Dick.

"What can we do?" Dick asked.

"Let me keep working on him. I'll ask Bonington to lean on him harder, too."

Breashears sent another letter to Naess, and the reply came two weeks later. It was now mid-December.

"He says he's sorry, but they can't take you," Breashears told Dick.

"We can't give up. We have to turn him around somehow. Got any ideas?"

"Not really. Unless I just keep bugging him so much I wear him down. Even if we do change his mind, I'm sure it will cost you a pretty penny."

Breashears tracked Naess to the Caribbean, where he was vacationing on a yacht, and called him daily via ship-to-shore. He next traced him to his ski chalet in the Swiss Alps. Then to his office in London. Then back to Norway.

The day after New Year's Breashears called Dick.

"We've got it. Naess says you can go, but it will set you back $75,000. And that only pays for getting on their permit and using their route. We'll still be responsible for all our own food, equipment, and Sherpas."

"You've got to be kidding!"

Dick now faced a terrible dilemma. On one hand he felt a surge of excitement thinking he had another chance to complete the Seven Summits—even becoming the first person to do so—but on the other hand his finances were at rock bottom due to cash-flow demands of a major lodge he had started at Snowbird (the same one whose blueprints he had been backpacking on all seven mountains). His business manager, Thurman Taylor, as well as his banker, had been telling him he couldn't afford *any* unnecessary expenditures for the foreseeable future, and Dick figured he didn't even need to ask to know their answer about spending seventy-five grand on another climbing extravaganza.

But this time Dick misjudged his business manager.

"We'll scrape up the money somehow," Thurman told him.

"I don't believe what I just heard."

"You've got too much time, energy, and money in this thing not to finish it."

"Thurman, if we didn't have the same type plumbing I'd kiss you."

So Dick agreed to pay what the Norwegians wanted, and Naess telexed Katmandu notifying the mountaineering officials of the additions to his team's roster. Everything was set. Dick figured he had plenty of time to organize their food, equipment, and oxygen. Then a week later Naess called Breashears to say he had just received a cable from Katmandu.

"I'm afraid it's bad news. The Nepalese say they have a new policy prohibiting foreigners from joining national climbing teams, and consequently they prohibit you and Dick from joining the expedition."

"That's crazy. We can't accept that."

"I agree. Listen, I have to come to New York in two days. You and Dick meet me there, and we will decide what to do."

"It's just a bunch of B.S. they're laying on us," Dick told Naess when they rendezvoused. "You've got Bonington on your team, and he's British."

"I know," Naess agreed. "It's ridiculous. So I suggest we do this: I will write a letter to the Nepalese saying I must have David here on the team as the cinematographer, and you because we need your monetary support. All of which is true. Then David should leave immediately for Katmandu and hand-deliver it."

Three days later Breashears walked into the familiar Katmandu office of Mr. Sharma, the same Nepalese Undersecretary of Tourism in charge of Mountaineering whom Dick had pleaded with a few months before.

"I am sorry," Sharma said, "but this is a new policy."

"But it's nonsense," Breashears replied. "You have people of mixed nationalities on these teams all the time. Bonington is on this team."

"But the new policy also says all team changes must be made at least four months before the expedition begins."

"That's also nonsense. You know on these big expeditions the team rosters change up to the last minute."

"Again, I am sorry. At any rate, I cannot make the decision. Your petition must now go to the Minister of Tourism."

Breashears knew it was essential to get a personal audience with the Minister before he had the all-too-easy opportunity to scribble on the petition "request denied." So the next day Breashears went to the Minister's office.

"I am sorry, the Minister is not available," said the young man at the front desk.

Breashears told him he would wait. He waited until the office closed that afternoon. Then next morning he was back, and he kept his vigil through the day. Finally he got a short audience late that afternoon.

When Breashears saw the Minister he wasn't sure if his sullen face was a basic mannerism or just a bad mood from having to deal with Dick Bass again. Either way, Breashears sensed it would be an uphill battle getting this guy to approve the petition.

"You must know by now about our new policy," the Minister said bluntly. "It's a rule, and there's nothing I can do about it. The only person who can change it is the Minister of State. The petition must go to him. So why don't you go back to your country, relax, and we will telex the reply in three or four days."

Fat chance of that, Breashears thought.

He figured his only hope now was to get in to see this Minister of State before the petition arrived on his desk.

"I am sorry, but the Minister is a very busy man," the secretary at the front desk told Breashears the next morning. "It will take maybe one week to arrange such an appointment as you request."

"But I don't have a week!"

"Again, I am sorry."

Breashears wasn't sure what to do. He let out a sigh as he gazed around the office.

Wait a minute, he said to himself. Who's that at that other desk? Isn't that Mr. Ale?

Mahabir Ale was the Liaison Officer on Frank and Dick's 1983 Everest Expedition, the same man who had spent the entire two months of that climb in base camp. Breashears had come to know him quite well.

"Mr. Ale, what a surprise. Remember me, David Breashears?"

"Yes, of course. Nice to see you."

"I didn't know you worked here."

"I am the personal assistant to the Minister of State."

"You've got to be kidding. Listen, it really *is* nice to see you. Say, why don't we go to lunch over at the Yak and Yeti? I want to tell you what I've been up to lately . . ."

Breashears got the appointment next morning. He walked into the Minister's office and his first impression was encouraging. The Minister was about sixty years old, with a grandfatherly face and cheerful smile.

"First, it was unfortunate what happened to Mr. Bass last year," the Minister said. "The police tried to ignore our standard procedures, and I had no choice but to ask you and Mr. Bass to come down the mountain."

Breashears realized this Minister had been intimately involved in the clean-up expedition, but he didn't know if that was good or bad.

"We weren't aware of what the police had done until it was too late," Breashears said diplomatically. "But when we did get our final order to descend the mountain, we obeyed. Now we have this very up-and-up deal with the Norwegians, and frankly, sir, I believe Dick Bass deserves one more chance."

"Oh, yes, so do I."

"You do?"

"Yes, I signed the paper as soon as I saw it."

"What did you say?"

"That Dick Bass can climb the mountain."

"Are you sure you said that?"

"Young man, of course I am. Listen, I know all about Mr. Bass. Last fall he had a press conference where he issued a statement to make sure everyone understood his position. Well, I read the statement very carefully. I know that Dick Bass is an older man like me, and I know about why he wants to climb this mountain. Now I think it would be encouraging to all people my age if Mr. Bass were able to climb Mount Everest. So you go right now and call Mr. Bass, and tell him to start doing his exercises."

Breashears rushed back to his hotel room to make the call.

"This guy just up and said flat out you can come and climb Everest."

"How come he was on our side?" Dick asked.

"Sounds like it was that press statement you handed out last year."

Dick recalled how at the time he wrote the statement he wasn't sure anyone would bother to read it.

"It just goes to show," Dick said, "by what slender threads our fate hangs."

Breashears and Dick had less than a month to gather together food, oxygen, and equipment. But now they had done it so many times they had everything ready in two weeks. Breashears left for Nepal on March 13, but Dick wasn't able to get away until March 25. By the time he flew to the Lukla airstrip on March 29 the rest of the team, including Breashears—who was filming—were through the Icefall and on their way to camp 2.

A normally prudent person might have been concerned about falling behind, but Dick was confident, perhaps to a fault, he wouldn't have any problems. Even without the normal lengthy acclimatization, he felt he could march right up the mountain. After all, he rationalized, this was his fourth expedition to Everest in approximately three years (a record in itself). He knew every step of the way (other than the last 1,200 feet of vertical) and consequently he had "no anxiety or fear because of the unknown."

He also had what he called his gameplan. This was to pick up Breashears at base camp and for two weeks trek the Khumbu area, climbing three lesser mountains, each around 20,000 feet. Dick felt this would help him to acclimatize as well as improve his climbing strength and proficiency. After the two weeks he would return to base camp and climb from one camp to the next straight up the mountain, with an acclimatization layover of only two days at camp 2.

"From base camp we'll be able to reach the summit in five or six days," Dick had said when he and Breashears had first devised the plan.

So now, as he walked from Lukla toward base camp, he left most of his climbing equipment and clothing stored at a Sherpa's house in Namche Bazar, thinking he would pick it up in a few days when he returned en route to the first of his three fitness climbs. When he got to base camp, however, Breashears, who descended from camp 2 when he heard Dick had arrived, had a new proposal.

"The Norwegians are zooming right up this thing," Breashears said, "and at this rate they'll be on top in a couple of weeks. So there's no time for practice climbs. You should stay here a few days, hike over to Kala Patar, then go up to camp two and spend a week or so to finish acclimatizing."

"But I left all my gear in Namche."

"We'll send a note down and have a yak herder bring it up."

The next morning, though, Dick said he wanted to pick it up himself. "I need to sort through my things, and besides, hiking down and back with a fairly heavy pack and at a fast pace will help me get aerobic."

"Okay, but be careful. Don't twist an ankle or get any blisters."

Dick was confident he could make it to Namche Bazar in one day, a distance that normally would take two or three. He was "feeling like gangbusters" as he hefted his forty-pound pack and left base camp late in the morning. He made very good time down the glacier and through the upper villages, but by late afternoon his right foot was starting to bother him. He was trying so hard to get to Namche before nightfall, though, that he didn't take off his shoe and have a look at the areas of discomfort until shortly before the Tengboche Monastery. He was mortified to discover several huge blisters on the ball and toes as well as the heel.

Oh Lord, he thought, I've blown an inner tube and Breashears is going to kill me.

He slept at the monastery, and next day the blisters looked not only worse than he feared, but he had deep painful bruises as well. In addition, the long downhill trek had jammed his foot forward so much that he had a swollen big toe with a blackened nail he was sure to lose. He hobbled the remaining five miles to Namche and spent the next two days with his foot propped in the sunlight, draining the blisters with his Swiss Army knife. Then he bandaged the wounds as best he could and took five days to limp back to base camp, arriving on April 16. There he radioed Breashears, who had been up the Lhotse Face filming the Norwegians and was now back in camp 2.

"I have a couple of blisters on my foot. I'll be fine, but I think it might be a good idea to rest a day or two before coming up."

"I told you to be careful with your feet!"

"Don't worry, it's not bad."

It wasn't bad—it was horrible. There were actually blisters within the blisters, exposing muscle and tendon. Despite what he told Breashears, Dick was not only concerned about his foot but also his lack of conditioning. After resting for two days he decided it would be a good idea to force himself to make a carry up the Icefall to camp 1 and back down, as he needed to accelerate his acclimatization.

Halfway up the Icefall his heel hurt from having gravity push it back in his boot, so he decided to turn around and go back to base camp. But going downhill put the pressure on the front of his foot so that it hurt even more than the heel. Now he really was in a fix. Obviously he couldn't stop and sit down in the middle of the Icefall. He felt he had no choice but to turn around again and continue uphill.

No one was at camp 1 so he decided to bite the bullet and continue the rest of the way to camp 2. He told a Norwegian who was on his way to base camp to tell the others what he was doing.

Dick found a first aid kit in camp 1 and changed the dressings on his wounds. He limped out of camp. He was halfway up the Western Cwm when he spotted Breashears coming down to meet him.

"Base camp radioed me you were coming up," Breashears said. "I can't believe you did this to yourself."

Breashears' exasperation changed to pity, though, when he saw Dick's face. His brow was furrowed and he limped with his right foot splayed in a kind of duckwalk. He was clearly in pain.

"It's bad," Dick admitted. "The pain's making me nauseous."

"Look on the bright side," Breashears said. "At least until your blisters heal you won't be able to gallivant off and really hurt yourself, or do something else as stupid as this."

It took Dick five hours to make it to camp 2, and there the Norwegian team doctor instructed him to stay off his foot until the blisters healed. The next day Breashears said he was descending to base camp to pick up a lightweight movie camera he planned to take to the summit. He also wanted to rest a couple of days at a lower altitude; he was feeling debilitated both by his relatively rapid ascent up the Lhotse Face and the hard work of filming for the Norwegians.

As he left camp 2 Breashears issued a final admonition to Dick: "Stay put and don't do anything foolish."

It took only one day, however, before Dick was going stir-crazy. So he decided to bandage his blisters and take a walk to the base of the Lhotse Face. It took about an hour from camp 2, and while his foot was tender it didn't hurt as much as he expected so he decided to repeat the walk the next day.

The following morning at 5:30 he left camp with the Sherpas, who were carrying loads to camp 3. Since Dick wasn't carrying a pack, he soon pulled ahead. He maintained a steady rhythm, moving one foot after the other. He felt good, and his foot wasn't hurting him too much. It was a clear day, and the morning snow was firm.

For the first half hour the glacier floor was fairly flat, and since he didn't have to pay much attention to his footing he started to daydream, thinking about what he would do when he got to the summit. Over the last several days he had composed a prayer he wanted to say once he got on top, and now he reviewed it in his mind, making sure he had it set to memory. He also wanted to compose another kind of spiritual message—a card addressed to Marty Hoey that he would put in a plastic bag and throw off the summit down the North Wall —so he spent some time thinking about how he might write it.

As he continued his steady step-step his mind drifted to a fantasy about what it would be like to climb Everest without supplemental oxygen.

That would really be something, he thought. I wonder if I could pull it off?

His reverie was interrupted when he noticed the snow starting to get harder and also steeper as he neared the base of the wall. Soon he had to begin kicking small footholds in the slick surface as he climbed the final hill to the beginning of the fixed ropes.

Maybe I ought to put my crampons on, he thought. But I've only got a hundred feet to where I turn around. Probably not worth the bother.

Suddenly his feet shot out and in a split second he was on his back sliding. He tried to roll over and dig in his ice axe pick, but it bounced off the hard snow and flew out of his hand. In three seconds he had accelerated beyond control.

My God, just like Marty, he thought. This might be it.

Suddenly he hit a patch of soft snow and stopped—just a short distance above a deep crevasse. He lay for a moment, wondering if he was injured. His right leg and arm hurt, his pants were ripped, but he decided that other than some possible bruises he was okay. He slowly started climbing back to the Sherpas, who had watched the entire slide and now were standing wide-eyed and speechless. He had slid about 350 feet.

"Whatever you do," he told the Sherpas when he got back to them, "don't tell David-sahib about this. He'd kill me for sure."

Dick was worried that if Breashears found out, he might question Dick's ability and judgment and perhaps even have second thoughts about wanting to take him to the summit. Back in camp 2 Dick was further chagrined when he found out some of the Norwegians' Sherpas had seen the fall, and he had to swear them to secrecy as well.

As Dick walked to his tent he thought, Every time Breashears tells me not to do something, I end up doing it. That boy's putting a hex on me!

Inside his tent he pulled down his torn pants to discover a huge hematoma on his right thigh that was already turning red and even purple.

I'm really a mess now, he thought as he bathed his leg, arm, and backside with Absorbine Jr. Black, blue, and blistered. Maybe the weather will turn bad, slow down the Norwegians, and give me a few days to heal before I have to make my summit bid.

As it turned out, the next afternoon Dick got the few days he would need to convalesce when Breashears returned to camp 2 complaining of aching muscles and nausea.

"Feels like the flu or something," he said as he crawled in his tent.

Breashears stayed in his sleeping bag for three days. Meanwhile the Norwegian team had maintained their rapid progress and two days later the first summit team, including Chris Bonington, reached the top. For Bonington, who had led three previous Everest expeditions but had never reached the top himself, it was an intensely satisfying personal achievement.

Breashears forced himself to come out of his tent to hear Bonington describe his ascent.

"We were unroped above the South Col because you simply don't have time to set up proper belays," Bonington said.

"We should do the same," Breashears told Dick. "Wearing a rope would mean two people getting killed instead of one if either of us slip. Also, I think it's important for you to start on oxygen above camp three."

"But in eighty-three I climbed to camp four twice without oxygen," Dick protested, "and felt fine."

"But you're not in as good shape, you're not as acclimatized, and you're two years older."

Dick reluctantly agreed. The plan now was for the second Norwegian summit team to make the next bid, then Dick and Breashears would have their turn. The second team was scheduled to leave the next day, but then a storm moved in and they had to wait. Three days later, when it looked like it was clearing, Arne Naess, on the second summit team, came to Dick and Breashears with a new idea.

"What do you mean you don't know?"

"Maybe I got it when I slipped in camp two on the way to the cook tent. Yeah, that must have been it."

"Dick, you're the only person I know who could have a bruise the size of a watermelon and not know where you got it."

About 3:30 that afternoon the first of the climbing team staggered back to camp. Their whole group, four Norwegians and four Sherpas, had made it. One of the Norwegians was so exhausted he collapsed about a hundred feet from his tent. Breashears took some oxygen and water to him, and with this he was able to get up and make the final few feet to his sleeping bag.

"It's a long way up there," Naess told Dick and Breashears later that afternoon. Shaking his head, he added, "It's absolutely ridiculous that a mountain should be that *big*."

"Arne, I've climbed this thing already," Breashears said, "so I know what you mean. It's going to take everything Dick and I have to get up there and back. So I was wondering, could you leave one of your Sherpas here at camp, in case we need any help getting down? I was thinking of Ang Rita."

Ang Rita was the same super Sherpa who had reached the summit with Breashears in 1983, the one who had climbed without oxygen and then had assisted Breashears with the microwave transmission from the summit. He had now just been to the summit for the third time—all without oxygen—and when Naess asked if he would mind staying he smiled and said, "Oh, no problem."

"That makes me feel better," Breashears said to Arne. "Thanks for asking him."

When Naess left, Breashears said, "Dick, it really is a long way up there. We've got our work cut out, believe me."

Breashears paused, then added, "That's why you've got to remember not to think everything's over once we get to the summit. That's when the difficulties really begin. So let's make a pact right now. Let's promise not to congratulate ourselves until we're all the way off the mountain. All the way down safe in base camp. That way you won't be tempted to let your guard down."

Dick understood, and they spent the rest of the afternoon melting snow. Breashears made sure each man's water bottle was full.

"That will give us a head start melting snow in the morning," he said. "Make sure you sleep with your bottle in your sleeping bag so it doesn't freeze."

They got to bed about 7:00, knowing they would have to start the stove again even before midnight.

"What time is it?" Breashears asked.

"Eleven-fifteen."

Dick lay in his bag as Breashears lit both stoves.

"Let's drink the bottles we slept with right now," Breashears said. "Then we'll have a hot drink as soon as the water's ready."

When they had each had two cups, Breashears refilled the water bottles.

"We'll each take a quart with us," he said. "Make sure you pack it inside your parka or something, so it doesn't freeze."

They finished dressing, then attached their oxygen regulators to the aluminum cylinders and passed them outside. Breashears and Dick would each take one, and Ang Phurba would take two, one for himself and an extra for Dick, who would need it later in the day because he was climbing at a higher oxygen flow rate than the other two.

"You ready?" Breashears asked Dick.

"Two more minutes."

Dick was packing the few things he wanted to have on the summit: pictures of his wife and kids, an American flag, a Nepal flag, a Seven Summits flag on a string, a Snowbird banner, and the plastic bag containing his card to Marty.

"Okay," Dick said, "let's get this show on the road."

It was 2:00 A.M. and about twenty below zero. They strapped on their packs and left. Ang Phurba took the lead, following the footprints left by the Norwegians the previous day. For a half hour there was a gibbous moon, then it set and although the night sky was clear, it was very dark and they had to rely on headlamps to see their way.

Dick followed Ang Phurba, thinking this was it, his best and probably his last chance to climb Everest.

But will my lack of acclimatization pre-empt my bid? he thought.

He felt good except for his foot, which now was more of a dull ache than sharp pain.

The slope gradually steepened, and after an hour the snow gave way to exposed rock. Dick lowered his oxygen mask and asked, "Why don't we move over to the right and stay on the deep snow like we did in eighty-three?"

"The Sherpa knows the way," Breashears answered.

It was still very dark, and Dick had to pay attention to his moves, especially since they were climbing without a rope and he was not very experienced using crampons on steep rock. Breashears stayed just below Dick to steady him in case Dick started to lose balance.

Just as well I can't see down, Dick thought.

Then Dick's headlamp battery went dead.

"Good Lord," he said, "what timing."

"We can make it with just my headlamp if we stay close," Breashears said.

"Listen, why can't we just go over there to the right, in the snow?"

"It's too soft."

"But that's where we were in eighty-three . . ."

Dick started to say more, then checked himself.

Don't get aggravated, he thought, because that's a negative thought, and negative thoughts will drain you.

After a number of scary sections, they finally climbed through the rock and back onto snow. Breashears continued to shine his headlamp ahead of himself to help Dick, but now Dick was able to see a little without the lamp.

"It's getting light," Dick said.

In a half hour they stopped to rest at the base of a snow gully. It was 5:30. About twelve miles to the southeast, dawn painted the granite pyramid of Makalu—the world's fifth highest peak—a soft pink. Sixty miles to the east the early morning light glowed on the mighty Kanchenjunga Massif, the world's third-highest summit. The sky was clear, and there was no wind.

"How are you doing?" Breashears asked Dick.

"I'm going to make it. But no more of those rock sections, okay?"

They climbed up the snow gully following the frozen path left by the Norwegians. Unfortunately the Norwegians had descended the same path they had climbed, and in the soft afternoon snow their plunging steps had left long skid marks that were now frozen and made footing difficult. Dick had to concentrate on placing each step so the metal crampons firmly spiked the hard snow, and he knew this extra effort was taking valuable energy.

The gully led to the crest of the southeast ridge where they climbed into sunshine. Now they could gaze across the peaks to the south and west. It looked like they were about even with neighboring Lhotse, the fourth-highest peak in the world.

Lowering his mask Dick asked, "What's the altitude?"

"Must be about 27,800," Breashears said.

"This is the spot where we turned back last time," Dick replied. "Let's rest here a minute and change your oxygen bottle."

The bottle Dick was using still had 40 percent of its gas remaining but Breashears had earlier judged it a good plan to switch him at this point to a full bottle, which would give eight hours of use at three liters per minute, a 25 percent to 30 percent safety margin for summitting and then returning to this spot. The initial bottle could then be used for the final descent to the South Col. Although Breashears and Ang Phurba would have only one bottle for the whole day, Dick was far less experienced and acclimatized—as well as being fifty-five years old, compared to their ages of twenty-nine and twenty-five.

Nearby there were a couple of empty oxygen cylinders the Norwegians had discarded, and they placed Dick's partially filled bottle next to those. Then they continued, with Ang Phurba and Breashears alternating the lead position. The slope steepened, and the snow, now unconsolidated, was only a thin covering over a loose slate section that downsloped like roof tiles. Dick found himself fighting not only to maintain his footwork, but also to control his fear. They were climbing on the Tibetan side of the ridge, and looking down he could see the glacier nearly two vertical miles below him. Without a rope, and with no hope of arresting himself should he even start to slip, he needed no reminding of the consequences of a fall.

Above them and to the left side there were several rock towers looming into the sky that to Dick appeared as enormous mountain spires. When he got closer, though, he could see they were actually quite small. It was odd, but it seemed like his perception was off. Maybe it was his fatigue, the lack of oxygen, making things appear larger than they were.

The altitude was approaching 28,500 feet, higher than Dick had ever been. He still had reserve strength, but the steep climbing, his great fear, his lack of proper acclimatization, his lack of physical conditioning before the climb, all were beginning to take their toll.

The loose snow and slippery rock gave way to snow so hard the crampon points barely pricked the surface. The slope steepened even more as they climbed back onto the ridge crest, and now it fell away suddenly on both sides.

Looking up he could see Breashears gracefully climbing with apparent ease, and he wished he had the same years of experience that allowed such confidence and economy of movement.

Bass, you stupid ass, Dick thought to himself. What a ridiculous place to try to improve your climbing proficiency.

The absurdity of it all made him laugh, and for a moment broke his fear.

Then he glanced down to his left and all he could see was the glacier floor of the Western Cwm on the Nepal side, 7,000 feet below. To his right, on the Tibetan side, the slope quickly dropped away to the Kangshung Glacier 19,000 feet below. He felt a gasping faintness and decided he had better not look down any more. He would instead focus on each step, repeating to himself Marian's words, the same message that had sustained him on the last steep face of Vinson:

"Never let your guard down. Remember how much you have to come home to. I love you."

He reminded himself again that he was unroped.

If this continues, Dick thought, I don't see how I can make the summit without slipping off somewhere. And even if I do, how in the world am I going to get back down?

As soon as he had that thought, he tried to force it out of his mind.

Get to the top first, he told himself, then worry about getting down.

He had to balance around a knob on the ridge that made correct placement of his crampon points even more critical.

This is the same kind of hard snow I slid on ten days ago, he thought, but that wasn't nearly as steep—and nothing compared to the mile and a half of vertical below me now.

He got around the knob and thought, That earlier fall was just a warning to let me know how quick things can get away from you.

He glanced up and saw Breashears and Ang Phurba resting. There was only open blue sky behind them and it looked as though they were on the summit. He made a step, breathed twice, made another step, and another, until he was only a few feet from Breashears.

"Five more steps and you're on the South Summit," Breashears said. "28,750 feet."

Breashears wasn't rejoicing, though. There were clouds wisping over the ridge, and a wind was picking up. He knew the clouds were most likely caused by normal daytime evaporation, but they might be the front edge of a storm. He was also concerned about both his and Dick's growing fatigue. He was now feeling the debilitation of his illness, and he was much weaker than he had been at this point when he climbed the mountain two years before. He could see Dick was slowing, too, and although it warmed his heart to watch how carefully Dick was climbing, Breashears could tell the concentrated effort was taking a lot out of him.

Dick reached the top of the South Summit.

"Take a short rest," Breashears said.

Dick sat, looked toward the summit, and felt his heart come to his throat. The ridge that continued toward the true summit fell away on the left side down the southwest face, and was guarded on the other side by a large cornice. Partway along the ridge Dick noticed a steep slot that he knew must be the landmark rise called the Hillary Step.

Thinking about the difficulty of the climbing he had just finished, and pondering the challenge that yet lay ahead, Dick realized that on his previous summit attempt in 1983 no one on that team would have had the expertise to safely lead these sections. Ed Hixson was certainly prudent when he insisted we turn around, Dick thought. And I was off-base in being miffed at him.

"We can't waste any time," Breashears said as he stood and began the descent off the South Summit into the notch at the base of the Hillary Step.

Ang Phurba followed. Dick got up, breathed deeply of the precious gas flowing into his mask, and cautiously worked his way along the descending ridge, finally joining Breashears at the base of the Step. It was about forty feet high and nearly vertical. There were two ropes fixed on it: an older one that disappeared into the ice short of the top of the Step, and another more recent one—apparently left by the Norwegians—that was strung top to bottom. Ang Phurba went first.

When Dick arrived Breashears was untying the Norwegian rope from the base of the Step.

"I'm going to tie you in with this," Breashears explained. "Then I'll climb up the Step and belay the rope as you climb. But remember, *do not* climb under that other fixed rope or you'll get hung up in it."

Dick nodded, and Breashears—himself unroped—skillfully ascended the icy, steep gully.

"Okay, Dick. Your turn."

Again Dick focused on his feet, trying to move with smooth economy.

Wait a minute, he said to himself. I'm caught in something.

"Dick, I told you not to climb under that fixed rope," Breashears yelled. "It's snagged on your regulator."

Dick struggled to reach back and clear it. He made two tries, then had to pause to catch his breath. It was difficult with all the clothing on, the oxygen mask covering his face, the backpack weighting him. He tried again, but couldn't get his hand on it. And he was hanging on to the vertical ice slot by only his ice axe and front points of his crampons.

"Stay there," Breashears yelled disgustedly. "I'm tying you off and coming down."

Breashears climbed down to Dick and cleared the rope.

"Every time I tell you not to do something you do it!"

"I was concentrating on my crampons and ice axe."

"Stay here until I get back up so I can belay you."

When Breashears was in place he signaled Dick to climb. Dick moved upward slowly and carefully, and was soon on top. He leaned over his axe to catch his breath.

Breashears lowered his oxygen mask and said, "You have to be careful on this next section. Stay exactly in my tracks. It's corniced on the right, and it drops off steeply to the left. So whatever you do, don't slip."

"Don't tell me that," Dick said through his oxygen mask. "You'll be hexing me again."

Dick was still hunched over his axe as Breashears and Ang Phurba set out. He took a few more breaths and stood up.

He pulled his axe from the snow and began making his slow, careful steps. He had to climb exactly in the line of footprints less than six inches wide. With each step he pushed his crampon points into the narrow surface, careful to place his boot as close as he could to the uphill side of each footprint left by Breashears and Ang Phurba.

Never let your guard down. Remember how much you have to come home to. I love you.

It wasn't necessary to look to his left—he could feel the empty air as the slope quickly dropped into space.

Angulate your ankles so all crampon points are in. Place your axe solidly. Make another step. *Never let your guard down. Remember how much you have to come home to . . .*

Breashears yelled back at him, "Be careful of the icy section just in front."

Dick had already noticed the telltale sheen of ice on the steep slope, and he knew that he didn't have the skill to walk confidently across this fifteen-to-twenty-foot section. In fact, he didn't see how he could keep from slipping right off the mountain.

He neared the ice and felt fear grip him.

He thought, Why Lord, does there have to be another test? Haven't I been through enough? This close, and it'd be just my luck to lose it all right here.

He knew if he dwelled on it he would freeze. So just as in a number of places earlier that morning, he concentrated with all his power.

He formed a mental image of himself quickly and lightly stepping over the icy section. As soon as he crossed, he would jam his ice axe and crampons in as quick and as deep as he could, hoping that would give a secure stop. He prayed the snow on the other side was firm enough to hold him.

And that's just what he did. The snow was firm—and held.

What the mind wills, the body follows, Dick thought as he regained his composure on the other side, leaning down on his ice axe and panting like he never had before.

"You're over the hard part, Dick," Breashears yelled. "It's easy from here."

Dick looked up. Ahead the slope broadened to what looked like an easy walk.

"But we've got to keep moving," Breashears added. "I don't like the looks of these clouds."

Ang Phurba and Breashears continued, and Dick fell in line a dozen yards behind. After a few minutes he looked up and saw them waiting on a small outcropping of rock.

"This is the last rock before the top," Breashears said.

Dick reached down and pried loose a small stone and put it in his pocket. Breashears and Ang Phurba got up and Dick followed. The slope was still gradual and easy, and Dick was making one step, breathing several times, then making another. The only sound was his muffled breathing in the oxygen mask. He looked up and saw Ang Phurba and Breashears sitting on top of a snow mound off to the right side. Breashears was waving and Dick thought once again that Breashears was exhorting him to keep moving.

Dick didn't realize it, but Breashears was actually motioning him to slow down so he could get the camera out of his pack and film Dick making the last distance. They were now within 150 feet of the top.

But Dick kept moving. He was in a groove, climbing with a steady rhythm. He made ten steps, fifteen, then paused and looked up. To his right he saw Breashears and Ang Phurba starting his way. He moved his head to the left and saw the slope rise, then stop. Behind was nothing but purple-blue sky.

Is that it? he thought. How far is it?

He couldn't tell. Fifty yards, maybe a hundred? He wasn't sure; again, his depth perception seemed off. But whatever the distance, he knew he could do it. He was too close not to.

He had no uplifting thought, no growing joy knowing victory was imminent. He concentrated on putting one foot in front of the other, on breathing evenly, on keeping a rhythm. He glanced up again.

Wait a minute, he thought. It's not a hundred yards at all. It's not fifty . . . my eyes are tricking me again. It's right here. I'm twenty feet away.

He felt a surge of energy—a sense of power—as the remaining distance closed. It was a sensation just like he had had on the other continental highs, only more extreme: that nothing in the world could stop him. He hummed in his mind the Colonel Bogie march from *Bridge on the River Kwai.* He straightened up, squared his shoulders, he was finishing in style, with class.

Thank you, God, thank you, God, he told himself. I'm here, I'm finally here. I can finally check "The Big Mother" off my list!

He stepped on top of the roof of the world.

He hunkered over his ice axe to catch his breath, then stood up. Breashears and Ang Phurba were only a few steps from joining him. He looked to the north, toward Tibet, but misty clouds hid most of the view. The other direction was also mostly obscured.

Too bad, he thought. I was hoping for a clear day. No, don't say that. Don't regret anything. Just thank the Lord I'm here safely, and ask Him to please help me get down alive.

He squatted down on one knee, arm over his ice axe. Now the exhaustion from his final charge hit him, and he was too tired for any emotion. Breashears and Ang Phurba made the top. Breashears lifted his oxygen mask, and hugged Dick.

"You made it, Dick . . . oldest man on Everest . . . first on the Seven Summits."

"It's our victory together," Dick said between gasps. "You got me up—and I know you'll get me down."

"Let me check your oxygen," Breashears said. He cleared the ice from the lens of Dick's regulator gauge.

"My God, Dick, you're on empty! We have to go down right now!"

"B.S.! We're not leaving until we get some pictures and I say my spiel."

Dick was definitely determined to do his summit routine and at the same time suspected that Breashears was making up a story about the oxygen bottle being empty in order to keep Dick from wasting time.

"I'm telling you, your gauge is on zero."

Without saying a word, Dick handed Breashears his camera from his parka and started fumbling in his backpack for his family pictures, flags, and note to Marty. He wasn't about to let an empty oxygen cylinder deter him from recording this moment to remember in his old age.

"First, get me holding pictures of my family."

"Okay, but let's make if fast." Breashears was reviewing what they had before them: getting down the Hillary Step, getting up the South Summit, descending the steep ridge below the South Summit, then the snow gully, then the steep rock sections they had climbed before sunrise. It was a long way, clouds were gathering, and Dick was out of oxygen.

Breashears took still pictures of Dick. Then he dug in his pack for the movie camera. While he was getting it ready Dick gazed down through the clouds that had broken enough so he could see patches of the Rongbuk Glacier, his expedition home in '82. There was only a light wind, and other than the sound of his breathing through the oxygen mask, it was quiet. It seemed the right time to recite the prayer of thanksgiving he had composed in camp 2. He said silently:

Thank you Lord for getting me here safely. And I pray You will get me down as well. Without You nothing is possible. And I want to thank my wife, Marian, our children, loved ones, friends and co-workers who have supported and backed me these last four years while I've played hooky much of the time. And I want to express my thanks and deepest friendship to my partner Frank, who stood by me on the other summits, and who is standing by me in spirit here on this, the highest one. And I want to dedicate this achievement to my climbing mentor, Marty Hoey, without whose inspiration and guidance I wouldn't be here, and who lies below me here at the base of the North Face, cradled in the lap of Chomolungma, Mother Goddess of the World. And finally I also want to dedicate this moment to all the plus-fifties in the world who share with me the conviction that the second half of life can and should be the best, as so beautifully expressed in Tennyson's immortal poem, "Ulysses," the last few lines of which are:

> *Though much is taken, much abides*
> *And though we are not now that strength which in olden*
> *days moved Earth*
> *and Heaven,*
> *That which we are, we are,*

One equal temper of heroic hearts
Made weak by time and fate,
But strong in will
To strive, to seek, to find, and not to yield.

Dick reached in his pack for the plastic bag with the card to Marty. He pulled it out and read it silently to himself:

> *30 April 1985*
> *Top of Mt. Everest*

Dear Marty,

Well, I didn't train for this one either—still frenziedly fighting the Snowbird battle—but I made it anyway because ol' "Thunder Thighs" was leading me all the way, looking over your shoulder periodically and giving me a thumbs-up. Thank you for throwing down the gauntlet with, "Bass, your hot air won't get you up that *mountain," and then paying your ultimate mountaineering compliment when I made it: "Bass, I don't believe you, you're an animal!" Those statements transformed my life and gave me a strength and will, as well as a mountaineering life-style I would never have known otherwise. I'll be forever indebted to you—just like all who knew and loved you, and those who their lives touch as well. Yours was truly a class act, and God evidently didn't want to dilute it by letting it stretch out too long. With your favorite lines of "Lasca" in mind, I'll close by saying: And I wonder why I do not care for the summits that are like the summits that were. Does half my climbing heart lie forever afar, by Everest's North Face below the Great Couloir? Requiescat in pace. Dick*

P.S. The enclosed Snowbird patch went to the top of all the seven continental highs with me. And so did you—just like you said you would.

Dick slipped the card back in the bag along with the Snowbird patch, then reached in his pocket and added the summit rock he had picked up a few minutes back. He then sealed the bag, kissed it and tossed it over the edge of the North Wall, in the direction of the Great Couloir.

• • •

"I'm not kidding, we have to start down immediately," Breashears insisted again after he finished a few frames with the movie camera. Ang Phurba was anxious to begin the descent too. Throughout the morning he had been removing his goggles because they were fogging, and now he thought he was starting to go snowblind.

"I'm telling you, this is serious," Breashears continued. "Without oxygen, it's going to be a close call."

"There must have been a leak," Dick said. "What are we going to do?"

Breashears checked his own bottle, which had about 400 P.S.I., enough to last almost an hour at two liters.

"I'll give you my bottle," Breashears said.

He took the bottle from his pack, and put it in Dick's. Then he said to Ang Phurba, "Keep your own regulator set at one liter a minute. When you get to the South Summit turn it off. Then when Dick's bottle runs out, we'll give him yours. Understand?"

The Sherpa nodded affirmatively, but Breashears wasn't convinced he understood.

"Remember, turn it off at the South Summit." Breashears felt it was fair to ask him to do this since at that point he was physically the strongest of the three. Ang Phurba started down, then Breashears, then Dick.

When they got to the narrow side slope traverse with the icy patch that was like walking a tightrope, Breashears said to Dick, "Remember, make each step count. There are no unimportant steps."

Never let your guard down, Dick told himself. *Remember how much you have to come home to. I love you.* Concentrate on each step. Just like David says, there are no unimportant steps.

Dick again skipped across the icy section and could see Breashears waiting at the top of the Hillary Step.

"To get down this," Breashears said, "wrap the fixed rope around your arm and over your shoulder, like this, then around your other arm. Then slide down slowly and carefully."

Breashears went first, then waited at the base to make sure Dick did it correctly. Dick was used to this technique and did it quickly and easily, for a change. When Dick was down Breashears told him to go first: they next had to climb uphill to the top of the South Summit, and Breashears knew that because he didn't have oxygen he would be slowest.

Even with oxygen, Dick was only slightly faster. Now he was starting to dig within himself to find the strength for each step. He recited some of his favorite maxims:

> *If you never stop, you can't get stuck.*
> *When the going gets tough, the tough get going.*
> *You're not a champion till you come up off the mat.*

Dick got to the top of the South Summit and waited for Breashears. "Where's Ang Phurba?" Breashears asked when he got there.

"He's already taken off. I think he's concerned about his snow blindness."

Now Breashears was really worried. He checked Dick's oxygen bottle: it was next to empty.

"I hope Ang Phurba waits down there," Breashears said. "Without his bottle I don't know . . ."

They rested a minute, then got ready to start off the South Summit.

"Let me know when you think your oxygen's finished," Breashears said. "And remember, there are no unimportant steps."

Now Breashears again went in front of Dick, stopping every few feet to turn around and check on him.

"Don't lean into the slope. Concentrate on your footing. Keep every point on the surface."

They had hardly left the South Summit when Dick started feeling his strength diminishing, like someone had pulled the plug on whatever reserve he had left. He made a step, breathed three times, four, five, made another step, breathed again, again, again, trying to catch his breath. He pulled the mask off his face.

"David, I must be out of O's."

Breashears knew it was only a matter of time anyway, but he knotted up at the thought it was happening so soon, so high on this dangerous section.

Dick descended to him, and Breashears unscrewed the oxygen cylinder and let it fall down the steep mountain face.

"There's seventeen pounds off your back. That should help."

This is what I get, Dick thought, for not acclimatizing more, for not getting in better shape before I left home.

He made another step, breathed, stepped, breathed. He breathed again, again, again. He halted, trying to catch his breath.

They continued to balance painstakingly down the hard-snow ridge where it was steeply exposed on both sides. Dick was too tired to have the same degree of fear he had earlier going up this section. Then it was a question of a lack of technique, of maybe slipping; now it was a concern about endurance, about just standing up. The angle eased slightly as they entered the section where loose snow covered the shinglelike shale rock. With each step Dick had to fight for his balance, and within five steps he had to stop and try to catch his breath. He gasped at air so thin it was like it didn't exist. His head was swimming, and it took a full minute or two before his breathing started to slow.

He shouted to Breashears, who was thirty feet below, "I can't handle this. I'm too weak."

Breashears, remembering how Larry Nielson had slid on his fanny down this section two years before, yelled back, "Sit down and slide."

I should have thought of that myself, Dick thought. He sat down, feeling like a kid about to have fun on a snow-covered slope. Unexpectedly, the tension in him broke, and he laughed. With all the fear, fatigue, uncertainty, here he was momentarily recharged and gleefully anticipating a slide down a snow slope.

The relief was only momentary. As soon as he pushed off with his hands he started going too fast. He was on the verge of losing control, of taking an 8,000-foot ride all the way down the Kangshung Face. He frantically dug in with everything he had: his heels, his buttocks, his elbows, his free hand, his ice axe. One second, two, three . . . he was still sliding and accelerating . . . four, five . . . then he slowed and stopped. He could feel his heart pounding against his chest, the pulse knocking in his temples. He was gasping for air and felt like he was suffocating.

It took a full five minutes for his nerves and breathing to calm. He was downslope from David's footprints, so now he tentatively started traversing over and back onto the track, still on his buns. He moved with all the deliberation he could muster.

Remember, there are no unimportant steps. Remember, there are no unimportant steps. Remember . . .

What just before he had guessed would take five minutes to get down was stretched to forty.

For God's sake, he said to himself, don't foul up now.

During this time Breashears was himself exhuasted. He felt he had enough reserve to get himself down, but certainly not enough to drag or carry Dick. He sat at the bottom watching Dick, motioning him to hurry.

This is the easy part, Breashears thought. Dick can slide here. But what's going to happen when we have to climb down those rocks? At this rate, he'll never make it.

The possibility hit him like a blow from a closed fist.

What will I tell his family, Breashears thought. And his friends. Everybody at Snowbird. It's not like he's just any climber. He's a close friend. Even more than that. I'm the one who pushed to get him on this permit. I'm the one who pushed him to climb from camp two directly to camp four. The Norwegians were always telling me I was pushing him too far. And that's how everybody will see it. That's how it will be when I get down. Everybody will say, David Breashears killed Dick Bass.

The thought echoed in his mind: David Breashears killed Dick Bass. David Breashears killed Dick Bass. David Breashears . . .

Wait a minute, Breashears thought. He's my responsibility: I have to get him down. If he quits moving altogether, I'll dig a snowcave. We'll crawl into that.

He paused, then thought, No, it's been too cold at night to survive that. He'd never make it. But I can't leave him. I could never do that—so that settles it. There's only one choice; I'll stay with him. It's the only way. If one dies, we both die.

Breashears looked up. It seemed like it was taking forever for Dick to reach him. He checked his watch; it was 1:30. They had now been climbing for eleven and a half hours with only short breaks and essentially no food and little water.

It's all closing in, Breashears thought. Dick's age, his lack of experience, his lack of acclimatization, his lack of oxygen.

Then Breashears remembered the oxygen bottle they had left behind that morning. That might be the answer.

Dick finally made it to where Breashears waited.

"We've got to get to that other oxygen bottle," Breashears said. "It's three or four hundred yards further. Can you make it?"

"I think so."

"Well, there's no choice. So you've got to keep moving. Even if it's only ten feet at a time. You've got to. Either you do it, or . . ."

Breashears was about to say, Or you'll never see your family again. But he checked himself, deciding to hold that one as the trump card. He would play it only when Dick was on his hands and knees. . . .

"So let's get going," Breashears said.

"Okay, but I just remembered I have some juice left in my water bottle."

That was good news. Breashears pulled the bottle from Dick's pack. There were a few ounces of fluid flavored with Dick's powdered energy drink. Breashears knew the sugar might give Dick a boost. Dick took a couple of swigs, and stood up.

"That seems to help a lot," Dick said.

"Remember, the goal is the oxygen bottle. Focus on it."

Again, Breashears went first in order to lure Dick downward. Dick would make ten feet, twenty, then stop. Breashears looked down the slope. There was the oxygen bottle, about 200 feet away.

But was it their bottle? He remembered the Norwegians had left a few empties in the area, and the possibility occurred to him that Ang Phurba, in his panic about going snow blind, had picked up the partially full bottle for himself.

Breashears quickened his pace toward the bottle. As he got closer, he tried to discern if it was the type of bottle he and Dick had been using, or the kind the Norwegians had brought. He got a little closer, craned his neck, and saw it was the one Dick had used early that morning.

Breashears looked up and saw Dick was still coming, but very slowly. Breashears took his pack off and sat on it. He was exhausted. He simply didn't have the strength to carry the partially full bottle up to Dick.

He's going to have to make it down here on his own, Breashears thought.

Dick leaned on his ice axe and lifted his head enough to see Breashears sitting next to the oxygen bottle. Breashears was about thirty feet away. Dick was now so exhausted, he wondered if he could make it that far.

Whatever I do, I can't sit down, he told himself. If I sit I'll never get up.

There was no energy left in his body. He hadn't known it was possible to be so tired. He was beyond extreme fatigue. His legs felt wobbly, like they were made of rubber. He felt they would buckle under any moment. He felt like a drunk who had to concentrate with everything he had left, just to keep standing.

He could still think clearly, however, and he knew the oxygen bottle would save him.

Got to get to it. Got to get to the oxygen. So find the strength. Use my secret weapon. Positive thoughts.

He thought of the couplet he had learned so long ago in high school: "Ability and Brain and Brawn/all play a certain part/but there is nothing better than/to have a fighting heart."

That's it! A fighting heart. A fighting heart, he repeated. There's nothing better than a fighting heart.

To strive, to seek . . . and not to yield. He repeated the lines two times, three times. Then he repeated his wife's message: *Remember how much you have to come home to. I love you.*

A fighting heart . . . Not to yield . . . I love you . . .

He made another step, breathed several times deeply, stepped, breathed more, stepped. He leaned down on his ice axe, panting deeply, fighting to remain standing.

Got to get to the oxygen bottle. Got to get to the oxygen bottle.

He lifted his head. There was Breashears, staring at him. There was the oxygen bottle. It was twenty feet away.

A fighting heart . . . Not to yield . . . I love you . . .

He lifted his boot, moved it forward, breathed, then lifted the other, breathed. He stood staring at Breashears, feeling his lungs heave in and out.

Now he began reciting Kipling's "If."

"If you can force your heart and nerve and sinew . . ."

He made a step . . .

"To serve your turn long after they are gone . . ."

And another step . . .

"And so hold on when there is nothing in you . . ."

And another . . .

"Except the Will which says to them: 'Hold on!' "

And another.

Have to rest, he told himself. Have to rest. But don't sit down. You'll never stand up if you do. You've got to hang on. You can't quit. Can't quit. Can't quit . . .

So this is how Mrs. Schmatz died, he thought. Just like this. She couldn't go any further, and she just sat down. Now I understand.

He formed a mental picture of her lying half-submerged in the frozen snow.

You can't sit down. Can't sit down and end up like Mrs. Schmatz. This must be what it's like to drown, to be so tired there is no anxiety, just relief at letting go, to slip into sleep. No! Don't sleep! Stay awake!

He snapped his head up and looked toward Breashears.

There's David, next to the oxygen bottle. And there, in front of him, who's that? Marty, of course. Now that I need her most. Ol' Thunder Thighs, standing, smiling over her shoulder at me, not doubting me anymore, but believing in me, signaling me thumbs-up, to get my butt in gear and get over to that oxygen bottle.

Okay, you little split-tail, I'll show you again I can do it. I'm coming.

Make a step, breathe several times, make a step.

We climbed this mountain together, Marty, and now we're gonna get down it together. You and me, the whole Seven Summits, just like we said we would.

So make a step, breath, breath, breath, make a step.

I'm making it, Marty.

Step, breath, breath, breath, step.

Marty! I'm here! We made it!

"You're incredible," Breashears said. "Absolutely incredible. Sit down here in front of me, and I'll strap these O's on you."

This oxygen's my salvation, Dick thought.

He sat with his back between Breashears' legs. Breashears fastened the regulator on the tank, opened the valve to the high rate of four liters a minute, and handed the mask to Dick, who leaned back on Breashears and took two deep breaths while Breashears put his arms over Dick's shoulders and gave him a tight hug. A few more breaths and Dick sat up straight.

"I feel like Popeye popping a can of spinach."

Then, in tune to the Popeye jingle, Dick yelled out, "Daa-Daaddle-de-daat-de daa!"

Dick couldn't believe what the oxygen was doing for him. More than any food or drink he ever had, it was giving him instant strength.

"It's starting to snow and could get heavy," Breashears said. "So let's get out of here."

Dick stood. He couldn't believe how much better he felt. He was far from his normal strength, but he knew he was strong enough to get down. He was going to make it after all, and the realization brought him close to tears.

"David, I just want you to know, I love you."

"I feel the same about you," Breashears said, grinning. "But before we get too sappy, let's get off this mountain."

Breashears turned and started down the gully. Dick followed. They made big, steady strides. Soon they were onto the rocks they had climbed in the predawn over twelve hours earlier.

The visibility was very restricted.

"We're heading too far to the right," Dick said. "We'll miss the Col and probably fall down the Southwest Face."

Then, like divine intervention, a few minutes later the sleeting mist opened.

"You're right," Breashears said. "Camp four is to the left."

A little later the weather blew through and the sky cleared. It was now late afternoon and the slanting rays of the sun cast long shadows across the rocks. There was no wind, and it was quiet and beautiful. God's benediction, Dick thought.

Occasionally Breashears would look back and Dick, always close behind, would signal that everything was fine. They reached the final snow slope descending to the South Col. Looking down, they could see the tents and also a lone figure walking across the Col toward them. They recognized Ang Rita, and it looked like he was carrying something. When they got closer they could see it was a thermos and cups.

"Hot tea, sahib," Ang Rita said, smiling widely.

They reached camp at 5:45, just before dark, with Dick a little behind, too tired even to disengage his oxygen cylinder, which had gone empty a half hour before. They had been climbing for nearly sixteen hours at altitudes above 26,200 feet. Ang Rita rummaged through the oxygen cylinders that littered the campsite until he found one with some residual gas. Dick and Breashears hooked on to it, but it ran out in an hour. They both had racking coughs, there was nothing left to eat, and they were too tired to care. It was a miserable restless night, but in the morning they both felt stronger and were able to break camp.

"Remember," Breashears said as they started down the Lhotse Face, "don't let your guard down. Not until we reach base camp."

They were now the only members of the expedition still on the mountain; all the others were in base camp waiting for them. They overnighted in camp 2, then next morning descended the Western Cwm, and, for the last time, the Icefall.

"Counting eighty-three, eighty-four, and this year, I've been through this mother ten times," Dick said.

"This is number forty for me," Breashears said.

It was noon when they walked out of the Icefall and knew without a doubt they were down safely. They stopped, shook hands, and hugged each other.

"I've got a bottle of Dom Perignon in my bag at base camp," Breashears said, "that I've been saving for this."

They climbed the last rise of a moraine that bordered base camp, and at the crest they were surprised to find the entire Norwegian team waiting for them. There were hugs and cheers all around.

"Did you get word out to Katmandu that we made it?" Dick wanted to know.

"As soon as you radioed us from the South Col," the Norwegians answered.

I bet Frank was beside himself when he got the news, Dick thought. I wish I could have called him direct. But I will as soon as I get to Katmandu.

"Could you send another message home that we're safely back in base camp," Dick asked, "and heading out tomorrow."

They walked into base camp and Breashears went to his tent for the champagne.

"It took four expeditions," Breashears said as he worked the cork off, "but you finally got it, Dick. Here's a toast to tenacity."

"Actually, I figure that first try on Lou Whittaker's team was only practice because I never had any expectation of getting a chance at the summit then," Dick said. "So it was really only three attempts. You see, I've got this thing. The third time works the charm."

"Whatever it is, I just want you to know I've never seen anybody with so much determination."

"Your compliment means a lot to me, David, but I'm not sure you would be so impressed if you knew the whole story. You see, there's something I've been keeping from you, and now that we're down I want to level with you."

"About what?"

"Well, about how I got this bruise on my leg . . ."

Frank was in New York on a business trip when he got the news from Katmandu. It was 4:00 in the morning, but he immediately got on the phone to call everybody.

For a few rings I didn't get out of bed, but when the phone persisted I had that hollow feeling you get when you realize someone has something important to tell you at 1:00 A.M.

"Hello."

"I just got news from Katmandu."

Frank always had the habit of returning your "hello" not with another "Hi, this is Frank," but instead by simply launching into the conversation, forcing you to quickly get your mind tuned to who it was and what he was saying. Because I had been expecting this call for the last couple of days, though, even in the middle of the night I instantly got my mental gears going.

There are only two possibilities, I thought. The news from Katmandu has to be that either Dick has made it, or something horrible has happened.

Frank's voice was two octaves above normal. My vague foreboding crystallized to a sharp fear.

"It's, it's Dick . . . Dick's . . ." Frank stammered, his voice now breaking. I felt the fear sweep over me, gripping my stomach.

"Dick's, he's, he's . . ." Frank's voice was now a high squeak.

"He's made it! He's climbed Everest! We've got the Seven Summits! And you, you lucky bastard, you've got the ending to your book!"

And now I could tell Frank was crying. Crying for joy.

THE IMPOSSIBLE
DREAM

A few days after Dick returned from Everest he got a phone call from Frank.

"Dick, you'd better sit down for this one. I just got a call from Giles, who has just received some appalling news from Antarctica. Apparently some scientists have recently resurveyed the Ellsworth Mountains, and they are right now recalculating the altitudes of several of the peaks."

Dick felt the blood drain from his face.

"Pancho, you're not going to tell me what I think you're going to tell me, are you?"

"They've just finished recalculating the measurements for Vinson. As you know, the old altitude was 16,860 feet."

"And the new?"

"Sixteen thousand sixty-seven feet."

"And the altitude of Tyree?"

"Well, it was 16,290 feet."

Dick leaned back in his chair.

"Oh, my aching back," he said. "Do you mean we climbed the wrong mountain?"

"Maybe not. See, they still haven't finished their calculations for

Tyree. Sixteen thousand two hundred ninety is the old altitude, and the scientists think there's a reasonable chance that since their new altitude for Vinson was lower than the older measurement, the same might be true for Tyree. If so, let's hope it's proportional."

"When are they going to know?"

"They say it will take another month or two to complete the calculations."

"I can't believe the good Lord would let us climb the wrong peak."

Dick recalled all too clearly the day he climbed Vinson and sighted down the range to Tyree, noting that it even *looked* higher than Vinson.

What am I going to do if Tyree is the highest? Dick thought after he had hung up with Frank.

A week later he had the answer. Dan Emmett, Yvon Chouinard, and a few other climbers were making a deal to charter the DC-3 Tri-Turbo for another trip to the Ellsworth Mountains, with the goal of climbing whatever peaks looked like the most fun.

"So if Tyree does turn out higher," Emmett told Dick, "we're saving one seat on the plane for you. But you'll definitely have to get up Tyree on the first go."

"Why?"

"Because Pat Morrow has made arrangements to charter the plane immediately after we do. He's heard the rumor that Tyree might be the highest, and he's set to climb it if that turns out to be the case."

"How long, O Lord, how long? When am I ever going to get this ordeal laid to rest?"

Dick decided it made no sense to worry about which mountain was higher until the final answer came in.

"Men spend most of their lives worrying about things that usually never happen," he told himself.

And if it does happen, Dick thought, I'll just have to pucker my tail to my tonsils and go back and climb Tyree.

Meanwhile, Dick followed through with his plan to have the gala Seven Summits banquet he had long dreamed of. It was set for August 4, 1985, on top of 11,000-foot Hidden Peak, overlooking Snowbird.

Everyone on any of Frank and Dick's expeditions received an invitation saying "tuxes for men and appropriate party dresses for women are required. Because of the rocky terrain on top of Hidden Peak both guys and gals are encouraged to wear climbing boots or hiking shoes."

Dick hired a camera crew to film the event.

"It'll be the perfect finale to our movie," Dick told Frank. "Just like I described to you that day on the Everest North Wall expedition in '82."

Dick also lined up the 80-piece Utah Symphony and the 150 member Jay Welch Chorale. When the big day came, the musicians and singers took a late afternoon tram to the summit of Hidden Peak. The rest of us—300 total, including many Snowbird employees— followed an hour later.

It was perfect weather. The symphony was located under a huge portable cover and the choir on raised bleacher seats. Next to them a forty-foot banquet table festooned with ice carvings and baskets filled with flowers was decorated with a whole pig with apple in its mouth, pheasants, lobsters, trays of snow crab, shrimp, smoked salmon and trout, white asparagus, caviar, and platters of exotic tropical fruit. Behind, running the length of the banquet table were huge three-foot-high letters carved from ice blocks that spelled out "Seven Summits," and nearby several chefs manned Texas-sized barbecues racked with whole strips of tenderloin and hundreds of roasting tiger shrimp. A phalanx of tuxedoed waiters was standing by on the sidelines, each waiter with a tray supporting a bottle of champagne.

I was standing next to a Dallas oilman friend of Dick's who I heard tell his wife, "You know darlin', even ol' Malcolm Forbes never put on a shindig like this."

Altogether, there were more than 500 people on the summit of the mountain. As Dick had promised when he first had the idea for the banquet, it was "a feast that would make Nebuchadnezzar envious."

Dick had carefully planned the feast from beginning to end, and as part of the plan he and Frank, instead of taking the tram, were hiking to the top of Hidden Peak. Now, with all the guests waiting with champagne in hand, and with the film crew rolling, the pair with packs on their backs crested the ridge to the reverberating crescendo of "Climb Every Mountain." They retired behind a temporary screen, then, as the symphony played "The Blue Danube," they doffed their climbing clothes and in time to the waltz tossed their hiking shoes and socks, soiled pants, shirts and underwear over the screen, emerging a few minutes later in black tie and tuxes.

They were each given champagne, and with their glasses raised to each other Dick spoke: "First, I'd like to say what I said on top of Everest," Dick told the crowd. He then recited the same message of thanksgiving to his creator, family, and friends he had said on the summit, ending with the dedication to Marty and "to all the plus-fifties in the world who share with me the conviction that the second half can and should be the best half."

The crowd cheered, and Dick then recited the last lines of Tennyson's "Ulysses."

"I've got one more thing to say, and this is to Frank. I really feel it's divine providence that we met, and the friendship and warm esteem we have for each other after what we've shared on the Seven Summits odyssey is as meaningful an achievement for me as the Seven Summits themselves."

Then turning to Frank, who was standing next to him, Dick added, "I mean it, Pancho."

"You have just heard the *second* most awesome fact of these climbs," Frank told the crowd. "And that is that after four years together, Dick Bass could say that to Frank Wells. The *first* most awesome fact is that after four years I can say the same thing back to Dick Bass."

A dozen waiters then popped champagne corks and the bubbly fountained into the air like a fireworks finale.

"Dick," Frank continued, "do you know what today is? Today is August 4, 1985—four years ago to the day we met at Warner Brothers Studio and shook hands agreeing to do the Seven Summits."

The crowd cheered again.

"And there's one more thing I want to say. A lot of people have asked me how I really felt when Bass made it to the summit of Everest, and I wasn't there. I've been trying to figure out an easy answer, some way to explain how I didn't feel bad at all because with my new job I'm as happy as a pig in mud. Well, here's my answer."

Frank then unbuttoned his tuxedo jacket, and pulling open his studded shirt exposed a T-shirt with a shoulder-to-shoulder image of Mickey Mouse. It brought down the house.

When the cheers and laughter subsided, Dick said, "Now for the banquet. Did you all see the movie *Tom Jones*? Well, we're about to have our eating scene."

"Wait a minute," Frank interjected. "First, I've got one more thing to say. I know this is liable to upset a lot of plans and a lot of celebration today, but I've just got a message, and I feel I must read it."

Frank then reached in his pocket and pulled out a sheet of paper.

" 'To Frank Wells from the U.S. Department of Interior,' " Frank read. " 'Thank you for your recent inquiries concerning the altitudes of the peaks in the Ellsworth Mountains of Antarctica. We understand your interest, and that of your mountain climbing associates, regarding the possibility that Mount Tyree rather than Mount Vinson may actually be the highest mountain in Antarctica.

" 'As you may know, our original measurements of the Ellsworth Mountains were made in the early 1960's and had some inherent inaccuracies. At that time, our measurement of Mount Vinson showed it to be 16,860 feet, the highest point on the continent.

"Recently a new survey using cross-reference measurements from five different satellite positions resulted in a new altitude for Mount Vinson. The new measurement is 16,067 feet.

" 'As you know, that makes Mount Tyree, by our old measurement, actually a few feet higher.' "

Dick's hand holding his champagne glass dropped to his side, and his ebullient bearing changed to incredulous dismay.

"Oh, my God, I can't believe this."

Frank paused, held up his hand, and said, "Wait, let me finish." He paused again, then slowly continued the message:

" 'However, we have just completed the new measurement for Mount Tyree. The final altitude is . . .' "

Frank paused again, smiling impishly.

" '. . . fifteen thousand nine hundred and three feet. So Mount Vinson is still higher than Mount Tyree—by 170 feet!' "

"Aah-eah-eaahhh!"

The waiters popped more champagne, the crowd cheered, and the symphony and chorus cut loose with "The Impossible Dream."